PSYCHOLOGICAL ASPECTS OF POLICE WORK

ABOUT THE AUTHOR

Bruce A. Rodgers holds a Bachelor of Science Degree in Criminal Justice from Texas State University, formerly Southwest Texas State University and a Doctor of Philosophy Degree in Psychology from The University of Denver. He has served for over 16 years as a police officer, federal agent, and police administrator. The author is a certified police officer in two states and is a graduate of the Federal Law Enforcement Training Center in Glynco, Georgia. He has received specialized training in mental health assessment, crisis intervention, and hostage negotiation. The author is a certified law enforcement training officer and field interrogation specialist. He is a member of The American Psychological Association, The Society for Theoretical and Scientific Psychology (Division 24), The American Police Psychology Association and the Fraternal Order of Police.

PSYCHOLOGICAL ASPECTS OF POLICE WORK

An Officer's Guide to Street Psychology

By

BRUCE A. RODGERS, B.S., Ph.D.

CHARLES C THOMAS • PUBLISHER, LTD.
Springfield • Illinois • U.S.A.

Published and Distributed Throughout the World by

CHARLES C THOMAS • PUBLISHER, LTD.
2600 South First Street
Springfield, Illinois 62704

© 2006 by CHARLES C THOMAS • PUBLISHER, LTD.

ISBN 0-398-07608-1 (hard)
ISBN 0-398-07609-X (paper)

Library of Congress Catalog Card Number: 2005050582

With THOMAS BOOKS *careful attention is given to all details of manufacturing
and design. It is the Publisher's desire to present books that are satisfactory as to their
physical qualities and artistic possibilities and appropriate for their particular use.*
THOMAS BOOKS *will be true to those laws of quality that assure a good name
and good will.*

*Printed in the United States of America
UB-R-3*

Library of Congress Cataloging-in-Publication Data
Rodgers, Bruce A.
    Psychological aspects of police work: an officer's guide to street
psychology / by Bruce A. Rodgers.
        p. cm.
    Includes index.
    ISBN 0-398-07608-1 -- ISBN 0-398-07609-X (pbk.)
    1. Police services for the mentally ill. 2. Crisis intervention (Mental
health services) 3. Mental illness. 4. Psychology, Pathological. 5. Police
training. 6. Police psychology. I. Title.
HV8079.3.R63 2005
363.2'32--dc22
                                                                        2005050582

PREFACE

After serving 16 years as a law enforcement officer and administrator, the author entered the mental health field and soon realized that his new-found profession could help a great many brother officers both on the job and at home. Too often human behavior and police work are viewed as occupying opposite ends of a continuum. The assumption of the uninformed may well be that each merges toward the other; the more unacceptable the behavior, the closer the potential encounter with the police function. Assisting law enforcement officers in their role has not been a traditional function of mental health professionals. This book is intended to provide education and training to any level police officer, and the author hopes that it may help fill the gaps left in academy training.

During his law enforcement career the author noticed a disturbing lack of mental health training for officers. Even though officers are not trained as such, they deal as front-line mental health workers and in many cases possess the power to place people in mental health facilities on an emergency basis. The author cannot remember very many days during his career as a police officer that did not involve an emotionally disturbed person. The author has applied his education and training in psychology with his experience in law enforcement to create this book. The book is a simple guide for officers to follow when dealing with mental health issues. The book's main objective is the presentation of comprehensive, up-to-date information for the police officer about human behavior – which is still the main focus of his or her job. It is the author's hope that this book will equip officers with important information and mental health skills that will lead to a more efficient integration of the police role in mental health situations, thereby decreasing an officer's liability and possibly saving lives.

B.A.R.

CONTENTS

Page

Preface   v

Chapter

PART I
Introduction

1. The Changing Role of the Police Officer   5
2. Foundations of a Professional Attitude toward Human Behavior . . 12

PART II
The Origins and Complexities of Human Behavior

3. Normal Personality Development 19
4. The Normal Personality in Operation: Conflicts and
   the Mechanisms of Defense 25
5. Abnormal Behavior: What It Is and What to Do 34

PART III
Understanding Mental Illness

6. Personality Disorders 47
7. Neurotic Disorders 53
8. Psychotic Disorders 68

PART IV
Assessing and Managing Abnormal Behavior in the Field

9. Psychopathic Behavior 81
10. Aberrant Sexual Behavior 94
11. Delinquent Behavior 111

12. Drug-dependent Behavior 117

13. Paranoid Behavior 129

14. Violent Behavior 135

15. Suicidal Behavior 156

PART V
Behavioral Aspects of Crisis Situations

16. Behavioral Aspects of Disasters 177

17. Behavioral Aspects of Crowd and Riot Control 187

18. Behavioral Aspects of Hostage Situations 200

19. Behavioral Aspects of Conflict Situations 220

20. Behavioral Aspects of Crisis Intervention with Victims 226

PART VI
The Stresses of Police Work

21. Job-related Stress 239

22. Special Situation Victims 255

23. The Brotherhood of Biochemistry: Its Implications for
    a Police Career 277

PART VII
Conclusion

24. The Role of the Mental Health Professional in Police Work 293

Index 305

PSYCHOLOGICAL ASPECTS OF POLICE WORK

PART I

INTRODUCTION

Chapter 1

THE CHANGING ROLE OF
THE POLICE OFFICER

POLICE WORK – 1890

Killers watched every move the ranger ace made. Slade [the Ranger] knew it. So he tensed to alertness as two shadowy figures approached in the poorly lit Juarez Street. They wore hoods and the flowing robes of brothers of the mission. But under the shorter robe of one, Slade spotted a pair of rangeland boots. Slade's guns streaked from their holsters as the "brothers" wheeled to face him. The quiet street exploded with gunfire. A slug ripped the crown of his hat. Then a stunning blow to his midriff sent him reeling, but both his guns pumped their lethal hail in the last few seconds of a duel to death! (Scott, 1973).

POLICE WORK – 1990

"Looks to me like he panicked," [Detective] Cardozo said. "Hitting on Hector for coke so hard that Hector let him have the gram and screwed up Debbie's delivery. Hector wouldn't have done that unless Loring had been in a very bad way."

"No, stick with murder one for a minute. Loring planned the killing. Afterwards he tooted a few lines to pull himself together, started taking the body apart with an electric saw, freaked, went to his girlfriend's to crash."

Her look seems to wonder at him. "Leaving the body half-dismembered?"

"It was a holiday weekend, no one was going to be around, he turned the air conditioning on so the body wouldn't cook, what was the rush."

"You're conjecturing that he reasons this way."

"Coke can lead to some pretty off-the-wall thinking. And we don't know what other drugs he was doing." (Stewart, 1988, 236)

Newspapers, magazines, radio, television, movies, and plays perpetuate the idea that the police are a "body of men engaged in the exciting, dangerous, and competitive enterprise of apprehending criminals. Emphasis on this one aspect of police functioning has led to a tendency on the part of both the public and the police to underestimate the range and complexity of the total police task" (President's Commission 1967, p. 13). The apprehension of criminals has been and will continue to be an important part of police work. However, this is not the only function of police agencies.

The daily experiences of many police officers provide evidence that their role as law enforcers is changing rapidly and extensively. There are some who do not regard this change as progressive and who are reluctant to turn from the methods and philosophies of the "good old days."

THE "GOOD OLD DAYS"

People who speak of the "good old days" of police work are recalling the past, when often the only things a police officer needed were a badge, a gun, and plenty of guts. Actually, it is doubtful if these alone ever sufficed. More likely then, as now, good police officers possessed other equipment and human attributes that contributed much to their ability to fulfill their assigned tasks.

Even back in the "good old days," police officers performed many social services, including distributing charity to the poor, helping the unemployed to find jobs, visiting the sick to check on communicable diseases, and escorting drunks safely home. J. E. Whitehouse (1973) concludes: "It would appear that police traditionalists have not read their police history closely enough. The police officer's dual function of performing law enforcement duties and peacekeeping community services has apparently been present as long as there have been municipal police departments" (p. 92). Nevertheless, the community perceived police officers primarily as enforcers of the law. They detected and apprehended criminals, and their presence deterred others from engaging in criminal acts. Emphasis was on the physical and mechanical aspects of police work. Officers were usually selected according to size and general toughness. They received little, if any, formal training and had low status in the community and even lower pay.

The common viewpoints of those days concerning crime and criminals might well be described by the old saying "There is more justice in the end of a nightstick [or gun] than in all the courts of the land." Crime was fairly rigidly defined as a function of the individual's will, and its complexity as a social, economic, political, and psychological problem was little appreciated by the general public. Officers were neither given nor expected to have flexibility in determining the enforceability of certain laws. Criminals were considered to be those who, with malice aforethought and free choice, elected to engage in criminal activity.

With this philosophy in vogue, enforcement of the law assumed first priority over other legal concepts such as civil rights, liberty, and sometimes – even freedom. As far as law enforcement practices were concerned, the end justified the means.

The Changing Role

Today, police officers patrolling a district in a large city are confronted with a variety of problems, few of which involve serious criminal activity. They probably recognize criminal activity as the essence of police work and may even succeed in convincing themselves that this is really why they are there. But most of their duty hours will involve such activities as helping a drunk, finding a lost child, settling a family dispute, preventing a suicide, taking a mentally disturbed person into protective custody, or helping a confused senior citizen.

Many officers do not feel that this is really police work and argue that these services should be someone else's responsibility. Yet none can deny the relationship between these services and at least the preventive aspects of crime. Family disturbances may result in homicides and assaults; the drunk may be robbed and/or assaulted; and on many occasions suicidal behavior can lead to homicide. Besides, there is no one else to perform these services – at least no one who is on the job twenty-four hours a day, seven days a week.

Furthermore, people in the lower socioeconomic classes are accustomed to calling the police for assistance in dealing with a variety of problems. The police are seen as their first, and sometimes only, resource. Specialized agencies and personnel are often unavailable to handle these situations, so police officers have to function as psychologists, social workers, and family counselors.

Police officers not only must deal with a broad range of tasks but also are expected to exhibit an equally wide range of skills in performing them, further complicating their job. As a careful observer of the police role has noted:

> Reviewing the tasks we expect of our law enforcement officers, it is my impression that their complexity is perhaps greater than that of any other profession. On the one hand, we expect our law enforcement officers to possess the nurturing, care-taking, sympathetic, empathizing, gentle characteristics of physician, nurse, teacher, and social worker as he deals with school traffic, acute illness and injury, juvenile delinquency, suicidal threats and gestures, and missing persons. On the other hand, we expect him to command respect, demonstrate courage, control hostile impulses, and meet great physical hazards. . . . He is to control crowds, prevent riots, apprehend criminals, and chase after speeding vehicles. I can think of no other profession that constantly demands such seemingly opposite characteristics. (Levy, 1966)

Increased complexity is but one aspect of the new reality that confronts police officers in their changing role. Society itself also is changing and no longer appears to present the solid front against unlawful behavior that it once did. What one segment of society may consider a serious crime, another may not. Today, the general public takes less responsibility in dealing with serious criminal activity. Despite the recent focus on crime, there is little desire to get involved. In contrast to the "good old days," police officers now feel more alone in enforcing the law. They often must perform in the midst of apathetic, indifferent, and often hostile surroundings. They must face situations in which emotions are high and danger is a constant threat.

As Eddie Donovan (1989), president of the International Law Enforcement Stress Association, notes: "Whether it is London, Miami, Seoul, Prague, Los Angeles, Toronto or Tampa, policing in the '80s has changed with the increase of drugs, guns, violence, unemployment and lack of housing. There seems to be little respect or fear of the authority of the police in the major cities of the world" (pp. 6–12).

A spokesman for London's Metropolitan Police observes: "There seems to be a general agreement that any police agency operating today has a much tougher task than it did 20, 10 or even 5 years ago" (Who Are We? 1989, p. 1).

Under these circumstances, today's police officers must rely on every personal resource they possess and not merely on a nightstick or weapon. In an oversimplified way, this is a measure of how the role of police officers has changed.

The Core Element

Although the role of police officers is increasingly complex, this is not to suggest that they now function in an endless state of confusion. There remains a single core element in the role of police officers.

The one thing police officers deal with — not just during duty hours, but during the entire waking day — is human behavior. This includes the behavior of criminals, of citizens, of fellow officers, and last, but by no means least, of themselves. Some of the behavior is criminal, some is not; some is sick, some is not; some is conscious, some is unconscious; some is simple, some is complex. Furthermore, they often deal with this behavior during conditions of emotional stress and in situations involving life-and-death decisions and personal danger. Therefore, officers must be like mental health professionals: devoted students of human behavior. But they must practice this psychology on the street rather than in a clinic or a university classroom. They must make decisions in a minimum of time (sometimes in only a few minutes or seconds) that might baffle the academic behaviorist — decisions whose ultimate resolution may involve months or even years of debate and legal consideration. More important, errors in the mental health professional's decisions are seldom critical; errors in a cop's judgment can be deadly and are often very public.

The author has advised new recruits that they have a far rougher job than the average mental health professional. No one expects psychologists to be police officers, but police officers are expected to be psychologists – practical, street-level psychologists.

Today's police officers must know as much as possible about human behavior. They can no longer regard this subject as the sole province of the mental health professional.

> The man who goes into our streets in hopes of regulating, directing, and controlling human behavior must be armed with more than a gun and the ability to perform mechanical movements in response to a situation. Such men as these engage in the difficult, complex, and important business of human behavior. Their intellectual armament – so long restricted to the minimum – must be no less developed than their physical prowess. (President's Commission, 1967)

"A fast-changing world by necessity requires law enforcement officers to be more experienced and sophisticated in carrying out their responsibilities. The 'tough' cop, today, is outdated and ineffective. The officers of the 80s need to be trained professionals" (Shea & Harpool, 1988, p. 380). This comment will be even truer of today's officers.

The view that J. W. Sterling (1972) presented three decades ago in *Changes in Role Concepts of Police Officers* is now shared by many:

> This knowledge can be of limitless value to police officers as they face a perplexing array of interpersonal problems which are always accompanied by confusion, distress, danger, and heightened emotions. . . . The police must act quickly, decisively, and lawfully, often with only a partial knowledge of the circumstances. However, their action orientation does not in any sense obviate the need for understanding behavior. Rather, it reinforces the necessity for a greater understanding of the self and others. (pp. 294–295)

More recently, London's Metropolitan Police state that training has changed from learning the law by tote to a focus on complicated and sophisticated management issues. "But we [police administrators] were told, most often by junior officers and the public,

that much more has to be done, especially in the area of interpersonal skills" (Who Are We? 1989, p. 9).

Knowledge of human behavior is essential to police officers, not only to ensure maximum effectiveness in their role but also for their safety. Statistics have indicated that approximately 20 percent of police officers killed in the line of duty were answering a family disturbance call. Another 40 percent of police officers' injuries occur on such assignments. Yet a group of officers with training in certain basic psychological techniques managed to handle over two thousand calls involving over one thousand different families in a tough ghetto area without suffering even a scratch. With proper training in certain psychological principles and techniques, police officers can perform more effectively and safely and can make a significant contribution to the care of those who live in their community. In addition, knowledge of deviant behavior will be of great value to police officers in preventing and detecting certain types of crimes. For example, knowledge of suicidal behavior will provide officers with an investigative tool to help determine whether the deceased was actually a suicide or met death by accident or through the violence of others. A sadistic sex murder may indicate either a psychopath or a paranoid schizophrenic. Knowing about these two disorders may significantly help an officer's investigation. With a knowledge of alcoholism and drug addiction, police officers may realize how alcohol can mask more serious neurological and psychiatric conditions that may bring death in a jail cell to a prisoner who is considered merely drunk and disorderly. The author will discuss these and other aspects of deviant behavior as well as certain principles applicable to police investigations in the subsequent chapters.

Reactive Versus Proactive Policing

Before closing this chapter, it must be noted that new developments in policing has the potential of altering even more drastically the traditional role of the police officers. James Q. Wilson, a noted authority in the field of police management, and George L. Kelling, a fellow at Harvard's Kennedy School, describe this change: "In what may be the most important change since radios were installed in police cars, police departments have been rethinking their basic tacts" (1989).

Traditionally, police response has been a reactive response – to murders, rapes, burglaries, citizens' complaints, and so on. This "incident" (reactive) type of policing may lead to arrests but does little to address the basic problem that caused the incident. Now some departments are seeking to do more than simply respond to incoming calls. They are trying to ascertain the causes of the problem and what it will take to achieve some positive change in the various factors involved in order to alleviate the problem. This is called "problem-oriented" or "community-oriented" policing.

Example: The New Briarfield Apartments in Newport News, Virginia, once had the city's highest burglary rates. For decades, traditional "incident-oriented" (reactive) policing had yielded no significant results. The deteriorating neighborhood kept deteriorating, burglaries kept occurring, and residents continued to live in terror.

In 1989, a detective named Tony Duke decided to interview the residents of the apartments about their problems. He found they were very concerned about the burglaries but were even more concerned about the physical deterioration of the neighborhood. Detective Duke began to investigate the buildings and found that the New Briarfield Apartments were a major headache to many city agencies. The report he wrote to Chief Darrel Stephens resulted in Stephens's recommendation that the apartments be demolished and the residents relocated. The city manager agreed. Barry Haddix, the patrol officer assigned to the area, worked with various city agencies to fix up the project pending eventual relocation. They removed trash and abandoned vehicles, filled in potholes, repaired streets, and

cleaned up the neighborhood. The burglary rate dropped by 35 percent after Duke and Haddix began this project (Wilson & Kelling, 1989). This approach has been referred to as "the problem of the broken window." If the first broken window in the building is not repaired, people who like breaking windows will assume no one cares and will break more windows until all are broken. Likewise, when neighborhood deterioration is not attended to and disorderly behavior is left unchallenged (drugs, burglaries, vandalism), the signal is given that no one cares. Neighborhood decay continues and disorderly behavior escalates, possibly to serious crime. "Community-oriented policing means changing the daily work of the police to investigating problems as well as incidents. It means defining as a problem whatever a significant body of public opinion regards as a threat to community order" (Wilson & Kelling, 1989, p. 49).

For example, citizens living near Mirasol Park in Tucson, Arizona, became very upset that crack dealers and transients had taken over their park. The citizens were afraid to use the park, even in the daytime. Tucson Police Chief Peter Ronstadt set up a two-man task force to patrol the park and to work not only with citizens and community groups, but also with the crack dealers and addicts. The two officers did not have any time limitations on what they did. They do not respond to regular calls. Chief Ronstadt states that the task force approach is designed to deal with problems rather than responding to problems.

In the past 20 to 30 years, police have been operating in a different mode – now we're returning to a neighborhood-by-neighborhood approach. When the officers first started on the Mirasol Task Force, they went to local community organizations, local churches and recreation centers to gather support.

Apparently, the officers have made the right connections. With a phone call, they can arrange for people to enter job training and placement programs, child-care facilities, computer literacy classes, even funds to help with utility bills. (Price, 1989, Accent 3B)

Community-oriented policing philosophy is also involved in such programs as Neighborhood Watch, the assignment of school resource officers, and community relations programs providing citizens with information on rape prevention, substance abuse, and so on. Many tradition-oriented police officers that were at first hostile to this problem-oriented approach have found that their conception of police work has changed after being assigned to a problem-oriented team. "They start meeting good people as well as bad guys and coming to grips with problems and not just complaints" (Wilson & Kelling, 1989, p. 47).

SUMMARY

The author has just described the differences between the role of police officers in the late nineteenth century and their present role, and the characteristics required of the officers in each. We have spoken of the changes in society itself and how these changes have affected the role of police officers. The author has argued that, regardless of the complexity of this role, the officers deal basically with human behavior and thus must be competently prepared in this area of knowledge.

The role of police officers is changing in our society. In the "good old days" that role focused on apprehending criminals, while in the present day it centers on controlling, directing, and regulating human behavior. In other words, the kind of activity described has changed – from apprehending to acts of control, direction, and regulation.

Further, the object of this kind of activity has changed from criminal to human behavior. Today's officers must function in relation to a more general objective than in the past, widening their concern from criminal activity to the larger area of human behavior. The approach emphasized in "problem-oriented" (proactive) policing versus the older, traditional "incident-oriented" (reactive) policing presents new challenges to police agencies and personnel.

Those who recognize in themselves a similar complexity can handle the greater complexity of the job facing today's police officers successfully. They must aim to be as well trained mentally as physically, as capable of using their minds as their weapons. Knowledge of how human beings – including themselves – behave is essential.

BIBLIOGRAPHY

Archer, P. (1978). *The role of the law officer.* London: Fabian Society.

Bard, M. (1970). Training police as specialists in family crisis intervention. In *Proceedings of National Institute of Law Enforcement and Criminal Justice.* Washington, D.C.: U.S. Government Printing Office.

Donovan, E. (1989). President's message. *Journal of Police Stress, 9*(1), 5.

Garner, G. W. (1979). *The police role in alcohol-related crises.* Springfield, IL: Charles C Thomas.

Levy, R. (1966). Quoted in *Proceedings of the Conference for Police Professions.* April 6–8. Lansing: Michigan State University.

President's Commission on Law Enforcement and the Administration of Justice. (1967). *Task force on the police.* Washington, D.C.: U.S. Government Printing Office.

Price, S. (1989). Two-man task force tackles drug scene. *Arizona Daily Star: Accent 3B,* July 31.

Salerno, R., & Tompkins, J. S. (1969). *The crime confederation.* New York: Popular Library.

Scott, B. (1973). *Killer's doom.* New York: Pyramid Books.

Shea, L., & Harpool, D. (1988). Tactical communications training for conflict diffusion. In *Police psychology: Operational assistance,* ed. J. T. Reese & J. M. Horn, pp. 379–390. Washington, D.C.: FBI.

Sterling, J. W. (1972). Changes in role concepts of police officers. Gaithersberg, MD: International Association of Chiefs of Police.

Stewart, E. (1988). *Privileged lives.* New York: Dell.

Terris, B. (1967). The Role of the Police. *The Annals, 10.*

Whitehouse, J. E. (1973). Historical perspectives on the police community function. *Journal of Police Science and Administration, 1*(1), 187–192.

Who Are We? (1989). *Journal of Police Stress, 9*(1), 6–12. Reprinted from Metropolitan Magazine.

Wilson, J. Q., & Kelling, G. L. (1989). Making neighborhoods safe. *The Atlantic Monthly,* February, 46–52.

Chapter 2

FOUNDATIONS OF A PROFESSIONAL ATTITUDE TOWARD HUMAN BEHAVIOR

In Chapter 1 the author suggested that police officers must perform as street-level psychologists to function effectively as professionals. Before proceeding in the next section to discuss several fundamental psychological concepts and theories, we will consider the topic of a professional attitude toward human behavior.

THE PROFESSIONAL ATTITUDE AND PERSONAL INVOLVEMENT

Professional police officers must learn to view behavior from a perspective similar to that of behavioral scientists in order to ensure maximal efficiency in handling the many complex situations they face. Although recruits may interpret this as an admonition to avoid involvement with others, this attitude is not desirable, especially toward the non-criminal public. For example, one police department received a citizen's complaint from a woman whose car had been stopped by an officer for speeding on a deserted street late at night. She was returning from a hospital emergency room where she had taken her sick baby. Her complaint was not that the officer had stopped her unjustifiably, but rather that he had shown no concern for the condition of her baby. As she said in her complaint, "He might have at least asked how the baby was."

The image of the aloof police officer runs contrary to practice. Police officers are involved each moment they are in contact with the public or with a criminal offender. They are certainly personally involved when their lives are in danger and when their action or decision can avert a crisis or solve a problem. However, this kind of personal involvement must be contrasted sharply with the behavior of officers who take a situation personally and then react emotionally to it. To further explore this distinction, the following analogy is pertinent. The psychologist does not get angry at the mental patient who calls him a potbellied pig, but accepts the remark as evidence of the patient's anger and hostility. He then directs his attention to the reason for the anger. Is it because the patient feels neglected on the ward, or because his wife failed to visit him that afternoon? The doctor tries to understand the patient's behavior by searching for the reasons behind it. Only with this understanding will the psychologist be able to alter or better understand it. As professionals, police officers also must try to understand the behavior they encounter so that they may have the opportunity to alter or control it.

In another sense, personal involvement is inevitable for police officers. They will often see behavior that is shocking, immoral, or degenerate. For example, they may encounter a father who has just beaten his four-year-old son to death, a rapist who has violated and tortured a seven-year-old, or an armed robber who has beaten an old man and left him to die in the streets. John G. Stratton (1984) reminds us that "academy training often encourages the violent and/or dangerous. Tragedies are part of the job, what you get paid for, and a nonemotional response is a necessity" (p. 226). But police officers cannot avoid experiencing feelings of anger, frustration, revenge, or disgust. Police officers are human beings with normal human reactions to deviant behavior. They cannot and should not stifle these personal reactions but should develop ways of handling them and turning them to good use. Police officers who learn to anticipate their reactions to offensive and difficult situations and who have developed ways of dealing with them not only have removed a serious barrier to effective performance of their duty but have also taken a first step toward the acquisition of a professional attitude toward behavior. They have discovered that although personal involvement is unavoidable, emotional involvement is controllable.

As pointed out in Chapter 1, contemporary police officers have as their primary task the regulation, direction, and control of human behavior. This is usually understood to refer only to the behavior of those persons, criminal and noncriminal, with which officers come in contact while performing their duties. But the officers' own behavior also must be under their control. They must handle their own feelings; whatever they are and in whatever situation they encounter them. Consider, as an example, the feeling of fear. During World War II, much was learned about the emotions experienced under conditions of stress and danger. Prior to that time, soldiers were taught that the feeling of fear was an indication of cowardice and that cowardice was despicable. General George Patton exemplified this attitude when he scolded and slapped an enlisted man who had been hospitalized for combat exhaustion. In what was perhaps an overzealous attempt to spur the man to greater effort, Patton accused the soldier of cowardice and demanded that he not be treated (Farago, 1963). Patton was apparently unable to understand or admit the existence of the normal emotion of fear. The alternative, though entirely out of character, would have been for the general to have openly recognized the emotions experienced by the soldier and to assist him in finding ways to cope with them. All-American military authorities did not share Patton's attitude. Army psychiatrists and field commanders know that in combat, fear is a constant companion. Everyone is afraid. The important thing is not whether soldiers are afraid but how they handle their fear. If they can admit to fear and use it positively (for example, fear can make one more alert or lead to a better effort), they can then perform effectively.

In a study comparing military units where it was possible to admit and talk about fear with those where it was never admitted or discussed, it was found that the former experienced fewer casualties, both physical and mental (Russell, 1965). Professional police officers, like professional soldiers, cannot let feelings of fear interfere with effectiveness. Officers with a professional view of behavior who acknowledge fear and learn how to deal with it will perform more effectively under conditions of emotional stress. As one police officer put it: "Fear is a natural response to danger which gives us that necessary shot of adrenalin. I don't think courage is the absence of fear, but rather the ability to control fear and maintain composure in the tightest of jams" (Stratton, 1984, p. 31). Thus, the first element in the foundation of a professional attitude toward behavior is the realization that in all stress situations, every human being will experience certain normal emotional reactions. This is as true for the professional police officer as for the ordinary citizen. What, then, differentiates professionals from citizens?

Professionals enter into these situations not only anticipating their own emotional reactions but also those of the person or persons with whom they are dealing. By anticipating what they and others may be feeling, professional police officers reduce the number of unknowns inherent in the situation. This will enable them to direct their attention to other factors and will enhance their effectiveness. As an added benefit, their knowledge of what to expect from their own emotions and those of others will permit them to achieve the second element of a professional attitude: the ability to control their own behavior. For example, they will see that recognition and control of their own fear will contribute to their efforts to cope with a hostile crowd.

The Professional Attitude in Operation

As described thus far, a professional attitude toward behavior rests upon several fundamental principles. Professionals who deal with human behavior must maintain control of their own emotional involvement in any situation. They must seek, with scientific interest, the motivations for that behavior, and they must strive objectively to understand how it was learned before attempting to change it. Unfortunately, this is easily discussed in the pages of a book but difficult to put into practice. A personal example may make this clearer. Several years ago, a colleague was requested to perform a psychological evaluation on a young man who had spent an entire evening torturing a small boy (his stepson) to death. He was very angry because the boy's mother had gone away with another man that afternoon, leaving him with the two children. In his extreme frustration and anger, he started drinking and, after becoming intoxicated, took both children in the bathroom, where he slowly and methodically

tortured the little boy while the ten-year-old girl was forced to watch. As part of the psychiatric team ordered by the court to examine this man to determine if he was sane and could stand trial, the author easily could have allowed his own personal feelings of disgust and anger to interfere with the important task of establishing the good rapport with the prisoner necessary to complete the psychological testing. Had he allowed his personal feelings to take control of his behavior, the author would have lost his professional attitude. In these situations, it is helpful to police officers to remember that people learn to be the way they are and that in all probability offenders who beat and torture victims were themselves subjected to similar treatment while growing up.

FBI agents who were assigned the task of interviewing serial rapists found that conducting such interviews was mentally and emotionally fatiguing. To quote from their research:

One cannot leave such an interview without experiencing a strong sense of sympathy for the victims of rape and an occasional feeling of empathy for the offender. There were documented instances of childhood physical, sexual, or emotional abuse suffered by some of the rapists. Those who read of such occurrences, or watch a man cry as he describes his father beating or raping his mother in front of him, cannot help but feel a sense of outrage toward the parents of the offender. Investigators must never cease to experience these essential human emotions. Without them, a person will become callous and lose effectiveness as an investigator or a researcher. (Hazelwood & Burgess, 1987, pp. 16-18)

This understanding will enable police officers to be professionally more tolerant and accepting of behavior that would otherwise alienate them.

SUMMARY

This chapter has discussed some basic principles in the development of a professional attitude toward human behavior. It has

pointed out that since personal involvement is unavoidable, it must be recognized, accepted, and handled. In the next chapters the author will present a more detailed discussion of personality development, function, and malfunction and their relationship to human behavior.

BIBLIOGRAPHY

Banton, M. (1964). *The policeman in the community.* New York: Basic Books.

Farago, L. (1963). *Patton: Ordeal and triumph.* New York: Dell.

Hazelwood, Robert R., & Burgess, Ann W. (1987). An introduction to the serial rapist. *FBI Law Enforcement Bulletin 55*(9):16–18.

Kelly, J. A. (1973). An appraisal of the attitudes of police officers toward the concept of police-community relations. *Journal of Police Science and Administration 1*(2):224-231.

Peckham, M. (1979). *Explanation and power: The control of human behavior.* New York: Seabury Press.

Russell, H. E. (1965). Combat psychiatry. Fort Sam Houston, Tx.: U.S. Army Medical Field Service School, Brooke Army Medical Center.

Stratton, G. (1984). *Police passages.* Manhattan Beach, CA.: Glennon Publishing Co.

PART II

THE ORIGINS AND COMPLEXITIES OF HUMAN BEHAVIOR

Chapter 3

NORMAL PERSONALITY DEVELOPMENT

To this point the author has discussed behavior – police officers' concern with it and the professional attitude toward it. We will now focus on personality – its basic structure, course of development, manner of function and malfunction, and its relationship to behavior. Professional police officers that constantly encounter both normal and abnormal behavior must have some understanding of how personality normally develops. There are three major influences on normal personality development: constitutional or hereditary factors, developmental factors within people themselves, and situational factors that arise from the interaction between people and their environment. Today, the interaction of these three influences is known as the bio-psychosocial model.

CONSTITUTIONAL FACTORS

Constitutional factors exist at birth and represent heredity's part in personality development. They include, among others, potential for growth in terms of height and weight, color of hair, intellectual potential, and sex. Less commonly, hereditary factors can include a predisposition toward various diseases such as diabetes and bipolar manic-depressive disorders, or a variety of anatomical defects, such as harelip. Each of these features or conditions may influence the development of personality, helping in some ways and hindering in others. For example, whether one is born a male or a female has profound implications for personality development. A serious anatomical birth defect can pose problems with which the developing personality may or may not successfully cope. Will the person become too dependent or feel inferior as a result of the defect, or will he or she adjust to the situation and even compensate by a greater effort in other areas? Hereditary factors can therefore be considered the physical foundation for all subsequent personality development. They determine the outer boundaries of the personality's development. For the most part, they do not change during the course of life, although many congenital defects can be corrected surgically.

DEVELOPMENTAL FACTORS

Sigmund Freud, one of the earliest and most influential students of personality development, constructed a theory based on assessment of those mental functions that he encountered in his adult patients. In his theory, Freud postulated a series of concepts con-

19

cerning the workings of mental processes that, through their interaction, influence personality development. His concepts of the id, ego, and superego represent interdependent aspects of mental functioning that relate dynamically to influence personality and behavior (Arcaya, 1988).

The Id

According to Freud, from birth and through almost the entire first year of life, the newborn's mental processes are influenced entirely by the id. The id may be conceptualized as a mental inheritance, a complex of biological urges and needs (instincts). Examples include hunger and the instinct for self-preservation.

Newborn babies do not learn to be hungry. They are hungry because their biological need for food makes their stomachs uncomfortable, leading to a behavior pattern that can be altered by providing food. Likewise, the instinct for self-preservation is common to all living things, ranging from the plant that turns to face the sun and sends roots deep into the soil for water, to the infant who reacts with a startle-withdrawal pattern to a painful stimulus.

Libido is a term that refers to the energy of the id. It may be compared to electricity flowing through a wire. Just as turning on an electric switch sends current through the bulb, so the libido finds expression when a "connection" is made between the needs of the id and suitable fulfillment for them in the environment. Psychologists call this process need gratification.

The Ego

The ego, Freud's second basic mental concept, first makes its influence on mental processes felt toward the end of the first year of life. Until then, newborn babies' psychological functions are influenced entirely by biological urges and needs (id) and the desire to gratify them. They are unaware of any distinction between self, needs, and the world outside. Nipple, breast, bottle, mother, and self and are mentally fused into one unit and

experienced as such. However, as they begin to grow older, children become aware that, unlike the situation in the womb, they are no longer protected from outside stimulation. Hunger and elimination needs are no longer automatically and immediately gratified. Now when they are hungry, they begin to recognize that there is often a delay before the caregiver – usually mother – feeds them. Bright lights and noises intrude, and elimination can produce uncomfortable, even painful results if children are not changed promptly.

They slowly begin to realize that something exists outside of the self and that their own well-being depends on this outside caregiver for gratification. As their recognition of her increases, they also become more aware of themselves as a separate person (individuation). As this awareness grows, the ego begins to form and assumes a role in the mental processes. The ego functions somewhat analogously to a corporate executive. Just as the executive gathers information on all aspects of the company and its place in the total economy, then makes decisions on corporate actions to be taken, the ego gathers information about the body, its needs, and its relation to the environment, then decides which course of action to take. The ego acts as the mediator or negotiator between the basic desires of the id and the outside world. The ego should not be seen as totally antagonistic to the id. Rather, the ego and id may be conceptualized as partners, since it is the function of the ego to find realistic ways of gratifying the id's desires. To return to the analogy, the corporate executive acts within the economy as a whole to best serve the interests of corporate stockholders.

Not only does the ego mediate the influences of the inner world through contact with the outer world, but it also serves a protective function to the individual. Should the ego fail in its protective and executive function, serious mental illness will ensue. Thus, an important function of the ego is to maintain a tolerable state of psychological equilibrium, or balance. Scientists refer to this equilibrium as homeostasis. Coined by physiologist Walter

Cannon, this term was first used to describe the system of physical checks and balances existing within the body to help maintain physiological equilibrium. For example, if a person goes out into the hot sun from a cool room, the body temperature does not change. A temperature-regulating mechanism in the body maintains constant body temperature regardless of the outside environment, thereby preserving physiological homeostasis. This concept also can refer to the psychological state. The ego is analogous to the physiological temperature regulating mechanism and helps keep the individual in psychological homeostasis.

The Superego

In Freud's postulates, the third aspect of mental functioning is the superego, a psychological construct closely related to the concept of conscience. As children grow up, they acquire from their parents a system of values — things they should or should not do. At first, these are forced on children from the outside (for example, by parents, church, and school), but eventually they become internalized so that even in the absence of parents or other authorities, children will follow them. The values that are first learned from parents form a rather primitive superego, which judges conduct (an upright citizen, a charming woman, a successful executive), or an ideal of desired accomplishments (to stand for honest city government or to protect the consumer). When this ego ideal is threatened, anxiety, fear, and/or anger can occur. While some people may have a very poor ego ideal that is easily threatened, others may possess an exaggeratedly superior one. The latter is often a defense against hidden powerful feelings of inferiority and inadequacy that would overpower the ego ideal if recognized openly.

Situational and Environmental Factors

Although the Constitution states that all men are created equal, reality can be very different. Even in the uterus, the yet-to-be-born baby is affected by social, economic, and environmental conditions. If the mother lives in a ghetto, she may not receive adequate prenatal care. Her diet may greatly affect her unborn baby's development. The incidence of complications at delivery may increase, and the baby may suffer some type of brain or physical damage. After birth, environmental forces are also influential. Studies have shown that prejudice and discrimination adversely affect personality development. They may lead to a very negative self-image.

The theories of psychologist Erik Erikson (1964) are helpful in understanding the influence of social and environmental factors on personality development. Erikson postulates that the first stage of personality development involves formation of a basic sense of trust. He emphasizes the importance of adequate mothering during the first year of life and claims that to be effective, it must move beyond the satisfaction of only physiological needs. Psychological needs must also be met: to be rocked, cuddled, sung to, comforted, and loved. If the mother adequately fulfills these needs during the first year of life, the infant will develop a basic sense of trust. If infants do not receive this mothering — if cries go unattended for long periods, if they are not cuddled — this basic sense of trust will not develop and infants will perceive the world as hostile and not gratifying.

In Erikson's conceptual framework, the second stage of personality development is the time of the growth of a sense of autonomy. This begins at approximately twelve to fifteen months of age. For the next two years, children's energies are centered on proving that they are separate people with a will of their own. In this stage, children must be allowed to make choices in order to develop a sense of self-reliance. At the same time, they must be protected from exceeding the boundaries of self-determination of which they are capable. The interaction between child and parents will again determine success or failure in developing this sense of autonomy.

In Erikson's third stage, at four years, children begin to want to find out what kind of person they can be and to develop initiative. They observe others, especially parents, and try to imitate their behavior. At no other time in life will most people be as eager to learn and to do. Parents should always encourage and support initiative, but it is especially important that they do so during this time of life.

Very soon, children move into the fourth stage. They want to be engaged in tasks that will give them a sense of accomplishment. During this period, children acquire not only knowledge and skills but also the ability to cooperate and interact positively with others. If they encounter situations in which they are labeled too often as a failure, they will develop a sense of inadequacy rather than accomplishment. At this time in life, school and school personnel play an important interactional role with children. Positive or negative reinforcement in school can influence the development of a healthy or unhealthy personality.

The fifth stage occurs as children enter adolescence. At this time, the central problem becomes the establishment of a sense of identity. Who are they? What will their role be in society? What job or profession will they seek? Will they marry and when? Can they make it even though they are part of a minority? Will they be a success or failure? They worry about acceptance by the peer group. They worry about their future. They become fearful of developing sexual desires and of the whole experience of sexual relationships.

As adolescents mature into adulthood, they also must be capable of developing intimacy with others (Erikson's sixth stage). This ability to experience intimacy is necessary for the mature emotional give-and-take of a successful marriage. Some people, because of inadequacies in previous stages of emotional development, can never get close enough to others to achieve this. They tend to retire into psychological isolation and maintain interpersonal contacts on a formal level that lacks true warmth and spontaneity. In Erikson's view, positive movement through these stages

is the basis for normal personality development. As will be pointed out later, interaction between a person and his or her environment can be negative at any point in this process, leading to a variety of emotional problems, both minor and major.

The Three Levels of Mental Activity

The developmental theories of Freud and Erikson are associated with Freud's theory of mental processes, which introduces the concepts of the conscious, the preconscious, and the unconscious. He described these three layers of mental activity as follows: (1) the conscious – our immediate experience; (2) the preconscious – that which is currently outside consciousness but which can be recalled immediately into consciousness; and (3) the unconscious – that which is made up of events and feelings that cannot readily enter into consciousness or the preconscious.

The following analogy is useful in understanding these concepts. A person stands in the center of a room with a flashlight. That portion of the room within the beam of the flashlight is the conscious (what she is now thinking, seeing, hearing). She shines the flashlight into another portion of the room and stops it on a part previously darkened (the preconscious). The unconscious is that portion of the room beyond the reach of the flashlight, because of distance, objects that block portions of the room, or inadequate brightness.

Of all behavior, the unconsciously motivated is perhaps the most powerful and significant. Although Freud postulated this concept in a new framework in this century, it actually reaches far back into history. Socrates, the early Greek philosopher, said, "In all of us, even in good men, there is a lawless, wild beast nature which peers out in our sleep" (Mezer, 1960, p. 33). Other philosophers often warned that a devil lurks within each of us, awaiting the opportunity to destroy our souls.

Nevertheless, it was Freud who formulated the first clinically workable theory to explain the dynamic nature of the unconscious. He demonstrated that the unconscious is not merely a jumbled collection of past experiences, memories, and feelings but rather a dynamic system of primitive needs and urges, constantly seeking immediate gratification through entry into consciousness. Some of these unconscious thoughts are allowed expression under only certain conditions; others are never allowed into conscious expression.

Evidence of unconscious activity includes dreams, slips of the tongue, sleepwalking, psychosomatic symptoms, accidents, and the processes of remembering and forgetting. Freud called these behaviors "the psychopathology of everyday life" and gave many examples from clinical histories to illustrate how some feelings of guilt, jealousy, and hostility that are usually unconscious can find expression in consciousness through these mechanisms. For example, a woman may not

want to go out with her husband and another couple because she is unconsciously afraid and jealous of the other woman. She develops a severe headache, forcing cancellation of the evening's plans. In another case, a person hostile to a coworker may "accidentally" let a pipe slip through his fingers that strikes and injures the other worker. Or consider the fellow at the bus depot who approaches the buxom ticket seller and says "Two plickets to Tittsburgh." In this case there was no need for a mental health professional to interpret the slip.

As we shall see in the chapter on suicide, some people who "accidentally" fall from windows, are hit by cars, or fail to make the curve on a lonely highway may be satisfying an unconscious urge to do away with themselves. They may not consciously intend to commit suicide, but their unconscious urges interfere with their ability to avoid these situations or to take appropriate countermeasures.

SUMMARY

Police officers with professional attitudes toward behavior must be able to assess and understand the behavior of those with whom they deal. Why is the adolescent running away from home? Why are some people more violent than others? What causes abnormal sexual behavior? Why do some offenders always get caught so easily? To answer these and similar questions, officers must possess a frame of reference that includes appreciation of ingredients necessary for healthy personality development. Comparing the background of an offender with

the known requirements for healthy personality development will enable officers to evaluate more effectively that offender's motivation.

The basic psychological terms and theories presented in this chapter are part of the knowledge necessary to appreciate the complexity of human behavior and personality development. In the next chapter the author will continue the discussion of basic psychological principles by exploring the development of defense mechanisms and the part that they play in both conscious and unconscious behavior.

BIBLIOGRAPHY

Arcaya, J. M. (1988). The police and the emotionally disturbed: A psychoanalytic theory of intervention. *Journal of Police and Criminal Psychology* 4(11), 31–39.

Cameron, N. (1963). *Personality development and psychopathology.* Boston: Houghton Mifflin.

Erikson, E. H. (1964). *Childhood and society.* New York: W. W. Norton.

Kisker, G. W. (1972). *The disorganized personality.* New York: McGraw-Hill.

Marburg, G. S. (1977). *The development of the healthy and unhealthy personality: A comparison of those developmental processes that facilitate optimal growth, openness, and integration with those that culminate in ultimate constriction, closure, and disorganization.* Washington, D.C.: University Press of America.

Mezer, R. R. (1960). *Dynamic psychiatry.* New York: Springer.

Mohr, D. M. (1978). Development of attributes of personality identity. *Developmental Psychology, 14,* 427–428.

Staub, E., ed. (1980). *Personality: Basic aspects and current research.* Englewood Cliffs, NJ: Prentice-Hall.

White, R. W. (1968). *The abnormal personality.* New York: Ronald Press.

Chapter 4

THE NORMAL PERSONALITY IN OPERATION: CONFLICTS AND THE MECHANISMS OF DEFENSE

In the last chapter the author discussed normal personality development and some of the factors that influence it. Ideally, the id, ego, and superego work together to maintain a psychological balance that maximizes functioning. Before completing this discussion of the normal personality, it is important to understand how the ego handles daily stresses. All encounters upsetting events, nagging problems both small and great, dreams that never materialize, and plans that go astray. To ensure that they do not disturb the balance among the id, ego, and superego, the ego employs defense mechanisms to handle these stresses. The failure of these defense mechanisms to work effectively often leads to emotional problems and mental illness. A complete understanding of defense mechanisms requires knowledge of other psychological concepts, including conflict and frustration. An unsuccessful resolution of frustration and conflict can lead to anxiety or guilt.

FRUSTRATION AND CONFLICT

In Chapter 3, the definition of the id referred to a group of biological urges and needs. These needs also can be called motives or drives because they supply the power that motivates or drives the earliest forms of behavior exhibited by the personality. Psychologists refer to these early drives as *primary drives* because they are the basic inherited constituents of behavior. Those that appear later in development are *secondary* or *learned drives.* These include love and a need for acceptance. Behavior is the result of either primary or secondary drives or a combination of both.

Within the scope of these two types of drives falls a vast number of biological, psychological, and social needs, all seeking fulfillment. Not all of them can be fulfilled. All people experience the frustration of their drives. The experience of frustration can be represented by a diagram that shows the individual (I) striving toward some goal or objective (G) with a barrier (B) intervening (Kisker, 1972).

$$I \rightarrow B\ G$$

The barrier may be physical (time, distance, space, confinement), biological (lack of intellectual ability, physical deformities, lack of strength), psychological (personality factors, feelings of fear, guilt, or anxiety), or cultural (group norms, pressures, and demands). At each barrier a solution must be found or an adaptation made. Related to this concept of frustration is the concept of conflict. In this situation individuals must choose between two goals that are incompatible (G1 and G2).

$$G1 \leftarrow I \rightarrow G2$$

Individuals are torn between two goals of equal or near equal repulsion or desirability. They have difficulty choosing. If the choice is very important, the conflict can be very disruptive to psychological and even physical balance. If individuals resolve the conflict successfully, the probability of personality disturbance is slight. If not, some form of personality breakdown is likely to occur.

Reactions to Frustration and Conflict: Guilt and Anxiety

No one is immune or insensitive to frustration and conflict. If each frustration could be overcome easily and every conflict resolved quickly, there would be no inner turmoil. Anxiety and guilt, the common reactions to frustration and conflict, arise when problems in any area of daily living cannot be quickly resolved. Anxiety and guilt seem to operate as signals, warning the ego that the psychological balance is being threatened.

Anxiety

Anxiety is an emotion that is familiar to everyone. If it is *normal* anxiety, the reasons for it are usually obvious and the anxiety is in proportion to the cause. However, anxiety also can emerge when there seems to be no apparent reason for it, or it can be manifested out of proportion to the cause. This is known as *pathological* anxiety.

Doctors first thought that anxiety occurred secondary to a physical dysfunction of the nervous system. Freud, however, postulated that anxiety is psycho-genic, occurring secondary to mental processes rather than physical dysfunction. Erikson viewed anxiety as secondary to the conflicts that the child, adolescent, or adult encounters in each stage of life. This is not to suggest that anxiety has no

physiological components when it occurs. On the contrary, changes in body functions are often one of the ways anxiety is noted. Freud also pointed out the usefulness of anxiety. He claimed that anxiety also can act as a signal to the ego, informing it of impending or present danger. With this signal, the ego is better able to anticipate or recognize situations that threaten the psychological balance.

How does anxiety differ from fear? Fear is a relatively well-defined response connected to a specific object, event, or person, while anxiety is a vague, diffuse response whose relationship to any specific object, event, or person can be ill defined. Sometimes it is difficult to make the distinction. Fear and anxiety usually go together. Anxiety-producing situations, or stress situations, have physiological effects that manifest themselves through the autonomic nervous system and the endocrine system. When people's security is threatened, physiological changes occur and help prepare them to meet the danger. Thus, anxiety, uncomfortable as it is, is useful to healthy people. It puts them on physical alert by heightening perceptions and reactions. These physical changes vary. The heart may beat faster, blood pressure may go up, chest pain may occur, and respiration may increase. Digestion also can be disturbed, with a loss of appetite, nausea, vomiting, or diarrhea. Shaking or a sudden feeling of weakness can occur. Reactions may range from profuse sweating to cold and clammy hands and feet.

Psychologically, the expression of anxiety also may vary greatly, from mild worry or vague uneasiness to dread, apprehension, or panic. Associated feelings of gloom, depression, pessimism, inadequacy, helplessness, or hopelessness may also occur. Individuals may be unable to sleep, have nightmares, or awaken easily. In summary, anxiety may be both a normal sign of future or present danger or a symptom of psychological imbalance. As a signal, it can serve the useful function of alerting the organism and getting it ready to fight or flee. As a symptom, it represents a reaction to frustration or conflict that, if not dealt with, can impair functioning and lead to more serious emotional problems.

Guilt

Like anxiety, guilt is also a possible reaction to frustration and conflict. It may be conscious or unconscious. A person who must choose one of two unacceptable alternatives may feel guilty about the reluctant decision. Guilt feelings are first instilled in children by parents, as an aid in setting limits on behavior, as a form of punishment for misdeeds, or perhaps for not living up to their expectations. Even if parents have no conscious intent to create guilt, children may still feel guilty because of their own interpretation. Guilt is often associated with id strivings, particularly sexual and aggressive urges. In our society, the creation of guilt feelings is also used to control the "base" nature of man. Soren Kierkegaard, the noted nineteenth-century Danish philosopher, stated that guilt "guides the individual and keeps the more violent tendencies of the personality in check" (Kisker, 1972).

People may feel guilty for something they did not do because they had an unconscious wish to do it, but the superego would not permit that wish into consciousness. For example, a woman who has had to care for an invalid mother for many years blamed herself for her mother's death. In treatment, it became apparent that her guilt feelings resulted not from inadequate care while her mother was alive, but rather from her wish, at first unconscious, that her mother would die so she would be freed from her responsibility. Guilt feelings also vary in intensity. One person may feel little guilt in a given situation, while another may feel very guilty. Some may even worry for years about something that others would easily forget. For example, it is not unusual for the Internal Revenue Service to receive guilt payments for tax errors or evasions committed years earlier.

Police officers also are familiar with some of guilt's variations. All have encountered the criminal who seems to want to be caught. The authors know of a burglar who broke into the snack bar at police department headquarters and was easily apprehended. The police may also encounter subjects who voluntarily confess to crimes they did not commit. Most often the chief motivation for such confessions appears to be a feeling of guilt for some actual or perceived behavior.

Defense Mechanisms

To this point, we have described (1) how a person strives to achieve certain goals, either for conscious or unconscious reasons; (2) how these goals are frequently not achieved because of some barrier or because they are incompatible, leading to frustration and conflict; and (3) how frustration and conflict can lead to anxiety and guilt. We will now describe how the ego attempts to deal with these feelings of anxiety and guilt and maintain psychological balance. Of the techniques used by the ego, two are overt, physical, and always employed consciously. The others are internal and dynamic, representing a psychological process that may be conscious or unconscious.

Fight and Flight

The two overt and physical mechanisms are fight and flight. When people resort to fighting, they are trying to overcome anxiety and guilt through aggressive behavior. This behavior is intended to destroy the source of danger, thus protecting the individual. However, when aggressive, hostile behavior is allowed direct expression, it may arouse more guilt and anxiety that, in turn, may intensify the aggressive, hostile behavior and create a vicious cycle. Choosing to flee rather than to fight may also be damaging. People who constantly make this choice may become passive and withdrawn or even resort to drugs or alcohol as a means of flight.

Internal Defense Mechanisms

The internal mechanisms, however, are of the greatest importance. Among these are displacement, rationalization, compensation, projection, reaction formation, denial, repression, identification, substitution, fantasy, regression, sublimation, and isolation. These mechanisms are usually employed unconsciously. Just as the body does not need to be told to evoke certain physiological defense mechanisms, such as temperature regulation, when physical equilibrium is disturbed, the mind does not need to be told to activate these psychological defense mechanisms when the psychological balance is threatened. However, these mechanisms may occasionally become conscious through increased self-awareness or treatment.

With the possible exception of repression, none of these processes is necessarily pathological or harmful to individuals. All of us use these defense mechanisms daily to protect us against guilt, tension, anxiety, inferiority, and other uncomfortable feelings. It is only when these mechanisms are employed indiscriminately and in an over determined or exaggerated manner, or when they are inadequately developed, that they become pathological.

Displacement

In displacement, a strong emotion (such as anger) is displaced onto a person or object other than the one that originally aroused the emotion.

Case Example. Officer Hunt is sitting on her motorcycle observing traffic when she notices a car approaching the corner of First Avenue from Salina Street. There is a stop sign, but the car merely slows down before turning right onto First Avenue. Hunt pursues the vehicle and makes the stop. She intends to give the middle-age driver a warning rather than a citation. However, when she approaches the driver, she is greeted with violent verbal abuse, which ends with the driver's suggestion that she take the ticket and "shove it."

Officer Hunt was a victim of displacement. Just before the motorist left home, his wife had announced that her cousin, whom he disliked

intensely, was coming for a three-week visit. Although Officer Hunt may never know the reason for the displacement, she does not need to. She should be aware that a defense mechanism may be operating in this situation and recognize that the motorist is not really angry with her. In this way, she can avoid losing her temper and responding negatively to the motorist's hostility and aggression. Knowledge of this mechanism may also help Officer Hunt become more introspective about her own behavior in situations where she loses control of her anger without sufficient cause.

Rationalization

Rationalization is the defense mechanism that enables individuals to justify their behavior to themselves and others by making excuses or formulating fictitious, socially approved arguments to convince themselves and others that their behavior is logical and acceptable.

Case Example. Sergeant Maloney is overweight. The chief has told him to lose pounds or face dismissal for physical unfitness. His own physician has advised him that his health is seriously threatened by his obesity. He is fully aware of his need to diet and has been trying to follow his doctor's orders. His wife nags him about losing weight but continues to cook many fattening foods because she feels the rest of the family shouldn't have to diet just because he has a problem. The sergeant had been losing weight, but one night after a particularly exhausting and frustrating tour of duty, he opens the refrigerator door and notices a single piece of apple pie (his favorite) left over from supper and eats it. However, Maloney could not have eaten that pie without feeling guilty or anxious (since his doctor told him dieting was necessary) unless he had first found a way to justify his action. This was possible through rationalization.

How did he rationalize this action? He might have convinced himself that (1) it is a fact that many people all over the world are hungry; (2) it is a sin to waste food; or (3) if someone doesn't eat this piece of pie tonight, it will be too dried out by morning and will have to be thrown away. In any one of these ways, it becomes not only excusable for him to eat the pie and thus avoid wasting food, but also his duty to do so even if he sacrifices his own welfare. With these rationalizations, Maloney can avoid guilt and anxiety. He is able to eat the pie, as he wanted to, and has justified his behavior to himself (and to others), thereby avoiding anxiety and guilty.

Compensation

Compensation is the defense mechanism through which people attempt to overcome the anxiety associated with feelings of inferiority and inadequacy in one area of personality or body image by concentrating on another area where they can excel.

Case Example. Scholastically, Recruit Thomas is the low man in his class, but he is the top marksman and judo expert. He spends every available extra hour either on the range or in the gym, perfecting these skills in which he is already overly qualified, even though his classwork continues to suffer.

Compensatory behavior may be healthy and constructive. For example, Recruit Thomas compensates for academic inferiority by concentrating on judo and marksmanship. Excellence in these two areas helps his ego cope with anxiety generated by marginal performance in the classroom.

Projection

In projection, people ascribe feelings and ideas that are unacceptable to the ego or the superego to others, so that those persons will seem to have these feelings or ideas. People thus free themselves from the guilt and anxiety associated with those feelings. This process is analogous to a motion picture. There is a picture on the screen, but the real image is on a small piece of film inside the projector.

Case Example. Sergeant Bucko is one of the first motorcycle officers in the department. He is not too smart and lacks a high school diploma. Things go well for him until a new lieutenant takes charge of the squad. The sergeant has never had any trouble with lieutenants in command. However, this new lieutenant places demands on the sergeant that have made his life miserable. Sergeant Bucko informs the chief that he can't continue to serve under his new lieutenant because he thinks that the new man does not like him. Although he has made no plans for retirement and could continue on the force for another ten years, and even though the chief urges him to reconsider, Sergeant Bucko resigns.

The sergeant has been confronted with duties that he cannot perform well. He feels inadequate, inferior, and harbors unconscious dislike for and anger toward the lieutenant. He avoids dealing with these feelings and emotions by projecting his anger and dislike onto the lieutenant. Thus, it appears to Bucko that the lieutenant is angry with him and also dislikes him.

Reaction Formation

The defense mechanism of reaction formation refers to development of a trait or traits that are the opposite of tendencies that we do not want to recognize. Individuals are motivated to act in a certain way but behave in the opposite way. Consequently, they are able to keep their impulses under control.

Case Example. Mr. Brewster is a middle-aged van driver who was raised in a strict religious family. He has never had a real date and considers sexual activity sinful and animalistic. He constantly calls his local police department with complaints about the goings-on in lovers' lane, urging patrol of the area twenty-four hours a day. He is the loudest voice in the community against indecency, advocating strict moral censorship of all movies, plays, and books.

If Mr. Brewster's personal history was carefully examined, it could be learned that stern, moralistic parents who regarded sexual activity as dirty and disgusting reared him. They considered the sex act acceptable only between married people, although they never explained how their son could change his attitudes and emotions when he did marry. The idea that a couple might enjoy sex was beyond his parents' comprehension.

Mr. Brewster grew up to be a physically healthy man with a normal sex drive. He cannot entirely repress these urges. They emerge in dreams, threatening to break forth into consciousness. His strict superego does not permit any direct expression of these drives. Mr. Brewster seeks to reduce his anxieties arising from personal conflict by becoming overly concerned about community morality. By badgering the police department with complaints about pornographic movie houses and lovers' lane, he can be preoccupied with sexual matters in a way that quiets his own unacceptable sexual urges and also supports his superego.

Denial

When people use the mechanism of denial, they refuse to recognize and deal with reality because of strong inner needs.

Case Example. Patrolman Click has been experiencing shortness of breath and occasional chest pains, but he tells himself that these symptoms are probably muscular and of minor importance. While riding in a patrol car with his partner one day, he suddenly experiences crushing chest pain. His partner rushes him to the nearest hospital, where he remains for a week for tests. The doctor tells him he has heart trouble but it is not too serious. He will have to lose some weight, give up smoking, and take medication. He will also have to leave patrol duty and transfer to a desk job. Officer Click doesn't believe the doctor and insists on returning to full patrol duty. He even goes to another doctor, at his own expense and without telling anyone. Even

though he receives a similar evaluation, it does not alter his thinking and he persists in demanding a return to full patrol duty.

Click refuses to believe that he has heart trouble because it is too threatening to his self-image as an active patrolman. He loves the duties of a patrolman and can't see himself in a desk job. To him, being on the streets is real police work. He therefore persists in his denial of medical reality as communicated to him by two competent doctors.

Repression

Repression is an unconscious process whereby unacceptable urges and/or painful, traumatic experiences are completely prevented from entering consciousness. Suppression, which is sometimes confused with repression, is a conscious activity by which an individual attempts to forget emotionally disturbing thoughts and experiences by pushing them out of mind (for example, a person may attempt to forget grief by losing him or herself in work).

Case Example. A motorist who found her wandering dazed and confused on the highway brought Helen Smith to the police substation. Her clothes were torn and she had obviously been beaten. A medical examination indicated probable rape. Helen could give no account of what happened and was hysterical. Investigation revealed that she had left a local bar with a man, later identified as a habitual sex offender who had served time for rape and assault. Days later, Helen could still not recall details of the incident and met all attempts to gather information with "I don't know . . . I can't remember."

Helen has apparently repressed the entire rape incident. Perhaps the experience was too frightening for her to assimilate and deal with consciously. Possibly she also feels some guilt and questions her own judgment. The physical pain of the beating, the terror of her experience, and her possible guilt feelings create a traumatic experience that she can deal with only through repression. She is not lying when she says she can't remember, nor is she trying to protect anyone.

Identification

In the defense mechanism of identification, people seek to overcome feelings of inadequacy, loneliness, or inferiority by taking on the characteristics of someone important to them. For example, children identify with parents, whom they see as models of strength and competence.

Case Example. Police were called when the body of an unidentified man was found in a local swimming pool with his feet tied together. Investigation established his identity and also that his wife died by drowning a few days before while they were on a fishing trip.

In this case, we have a specialized form of identification: introjection. People have an unconscious tendency to assume (interject) characteristics of someone close to them who has died recently. When this man's wife died by accidental drowning, grief and despondency drove him to employ introjection in his suicidal behavior (Kisker, 1972). Knowledge of this defense mechanism could be of great value to the officer investigating whether the man's death was homicide or suicide.

Substitution

Through substitution, individuals seek to overcome feelings of frustration and anxiety by achieving alternate goals and gratifications. Unrequited loves, unfulfilled longings, unattainable plans and ambitions, and unacceptable urges and impulses will create feelings of anxiety and guilt unless people find some substitute gratification.

Case Example. Fifteen-year-old Marie Smith is arrested again as a runaway juvenile. She is found living with a thirty-eight-year-old man. This is the fourth time in two years this has occurred, each time with a different man. She always promises it will not happen again.

However, when it does, she is at a loss to explain why.

It is likely that Marie is trying to find the love and affection she lacks at home by having sexual relationships with older men. If her father had given her normal love and affection, she would not have to seek it by running away and engaging in promiscuous behavior with a father substitute. The officer who finds Marie Smith might be more helpful if he understood the reasons behind her behavior.

Fantasy

Fantasy is one of the most useful defense mechanisms. Its content is determined by unfulfilled ambitions and unconscious drives.

Case Example. Officer Jeffers sometimes has trouble keeping her mind on academy lectures. She finds herself daydreaming that she will become the Dirty Harry of the department and imagines herself overcoming all sorts of obstacles in solving the case of the century. These fantasies occasionally lead to inappropriate behavior, such as the time she tried to arrest a dangerous criminal by herself.

Regression

A person who regresses reverts to a pattern of feeling, thinking, or behavior appropriate to an earlier stage of development.

Case Example. Officer Riley's husband seems mature to most people. However, whenever he cannot have something he really wants (like a fishing trip), he throws a temper tantrum. Even though they can't really afford it, Officer Riley finally agrees to her husband's demands to halt his tantrum.

While growing up, Mr. Riley never learned to deal maturely with denied gratification. He never had to learn because his father and mother gave in immediately whenever he started having a temper tantrum. Today, when he thinks he is denied something, he is only repeating the successful behavior learned in childhood.

Sublimination

Sublimation is the diversion of unacceptable id impulses into socially and culturally acceptable channels.

Case Example. Charlie Smith has always been hostile. Since early childhood, he has had frequent daydreams of hurting or killing someone. When he entered high school Charlie did not enjoy regular sports, such as baseball and basketball. One day a friend took him down to the local gym. Charlie soon realized that he had found what he wanted – to become a boxer.

Boxing allowed Charlie to release his aggression with social approval and possible financial reward. Sublimation proved a positive and constructive defense against otherwise unacceptable impulses and needs.

Isolation

According to Henry P. Laughlin (1979), isolation is in use when an idea or object is divorced from its emotional connotation. "Police officers see it in killers and rapists who speak about their crimes expressionlessly. They see it in hospitals where medical and nursing professionals cope with patients with such detachment that they seem cold and indifferent. And they see it in themselves when they stand over a pitiful victim and calmly order an investigation" (Reese, 1987, pp. 67–74).

This mechanism permits officers to distance themselves emotionally from the immediate reality of the situation and enables them to appear in control. They maintain their police image and deny any emotional involvement in the situation. This defense mechanism is useful in that it allows officers to get the job done. However, it is one of the most deceptive and, if not controlled, emotionally dangerous defenses used by officers. If carried over to home and family, it seriously interferes with their role as spouse, parent, and neighbor. They will hear their spouse complaining "I just can't seem to get through to you anymore – you have no feelings" (Reese, 1987, pp. 67–74).

SUMMARY

This chapter has pointed out that the dynamic interaction of the id, ego, and super-ego, occurring on both a conscious and unconscious level, can often lead to frustration and conflict, creating feelings of anxiety and guilt.

Defense mechanisms, such as displacement, rationalization, and compensation, may operate automatically to protect individuals from these unpleasant feelings and to maintain psychological balance (homeostasis). When people use these defense mechanisms constructively and positively, they are acting in a healthy way; when people employ them indiscriminately and inappropriately, they are heading toward ill health. When people's defense mechanisms break down completely or have not been adequately developed, the individuals are likely to become mentally ill.

Reading this chapter should impress upon police professionals that there is some motivation for every action and that most persons are not necessarily aware immediately of the reason for their behavior. However, the basic concepts considered here is only the starting point for understanding specific behaviors. Therefore, police officers must be cautious in drawing any conclusions regarding the underlying causes of a person's action. If people themselves are unaware of why they act in a certain way, officers will come to understand this behavior only after thorough investigation and study. Police officers also should resist instant diagnoses of behavior. However, they may legitimately use their understanding of behavior to help form preliminary judgments that will guide their actions, recognizing that all the facts may not appear on the surface. In addition, knowledge of defense mechanisms should afford police officers some insight into their own behavior, especially in stressful situations. For example, are they displacing some personal, private anger (perhaps from home or from an encounter with an angry supervisor) onto the hapless citizen, thus increasing the stress for both?

Knowledge of defense mechanisms should encourage police officers to examine the effect of their own presence on the behavior of others. In many cases, people may view officers' presence as a barrier to their desires, or as another factor they must consider before deciding on further action. With this knowledge, police officers can better anticipate the behavior they are likely to encounter and, by anticipating it, control their own reactions and increase their effectiveness.

BIBLIOGRAPHY

Brenner, C. (1982). *The mind in conflict.* New York: International Universities Press.

Cramer, P. (1979). Defense mechanisms in adolescence. *Developmental Psychology, 15*, 476–477.

_____. 1987. The development of defense mechanisms. *Journal of Personality, 55*(4), 597–614.

Freud, A. (1946). *The ego and the mechanisms of defense.* New York: International Universities Press.

Freud, S. (1961). Inhibitions, symptoms and anxiety. In *The Standard Edition of the complete psychological works of Sigmund Freud*, ed. J. Strachey, vol. 20, pp. 87–172. London: Hogarth Press.

Kisker, G. W. (1972). *The disorganized personality.* New York: McGraw-Hill.

Laughun, H. P. (1979). *The ego and its defenses*, 2nd ed. New York: Jason Aronson.

Martin, D. G. (1976). *Personality: Effective and ineffective.* Monterey, CA: Brooks/Cole.

Reese, J. T. (1987). *Behavioral science in law eEnforcement.* Quantico, VA: U.S. Department of Justice, FBI Academy.

Chapter 5

ABNORMAL BEHAVIOR: WHAT IT IS AND WHAT TO DO

The last two chapters presented concepts of normal personality development and functioning. This body of knowledge is basic to understanding the complexities of human behavior. It is now appropriate to consider some aspects of abnormal behavior based on these concepts.

WHAT IS ABNORMAL BEHAVIOR?

Since *ab* means "away from," abnormal behavior is behavior that is away from, or deviating from, normal behavior. However, defining normal behavior is not as easy a task as may first appear, since many variables are involved. Some people regard their own behavior as quite normal. They therefore conclude that people who behave as they do are normal, while those who do not behave similarly are abnormal. This personal standard of definition is illustrated by the old Quaker proverb:

Everyone is queer
Save thee and me
And sometimes I think
Thee a bit queer too.

Normal behavior also can be defined as the embodiment of an ideal (the ideal soldier, the ideal husband). If normal behavior is that which emulates an ideal model, then abnormal behavior is that which deviates from it. Normality also can be conceptualized statistically. Here the average (mean) is considered normal. The more one's score deviates from the mean, the more abnormal one is. The deviation can be in a positive or negative direction (for example, a child may be exceptionally dull or exceptionally bright depending on whether her IQ is far below or far above the mean). However, this approach does not lend itself well to the study of the individual because there are always exceptions to the rule and because human behavior is too complex to be reduced to a curve or set of curves.

Culture also plays an important role in determining what is normal or abnormal. One culture may approve of sex play among children; another may strongly disapprove. One culture condones homosexuality; another condemns it. Otto Klineberg, a noted social psychologist, stated: "Abnormality is embedded in the very structure of our society and can only be understood against the background of the culture in which it occurs" (Klineberg, 1954). This interconnectedness between the individual and society is pointed out by C. Wright Mills: "Neither the life of an individual nor the history of a society can be understood without understanding both." In

34

this view, no behavior is intrinsically abnormal; it becomes abnormal only in relation to the whole range of social and cultural preferences. In our own society, the professional judgment as to whether behavior is significantly abnormal depends on the presence of certain symptoms characteristic of mental illness. For example, are patients hearing voices that do not really exist (hallucinations)? Do they cling strongly to false beliefs despite all tests of reality (delusions)? Are they depressed?

In judging the seriousness of the illness, professionals also look at the degree of ineffectiveness of the individual's behavior. Is the person able to continue working, or does his or her behavior interfere to such a degree that work is impossible? Is the person able to fulfill the role of husband or wife, father or mother? In this view, behavior that is ineffective, self-defeating, self-destructive, and that alienates the individual from those who are important to him or her is regarded as abnormal.

Common Misconceptions About Abnormal Behavior

Regardless of these definitions of abnormal behavior, most people associate it with the strange, the alien, and the unknown. Consequently, abnormal behavior and mental illness frequently cause fear, repugnance, and misunderstanding. Attitudes are shaped more often by rumor and popular stereotypes than by direct experience and sound information. The following misconceptions are common.

1. There is something evil about mental illness, and people who suffer from it are themselves evil, violent, and homicidal. This misconception is a carryover from the days when the mentally ill were regarded as possessed by evil spirits or as having willingly made a pact with the devil in return for certain favors. Many stories, plays, and movies have perpetuated this belief through tales about mad scientists, witches, maniacal killers, and sex fiends. A typical opening scene in many horror movies shows a state hospital or

insane asylum set forlornly in the middle of nowhere. A violent thunderstorm is raging, and as the camera moves inside the institution, a mad scientist-type character is pacing to and fro along a darkened, eerie corridor. Is it any wonder that many people are afraid of mental institutions and the people within them? The truth is that there is nothing at all evil about mental illness. Most of the mentally ill are neither violent nor dangerous. A better word to describe them is *afraid*. They are afraid of many things – of what is happening to them, of the people around them, and of the world in which they live. This is true even of the person who is brandishing a knife and threatening to kill whoever comes near. If police officers recognize this fear, they can use it to their advantage when taking the person into custody by offering help and protection instead of a confrontation.

2. Mental illness is an "all-or-nothing" affair. The concept of mental illness is easily dichotomized. A person is often regarded as insane or normal, yet nothing could be farther from the truth. Mental illness, like physical illness, is both a matter of type and of degree. Years ago, the army made a training film whose purpose was to acquaint line commanders with different types of psychiatric casualties and how and why such casualties occurred. The title of the film was *Shades of Gray*, and it opened with vignettes about various types of psychiatric disorders. The film begins something like this:

"It's a big day for the recruits on the grenade range. For the first time they are throwing live grenades. Suddenly, something goes wrong in pit number 5. Private Smith pulls the pin on the grenade then freezes with the grenade clutched tightly in his hands. The sergeant grabs the grenade from the recruit and throws it just in time." "What went wrong?" the narrator asks.

Another scene begins: "This soldier has been acting strangely recently, keeping more and more to himself. He seems suspicious of his buddies. Suddenly, while eating in the mess hall, he grabs the soldier next to him and accuses him of poisoning his food." The scene ends with the soldier being forcibly taken from the mess hall to the Mental Hygiene Consultation Center.

Another vignette depicts a soldier walking guard on a lonely, desolate post in the far north. "Suddenly," the narrator tells us, "this soldier is overcome by a wave of depression." He drops his weapon and leans against a stunted tree, staring blankly into the distance with tears in his eyes.

The film then discusses mental health and mental illness. It points out that if physical examinations were given to every soldier in one of the most elite units, not one man in that platoon would be rated perfect. For example, a few might be coming down with a cold; others may have a minor stomach upset; and hardly anyone would have a perfect set of teeth. On the other hand, there would also be no one who would merit a completely negative physical rating. All would be a "shade of gray." The same is true of mental illness. As no one is perfectly healthy, no one is perfectly adjusted. Some may be too sensitive to what others say; some may worry too much about an overdue letter from home or unpaid bills; others may feel without justification that they are not up to the standards of their peers and are inferior or inadequate. On the other hand, even the chronic mental patient will have some area of health, no matter how small. Mental health, like physical health, is not a dichotomy; it is not an all-or-nothing affair. It is a matter of degree. It is also a matter of kind. For example, someone who has a common cold is not suffering from the same disease as the person suffering from strep throat, even though both are ill. Nor is either of them suffering from the same kind of disease as the person with terminal cancer.

In mental health, the person who experiences mild feelings of inadequacy and tension at social gatherings is not suffering from the

same type of illness as the individual with a strong and unrelenting fear (phobia) of crowds. Nor is either of them suffering from the same type of illness as the acutely disturbed person who locks him or herself in a room all day to avoid all contact with people. Variations in kind are as critical as variations in degree.

3. If people are mentally ill, they will always be mentally ill and their condition will not vary significantly from day-to-day. Illness, mental or physical, is like health. It is dynamic and does not remain constant. A person may show signs of emotional disturbance one day and not another. Even the sickest person in the state mental hospital has good days and bad days, just like all of us. Those with mental illness can be treated and become functional again. Like physically ill patients, they also may get sick again, receive appropriate treatment, and recover.

4. The feelings and behavior of the mentally ill have no relationship to the feelings and behavior of the mentally healthy. Nothing could be farther from the truth. Have you ever had a day when you were down in the dumps, when everything around you made you feel more depressed? The bipolar patient (formerly called manic-depressive) experiences similar feelings. The difference is that your feelings of ups and downs are usually connected with things that are actually happening, while the bipolar patient is more often responding to inner feelings and thoughts unrelated to reality. While your depression could be lifted immediately if you were told that you had won $10,000 in a sweepstakes, bipolar patients are not necessarily cheered by such news. They even may interpret winning as another example of how unworthy they really are.

Consider another example. Some mentally ill patients experience delusions. A delusion is a false belief that is strongly held despite all tests of reality. All of us have experienced beliefs that later turn out to be false. The difference is that the mentally healthy person is able to check beliefs against reality and modify thinking based on evidence presented. The delusions of the mentally ill person are not subject to the challenge of reality. For example, any attempt to convince such a person that, say, his belief that all doctors are out to kill him is not true may turn him against you. He may conclude, because of disturbed thinking, either that you are a fool for not believing him or that you are in league with those plotting against him.

5. Nothing a mentally ill person tells you can be believed. Many times people (including police officers) refuse to listen to (or believe) a person they suspect to be mentally ill because they feel the person is "too crazy to make sense." However, most mentally ill people can (and do) answer questions sensibly and give reliable information unless they are acutely ill and hallucinatory or delusional. Police officers would do well to keep in mind the admonition frequently given to medical students: "Listen to the patient."

These are some of the popular misconceptions about mental illness and the emotionally disturbed. Understanding these misconceptions is important because they tend to bias people against those who are mentally ill and prevent them from dealing with such persons in a more accepting, humane, and professional manner.

Guidelines for Judging Abnormal Behavior

Officers on the street often will have to decide whether a person's behavior is normal or abnormal. If it is abnormal, they will have to decide whether it can be handled without police action or whether official intervention is necessary. They must judge how serious the abnormal behavior is and whether it is dangerous to the person himself and/or others. To trained law enforcement officers, recognition and handling of abnormal behavior is critical to the effective execution of their duties. We will now turn to those general and specific characteristics of behavior that police officers will assess to reach conclusions about

the meaning of the behavior, as well as how to handle it.

Appropriateness

Normal behavior tends to be appropriate to the situation; abnormal behavior tends to be inappropriate. The judgment of a behavior's appropriateness involves assessment of not only the behavior itself, but also of the situation in which it occurs. For example, suppose you are standing in the foyer of a Catholic church during a noon Mass. Mr. Smith enters the church, comes up beside you, kneels, makes the sign of the cross, and starts to pray. This is appropriate behavior since it takes place in a Catholic church during Mass. However, suppose the locale, but not the behavior, is changed. It is Sunday noon at a busy intersection. You are in the center of the street directing heavy traffic. Suddenly Mr. Smith appears, kneels by your side, crosses himself, and starts to pray. In this different setting, not only is the behavior inappropriate, but it is also dangerous. Note that the behavior itself has not changed; only its appropriateness has changed.

Similarly, most of the time emotions are directly related to what is happening or what has happened. If individuals experience great emotion after a major tragedy, that is appropriate. If, on the other hand, they fall apart following minor frustrations and conflicts, it may not be appropriate. Perhaps you can recall a relative or acquaintance that became greatly upset under conditions that surprised you. Or if you have been in the military, you may have noted some recruits who broke down and cried or went absent without leave after only a minor reprimand. In most instances, the degree of sadness or happiness is usually related to what is actually happening. Emotionally disturbed persons, however, may be so depressed that they want to kill themselves, even though another person with the same problems is neither as depressed or suicidal. Persons suffering from other kinds of mental illness may also show marked discrepancies between degree or type of emotional response expected in a particular situation and the actual degree or type of emotion demonstrated.

Flexibility

Normal behavior tends to be flexible; abnormal behavior tends to be inflexible. Normal behavior, regardless of setting, tends to be flexible in that it is altered to fit the situation. As an example, a police officer's behavior toward the chief of police is flexible if he adopts a different approach when he is talking to him in the office on an official matter than when they are at a department picnic where they are both dressed in sport clothing and drinking beer together.

These criteria for examining behavior are closely related to appropriateness. However, while a person's behavior may be appropriate, it may lack the flexibility characteristic of healthy behavior.

Impulsivity

Since abnormal behavior is related in part to uncontrolled or partially controlled needs and drives, it tends to be impulsive. A person with normal behavior is more likely to consider its consequences and give important decisions careful thought before implementation.

During the Vietnam War, a young soldier was referred to an Army Mental Hygiene Consultation Clinic shortly after entering basic training. He sat weeping in a chair, crying with dismay and desperation at how he could not cope with the army and had to get out. Asked when he was drafted, he replied that he had enlisted. When asked why he enlisted if he hated it so much, he related the following story:

> He had never wanted to go into the service. He had been under the care of a psychiatrist for some time and had prevailed upon his doctor to write a letter that he could take to his draft board declaring that he was unfit for military service. He took the letter to his draft board, expecting to be told that he

would never be called. Instead, the board told him that when his number came up, this letter would be considered in determining whether to call him up. This made him so angry that he went across the hall to the Army Recruiting Office and enlisted for four years – an obviously impulsive act.

Not all abnormal behavior signals mental illness. As we stressed earlier, there are degrees of mental health and illness, just as there are degrees of physical health and illness. However, if a person's behavior is abnormal according to one or more of the three general characteristics discussed earlier, the need for additional action should be analyzed further. In their book *How to Recognize and Handle Abnormal People*, Matthews and Rowland suggest the following specific criteria (Matthews & Rowland, 1974).

Big Changes in Behavior

Since behavior is dynamic, not static, everyone's behavior changes over time. However, one should be especially alert for sudden, big changes in an individual's lifestyle. For example, if a man who always stays at home during his leisure hours, loves his wife and children, never quarrels with his neighbors, and works faithfully at his job suddenly becomes quarrelsome, misses work, spends his time in bars, starts drinking excessively, and abuses his wife and children, it is likely that he is suffering from a serious mental disorder. The officer should inquire about the individual's present behavior compared with his past actions. Has he behaved this way before? If so, when and under what circumstances? When was this current change in behavior first noticed?

Losses of Memory

All of us have memory losses at one time or another. We may forget dental appointments, miss birthdays and anniversaries, or fail to recall material studied the night before. These memory losses are normal. However, if a person cannot remember who he is, where he is, or the day, month, or year; if a woman has been raped and cannot recall any of the details; or if a man who has had an auto accident cannot remember anything after the crash, the possibility of a brain injury or psychological dysfunction arising from serious conflict should be considered.

Feelings of Persecution

Police officers know that people plot against other people. A person who is realistically worried about being killed usually will be able to tell officers who might want to kill him or her and offer plausible reasons why. Abnormal persons, however, may *imagine* that someone (or some group) is planning to kill them. They may specify that group, but the choice is usually unrealistic. Furthermore, the reasons, if they are able to offer any, are likely to be bizarre and not readily understood by officers. For example, a person may say that "the communists" want to kill him because "they know my message to the President will end the war and dissolve the international conspiracy of communism."

Grandiose Ideas

An individual may claim that he represents the second coming of Christ or that she is the Virgin Mary. In other situations, people may indicate how important they are by telling you that everybody is plotting against them. They must be very important if everyone is after them. Or individuals may believe that they have committed the world's worst sin and that they are the most miserable, unworthy humans ever born. Even in these negative statements, they are emphasizing their importance. It is important to keep in mind that some seemingly grandiose ideas may turn out to be true after investigation. For example, a soldier, suspected of being somewhat paranoid, was speaking to a doctor about his father. He said that his father, who was retired, had been a German intelligence agent

in World War I and that during World War II, after immigrating to America, he had parachuted behind German lines for the OSS to make contact with and escort to freedom a famous Dutch scientist who was being forced by the Nazis to work on V2 bombs. His story sounded like a James Bond novel. The doctor calculated that the patient's father would have been in his sixties during World War II and considered the whole story delusional. However, later interviews with the father revealed that the boy's story was true.

Talks to Self

All of us occasionally talk to ourselves, especially if we are angry or emotionally upset. However, mentally ill adults can carry on entire conversations with imaginary people or animals for considerable periods of time.

Hears Voices

Occasionally, in talking with people who demonstrate feelings of persecution or grandiosity, police officers note that the people appear easily distracted and are not paying attention to what is going on around them. On further inquiry, officers might determine that the people are hearing voices. These voices are actually the people's own thoughts, projected from the self to the outside (auditory hallucinations). However, some who hear voices may tell you that they do not know where they are coming from or who they are, while others may tell you they are coming from a radio (which is not on) or from someone who is not there.

Sees Visions, Smells Strange Odors, or Has Peculiar Tastes

Instead of or in addition to hearing voices, people may say they have seen their dead mother standing by their bed before they go to sleep or that they have seen God or the devil (visual hallucinations). Unlike voices, however, these types of hallucinations are more often related to physical influences or abnormalities, such as the effect of alcohol on the brain or brain tumors. Similarly, people may smell strange odors (gas in the apartment) or complain of peculiar tastes (poison in the food). In these instances, the possible presence of a physical illness should be thoroughly investigated.

Thinks People Are Watching or Talking about Them

Sometimes people will complain that they are being watched or that people are talking about them. Because of their own conflicts, they have become supersensitive to other people through the mechanism of projection (Chapter 4). They see two people talking and are sure they are the topic of conversation. They feel that they are being followed, but when they look over their shoulder no one is there. They interpret remarks made within their hearing as pertaining to them even though the person speaking may have no idea that they exist. At first they are not sure about these things. They try to check them out. However, as they become more disturbed, they become more convinced of the accuracy of their perceptions and resist attempts to convince them that their beliefs are wrong. Finally, these *ideas of reference*, as they are called, can become fixed delusions of persecution or grandeur.

Unrealistic Physical Complaints

All people have physical complaints at one time or another. However, people who exhibit abnormal behavior or are mentally ill often believe that things are wrong with or happening to their bodies that are not anatomically or medically possible. They may tell you, for example, that their brain is decaying or that half of the body is different from the other half. They often will tell you these terrible things with little or no emotion. If they are convinced that they have an incurable disease, they may try to take their own lives. It is important to realize that these symptoms are very real to the individuals and that they can suffer as much as anyone with a physical ailment.

Extreme Fright

Some people become frozen with fear, while others panic. A person may tremble, speak haltingly, glance about in terror, or demonstrate a marked startle reaction at the slightest sound. Officers should protect such people from injury that may result from efforts to get away from what is feared. Such persons may attack officers if the latter attempt to stop them.

Dangerous or Destructive Behavior

As we shall see in a Chapter 9, some emotionally disturbed people will not show any of the above-mentioned symptoms but, time after time, will do things that are destructive or dangerous to themselves or others. Although they may get hurt or hurt others, they do not seem to learn from the experience or show any emotion about it.

Depression

Officers should be alert for individuals who do not respond to questions and seem very depressed. These people may be potential or acute suicidal risks.

How to Handle the Mentally Ill

Police officers not only must be able to recognize abnormal behavior and mentally ill persons, but also must be prepared to guard, restrain, or take into custody people whose behavior suggests the presence of a mental illness. The following are suggestions for handling these difficult situations.

1. Calls involving known emotionally disturbed individuals should be answered by more than one officer. If it is not known that the call involves a disturbed person, the officer who arrives first on the scene should immediately ask for backup. Do not try to handle the case alone. Handling it alone does not prove you are a better officer than if you ask for help.

Psychiatric attendants, doctors, and nurses who have worked with very disturbed people, including both homicidal and suicidal patients, suffer very few injuries. Even prior to tranquilizers, mental health professionals have been able to work on a ward housing forty to fifty such patients without difficulty. One reason for this is their ability to use the *show-of-force* principle effectively. For example, an attendant might approach Mr. Brown and tell him that he has to go to X-ray. He should, of course, try to convince Mr. Brown to go. If Mr. Brown shows signs of resistance and refuses, the attendant would not argue or try to force him. Instead, he should withdraw and reappear with three or four more attendants and again tell Mr. Brown that, for his own welfare, the doctor had ordered X-rays and that he has to go to X-ray. He should be told, without anger or threats, that he can walk to X-ray under his own power or be carried by attendants. He should also be told that more attendants can be called if needed. Faced with this show of force, most patients usually elect to proceed under their own power. This show of force does two things for disturbed individuals: It gives them a face-saving out if they have been bragging how tough they are or that no one can force them to do anything they do not want; and it shows them that many people are interested in them and that they care enough to ensure that treatment orders are carried out.

This process can work the same way on the street. If a disturbed person has been boasting that no cop is going to take him anywhere, he may feel required to put up a battle against one policeman. With two or three officers present as backup, he has a face-saving out. The officers also can use their numbers to assure the person that they are able to offer him protection against any threat. As with the

hospital patient, their numbers also give him a sense of importance and show him that somebody does care about him. An acutely disturbed subject should be taken to a hospital emergency room for evaluation and assistance (Leff & Simon, 1984).

2. Stay with disturbed persons until additional help arrives. If necessary, ask someone else to phone for assistance rather than leaving the person.

3. Move slowly. Resist the impulse to act hastily. This may be difficult since most police training teaches the importance of quick decisions. With the emotionally disturbed, it is better to take time and carefully assess the situation. Immediate action is necessary only when handling an *immediate* danger.

4. Reassurance is important. Acutely disturbed individuals are generally very frightened.

5. As a matter of policy, it is usually a good idea to send uniformed officers. Avoid emergency lights and sirens since they tend to attract unwanted crowds. Keep spectators away if possible.

6. Solicit help from friends, relatives, and others known to the emotionally disturbed individuals. The time spent in obtaining this help may prevent violence and harm from coming to the individual, yourself, or others. Be cautious, however, in allowing these people to talk to the disturbed person. Their presence may further upset him or her.

7. Don't lie or try to deceive emotionally disturbed persons. If they are aware of deception, dealing with them will become more difficult. If you lie, you also create a barrier to their acceptance of future help.

8. Do not rely on your weapons. The threat of a gun is quite meaningless to people who are acutely disturbed. They may grab it and use it, or you may be tempted to use it. A weapon should be used only in the very rare situation when it is necessary to save a life.

9. Don't be fooled by the individual's size. For the same reasons that some people are impervious to intense pain during periods of emotional stress, others may have unusual physical strength at these times. Experienced police officers are familiar with this phenomenon and can cite cases where several officers have found it difficult to subdue a 125-pound senior citizen.

10. Don't meet hostility with hostility. This is often a natural reaction since hostile people tend to elicit hostility in others. It is important to maintain a professional attitude. Meet hostility and anger by being calm, objective, and accepting. Ask why they are angry or afraid. If they will tell you, they may begin to calm down.

11. Don't argue with delusions, but don't agree either. Rather, try to steer people away from whatever subject is exciting them. If they demonstrate by actions, facial expression, increased agitation, or bizarre behavior that the subject discussed is making them upset, switch to another subject. Try to bring them back to reality by asking concrete questions, such as: "How long have you lived here?" "Who is in your family?" and "Where do you work?" By maintaining control of the discussion, you will reassure them. Sensing that you are in control of the situation will help them to gain control.

12. Don't be fooled by a sudden return to reality. Emotionally disturbed individuals can return to their delusions just as quickly. Consider them potentially dangerous because their behavior is unpredictable, and remain alert even if they calm down. You can remove any restraints that have been applied if, in your judgment, behavior warrants it; but be ready to reapply them if behavior makes it necessary. If available, leather cuffs similar to those used in mental hospitals are best. Agitated people have been known to pull tendons and cut wrists while in handcuffs. If handcuffs have to be used, check frequently to see that circulation has not been cut off. When restraints are unavailable, safety devices can be made on the spot using pillows, mattresses, and belts or by reversing an ordinary coat or jacket.

13. Take all suicidal behavior seriously. Ten to 20 percent of all crisis calls are likely to involve suicidal persons (France, 1982). People making threats, gestures, and suicidal attempts should be referred for professional psychiatric help. Do not excuse or gloss over a person's behavior just to reassure anxious relatives.

14. Make sure individuals are not physically ill or injured. Diabetic coma, fever delirium, brain tumors, convulsive disorders, and other physical illnesses could be mistaken for drunkenness or combativeness. Head injuries often go unnoticed, especially if there is an odor of alcohol on the breath. If any doubts exist, get medical attention.

15. Keep a record of a person's complaints regarding plots against him or her. If the complaints change from a vague "they" to a particular person or small group of people, the safety of those named may be at risk. Officers or mental health professionals may have a legal obligation to warn anyone who is threatened. Try to persuade someone who knows the person to take him or her to the family doctor, clergy, or local psychiatric facility.

16. Learn what community facilities are available. These exist to help the mentally ill and their families, especially in an emergency.

17. Remember that most disturbed people are afraid. They experience extreme fear because they do not understand their feelings and because they are not certain how others will treat them. When emotionally disturbed persons become aggressive, it is almost always because of fear. Therefore, officers should attempt to handle them in a calm, understanding, and humane way. This will often reassure the people that officers are there to help.

18. Don't make fun of other people's troubles. It is easy to become callous, especially in dealing with disturbed persons.

19. Maintain your sense of humor. This is important, especially in stress situations. Many a day has been saved because someone did.

SUMMARY

This chapter has presented some differences between normal and abnormal behavior and has discussed some misconceptions regarding abnormal behavior and mental illness. Certain guidelines have been offered to help police officers decide whether the behavior they are dealing with is abnormal and, if so, to what degree. The author has pointed out that abnormal behavior differs from normal behavior in three general characteristics – appropriateness, flexibility, and impulsivity – and that certain specific signs and symptoms indicate mental illness. Finally, The author has offered various suggestions on how officers can handle individuals manifesting abnormal behavior in order to increase officers' effectiveness and decrease the chances of injury to self or others.

BIBLIOGRAPHY

Altrocchi, J. (1980). *Abnormal behavior.* New York: Harcourt Brace Jovanovich.

Arcaya, J. M. (1988). The police and the emotionally disturbed: A psychoanalytic theory of intervention. *Journal of Police and Criminal Psychology, 4*(1), 31–39.

Goldenberg, H. (1977). *Abnormal psychology: A social/community approach.* Monterey, CA: Brooks/Cole.

Klineberg, O. (1954). *Social psychology,* 2nd ed. New York: Holt, Rinehart and Winston.

Matthews, R. A. (1970). Observations on police policy and procedures for emergency detention of the mentally ill. *Journal of Criminal Law, Criminology and Police Science, 61*(2), 283–295.

Matthews, R. A., & Rowland, L. W. (1974). *How to recognize and handle abnormal behavior.* New York: National Association of Mental Health.

Olfson, M. (1987). A characterization of police-referred psychiatric emergencies. *American Journal of Forensic Psychology, 8*(3), 5–13.

Reid, W. H., et al., eds. (1986). *Unmasking the psychopath.* New York: W. W. Norton.

Sokol, R. J., & Reiser, M. (1971). Training police sergeants in early warning signs of emotional upset. *Mental Hygiene, 55*, 303–307.

PART III

UNDERSTANDING MENTAL ILLNESS

Chapter 6

PERSONALITY DISORDERS

In the next three chapters, the author will discuss the three most commonly encountered categories of abnormal behavior. We will examine their major characteristics and provide case examples illustrating situations often associated with these conditions.

Diagnostic terminology used is consistent with the DSM-IV-TR (the most recently adopted version of the *Diagnostic and Statistical Manual of Mental Disorders* of the American Psychiatric Association) except in Chapter 7, where we have chosen to retain the term neurotic disorders because of its familiarity to nonmental health professionals. With one exception, not discussed are diagnostic categories of abnormal behavior characterized primarily by psychological factors in association with physical conditions, such as specific disorders first evident in infancy, childhood, or adolescence (excluding mental retardation); mental retardation; and organic mental disorders (caused by or associated with impairment of the brain or its associated functions).

GENERAL CHARACTERISTICS OF PERSONALITY DISORDERS

Patterns of normal and abnormal behavior originate during early development. Personality disorders result from aberrations in this developmental process, influencing patterns of perceiving, relating to, and thinking about the environment and the self. The path from normal personality development to personality disorder is *not* analogous to a divided highway where a normal personality becomes a personality disorder as soon as the center divider is crossed. Rather, the path is more analogous to a two-lane highway divided by a dotted line, where an individual with certain traits may use them to his or her advantage at times (for example, stay in the proper lane), but also may use them dysfunctionally (for example, crossing over into the opposite flow of traffic), leading to behavior that does not serve the individual's best interest.

There are many significant periods in childhood development in which a failure to receive appropriate care from parents and others can lead the child to develop abnormal behavior patterns. These can serve initially as a defense against increased environmental stress. However, once adopted, they are very difficult to give up, especially if the child is not encouraged to change but is instead rewarded for maladaptive behavior. For example, if Johnny gets what he wants by having a temper tantrum, he may repeat this behavior because it has been rewarding. Other negative early experiences may include the unreasonable demands that parents sometimes place on their children by failing to accept excuses when the child's behavior does not meet their expectations. Faced with this situation, a child may adopt a behavior pattern in which he or she quickly mobilizes energy to meet each demand, not necessarily with the goal of being successful but simply to avoid punishment if he or she fails.

Those with personality disorders often lack flexibility in responding to situations. While the normal personality is flexible and responds with appropriate patterns of behavior to different environmental events, the person with a personality disorder cannot significantly alter or change the pattern of behavior toward events that require different responses. As a result, the person experience distress and often has trouble in social and occupational situations. In contrast to neurotic disorders, personality disorders are generally ingrained in the development of a person's life-style over a long period. Those with neurotic disorders more often exhibit specific symptoms, such as anxiety or depression, rather than a pattern of behavior. Thought disorders, delusional thinking, or hallucinatory experiences are indicative of psychotic disorders.

This chapter will describe four types of personality disorders most commonly encountered by law enforcement officers. Other personality disorders include the schizoid (in which the major defect is in the capacity to form social relationships), the narcissistic (in which the major defect is a grandiose sense of self-importance), and the borderline personality disorder (in which there is an instability in interpersonal relationships, mood, and self-image). The psychopathic personality disorder will be discussed in Chapter 9.

The Passive-Aggressive Personality Disorder

The passive-aggressive personality disorder is a major cause of failure in jobs, school, and interpersonal relationships. The essential feature is a direct or indirect resistance to demands for adequate performance. Those with this disorder often passively express hidden

aggression. Their behavior may be characterized by procrastination, stubbornness, intentional inefficiency, forgetfulness, and delaying tactics. Despite their aggressiveness, these people are often dependent and lack self-confidence. They may express pessimism about the future, but at the same time are unable to recognize that their behavior is responsible for the difficulties they encounter. They frequently blame others. Authority figures are a favorite target for resistance and resentment. Many of these people also have a magical anticipation that all their needs will be met regardless of their behavior.

Case Example. Gregory Martinez, who is twenty years old, came to the police's attention one evening when his mother called the emergency number. She said that her son was lying on the bathroom floor and that his arm was bloody. Upon arrival, the paramedics administered emergency first aid and took Gregory to the hospital, accompanied by his mother.

While the doctor was treating the cut Gregory had inflicted on his arm, the officer obtained the following information. Gregory had just graduated from a vocational rehabilitation program after taking courses in automobile bodywork. He had entered it after his parole, having served one year for felonious assault on the boyfriend of a girl Gregory had dated earlier. More recently, his mother said he had been very upset because even with his diploma, he could not find work. In the days before cutting himself, Gregory had been complaining bitterly of the prejudice he felt from others because of his past prison record and his Mexican-American heritage. In reality, however, it was a period of high unemployment in the community and jobs were scarce all over.

Gregory had been a spoiled only child and until recently had never demonstrated any motivation to help himself. Even entrance into the rehabilitation program had occurred only after his parents, girlfriend, and other friends had cajoled him. Gregory's mother said, "He always seems to want everything to happen for him, and when he doesn't get his way, he strikes out." When asked to explain further, she recalled how, as a teenager, he had many problems in school with both classmates and teachers because he would not accept direction. His teachers told his mother that he couldn't handle criticism no matter how small and that his typical response was to become more disruptive. They all felt he could do better, but noted that he was his own worst enemy, always managing one way or the other not to do what he was asked.

The Histrionic Personality Disorder

Those with histrionic personality disorders are easily excited and overreact to many situations in a dramatic manner. Minor stimuli lead to emotional hyper responsiveness. This dramatic behavior is always attention seeking and may appear seductive. Furthermore, histrionic people are generally self-centered, immature, and tend to be impressionable. They are easily influenced by others, particularly by authority figures. Police sometimes encounter them as victims of sexual attack. In presenting their stories of the attack, they are likely to embellish dramatically the details of the event, missing nothing in their description. Those with this disorder are often incapable of forming mature heterosexual relationships; they act dependent and helpless while constantly seeking reassurance. Others perceive them as shallow, even if they are superficially warm and charming.

Case Example. Hilda Davis is twenty-two years old and twice divorced. She was brought to the emergency room after she had reportedly fainted at home. She had been living with her sister and brother-in-law and their children in a small trailer following her most recent divorce. She remembered feeling nervous almost as soon as she moved into the house. On further questioning, Hilda revealed she had had an affair with her brother-in-law several years earlier. Although she did not see any connection between this event and her

feelings of nervousness, Hilda revealed, perhaps inadvertently, that she felt edgy and dizzy at night when she was alone with her sister and he was working, and got better during the day when he was there and her sister was working. Hilda was given some tranquilizers and asked to return to the clinic the next day. When she appeared, the doctor immediately noticed a remarkable change in her appearance. Instead of the disheveled young woman he had seen the night before, Hilda was now seductively dressed with somewhat overdone makeup. When invited into his office, she immediately said, "I'm so glad to be here. That medicine you gave me last night made me feel so much better." More than seeking a sexual relationship, these people seek attention. When this attention was lacking during childhood, they learn to get it by dramatizing their behavior or feelings. If this is not successful they may try other routes, such as feigning illness.

The Paranoid Personality Disorder

Hypersensitivity, rigidity, unwarranted suspicion, jealousy, and feelings of excessive self-importance, coupled with a tendency to blame others for any failure that they encounter, characterize those with a paranoid personality. They often use projection as a defense mechanism and see the entire world through a very personal set of references. They view their frustrations as further evidence that their suspicions about the world are true. These people often have an exaggerated sense of importance. They see themselves as the focal point of all activities that surround them, whether or not this is true. They make mountains out of molehills and are often concerned with hidden motives and special meanings. Usually appearing tense, they are rejected by others because their underlying hostility and lack of humor make others very uncomfortable.

Case Example. Mary Rutherford is twenty-six years old and single. She is employed as a secretary and is the least liked woman in the office. She is impossible to get along with because of her constant accusations that others are picking on her, giving her too much work, or not treating her properly. This is puzzling because she appears intelligent and ambitious. A woman who used to share an office with her remembers one encounter that illustrates why Mary is not well liked. One day this woman was called into the office of one of the people for whom she and Mary worked. The two women had been proofreading a manuscript. When Mary's coworker got up to go into the office, she said, "Be back in a minute." Unfortunately, her return was delayed because the boss had a lengthy task to explain to her. When she finally returned to her desk, Mary was enraged, sarcastic, and jealous. Without provocation, Mary immediately launched into a tirade, accusing her office mate of trying to seduce the boss. Attempts to quiet Mary were unsuccessful, and both the conversation and the accusations ended only when the woman excused herself, went to the powder room, and remained away from Mary the rest of the day.

Paranoid personalities usually grew up in a home filled with parental conflict. One parent is usually domineering and the other submissive. Not only are the children unable to deal with the domineering parent, but they also do not receive help from the submissive one. As one way of handling this devastating situation, the children adopt a behavior pattern in which they may react defensively to almost any situation in which a threat is felt from the domineering parent. The children become constantly vigilant and fearful of individuals and situations, whether or not the fear is justified. Feelings of rejection are exaggerated and further reinforce this vigilant attitude.

The Compulsive Personality Disorder

Excessive concern with rules and conformity, adherence to strong standards of perfectionism, an inability to relax and to tolerate ambiguity, a characteristic rigidity that makes it impossible for them to change their minds after arriving at decisions, and a failure to express warm emotions characterize those with a compulsive personality. At work they often initially draw the positive attention of superiors because of an ability to organize their thinking and to conduct affairs in an orderly fashion. However, these positive traits quickly become obscured by their stubbornness and by the eventual recognition of their inefficiency.

Case Example. After several years as a patrolman, Mike Morris was promoted to sergeant. While complimented in the past for his attention to detail, excellent reports, and seemingly appropriate observance of the rules of safety, he was a total failure as a supervisor. Those who had been his peers and were now his subordinates quickly found it impossible to work for him. With his new responsibility of enforcing rules and regulations rather than following them, he made life miserable for his subordinates. His attention to detail, while admirable as a patrol officer, interfered with the ability of other officers to perform their work. His demands for more and more reports and his tirades when officers did not "go by the book" created a morale problem. While his peers ignored his excessive attention to orderliness when he was at their level and was complimented by his superiors, it now became obstructive and antagonistic. Initially officers under him tried to please him but soon found they could not succeed. Finally they gave up and began devising ways of getting around him and discrediting him. The situation deteriorated, and finally the officers felt forced to go to Mike's superior and ask for his removal or their transfer. Mike's compulsive personality disorder nipped a promising career in the bud. However, like most compulsive personality disorders, his never received psychiatric attention. Many such people can function effectively, provided they are placed in a suitable environment.

This need to maintain rigidity is an outgrowth of early developmental problems involving parental control. Faced with the need to comply with parents and overly threatened with loss of love if they do not, children may either be overly compliant and compulsive or become rebellious. Children often give up the latter alternative quickly because of parental demands and the children's need for love. The children learn quickly that parental approval and love will come if they are compliant. By paying attention to detail, they avoid dangerous feelings of fear and anger directed at the parent for enforcing this standard of behavior. In attempting to gain control of anger, they pay the price of giving up opportunities to express this emotion. If they encounter a stressful situation in which these emotions are overwhelming, the compulsive behavior pattern can break down and a psychotic reaction occur with severe depression. Even in this decompensated state, they may continue to pay attention to detail. A well-known example of this is Lady Macbeth who, while psychotic, focused on a spot of blood and compulsively repeated, "Out, damned spot!"

HELPFUL HINTS TO LAW ENFORCEMENT OFFICERS

The interpersonal relationships of those with personality disorders present a unique problem for law enforcement officers. Police officers who are called into a situation involving someone with a personality disorder often find behavior out of control and violence looming. Officers should remember that this person has adopted a disorderly behavior pattern to protect him or herself from life's stresses. When this pattern is threatened, the person may become dangerous and likely to act impulsively in a desperate attempt to protect the self. In handling these situations, law enforcement officers should work in teams. The team approach enables officers to assess the situation quickly and to divide up those responsibilities that will help to bring the situation rapidly under control. When a person is in tense conflict with another, officers should remember that it will not be enough to direct all attention toward the individual with the personality disorder, even if it is obvious who that person is. Since the person is reacting to a stress from another individual, he or she will be reassured if officers also direct their attention to that other person. It is important to remember that since those with personality disorders may do poorly under acute stress, they will respond positively to any activity that helps remove that stress. This does not mean that officers should be lulled by magical expectations. Rather, they can help remove the stress by indicating to the person in forceful, clear, and tactful terms that there is no way that the wish can be granted. This direct confrontation with reality, in clear and nonargumentative terms, can have a calming influence because it helps the person reestablish contact with a reality that has been lost temporarily as emotions gained control.

SUMMARY

In this chapter the author has described those personality disorders that police most often encounter. Officers can learn to recognize the signs of passive aggressive, histrionic, paranoid, and compulsive personality disorders in a variety of situations. Officers can act more effectively if they are aware of the characteristics of these disorders and their influences on behavior. Although the clinical examples in this chapter tend to focus on noncriminal aspects of law enforcement, those with personality disorders can readily be found in criminal situations. This will become clearer when we later examine psychopathic behavior, deviant sexual behavior, delinquent behavior, and drug abuse.

BIBLIOGRAPHY

American Psychiatric Association. (2000). *Diagnostic and statistical manual of mental disorders*, 4th ed. revised. Washington, D.C.: American Psychiatric Association.

Cameron, N. (1963). *Personality development and psychopathology*. Boston: Houghton Mifflin.

Dally, A. G. (1978). *The morbid streak: Destructive aspects of the personality*. London: Wildwood House.

Friedman, A. M., Kaplan, H. I., & Sadock, B. J. (1975). *Comprehensive textbook of psychiatry*, 2nd ed. Baltimore: Williams & Wilkins.

Redlich, F. C., & Freedman, D. X. (1966). *The theory and practice of psychiatry*. New York: Basic Books.

Widiger, T. A., Frances, A., Spitzer, R. L., & Williams, J. B. (1988). The DSM-III-R personality disorders: An overview. *American Journal of Psychiatry, 145*(7), 786–795.

Wishnie, H. (1977). *The impulsive personality: A manual for understanding criminals, drug aAddicts, and sociopaths*. New York: Plenum Press.

Chapter 7

NEUROTIC DISORDERS

Having reviewed the major personality disorders, The author now will focus attention on the next major category of emotional disturbance – neurotic disorders. Whereas personality disorders are generally characterized by maladaptive behavior patterns that evolve into a life-style, neurotics constitute a group whose abnormal behavior is usually characterized by the episodic presence of anxiety or depression in one form or another. Neurotics, unlike psychotics, are not divorced from reality. They live in the same world as we do. Instead of acting out their conflicts as those with personality disorders do, neurotics cannot resolve their conflicts and develop neurotic systems as an expression of them. Before we discuss the specific symptoms of each of the major neurotic disorders, it will be helpful to understand some of their general characteristics.

GENERAL CONSIDERATIONS

The most important element in the development of symptoms is the presence of an impulse, generally coming from the id, which is likely to create anxiety if allowed into consciousness. If it becomes conscious, symptoms also may occur if the impulse is not dealt with appropriately. Defense mechanisms are used to ward off anxiety, but symptoms may occur if the defenses do not work effectively or work so well that the behavior resulting from them impairs functioning. This is a simplified description of the process of symptom formation and does not do justice to its complexity. The complexity results in part from childhood experiences. Consequently, another may ward off a specific impulse that creates anxiety in one person. Similarly, the way one person wards off anxiety may differ from another person's method. An illustration will help clarify this point. Suppose that the unacceptable impulses coming into consciousness are sexual. Let us say that they involve a woman. One woman might handle these impulses through sublimation by choosing a job, such as modeling, that helps her successfully channel her unacceptable sexual impulses. Another might use projection and channel unacceptable sexual impulses into a belief that others are looking at her on the street and thinking about picking her up. Why one person chooses sublimation and another projection to handle the same unacceptable sexual impulses may be a reflection of early developmental factors, including those defense mechanisms that the child used to handle positive or negative reactions from parents. Both women could develop neurotic symptoms if their defenses came under attack. Suppose that the first loses her modeling job or the second is picked up on the street. Both events could generate great anxiety or depression.

While neurotic symptoms may be disturbing, they also can serve a positive purpose. Freud called these advantages *secondary gain*, referring to the benefits obtaining from being sick, when others may pay more attention and do things that they would not ordinarily do if the person were well. Although secondary gain may not play a major role in the onset of neuroses, it may support their continuation. If its benefits are great, there is less motivation to give up the neurotic symptoms. The pursuit of secondary gain is not conscious. When it is, it is called *malingering*. Sometimes it is difficult for the professional to distinguish between conscious malingering and unconscious secondary gain.

Anxiety Neurosis

An anxiety neurosis (also referred to as a anxiety disorder) is defined as an episode of "generalized, persistent anxiety of at least one month's duration" without the specific symptoms that characterize other mental disorders. It is characterized by apprehensive expectation, physical complaints, and hyperattentiveness, but should be differentiated from normal apprehensiveness or fear (DSM-IV-TR 2000).

Historical Background

Many psychiatrists and psychologists have used the concept of anxiety neurosis in their attempts to explain the dynamics of personality development, abnormal behavior, and emotional disturbance.

In his early theory, Freud viewed anxiety as resulting from an inability to discharge physical tension. In his later theory, however, he adopted a more psychological orientation and made an important contribution to our understanding by recognizing the protective function of anxiety. In his concept of *signal anxiety*, he described a state in which the individual first perceives danger and then uses signal anxiety to mobilize defense reactions to avoid the danger. If these attempts to avoid danger are not wholly successful, anxiety may increase and become a diffuse state that affects all behavior, thereby contributing to the development of a more generalized anxiety disorder.

Harry Stack Sullivan, a later theoretician, stressed the early mother-child relationship in the origin of anxiety neuroses. He proposed that the original model for adult anxiety could be found in the child's fear of mother's disapproval. This early anxiety is related not only to the child's knowledge that maternal approval is essential to his or her own comfort, but also can serve as an *alerting mechanism* in situations where maternal disapproval might be forthcoming.

Characteristics

The person with an anxiety neurosis may have a history of chronic anxiety not necessarily related to any specific situation. This anxiety can become more acute in some situations, but there is usually not any particular pattern to the casual observer. Physical complaints can be wide-ranging and involve almost every organ system of the body. Headaches, nausea and vomiting, shortness of breath, palpitations, menstrual dysfunction, and insomnia are often associated with anxiety neuroses. In addition to these specific physical complaints, general uneasiness may be present, characterized by such statements as "I feel uptight," "I can't sleep," "I don't like to be by myself," or "I'm always worried."

Mild depression symptoms, along with anxiety, are common. It is not rare to encounter abuse of alcohol, barbiturates, and tranquilizers, especially in those whose anxiety is persistent or where episodes have occurred frequently. The following example will further illustrate the characteristics of the anxiety neurosis.

Case Example. Hazel Newton is a twenty-one-year-old college junior who was brought to the hospital after police were called to the campus. Her roommates had found her apparently unconscious with a half-empty pill bottle by her bed. After receiving medical attention, she told the following story to the psychiatrist who interviewed her.

Although she had never gone for help, she recognized that she had not been her normal self for at least a year. During the summer between her freshman and sophomore years, she had broken up with the fellow she had been dating since her sophomore year in high school. Up to that time, he was the only man she had dated. Since then, she said, "I have been uptight all the time." Upon further questioning, she also told the doctor that she had had insomnia for two years. She had made many visits to physicians because of vague physical complaints and had many tests to find the cause of these symptoms but without success. Furthermore, her grades, excellent during her first year of college, had gone steadily downhill. When asked about the suicide attempt, she revealed that several days previously, she had been called into the dean of women's office and told that if she did not pull her grades up, she would not be able to graduate. Hazel also stated that she no longer felt comfortable with men and that no man she had dated in the past year had asked her out again. She commented, "I just can't seem to relax on dates."

Underlying Factors

Hazel's anxiety is consistent with the definition of an anxiety neurosis, since it is diffuse and not restricted to specific situations or objects. Her case illustrates another common characteristic: the inability to link the onset of the neurotic behavior with any single precipitating factor. In Hazel's case, the breakup with her boyfriend two years previously and the prospect of failure and rejection conveyed to her by the dean several days before her suicide attempt were critical factors in the original onset and recent worsening of her anxiety disorder.

As previously suggested, events in early childhood serve as the focus for the development of the condition. In Hazel's case, her mother's long absences from home because of work and illness may have been an important underlying factor. Prior to breaking up with her boyfriend, Hazel had been able to cope with her fears of abandonment and rejection through a close and clinging relationship. However, after the relationship ended she could no longer handle her fears of abandonment. Her anxiety grew and grew until it culminated with the suicide attempt.

Depressive Neurosis

Depressive neurosis (also referred to as *dysthymic disorder*) is a condition in which there is a chronic disturbance of mood or a loss of interest in almost all usual activities. It differs from a major depressive disorder (Chapter 8) in that the person with a depressive neurosis does not experience the severe or lengthy distortion of reality and behavioral disorganization that characterizes a psychotic disorder; also, the genetic predisposition noted in the latter is not present in a dysthymic disorder.

Historical Background

During the past seventy years theoreticians, clinicians, and biologists have paid much attention to the differences between the various types of depression. These differences have become more critical since the advent of medication because it appears to have a variable effect on different types of depression.

Characteristics

Persons with symptoms of depressive neurosis feel disturbed, sad, blue, miserable, and depressed. Along with this alteration of mood, these people may show a general loss of interest in the environment, including their home, family, work, or schooling; a tendency to be more self-critical without apparent reason or justification; and an increase in physical symptoms, such as a sleep disturbance, loss of appetite, and a marked change in weight. Suicidal thoughts may be present, often associated with a pessimistic attitude toward the future. Like the anxiety disorder, this depressive disorder is pervasive. In full force, the depressed mood colors all life events. A specific precipitating experience may be identifiable, although it can also be absent. The following example will illustrate.

Case Example. Martin Dine, a twenty-six-year-old police officer, had recently been divorced. He took twenty-five Nembutal after drinking beer for several hours and was found by the police, whom he had called just prior to passing out. He was taken to the emergency room and interviewed after receiving medical attention. He had been depressed for some time since his wife told him she was involved with another man, did not love him anymore, and wanted a divorce. When she was interviewed later, she said that Martin seemed to take the news very well initially, that he recognized their marriage was on the rocks and perhaps a divorce was for the best. However, shortly after the divorce became final and six weeks prior to his suicide attempt, he became very depressed. His fellow officers noticed that he was paying less attention to his work and occasionally took unnecessary risks. Furthermore, he was obviously losing weight, as he was not eating when his squad took a dinner break. On the day prior to his suicide attempt, he was called into the sergeant's office and told that his poor work was noticeable and that if it did not improve, he faced disciplinary action and possible termination. Later that day his former wife called him to say that she could not care adequately for their two children on his alimony payments. Feeling even more depressed and seeing his situation as hopeless, Martin decided to kill himself.

Underlying Factors

Those with a depressive neurosis, like those with an anxiety neurosis, have usually encountered difficulties in early childhood that contribute to a personality foundation that is highly susceptible to development of a neurosis. These early factors may include a poor self-image, which develops either as a result of a lack of positive parental reinforcement or in the presence of overcritical parents. People with depressive neuroses usually have very strict superegos, developed as a result of identification with the overcritical parent. Thus they become overcritical of themselves.

When faced with failure, as Martin was when his marriage ended and his job was threatened, they perceive these events as a natural consequence of their own inabilities, a point of view consistent with their underlying poor self-image. Prior to the onset of the full-blown disorder, they may have experienced less severe episodes of depression as they attempt to compensate for their poor self-image. If they fail, they also experience guilt because they have been unable to live up to not only their own expectations, but also those of their parents and their profession.

In a depressive neurosis, one of the principal underlying characteristics is an inability to handle feelings of anger appropriately. The unexpressed hostility Martin felt toward his wife at the time she told him about her extramarital affair was an important contributing factor to the onset of his acute illness. In treatment, Martin later learned that one of the reasons he was unable to express this hostility was because of the non-acceptance of hostility in his early childhood surroundings. He was forced to hold back these feelings unless he was willing to run the risk of further criticism and rejection from his parents.

Obsessive-Compulsive Neurosis

The obsessive-compulsive neurosis (also known as obsessive-compulsive disorder, or OCD) is characterized by ideas, thoughts, or impulses that are repetitive (obsessions) and by actions that are repeated for unexplained reasons in a patterned form of behavior (compulsions). These obsessions and compulsions are usually perceived as unwanted or unacceptable. The person usually recognizes the senselessness of these thoughts and derives no pleasure from this behavior, other than a relief of tension.

Historical Background

Observations of obsessional thinking patterns and compulsive acts date from medieval times, when these people were often thought to be under the devil's influence. Consequently, many early theories about the origins of obsessive-compulsive neuroses dealt with spiritual forces or witchcraft. By the nineteenth century, however, theorists began to view obsessive-compulsive neuroses differently. Pierre Janet was among the first to assume a more modern view of this emotional disturbance, describing a biological base in which the central disturbance was the result of a lessening of mental energy. However, it was Freud who recognized the importance of the unconscious and conflict, and devised the first modern theory. He viewed obsessive-compulsive symptoms as related to three defense mechanisms: isolation, undoing, and reaction formation. He saw obsessive thinking as an attempt to remove from consciousness any feelings associated with the thought. Only after fully isolating these feelings successfully could the individual allow the previously unconscious and dangerous thought into consciousness.

The amount of energy required to keep the emotional component isolated often involves the entire personality in the process. In the pre-neurotic state, this defense mechanism of isolation begins to break down, and the emotional component of the thought or impulse constantly threatens to break through into consciousness and escape the controls placed upon it. Other defenses must then be employed to counter this threat. The defense mechanism of undoing is a behavioral attempt to handle the obsessional thought that makes the person anxious. This leads to the compulsive act. For example, a mother's compulsion to check the baby's room three times before going to bed might be her way of unconsciously undoing a death wish that she has toward the baby.

In *reaction formation*, the third defense, the person tries to handle unwanted thoughts and emotions by channeling them into a pattern of behavior that is the opposite of the behavior associated with the underlying impulse. For example, the overprotective mother may really be a rejecting mother who deals with this unacceptable impulse by becoming over concerned about her child's welfare. These formulations will be clearer as we talk about the characteristics of obsessive-compulsive disorder and present an example.

Characteristics

As described previously, the characteristics of all OCDs are the presence of obsessional thinking, accompanied by a pattern of compulsive and ritualistic behavior. Kleptomania (compulsive stealing) and pyromania (compulsive fire setting) are variants of the compulsive neurosis occasionally encountered by police officers. These kinds of behaviors protect against the release of even more dangerous, usually aggressive, impulses. In later stages of the illness, the person may give in to them, no longer having the desire to resist them.

Neurotics may not recognize or accept this aggressive content because it is too threatening, but it is usually obvious to a trained observer. Likewise, the person who experiences the compulsive behavior pattern that is designed to ward off the obsessional thoughts is not able to make the connection between the acts and the thought pattern. The following case is an illustration.

Case Example. Michael Monroe was eighteen years old when he was admitted to the hospital's psychiatric unit because he felt he was going crazy. He told the interviewing psychiatrist that for the past three months he had been constantly preoccupied with thoughts about cleanliness and more recently had been spending great amounts of time washing himself and his clothes. His mother confirmed his story and said she also had noticed other changes in his behavior, including an increase in nail biting, a willingness to eat only certain foods, and a peculiar pattern of leaving notes all over the house to avoid talking with family members. Several days prior to admission, a new behavior pattern emerged whenever Michael left the house in which he would walk out the door three steps and back up four steps into the house. This would be repeated four or five times before he could leave the house. When questioned, Michael was unable to present any reason for these actions. He could only state that his behavior had completely interfered with his schoolwork and was seriously threatening his expected graduation from high school in June. He also admitted that the reason he had agreed to come to the hospital was that he had begun to have thoughts of violence toward his father.

Underlying Factors

In Freudian theory, an obsessive-compulsive neurosis has its origins in early childhood, particularly during the period of toilet training. According to this theory, there is a marked degree of ambivalence and uncertainty during this phase of development. This early ambivalence – of not knowing what to do, accompanied by a frequent changing of one's mind – can evolve into a ritualistic pattern of compulsive behavior when stresses are great enough. This ambivalence is exemplified by Michael's inability to make up his mind whether to leave the house. He must first go through a compulsive behavior pattern before he can give himself permission to go. When obsessive-compulsive patterns begin to fail to accomplish their purpose, regression may become the last defense available as an escape from the ambivalent bind. This regression is illustrated by the observations of Michael's psychiatrist. Although

Michael reported being obsessed with cleanliness, he appeared as a dirty, sloppily dressed young man who had not paid attention to his personal hygiene for at least several days.

Michael's mother revealed that just prior to the onset of this obsessive compulsive pattern, his father had been seriously injured in an auto accident. Later, in treatment, the therapist was able to identify that this precipitating event had been a magical carrying-out of Michael's previously unconscious hostility toward his father. A characteristic of the obsessive-compulsive neurotic is an inability to deal with rage, leading to the ambivalence. In this case, the accident had served as the trigger that brought many of these formerly successfully repressed hostile impulses to the surface. The obsessive-compulsive neurosis represented Michael's frantic attempt to prevent these hostile, aggressive impulses and thoughts from breaking through to the surface, which they had finally done in the days immediately prior to his admission to the psychiatric unit.

Phobic Neurosis

Phobic neurosis can be distinguished from the preceding three neuroses because its symptomatology is usually limited to a specific *phobic object* or *phobic situation*. A person with a phobia restricts some normal activities. The phobic neurosis often coexists with other neurotic symptoms, such as anxiety and depression.

Historical Background

The term *phobia* did not appear until the nineteenth century. In 1872, Kurt Westphal, a German theoretician, reported on three male patients who had specific fears of open places, a condition he labeled *agoraphobia*. Today we recognize a variety of phobias that are generally named after a particular fear. Other examples include *claustrophobia*, a fear of closed-in places, and *acrophobia*, a fear of high places.

Characteristics

A phobia must be distinguished from a normal fear. It refers to a *morbid* fear of a particular object or situation – a fear of something that normal persons do not perceive as any great threat or danger. However, this distinction is not always entirely clear. Some phobic objects or situations may create normal fear. When this occurs, we have to look at the strength of the individual's reaction to the object or situation and judge whether a phobia is present by the degree of fear. When anxiety about a specific object or situation cannot be handled appropriately, it is displaced in a phobic neurosis onto a previously neutral object or situation that then becomes the phobic object or situation. Phobias are always accompanied by anxiety when the person is in the presence of the phobic object or situation. However, this anxiety is secondary; it is not the original anxiety.

In the phobic neurosis, displacement is used as a defense. The unacceptable feeling or thought is unconsciously transferred from its source to a less threatening substitute. Through displacement, the neurotic combats the original anxiety. If this person avoids the phobic object or situation, he or she can function effectively. Occasionally, however, the phobic neurosis becomes more severe because the anxiety generated becomes so great that the person develops a phobia for almost every object or situation. Sometimes one or more of the phobic objects or situations becomes so important to the individual's lifestyle that they cannot be avoided. An example will help illustrate this point.

Case Example. Judith Rosenberg is a forty-three-year-old woman who was accompanying her husband when he had an auto accident. Mr. Rosenberg told the investigating officer that his wife made him so nervous when he drove that she really caused the accident. In response to the officer's questions, he said that his wife was much less nervous if she drove the car. The officer suggested that

Mrs. Rosenberg might seek professional help about her nervousness. She did not do so at first, but when her anxiety became so great that it was almost impossible for them to go anywhere unless she drove, she agreed to professional help. The psychiatrist learned that Mrs. Rosenberg's aged mother, Mrs. Schwartz, had died after a twelve-year illness six months ago. During the terminal phase of her illness, Mrs. Schwartz had been in a nursing home. Prior to that, she had lived with the Rosenbergs for close to twelve years. During this time Mrs. Rosenberg had the principal responsibility for caring for her mother.

Underlying Factors

Those who are prone to phobic neuroses as adults have a history of observed anxiety, even as children, in association with certain impulses. Most commonly, the impulses are sexual and aggressive. In normal personality development, the person develops appropriate defense mechanisms that channel these unacceptable impulses.

Prior to devoting all of her energy to her invalid mother, Mrs. Rosenberg had spent much time doing volunteer work for the sick. Consequently, it was natural for her to assume the responsibility of caring for her ill mother. At the outset, before her mother moved into her home, the physician had told Mrs. Rosenberg that he anticipated that Mrs. Schwartz had only a year to live. However, Mrs. Schwartz lived for twelve years, and Mrs. Rosenberg devotedly cared for her every day. Through this attention, Mrs. Rosenberg could continue, through sublimation and reaction formation, to channel many of her unacceptable aggressive impulses. She had begun this pattern with her volunteer work and continued it through her care for her mother. Only when her mother became so ill that she was unmanageable at home was she moved to a nursing home. This was done against Mrs. Rosenberg's wishes, but at her husband's insistence. Mrs. Schwartz died several weeks later.

In treatment, it became clear that the onset of Mrs. Rosenberg's phobic neurosis was directly related to her failure to develop adequate mechanisms for handling her unacceptable aggressive impulses. When her mother died, her mechanism for sublimating this aggressive impulse was also lost. Her choice of the car as the phobic object was related to the corollary phobia of an accident. This latter phobia represented both a displacement and projection of her hostile impulses. She could feel more comfortable if she was in control of these impulses by driving the car but was more anxious when she was not in control and her husband was driving.

Conversion Neurosis

In conversion neurosis, also referred to as hysterical neurosis or conversion disorder, individuals convert the unacceptable impulse threatening them with overwhelming anxiety into a physical symptom, usually associated with the parts of the body under voluntary control. These symptoms lessen anxiety and are often symbolic of the underlying conflict. Conversion neurosis is both similar to and different from phobic neurosis. The similarity is in the use of the defense of displacement; the difference is that the displacement is to a part of the body rather than to an outside object or situation.

Historical Background

Like obsessive-compulsive neuroses, the unusual symptoms of conversion neuroses contributed to an intense mythology during the Middle Ages, the seventeenth, eighteenth, and early part of the nineteenth centuries. Only in the latter part of the nineteenth and early part of the twentieth century was a psychological basis for these symptoms recognized and their causative mechanisms worked out by Freud and his predecessors, Jean-Martin Charcot and Hippolyte-Marie Bernheim.

In Freud's theory, the emotions associated with a specific psychological trauma cannot be expressed directly because they would lead to unacceptable impulses and behavior. Consequently, these feelings and impulses are displaced and converted into physical symptoms. Furthermore, they are so well blocked that the person is characteristically indifferent to physical symptoms. If he or she is hysterically blind, for example, the emotional concern that most of us would display is not evident.

Characteristics

The physical symptoms associated with conversion neuroses are either motor or sensory. Motor disturbances usually take two forms: impaired movement and paralysis. In both cases, a complete neurological examination will not reveal any organic basis for the symptoms. The symptoms are often inconsistent with known anatomical pathways. In sensory disturbances, the areas affected also will not be consistent with known anatomical pathways (for example, in stocking anesthesia, the patient's insensitivity will cover the same area of the leg that a stocking would — an anatomical impossibility). While it is more likely that those with repeated episodes of conversion neuroses will experience the same symptom during each episode, it is also possible that the conversion symptom may vary in site and nature. Usually the symptom appears suddenly in a situation where extreme stress is present.

Case Example. Officer Clarence Kanner had been transferred to Vice from Patrol about six months prior to his admission to a hospital. He complained of blinding headaches and feared a brain tumor. Thorough medical and neurological examinations were negative. A consulting psychiatrist was called in, and he established the following sequence for the development of the symptoms.

The officer had led a rather protected life as a youth and had dated only one woman since high school. Shortly after graduation, they were married. After several short-term jobs that did not interest him, he joined the police department. After he had been in Patrol for about four years, he was transferred to detectives and assigned to Vice. Here he was thrown into association with many young women who, despite their lack of an acceptable moral code, were physically attractive to him. It was evident that a number of them also found him attractive. When he came home from work to his wife and family (he had two small children), the problems of family living contrasted sharply with the nightlife environment of his job. His own strict moral code and sense of responsibility as husband and father were in conflict with the role he had to play at work. Unable to resolve this emotional conflict, he developed blinding headaches – sometimes on the job (perhaps when temptation was becoming too great for his unconscious desires) and sometimes at home (when family pressures built up). He began to suspect that he had a brain tumor, and this aggravated his symptoms. His emotional conflicts were thus converted into physical symptoms that had no organic basis.

Underlying Factors

The benefits of a conversion symptom to the neurotic are twofold: the person achieves a primary gain by keeping an internal conflict or need out of conscious awareness; and the person also may achieve a secondary gain by using the conversion symptom to avoid a specific activity that is unacceptable or by obtaining support from important people who would not otherwise provide it. In contrast to other neuroses that have their origins in conflicts surrounding very early stages of development, the roots of the conversion neurosis are related more directly to the sexual conflicts that the child encounters between ages three and five. As in Officer Kanner's case, conversion neuroses and conversion symptoms occur as a result of the displacement of unacceptable sexual impulses that, if allowed to come into consciousness, would cause overwhelming anxiety.

Dissociative Neurosis

The dissociative neurosis (or dissociative disorder) is especially important to law enforcement officers. It is in this category that psychological amnesia falls. This psychological forgetting is often difficult to distinguish from a true amnesia based on organic injury or disease.

Historical Background

In early theories, dissociative neuroses and conversion neuroses often were included together under the general label of hysteria. However, later theoreticians, including Freud, differentiated between the two on the basis of the physical symptoms present in conversion neuroses. In the *Diagnostic and Statistical Manual of Mental Disorders* (DSM-IV-TR; APA 2000), the distinction is even greater; conversion neuroses are considered part of the class of somatoform disorders, while dissociative neuroses are a separate class altogether.

Characteristics

Because of their many forms, the dissociative neuroses form a complex group of emotional disturbances. It is important to know whether the temporary alteration of personality integration is in the area of consciousness, identity, or motor function. Depending on the form, the illness will be hysterical amnesia, multiple personality, a sleepwalking trance, or, of special interest to law enforcement officers, the phenomenon of highway hypnosis. All are related by the phenomenon of *dissociation*, in which events originally blocked from consciousness because of their unacceptable nature become so overwhelming that the only way to deal with the problem is to dissociate completely from the environment. A case of highway hypnosis will serve as an illustration.

Case Example. It was a clear day when John Vincent, twenty-seven years old, died at 2:14 P.M. in a single-car accident on an interstate highway in northwestern Arizona. The investigating officer reported that a thorough perusal of the highway on which John had been traveling just prior to crashing into a telephone pole did not reveal the characteristic pattern of weaving associated with falling asleep at the wheel or the skid marks commonly noted when the brakes are applied abruptly after the victim awakes. John's death was probably a result of highway hypnosis.

Underlying Factors

In highway hypnosis, the victim becomes dissociated from the environment as a whole, losing track entirely of the passage of time and place. Mild cases of highway hypnosis are known to all of us. When we emerge from our dream state, we recognize that we have been driving for seconds or minutes and have passed several familiar landmarks without realizing it. In serious cases, such as led to John Vincent's death, this trance state leads to complete immobilization at the wheel. Because of it, the driver is often unable to negotiate a curve. Highway hypnosis associated with fatal traffic accidents is most likely to occur on long, straight, monotonous stretches of turnpikes where curves are few and far between, offering little challenge to the motorist to pay attention to the road.

NEUROTIC DISORDERS AND SITUATIONAL TRAUMA

Recent manuals of psychiatric diagnosis include two specific types of disorders that arise in response to what is perceived as severe life-threatening circumstances: post-traumatic stress disorders (PTSD) and panic attacks. Either PTSD or panic attacks can expand into a "full-blown" anxiety disorder or neurosis – usually as a result of interaction with preexisting stress conditions and/or with preexisting psychological disorders, such as those previously described. Police officers are exposed to both of these disorders much more frequently than the average person. They occur not only in the people police officers deal with in the line of duty but also in police officers themselves and in other emergency service personnel. It is especially important for officers to be alert to their symptoms.

PTSD and panic attacks are fairly common during or following major traumas or life-threatening situations. Rape, other violent crimes, sexual molestation or abuse (of adults or children), family violence, natural disasters, and cataclysmic accidents with mass casualties (for example, airplane crashes) are some of the situations or circumstances that often lead to one or both of these disorders.

On occasion, automobile accidents can also produce a post-traumatic stress disorder or a panic attack.

Post-Traumatic Stress Disorder

Post-traumatic stress disorder often continues to produce symptoms long after occurrence of the precipitating trauma. Police officers may be exposed to acting-out or aggressive behaviors that are delayed symptoms of PTSD, resulting from trauma that occurred months or years before (for example, as in the case of some Vietnam veterans). In fact, this diagnosis came into being largely as a result of the observations made by mental health professionals treating such Veterans Administration patients. However, the disorder is not limited to Vietnam veterans or to combat experiences. PTSD can occur as a result of experiencing *any* sudden trauma that is outside the range of "normal" or ordinary day-to-day human experience (such as rape/violent crime, accidents, disasters, and so on). Because a conflict is present resulting from the trauma, anxiety or depression are predominant symptoms. PTSD is considered a type of neurotic disorder.

Historical Background

Post-traumatic stress disorder is listed in the DSM-IV-TR as an anxiety disorder. Because it is triggered in children and adults by traumatic circumstances of all sorts, it is particularly relevant to those in law enforcement. PTSD appears to be the most prominent disturbance found among victims of rape and other violent crimes. In general, the situations that trigger PTSD are associated with feelings of intense fear, terror, and helplessness.

Characteristics

Criteria used to establish the diagnosis of PTSD include:

1. *Presence of a stressor that is easily recognized and capable of evoking distressful symptoms in virtually anyone.*
2. *Continuing experience of the psychically traumatic event as evidenced by uncomfortable and disquieting thoughts about the event that appear suddenly despite efforts to keep them out, disturbed sleep with recurring dreams about the event, and/or visual experiences that cause the victim to feel as if the disturbing event is happening again.*
3. *Psychic numbing or "emotional anesthesia" manifested most often by reduction of interest in activities that were previously important, feeling estranged from other persons, and/or loss of the ability to express emotions and feelings.*
4. *Appearance of specific symptoms not present prior to the disturbing event, such as feeling jumpy, edgy, and easily startled, fitful sleeping, feeling bad or guilty about some aspect of behavior during or after the event, difficulty with concentration or memory, avoiding activity that might cause the victim to remember the event, and/or recurrence of sudden distress when something occurs to remind the victim of the traumatic event or symbolizes it.*

In acute PTSD, symptoms of this disorder may become manifest within six months after the traumatic event; symptoms generally disappear within six months of their occurrence. In chronic or delayed PTSD, symptoms first appear more than six months after the event and persist for more than six months (Frederick, 1986).

Onset

The most common trauma involves either a serious threat to one's life or physical integrity; a serious threat or harm to one's children, spouse, or other close relatives and friends; sudden destruction of one's home or community; or seeing another person who has recently been or is being seriously injured or killed as the result of an accident or physical violence. In some cases the trauma may be simply learning about a serious threat or harm to a close friend or relative.

PTSD is a "family disease." Family members and/or close friends of people who suffer trauma, such as violent crime, can be the victims of PTSD just as much as the person who actually suffered the original trauma. Family violence is one instance in which police officers may find themselves dealing with several sufferers of PTSD in the same household, all experiencing emotional anesthesia, paranoia, hypervigilance, difficulty sleeping, and so on.

> Family violence may often be both a symptom and a cause of PTSD. That is, in situations where one member of the family has been exposed to extensive stress or suffered trauma, the violence may be one manifestation of the rage and depression that have grown since the original trauma. For those who are the victims of this violence, the violent event may be setting the stage for the later eruption of symptoms of PTSD. (Williams, 1987, p. 254)

Those who have survived a life-threatening trauma or traumatic death when others did not, often describe painful guilt feelings about surviving.

Managing PTSD

In an effort to control or prevent flashbacks and re-experience of the original trauma, sufferers not only avoid any situation or stimuli that might trigger it but also tend to avoid thoughts or feelings about the traumatic event. This avoidance may require a form of amnesia regarding an important aspect of the traumatic event. In the case of a violent crime victim, such amnesia or "denial" may make it difficult for an investigating officer to gather all needed information about the crime. For example, delayed recall is not at all uncommon among rape victims. If officers assigned the case are not sensitive to this symptom, they may have serious doubts about the credibility of the witness/victim and the information that is recalled weeks or even months after the crime.

Another element of PTSD that may confuse investigating officers is the characteristic "psychic numbing" or "emotional anesthesia." For example, the lack of feeling with which a rape victim may report the assault may cause interviewers to doubt the credibility of the facts or the witness. Officers should be aware that such flat affect or lack of feeling is common among PTSD sufferers. Post-traumatic stress disorder can also be the cause for sudden and severe aggressive behavior. This is particularly characteristic of combat veterans and police officers who have been previously involved in acts of violence. The reduced ability to moderate or control one's impulses may be expressed in unpredictable explosions of aggressive behavior, often in the family setting.

Case Example. Police were called to a family disturbance where the husband, a Vietnam vet who had been diagnosed as a PTSD victim, became enraged when his wife came home late from work. He accused her of having sex with her boss and other men and became physically violent. When she managed to leave the house and call the police, he refused admission to the officers, claiming they were really Viet Cong coming to kill him. His wife advised the officers that her husband had several weapons in the house, including guns. After several hours of negotiation,

he allowed the negotiator and police officer (both of whom had identified themselves as veterans) to enter the house. He kept them away with a bayonet for another hour before allowing them to advance and take the weapon. He then readily consented to be transported to the local veteran's hospital for treatment.

Panic Attacks

Case Example. It is about 3 P.M. on a sunny, hot afternoon. Captain Smith of the police department is on his way back to the main station, driving alone in his city car. Suddenly he feels pain in his chest, has difficulty breathing, and feels a tingling sensation around his mouth and hands. His heart is pounding in his chest. He pulls to the side of the street and radios for assistance. A Medic One unit from the fire department responds and rushes him to the nearest hospital emergency room. After extensive monitoring and evaluation, he is released with the diagnosis of "panic (anxiety) attack."

Case Example. Detective Brady gets up from his desk in sex crimes and starts to walk toward the snack bar for a sweet roll and juice. He suddenly feels faint, dizzy, and lightheaded. He begins to perspire heavily. He feels his body becoming numb. He's confused, somewhat disoriented. He wonders what's happening? What does it mean? How serious is it? He manages to return to his desk and collapses in the chair. Others notice his condition and someone calls an ambulance. Detective Brady spends some time in the emergency room and is released with a diagnosis of "panic (anxiety) attack."

Everyone, including police officers, experiences the symptoms of anxiety – even panic – from time to time simply because of the stress of everyday living: problems inherent in the job, in the home, and in our interpersonal relations. Most of us usually weather these symptoms and get on with living. However, these symptoms may involve such strong physical experiences that we become frightened and either try to deny them or seek out a physician in an attempt to find out what is wrong. Usually denial does not work and the consultation may result in little if any explanation for these attacks and no effective techniques for dealing with a recurrence. When the attacks do recur, we become more frightened and fear we are "losing control." DSM-IV-TR states:

> The symptoms experienced during an attack are: shortness of breath or smothering sensations; dizziness, unsteady feelings, or faintness, choking; palpitations or accelerated heart rate, trembling or shaking; sweating; nausea or abdominal distress; depersonalization . . .; numbness or tingling sensations . . .; flushes (hot flashes) or chills; chest pain or discomfort; fear of dying; and fear of going crazy or of doing something uncontrolled during the attack. (APA, 2000, p. 236)

Acute panic disorders can be associated with disaster situations (Chapter 16) and generally respond well to brief psychological therapy. In only a small minority of cases is recurring panic symptoms associated with a physical problem. Most difficulties, even if associated with a physical disorder, are caused by excessive and/or prolonged stress and are sustained by a pattern of thinking that reinforces their recurrence. R. Reid Wilson (1987) states that if the panic symptoms persist over a period of time, they are usually associated with one of the following categories of mental disorder: panic disorder, generalized anxiety disorder, phobic disorder, obsessive-compulsive disorder, and post-traumatic stress disorder.

Although the first panic attack may take place in a distinct situation, further episodes are unpredictable as to time or place. It is this unpredictability that so frightens victims. While the panic attack seems to have come "out of the blue," clinical experience indicates that its occurrence is usually associated with a period of severe and prolonged stress – not days of tension but weeks, even months. Life transitions (moving, marriage, divorce, job change, and so on) sometimes account for much of the psychological pressure. In the two examples given at the start of this section, Captain Smith had been under considerable stress in the past year. His wife was threatening divorce if he didn't retire, but he didn't want to because he had nothing to retire to. One of his children was using drugs; the new chief seemed to be looking for a chance to retire him. In Detective Brady's case, he had been working hard on his master's degree. The recent change in chiefs threatened his present assignment, which allowed him to continue school. His wife was threatening divorce because his excessive hours left no time for her and the kids. Both these officers were fortunate to have psychological help available from the department's behavioral science unit, but for many officers, such resources are not available. Because of the predominant physical symptoms, if they seek help at all, they are most likely to consult the family physician or some other medical specialist. If the doctor is not familiar with the symptomatology of panic (anxiety) attacks and/or does not know the treatment of choice or whom to refer the officer to, the officer will come away from the consultation with no effective help. This is sad because panic disorders are amenable to treatment.

HELPFUL HINTS TO LAW ENFORCEMENT OFFICERS

In handling someone with overwhelming anxiety, it is important to provide reassurance in order to help that person regain control over panic. It is not helpful for police officers to attempt to persuade the person that the anxiety or panic is unrealistic or unwarranted. Even if officers perceive the reasons for the anxiety and consider them ridiculous, they must recognize that they are not ridiculous to the person experiencing the anxiety. Instead of belittling the person's symptoms, they should offer reassurance and try to remove the person to a protective situation. Then they can begin to talk with the person about the anxious feelings.

When police officers encounter someone who is depressed, they should be alert to the seriousness of this condition. Even though they may not perceive any realistic cause for the depression, they should try to identify with the person's depression by recognizing how painful it must be and by empathizing with the person's pain. After all, it is not how the officers see it but how the depressed person sees it that will determine what that person will do. If the depression appears so great that a suicide attempt is possible, the person should be placed in a hospital immediately and watched very carefully until the depression has lifted. However, a word of caution: Many depressed individuals commit suicide just when they seem to be improving. It is thought that this false improvement is actually due to the neurotic's having made a final decision to commit suicide. Having done so, the person is able to put on a happy face because he or she knows that all worries will soon be over. This happy face sometimes fools even the professional, who may decide that the danger has passed.

Officers who have responsibility for prisoners should know that many depressed persons are encountered in jails. The stress of incarceration is likely to precipitate a depressive neurosis. Officers must be alert for depressed inmates so that they can make a judgment regarding suicidal potential. They should always be especially sensitive to the inmate who, several days before, was profoundly depressed but

now has undergone a remarkable mood alteration unrelated to any significant external event, such as imminent release. This person may have also made the decision that life is no longer worth living. Observant officers should then summon appropriate medical help. If officers encounter someone with severe obsessional thinking or a ritualistic compulsive behavior pattern, it is important for them to recognize that this person is disturbed and should not be assumed to be "crazy." It is easy to assume the latter, since compulsive acts in particular are often nonsensical and funny to the casual observer.

As professional observers of behavior, officers should recognize these obsessive thought patterns and compulsive acts for what they are: symptoms of an emotional disturbance. Knowing this, they will be able to guide the person toward a therapeutic setting. Because of the seeming irrationality of the behavior (and in most instances its apparent harmlessness), it is often easier to ignore it rather than to take the trouble to refer the person to an appropriate facility. However, it may prove to be rewarding to suggest a referral because neurotic persons are generally very receptive to the idea of seeking help. They are in full contact with reality and recognize that their obsessional thoughts and compulsive behavior are symptoms of illness. Their ambivalence stops them from seeking help on their own, but the officer's influence will generally help them overcome it. When officers encounter someone who is experiencing an unreasonable fear (phobia) in relationship to an actual situation, they also can help by reducing the person's panic through supportive intervention.

SUMMARY

The neuroses include many examples of emotional disturbance that law enforcement officers are likely to encounter. Awareness of the various types, their characteristics, and some of the underlying factors will enable

officers to assess their severity, the necessity for immediate intervention, and most important, their own response to the person who is experiencing the symptoms. Without this knowledge, law enforcement officers may respond inappropriately to neurotic people. With it, they are more likely to function as an ally of the medical and non-medical therapeutic professional by assessing these troubled persons correctly, responding appropriately, and referring them for treatment, if necessary.

In this chapter the author has presented basic information about post-traumatic stress disorders. The author has also directed the reader's attention to panic attacks, noting that these attacks occur with some frequency in police work as well as in other high-stress professions. Physical symptoms associated with panic attacks can be frightening, but the condition is often amenable to psychological therapy, combined in some instances with medication.

BIBLIOGRAPHY

American Psychiatric Association. (2000). *Diagnostic and statistical manual of mental disorders,* 4th ed. Washington, D.C.: American Psychiatric Association.

American Psychiatric Association. (1987). *Diagnostic and statistical manual of mental disorders,* 3rd ed. revised. Washington, D.C.: American Psychiatric Association.

Anderson, S. J. November, 1988. The dark void of depression. *USA Today, 117.*

Brett, E. A., Spitzer, R. L., & Williams, J. B. (1988). DSM-III-R criteria for post-traumatic stress disorder. *American Journal of Psychiatry, 145*(10), 1232–1236.

Card, J. J. 1983. *Lives after Vietnam: The personal impact of military service.* Lexington, MA: Lexington Books.

Chest pains may be warning (of treatable psychiatric disorder). October, 1988. *USA Today, 117:*13.

Domash, M. D., & Sparr, L. F. September, 1982. Post-traumatic stress disorder masquerading as paranoid schizophrenia: A case report. *Military Medicine 147.*

Fenichel, O. (1945). *The psychoanalytic theory of the neuroses.* New York: W. W. Norton.

Figley, C. R. (1985). *Trauma and its wake.* New York: Brunner/Mazel.

Fox, M. (1985). Panic patrol (care and treatment for panic attacks). *Health 17,* 19.

Frederick, C. J. (1986). *Post-traumatic stress responses to victims of violent crime: Information for law enforcement officials.* Washington, D.C.: National Institute of Mental Health.

Freud, S. (1961) (originally published 1936). Inhibitions, symptoms and anxiety. In *The Standard Edition of the complete psychological works of Sigmund Freud,* ed. J. Strachey , vol. 20, pp. 87–122. London: Hogarth Press.

Friedman, A. M., Kaplan, H. I., & Sadock, B. J. (1975). *Comprehensive textbook of psychiatry,* 2nd ed. Baltimore: Williams & Wilkins.

Gallacher, W. (1986). The dark affliction of mind and body (mental depression). *Discover 7,* 66(9).

Gossop, M. (1980). *Theories of neurosis.* New York: Springer-Verlag.

Gray, M. (1978). *Neuroses: A comprehensive and critical view.* New York: Van Nostrand Reinhold.

Green, B. L., Lindy, J. D., & Grace, M. C. (1985). Post-traumatic stress disorder: Toward DSM-IV. *Journal of Nervous and Mental Disease 173*(7), 406–411.

Hales, D. January, 1982. Women and depression: The pain is real. *Facets* 14–17.

Leerhsen, C., King, P., & Gosnell, M. 4 May 1987. Tender years, a terrible sadness: Children of depression. *Newsweek* 50–51.

Millon, T. (1981). *Disorders of personality; DSM-III: Axis II.* Somerset, NJ: John Wiley & Sons.

Redlich, F. C., & Freedman, D. X. (1966). *The theory and practice of psychiatry.* New York: Basic Books.

Rosenfeld, A. H. (1985). Depression: Dispelling despair; a look at the treatments now being used to help millions. *Psychology Today 19,* 28–34.

Slovinsky, L. J. 3 January 1988. Out of depression. Mental depression. *New York Times Magazine* 36.

Symonds, M. (1980). The second injury to victims of violent crime. *Evaluation and Change,* Special Issue, 36–38.

Ttrafford, A. 24 January, 1983. New hope for the depressed. *U.S. News & World Report.*

Williams, T., ed. (1987). *Post-traumatic stress disorders: A handbook for clinicians.* Cincinnati, OH: Disabled American Veterans.

Wilson, R. R. (1987). *Don't panic.* New York: Harper & Row.

Chapter 8

PSYCHOTIC DISORDERS

No one knows for sure what causes psychotic disorders – whether they are organic or functional in origin. In many instances, it may be a not-well understood combination of the two. Some psychoses clearly have an organic component – a head injury, biochemical imbalance, or genetic abnormality – while others appear to result primarily from developmental and situational factors – something that occurred in childhood or as the result of unusual trauma.

This chapter will focus on the two principal groups of psychoses: schizophrenic disorders and affective disorders. We will discuss how people with these disorders behave, with illustrations from several case examples. We will explore current theories related to some of the factors underlying the behavior and will briefly describe a personality disorder (organic personality disorder, explosive type) that is commonly mistaken for a psychotic disorder and describe its behavioral characteristics. The author will then provide helpful hints to law enforcement officers in handling people with such conditions.

COMMON CHARACTERISTICS

The common characteristics of all psychotic disorders are a *loss of contact with reality*. In addition, there are six other major psychotic symptoms: disturbances in thinking, disturbances in thought content, disturbances in perception, disturbances in judgment, disturbances in mood and emotions, and regression. The diagnosis of a specific psychotic disorder depends on the particular combination of these symptoms.

Disturbances in thinking occur when thought is no longer rational, logical, and goal-directed. Many terms are used to describe these types of disturbed thinking, ranging from the less serious, *circumstantiality*, to the more severe, *loosening of associations*. Officers listening to someone with an emotional disturbance will be better able to judge its seriousness if they understand these terms. In *circumstantiality*, people's thinking remains goal-directed, but they reach the goal only after a series of lengthy digressions. For example, by the time they answer a question, the person who asked may have forgotten what was asked. In *tangential thinking*, people never reach the goal, but their thoughts still have logical connections. In contrast to both of these, persons with a *loosening of associations* neither reach the goal nor connect between thoughts rationally. Other forms of disturbed thinking affect the flow of thought rather than the pattern of associations. These include the *flight of ideas*, in which persons go so rapidly from one connecting thought to another that the listener becomes lost trying to follow. In contrast to this increased flow of thought, *blocking* refers to a slowing down or complete cessation of thought expression because of threatened anxiety. In addition to disturbances in the forms and expression of thinking, another important characteristic of a psychotic disorder may be *disturbances in the content of thought.* The most common form is the delusion, a false belief arising without appropriate external stimulation that is maintained more or less unshakably in the face of all reason. These false beliefs are generally not shared by other members of this person's peer group. Delusions may be either persecutory or grandiose. Their presence may relate to the person's mood. Someone who is depressed is more likely to experience delusions of persecution (the Mafia has put out a contract on my life), while the hyperactive person is more likely to experience delusions of grandeur (my father was the President, and my mother was the Empress).

Closely related to disturbances of thought content are *disturbances in perception.* In many psychotic disorders, delusions are accompanied by disturbances in perception (hallucinations). A hallucination refers to the apparent perception of an external object, such as a voice, when no corresponding real object exists. In most psychoses, these hallucinations are auditory (I hear my mother telling me I'm no good), but in the organic psychoses, where brain damage is present, visual, tactile, gustatory (taste), and/or olfactory (smell) hallucinations are common.

The loss of contact with reality is also commonly associated with *disturbances in judgment.* If judgment is a mental function whose purpose is to ensure reality-oriented action, then psychotics are invariably impaired in this area. Police officers can assess the degree of impairment by posing hypothetical problem-solving situations (What would you do if you smelled smoke in a theater?) or by simply observing ongoing behavior.

In psychotic disorders, *disturbances in mood and emotions* are usually more severe than in the neuroses and interfere with effective functioning to such an extent that hospitalization is often necessary. These disturbances may include sudden changes in mood without accompanying changes in the person's situation, or the complete absence of mood change despite major changes in the environment that would normally result in change in the person's mood. Finally, psychotics may also show *regression,* in which the ego returns to an earlier state of development in an attempt to avoid the present tension and conflict. The result is a deterioration from a previous level of functioning (Chapter 4).

The degree to which some of these signs and symptoms are seen can assist police officers in deciding what type of psychosis is present. Disturbances in thinking primarily characterize the schizophrenias, while disturbed emotions are more prominent in the affective disorders. This does not imply, however, that disturbances in emotions do not occur in schizophrenia or, conversely, that disturbances in thinking do not occur in the affective disorders. Other disturbances described in this section are commonly associated with both types of psychoses.

Schizophrenias

Historical Background

Although observers recognized many symptoms of schizophrenia prior to the time of Christ, it was not described as a disease until the end of the nineteenth century. In 1898, Emil Kraepelin was the first to combine many of these previous observations into a single entity. In his paper *The Diagnosis and Prognosis of Dementia Praecox*, he included many of these symptoms as having in common an apparent lack of external causes, an occurrence in young and previously healthy individuals, and an impact that led to an ultimate deterioration of the personality as the disease progressed. Although Kraepelin was the first to bring together the signs and symptoms of schizophrenia, it was Eugen Bleuler who, several years later, substituted the term *schizophrenia* for dementia praecox. Bleuler's substitution reflected his disagreement with Kraepelin's concept of the disease's incurability and associated deterioration. He pointed out that only some patients deteriorated, while others recovered.

The current system of classification (DSM-IV-TR, 2000) identifies five subtypes of schizophrenia that derive from the thinking of Kraepelin and Bleuler but also reflects more recent diagnostic research. These include the undifferentiated type, the paranoid type, the disorganized type, the catatonic type, and the residual type. We will emphasize the first two types, in either their acute or chronic forms, since these are the forms most frequently encountered by police.

Underlying Factors

There have been many theories on the cause(s) of schizophrenia. Various genetic, biochemical, physiological, psychological, and sociocultural factors have been described, but none of them has been shown to be the sole cause. The cure for schizophrenia is still unknown. Some researchers believe that the origins of schizophrenia lie solely in developmental processes and, specifically, in the early interactions between the child and family. Disturbances in the mother-child relationship are considered crucial. These predispose the child to a weak ego, which in later life is not able to withstand stress. Consequently, the personality disintegrates, causing symptoms of schizophrenia.

Others believe that physical conditions are responsible for schizophrenia. Endocrine (glandular) problems, brain damage, and toxic poisoning have been offered as causes. More recently, researchers have concentrated on certain biochemical factors – substances in the body fluids that might play a role in schizophrenia's onset and occurrence. Still others suggest a strong genetic (hereditary) factor. Studies completed with identical twins indicate a higher incidence of schizophrenia in monozygotic twins (born from the same egg) compared to dizygotic twins (born from two different eggs). Although these data support the hypothesis that genetic factors may play a role in the development of schizophrenia, the mechanism(s) is not clear. Possibilities include genetic factors operating through a physiological defect, such as the absence of an enzyme, or some broader gene mutation.

Theorists also have stressed the importance of sociocultural variables in the development of schizophrenia. They remark on the greater prevalence of schizophrenia among the lower socioeconomic classes. Whether this finding is related to the cause or the result of schizophrenia (through the drift of people suffering from schizophrenia into the lower socioeconomic brackets because of poor functioning) is not known. In conclusion, our current knowledge is inadequate to account for the development of schizophrenia. Despite many years of research, sufficient data are not available to determine conclusively the relative importance of the psychological, physical, genetic, and sociocultural factors that may be involved in predisposing a person to schizophrenia, but it is known that a biophysical model is most likely.

Undifferentiated Type

The undifferentiated type of schizophrenia is characterized by a gradual deterioration of drive, ambition, and the ability to function. It is reflected in the absence of social relationships, the inability to work effectively at a job, or difficulty in functioning above a marginal level in school, and in generally disorganized behavior. This impairment is usually accompanied by delusions or hallucinations. While disturbed emotions (primarily depression) are characteristic, the major sign is a thought disorder, often accompanied by incoherence. An example will illustrate.

Case Example. Floyd Brown is twenty years old, single, and a recent college dropout during his sophomore year. His mother following a violent outburst called the police to his home one evening. When they arrived, Floyd's mother told them that her son had recently been very difficult to live with, pacing and yelling in an irrational manner most of the day and night. On the evening she called the police, he had hit her for the first time. The police officers obtained the following information. Following graduation from high school, Floyd entered the local university and did well the first year. However, during his second year his functioning began to deteriorate rapidly. Not only did he lose interest in his studies, which led to his dropping out of school, but he also became preoccupied with many bizarre ideas concerning science and the meaning of life. Totally consumed by the quest for "truth," he began to withdraw and spent most of his time at home despite the family's urgings to go out. He lost interest in his personal hygiene. The family found it more difficult to cope with him because, as his mother remarked, "We couldn't talk to him, and he didn't make sense." Within the past two weeks, he had talked about his special powers to control life and had even stated his conviction that his father, who had died the previous summer, had communicated with him and would soon be "returning home." When he was severely agitated, as on the evening he hit his mother, he talked about her as an agent of the devil, implying that she had something to do with his father's death. The police decided that Floyd was a danger to others. As he was unwilling to go to the hospital voluntarily, they contacted the hospital by phone and received permission to take him into protective custody so that he could be transported there for a psychiatric evaluation and possible involuntary admission.

Paranoid Type

The paranoid type of schizophrenia is characterized principally by delusions of persecution and/or grandeur. Hallucinations, usually auditory, are often present. Prior to onset, paranoid schizophrenics often display a suspicious and guarded attitude toward everyone. These persons usually show less impairment of functioning if they have not acted upon the delusional material. Severely disorganized behavior, as noted in the undifferentiated, catatonic, and disorganized types, is rare. A case example will illustrate.

Case Example. Judy Eden, twenty-eight years old and single, called the police to her home. When the responding officer arrived, Judy told him that she had a problem she wanted to explain. She began by saying that there were bottles of liquid in her home killing her and her dog and that the dog was already very ill. She took a wad of tissue from her purse and asked the officer to smell the odor. He did so and found no odor. When he did not confirm her suspicion, she told him that another officer had been to her home before and had told her to throw away the bottles. She said that she had done this but that both the bottles and odors had returned. In addition, she mentioned that her air conditioning was spreading the odors throughout the house. On further questioning, Judy revealed that lately she had received messages from the television set. She told the officer how most of the people on the television were talking to her and telling her that she was going to die if she did not mend her ways. The officer also learned that Judy had been widowed a year ago when her Air Force husband was killed in a plane crash while on a test flight. Initially she had seemed to make a good adjustment to this tragedy, continuing her job as a secretary. However, several months later her bizarre behavior began. She mentioned that her friends and coworkers had seemed concerned, but she soon realized that it was because "I have a pension and they want my money." Although Judy did not demonstrate evidence of violence, the officer recognized that Judy's illness had been progressive and that violence to herself or others was an eventual possibility. Consequently, he asked her if she would accompany him to the hospital and talk to someone else. She refused.

The officer left but immediately notified the local mental health center, which sent a social worker to see Judy the next day.

Residual Type

The residual category of schizophrenia applies to those who have had at least one prior episode of schizophrenia. While it is true that individuals with other types of schizophrenia may also have recurring episodes, the feature distinguishing the residual type is the recurrence of episodes without prominent psychotic symptoms. For example, while delusions, hallucinations, and grossly disorganized behavior are usually not present – or if present, occur in a very muted form – these people generally demonstrate illogical thinking, loosening of associations, emotional blunting, social withdrawal, and eccentric behavior. By definition, therefore, this is the most chronic of the schizophrenias. People with this disorder do not have repeated acute episodes in which severe symptoms of hallucinations, delusions, and disorganized behavior are present, except perhaps at the first episode. A case example will illustrate.

Case Example. The police picked up Mary Michael at 3:00 A.M. on an interstate highway. A patrol car had been notified that several motorists had seen her standing at the side of the street, throwing various items of clothing from a large suitcase into the middle of the road. When the police officers approached her and asked what she was doing and why, she replied, "I like to travel light, and besides, the last guy who gave me a ride didn't like the way I was dressed. He said I 'looked a mess' and put me out of the car. So there." Further questioning revealed that Mary not only was unable to explain where she had been and where she was going but also spoke about how she was hoping to find the "end of the rainbow" so she could be young again. Feeling that she represented a potential danger if left by the side of the road, the officers encouraged her to come with

them to the local hospital. She agreed to accompany them.

In the emergency room, the doctor who spoke with her learned that Mary was thirty-eight-years old and had been traveling for the past ten years from city to city, staying in one place no more than three months at a time. During this time, she had been hospitalized on at least six different occasions, once for as long as four months in a state hospital. Each time she was given medication that "helped her think better," but she usually discontinued it shortly after her discharge and headed on her way. The doctor agreed to admit her for a few days so that she could be put back on her medication. However, he was not optimistic that this would do much more than calm her down enough so that she could continue her travels without being an immediate danger to herself or others.

Catatonic Type

The catatonic type of schizophrenia is rare. Its importance to law enforcement officers lies in the extreme violence that may be associated with one of its forms – catatonic excitement – in which there is excessive motor activity, grimacing, talkativeness, and unpredictable emotional outbursts. When these symptoms are not present, the person is usually in a stupor, a state of total silence, and often bizarre posture. The person can remain in this single position for hours, seemingly paying attention to nothing and responsive to no one. This lack of verbal or physical response is accompanied, paradoxically, by an increased awareness of what is going on. This helps explain why, without warning; the person may fly into the rage of catatonic excitement, becoming extremely dangerous. In either case, careful supervision is required and hospitalization is indicated.

Disorganized Type

The disorganized type of schizophrenia is also rare. Knowledge about it, however, is important for law enforcement officers because of the severe disintegration of the personality. If an adequate history can be obtained, this clinical picture is usually associated with extreme social impairment, a lengthy history, early onset of the illness, and a chronic course. Generally people with this disorder are so disorganized that hospitalization is essential and should be arranged as quickly as possible.

Affective Disorders

In contrast to the schizophrenias, the affective disorders are psychoses in which the primary signs and symptoms are related to *disturbances in emotions* rather than to *disturbances in the form of thinking* (circumstantiality, tangentiality, and loosening of associations). However, disturbances in the flow of thinking, thought content, perception, judgment, and regression are also characteristic. The affective disorders may be classified into two types: manic-depressive (bipolar) disorder and major depressive disorder. Recent research suggests that although they are grouped together because of the primary disturbance in emotions, there also are differences between them.

Historical Background

Theories about affective disorders go back to the early writings of Hippocrates, who described the interaction of the four bodily humors (blood, black bile, yellow bile, and water) as closely related to the occurrence of mania (unusual elation) and melancholia (unusual depression). It was not until the passing of the Middle Ages, with its emphasis on demonology, that a modern classification of affective disorders could emerge.

In 1854, Jean Pierre Falaret published a description of an illness that he called *La Folie Circulaire*, the first description of the "circular" syndrome associated with the manic-depressive psychosis. In 1882 Karl Kahlbaum was the first to view mania and melancholia

as different stages of the same psychosis rather than as two different illnesses. Emil Kraepelin first proposed the diagnosis of manic-depressive insanity for this entire group of disorders. Although these are now more commonly referred to as affective disorders, the manic-depressive (bipolar) disorder is still recognized as one of the two major types – the other being the major depressive disorder.

Underlying Factors

Current research into the causes of affective disorders is slightly more advanced than research on the schizophrenias. A genetic (hereditary) factor has been suggested, and recent research confirms its existence. For example, affective disorders occur with significant frequency in the children of parents with affective disorders, in children of alcoholic parents, and in certain population groups like the Amish. However, the presence of an affective disorder in a family does not necessarily mean that it will occur in any or all of its children. Similarly, theorists have noticed many biological changes in those with affective disorders, but whether they are causes or symptoms of the illness has not been clearly demonstrated.

Earlier inquiries into these disorders focused primarily on developmental and psychological factors. For example, in the early twentieth century, Karl Abraham drew attention to the obsessive-compulsive personality structures of those who were most likely to develop an affective disorder in late life. Freud added to our understanding of this illness by pointing out the similarities and differences between normal mourning after the loss of a loved one and melancholia (depression). He viewed mourning as a period of appropriate grief, and melancholia as resulting from an inability to resolve that grief. In melancholia, the loss is no longer confined to the departure of the loved one but is also turned against the self, through a loss of self-esteem. However, today, biological origins are believed to contribute significantly to the development of affective disorders; it is believed that less serious forms of depression have more psychological origins.

Bipolar Disorder

In bipolar psychoses, either a severe psychotic depression or an acute manic episode characteristically occurs first when persons are in their late twenties or early thirties. If the psychotic depressive episode occurs first, it is often difficult to make the diagnosis until it has been followed by a manic episode. Sometimes it is also difficult to distinguish an acute manic episode from an acute schizophrenic episode.

In contrast to schizophrenics, manics are more apt to exhibit a flight of ideas rather than a loosening of associations. In addition, there is usually a marked increase in activity, either social or physical. Individuals in a manic state tend to be more talkative than usual and have a decreased need for sleep. They are usually quite distractible; their attention is easily drawn to unimportant or irrelevant external stimuli. Finally, they have a potential for excessive involvement in activities that may bring painful consequences that they do not generally recognize, such as buying sprees, sexual indiscretions, poor business investments, and occasionally reckless driving. While these are some characteristics of a manic state, it is important to recognize that people with bipolar disorder may also first experience a major depressive episode. However, in contrast to individuals with a major depressive disorder, bipolar patients who suffer a major depressive episode eventually develop a manic episode.

Case Example. Alan Farr, twenty-seven-years old, came to police attention in an unusual manner. He had been under a physician's care for his bipolar disorder for several months and had been placed on medication. One evening he found himself out of medication and planned to return to the hospital the next day to get more. However, he postponed his visit for several days because he did not have transportation and, as time elapsed, became increasingly manic. As he recognized the impending recurrence of his illness, he began to panic.

One evening he left the house and began walking. He passed a police officer on patrol and accosted him, demanding to be taken to the hospital so he could get his prescription. When the police officer refused, indicating that this was not within his duties, Alan, who at the time was standing in a gas station, took a book of matches out of his pocket. He lighted one and dropped it into a small puddle of gasoline on the ground. It immediately ignited, and Alan was placed under arrest for arson. He was taken to jail where, without his medication, he became increasingly manic and was eventually transferred to the hospital. Prior to his transfer from jail, the detention officer noted in the log the following comments about his behavior: "Won't stop talking, constantly making jokes, seems on the verge of losing control, doesn't sleep." In the hospital Alan was placed back on medication and his manic behavior subsided after a week. For a period of several weeks he appeared normal. Then he gradually became depressed, increasingly withdrawn, and slow of thought. His condition gradually worsened until he was no longer responsive to the staff's questions. He spent most of his time in bed, had a poor appetite, lost weight, and began to have suicidal thoughts.

Major Depressive Disorder

In contrast to the bipolar disorder, where the manic episodes are usually the most prominent feature of the illness, persons with a major depressive disorder display a marked loss of interest and pleasure in all usual activities. This may occur only once in a person's life or often, in similar episodes. The onset may occur at any time. Physical and psychological symptoms include marked agitation, restlessness, and depression. The person's appetite is either poor or absent, and sleep is disturbed. Many physical complaints may also be present.

Disturbances in thought content include delusions of sin, guilt, and unworthiness. Suicidal and paranoid thoughts are common. Delusions may also develop around somatic complaints (for example, the person may show an unrealistic concern over cancer). Hallucinations are less common. When they occur, they are usually auditory and have a condemning quality consistent with the delusions of sin, guilt, and unworthiness. An example will illustrate.

Case Example. On a Friday morning police were called to the residence of Karen Bragen, age twenty-four, by neighbors who heard gunshots. They found Karen sitting quietly in the living room with her face buried in her hands. In the bedroom they found the body of her three-month-old son, who had been shot twice in the head. From their interrogations of Karen, her husband, and family, the police obtained the following information. She had an uneventful pregnancy and, in fact, her husband commented how much happier she had seemed when pregnant. However, shortly after the baby's birth she began to be depressed. Initially, both she and her husband attributed this depression to postpartum blues, typically seen within several days after a baby's birth. However, her blues did not go away after a week or two, as is common in postpartum cases. Instead, she began to have bizarre thoughts, which initially occurred in the late afternoon or early evening, particularly when she was alone. These thoughts consisted of fleeting mental images in which she saw herself with a gun, killing her baby and husband. She tried to get them out of her mind by keeping busy. When this failed, she began a compulsive pattern in which she sat with a book, reading for several hours in the late afternoon and early evening while the baby was left in the bedroom. When this did not stop her violent thoughts, she began to lock the bedroom door so that she could not

reach the baby. This was also unsuccessful. One week before the murder, Karen began to hear the voice of her mother, with whom she had always had a poor relationship. The voice condemned Karen, saying that she was a poor mother and accusing her of not taking care of the baby. She began to hear her mother's voice coming from the television set.

Her husband told police that in the two weeks prior to the infant's death, Karen became increasingly withdrawn and was constantly finding fault with herself as a mother. He tried to reassure her, but to no avail. She never told him her violent thoughts. On the day of the murder, she heard a voice telling her to kill the baby. The voice said that then her problems would be solved because she would no longer have to be a mother. In her psychotic state, this seemed like a perfect solution. In response to the voice's continued urging, she took her husband's gun from the closet, walked into the bedroom, and fired two bullets into the sleeping baby.

This case underlines the serious homicidal and/or suicidal potential associated with this illness. If the possibility of a major depressive disorder exists, officers should always try to get the person to a hospital or a doctor.

Intermittent Explosive Disorder/Organic Personality Disorder, Explosive Type

Historical Background

The idea that there might be a psychological disorder characterized by sudden, unpredictable explosive or violent outbursts that is not the result of a known or identified psychiatric condition is relatively new. With the publication of DSM-III in 1980, the condition "intermittent explosive disorder" was described and placed under the category "impulse control disorders not elsewhere classified." By definition, this condition could not be the result of organic causes. Increasing empirical evidence led to a change in name and description of this condition in the

DSM-III-R. It became organic personality disorder, explosive type, and organic causes were acknowledged as the most common source (Yudofsky, Silver, & Yudofsky, 1988). While not a psychosis, this disorder is included in this chapter because the sudden violent acting-out behavior that characterizes it does not typically occur in other personality disorders and may be confused with the aggressive behavior associated with some forms of schizophrenia or with bipolar disorder.

Underlying Factors

It is important that law enforcement officers be aware that sudden and extreme aggressive outbursts can occur unpredictably as the result of head injury, epilepsy, cerebral tumors, strokes, multiple sclerosis, and Alzheimer's disease, as well as other organic causes. The change in diagnostic criteria from DSM-III to DSM-IV-TR resulted from increasing evidence that these organic causes can often produce symptoms of sudden explosive verbal aggression or physical aggression against objects, self, and other people (Yudofsky et al. 1986). Intoxication and withdrawal from alcohol use as well as the abuse of a variety of drugs and toxic reactions to prescription medications also can produce such symptoms (Yudofsky, Silver, & Yudofsky, 1988).

Characteristics

The key features of this disorder are "recurrent violent events, either verbal or physical in nature, which are out of proportion to the precipitating stress or provocation and which stem from organic etiologies" (Yudofsky, Silver, & Yudofsky, 1988, p. 6). People with this disorder change from states of relative calm to extreme aggression within an instant, often without objective warning signal. Such outbursts are rarely premeditated, and they are characteristically under less control than the aggressive acts of those with disorders that are solely functional.

Case Example. Michael Haynes was a sixty-three-year-old man who was struck in the head by a truck tire that exploded violently as he was filling it with air. He was in a coma for three weeks subsequent to the accident. Upon emerging from the coma, he began to develop agitation and episodic violent behavior. Over the year following the injury, his aggressive behavior intensified to the point that Michael would become angry and combative four to ten times per day, strike out dangerously at family members and nursing staff, and, uncharacteristically, scream profanities. Even minor frustration could result in an explosive discharge of violence. For example, during his hospitalization he requested a glass of orange juice. When the nurse replied that she would go to the pantry and be right back with the juice, the patient screamed, "No, I want the orange juice now!" With that he swung his fist at the nurse, knocked her glasses from her face, and scratched the cornea of her right eye. Later, when the patient was calmer, he expressed remorse and shame over the incident as well as concern for the injured nurse. He said, "I just can't help myself, I don't know what gets into me" (Yudofsky, Silver, & Yudofsky, 1988, p. 6).

It is important to note that sudden aggressive outbursts can occur in people with this disorder, even in the absence of the agitation or obvious disorientation that is more characteristic of someone in the midst of a psychotic episode. Further, this violent behavior may occur as a result of being stopped for a minor traffic violation or because officers have interfered in some way with the person's activities. As a result of frustration, the person explodes into unexpected aggressive behavior.

Helpful Hints to Law Enforcement Officers

Because of the psychotic's confusion, bizarre behavior, and capacity for violence, police officers are often the first to be called when a mentally disturbed person displays signs of psychosis. Officers' ability to handle the psychotic person appropriately is important not only for their own safety and the safety of others, but it is also important to the psychotic person, who is probably experiencing tremendous fear. In addition, the ability of officers to form a trusting relationship with this person may be very important in determining the outcome of further treatment efforts. The mental confusion, distortions of thought content, and disturbances of perception increase the possibility that psychotics will distrust everyone, even those attempting to help. They may then react with violence.

It is important for officers to remember to approach psychotics in the most nonthreatening manner possible. Any display of force, including guns and restraints, should be avoided, unless officers suspect that their own safety or that of others is threatened. The psychotics' sensory awareness is heightened. Consequently, it is important for officers to reduce sensory input in order to reduce psychotics' fear. This might include removing all nonessential people from the environment, speaking in a slow, soft voice, and reducing other sensory stimuli, such as police radios, bullhorns, and other equipment. By reducing sensory stimuli, officers help psychotic individuals gain control of themselves, making them more approachable.

Persons suffering from depression are frequently in an ambivalent mental state, unable to make decisions, vacillating between pros and cons. Consequently they may argue the opposite of whatever officers suggest. For example, should officers suggest hospitalization, psychotically depressed persons may immediately resist the suggestion, saying that they don't need to be in the hospital and offering all kinds of reasons why they can't go. Officers should stick firmly to their decision, regardless of the depressives' pleas. Therefore, it is important for officers to make up their own minds as to what must be done before revealing the decision to the person concerned. Once officers state their decision, they must act as if there is no alternative. Surprisingly, officers will find that their firmness is reassuring and that in response, the person may stop debating and arguing and instead follow their dictates. The officers' approach to persons who demonstrate delusional thinking is also important. They should neither argue with the delusions nor agree with them. Rather, they should listen and hear out the person's concerns. They can then suggest that there are others who would like to help the person. Mention of going to a hospital or a clinic may disturb some people, but they are more likely to go along with officers who handle the situation in a tactful and firm manner.

SUMMARY

Police officers frequently come in contact with psychotics who act in a strange or violent manner. Or they may come in contact with people with an organic personality disorder who give no sign that they are disturbed until they suddenly explode. In either case, officers should be aware of the strategies they can use to minimize the danger to others, the disordered person, and themselves. They also should be knowledgeable about the symptoms of these disorders so they can distinguish the psychosis from less serious conditions, personality disorders, and neuroses.

Chapters 6 to 8 have presented descriptions of each of the major classifications of mental illness. Since one of the primary responsibilities of law enforcement officers is to assess and manage deviant behavior, the next seven chapters (9–15) will take a closer look at the most common forms of deviant behavior officers are likely to encounter.

BIBLIOGRAPHY

American Psychiatric Association. (2000). *Diagnostic and statistical manual of mental disorders*, 4th ed. Washington, D.C.: American Psychiatric Association.

American Psychiatric Association. (1987). *Diagnostic and statistical manual of mental disorders*, 3rd ed. revised. Washington, D.C.: American Psychiatric Association.

Bleuler, E. (1950). *Dementia Praecox or the group of schizophrenias.* New York: International Universities Press.

Boffey, P. M. 16 March, 1986. Schizophrenia: Insights fail to halt rising toll. *New York Times 1*, 21.

Bower, B. 1 June, 1985. A closer look at bipolars. *Science News 127*, 344.

———. 27 June, 1987. What's in the cards for manic-depression? *Science News 131*, 410.

Bradford, J. M. (1983). The forensic psychiatric aspects of schizophrenia. *Psychiatric Journal of the University of Ottawa, 8*(2), 96–103.

Delgado-Escueta, A. V., et al. (1981). The nature of aggression during epileptic seizures. *New England Journal of Medicine 305*, 711–716.

Eckholm, E. 17 March, 1986. Schizophrenia's victims include strained families. *New York Times pt. 2*, 1, 13.

Eysenck, H. J. (1976). *Psychoticism as a dimension of personality.* London: Hodder and Stoughton.

Freeman, T. (1976). *Childhood psychopathology and adult psychoses.* New York: International Universities Press.

Freud, S. 1955. Mourning and melancholia." In *The Standard Edition of the complete psychological works of Sigmund Freud*, ed. J. Strachey, vol. 14, pp. 87–172. London: Hogarth Press.

Friedman, A. M., Kaplan, H. I., & Sadock, B. J. (1975). *Comprehensive textbook of psychiatry*, 2nd ed. Baltimore: Williams & Wilkins.

Gapen, P. (1985). One-third of D.C.'s homeless are schizophrenic, study says. (Public Citizen Health Research Group Study). *American Medical News 41.*

Gelman, D., et al. 4 May, 1987. Depression. *Newsweek* 48–57.

Goleman, D. 19 March, 1986. Focus on day-to-day life seen as hope for schizophrenics. *New York Times pt. 4*, 1.

Hunting the black dog. 9 March, 1987. *U.S. News and World Report*, p. 8.

I feel like I am trapped inside my head, banging desperately against its walls. 18 March, 1986. *New York Times pt. 3*, 5.

Kisler, G. W. (1972). *The disorganized personality.* New York: McGraw-Hill.

Kraepelin, E. (1918). *Dementia Praecox.* London: E. and S. Livingstone.

Lewis, D. O., et al. (1985). Biopsychosocial characteristics of children who later murder: A prospective study. *American Journal of Psychiatry 42*, 1161–1167.

Monmaney, T. 4 May, 1987. When manic depression is part of the family legacy. *Newsweek* 53.

Redlich, F. C., & Freedman, D. X. (1966). *The theory and practice of psychiatry.* New York: Basic Books.

Schmeck, H. M., Jr. 17 March, 1986. Schizophrenia focus shifts to dramatic changes in brain. *New York Times.*

Silver, J. M., & Yudofsky, S. C. (1987a). Aggressive behavior in patients with neuropsychiatric disorders. *Psychiatric Annals, 17*(6), 367–370.

———. 1987b. Documentation of aggression in the assessment of the violent patient. *Psychiatric Annals, 17*(6), 375–384.

Tteiman, D. M. (1986). Epilepsy and violence: Medical and legal issues." *Epilepsia 271*, S77–S104.

Yudofsky, S. C., Silver, J. M., Jackson, W., Endicott, J., & Williams, D. (1986). The overt aggression scale for the objective rating of verbal and physical aggression. *American Journal of Psychiatry, 143*(1), 35–39.

Yudofsky, S. C., Silver, J., & Yudopsky, B. January, 1988. Treatment of patients with organic personality disorder, explosive type. *Panel on treatment of organic mental syndromes, task force on treatment of psychiatric disorders.* Washington, D.C.: American Psychiatric Association.

PART IV

ASSESSING AND MANAGING ABNORMAL BEHAVIOR IN THE FIELD

Chapter 9

PSYCHOPATHIC BEHAVIOR

Psychopathic behavior is of particular importance to police officers. W. H. Reid has noted that this personality disorder is to be found "not only in prisons or in socially underprivileged settings, but also practically anywhere in society where antisocial traits have survival value, including business and political circles" (1985). A list of psychopaths includes not only homicidal serial rapists like Ted Bundy, Albert DeSalvo (the Boston Strangler), and Kenneth Bianchi (the Hillside Strangler), but also unprincipled and unethical businesspeople, lawyers, physicians, and politicians. The terms *sociopath* and *antisocial personality* are also used to describe such individuals.

The cases that follow represent a wide variety of abnormalities associated with psychopathic behavior. (The sexual psychopath will be explored in more detail in the next chapter.) These cases will serve to focus discussion on the psychopath's characteristics and the underlying factors behind this behavior. The discussion will provide helpful hints to law enforcement officers in handling this behavior.

Historical Background

An English psychiatrist, James Prichard, originally described psychopathic behavior in the nineteenth century. He called those with an unimpaired intellect who had lost their power of self-control *morally insane*. After he introduced this concept, it was first thought that these people might have an organic disease

of the central nervous system that caused this morally insane behavior. The term *constitutional psychopathic inferiority* was used to indicate this organic component; some observers still believe it exists.

In this century, the person who has had perhaps the most impact on the way we view the psychopath is Hervey Cleckley. In his classic work *The Mask of Sanity* (1955), Cleckley provided a conceptual framework for this disorder that has so mystified and frustrated mental health professionals. Cleckley committed his professional career to studying and understanding this personality disorder.

Case Histories

Case Example. After being persuaded to give up his precarious position on the window ledge of a hotel high above Louisville, Kentucky, Michael Crawford sobbed a tale of despair to sympathetic listeners. Newspaper reporters called to the scene gave considerable attention to his story.

John Flynn, a local policeman, read his morning newspaper the next day and recalled a similar incident that had taken place in Boston several weeks earlier. Details of the events were so similar that, out of curiosity, he decided to check further. To his surprise, Michael Crawford and the man rescued from the hotel window ledge in Boston were the same person. With heightened interest, he checked further and discovered that Michael was absent without leave from an army hospital, where he had been taken after his first suicide attempt in Boston.

Louisville police quickly returned him to military control, and he was admitted to an army hospital for evaluation and treatment. After several days on a locked ward, he was transferred to an open ward and allowed to roam the hospital. He soon found his way to the Red Cross building, where he offered his services to the overworked staff. Soon he was their "right hand," showing movies, setting up chairs, serving refreshments, and being helpful in every possible way. Volunteers began to comment on how charming, earnest, and hard-working he was. They began to talk on coffee break about the patient, the heroic combat record he described (which was not true), and his desire to leave the army and return to college (he had never finished high school). The impression that he made was so great that they began to discuss ways they might help him achieve his goals after discharge.

Early discussions of possibly assisting him became even more positive following a fire in one of the hospital buildings. Michael led other patients to safety, helped drag equipment out of the building, and performed heroically. However, the impressed, appreciative volunteers lost their enthusiasm several days later when they discovered that Michael had set the fire. Following his arrest, he was taken to the stockade to await a court-martial. While there, his behavior became so unmanageable that he had to be sent back to the hospital and was admitted to the locked ward. After his return, he made many dramatic suicidal gestures, organized a small patient rebellion, and finally escaped from the facility, never to be heard from again.

Case Example. Some citizens in Crescent City and in Hollywood would like to talk to Billy Dalton about a grand hoax on local businessmen involving the filming of a television show. A small man in his late thirties, dressed in western-style clothing, Billy arrived in Crescent City on Sunday and was gone by

Tuesday. Within these forty-eight hours, he left a trail of actions that are still talked about.

He came to town with a briefcase marked "Paramount" and represented himself as an advance agent for a currently popular television series. He checked into a local motel and told the manager that he needed accommodations for 210 cast and crewmembers that would be arriving within several days to film a segment for the show. He also booked seven rooms for the next night, to be used by production company members who would be coming early. He then contacted the new owner of a local theater, Mr. Chapman, and gave him the same story. He obtained the use of the theater as well as a promise to help him put together a Monday night dinner party for the star of the show. He also secured the local fairgrounds building as a mess hall for the arriving cast and crew. As Mr. Chapman later recalled, "He struck me at precisely the right moment." The prospect of having a well-known actor help publicize his theater interested Mr. Chapman. Consequently, he not only accompanied Billy to a local bakery and ordered refreshments for the party but also gave him close to $300 to go out and buy the rest of the food for the party. At 3:30 P.M. on the day of the party, Billy told the hotel manager that he was going to meet the star at the theater. Shortly thereafter, the manager received a call from a man who identified himself as the star and asked him to tell Billy that he would be a little late. When the dinner began with no sign of production company members, but with others invited by Mr. Chapman present, Mr. Chapman received a phone call from an unidentified person who told him that the star had been delayed in another city but would arrive later. He never appeared. Mr. Chapman picked up the entire tab and began to get suspicious. The next day he called Paramount Studios and was informed that they had never heard of Billy Dalton and that there were no plans to film anything in Crescent City. At approximately the same time, Billy was leaving the motel, telling the manager that he was going to a local laundry to wash some clothing. No one in Crescent City has seen Billy Dalton since.

Several months later in another state, Billy Dalton was arrested and charged with obtaining property through false pretenses. His rap sheet showed fifteen arrests in the last five years for bogus checks, grand theft, and drawing checks on insufficient funds, theft by fraud, and other similar offenses. Pre-sentence evaluation included the following excerpt from the report of the court psychologist:

> Mr. Dalton presents himself as a mousy, insecure, extremely nervous little man who is overwhelmed by society's callous disregard for his obvious virtue. This attitude is difficult to understand in view of his record of collisions with the law. His history illustrates his incapacity to learn from experience and his inevitable failures. He does not appear to be consciencestricken for any of his acts and avoids accepting blame for them.

Case Example. Larry Lindgren graduated 229th out of 240 students in his high school class and began to work in the auto plant where his father had worked for many years. Although he was soon offered an opportunity to become a sponsored trainee, who would eventually mean a better-paying and more responsible position, he decided that this job was too dull. Although he had never been interested in college, he told his father after quitting his job that he was going to a nearby university to look things over. However, he was refused admission because he did not have credits in certain subjects that he had failed in high school. Instead of returning to another regular job, he continued to wander about the campus and attend classes without formally enrolling. After a while he became quite comfortable with his masquerade and began to fake report cards to send home to his parents, telling them that he had won a scholarship.

He became interested in the human body in his biology class. He bought a secondhand stethoscope and a record that played the sounds of normal and abnormal heartbeats. After he had listened to this record diligently and compared the sounds to those of his own

heart, he began to walk through the corridors of the university hospital wearing an intern's white coat and carrying the stethoscope protruding conspicuously from the pocket. Because of his large size he looked older than his age and, consequently, no one questioned his masquerade. He later recounted, "I knew what I was doing. I was the perfect image of the young doctor." Larry spent three years in this environment, observing everything as he walked around the hospital, becoming friendly with the staff, but always being careful not to overact. He became enamored of this way of life. One day the idea occurred to him that, if he could keep it up, he might eventually be able to become a doctor. For the next three years, while holding down a job, he continued to go to the hospital and mingle with the students. He became fast friends with many of them, telling them that he worked elsewhere in the hospital. Larry finally felt ready and "his class" graduated. He even attended graduation, standing in the back as the dean conferred the degree of Doctor of Medicine on the students. Shortly after his "graduation," Larry had a fake diploma printed and moved to another town, where he hung up his shingle and waited for patients.

His co-tenant in the building was a dentist, who complained to Larry about feeling tired most of the time. From what he had learned and his powers of astute observation, Larry diagnosed his condition as anemia and discovered a bleeding ulcer, which he treated. The dentist was grateful and became one of Larry's strongest boosters. Soon patients and money began to roll in. One patient later recalled, "He made us feel so cheerful and healthy because he was young. Children loved him." Within seven months after opening his practice, Larry was seeing an average of two hundred patients a week. His practice grew; at the time he was exposed, he was netting many thousands of dollars a year. He had married several years earlier, but his wife was not aware of his masquerade. They enjoyed their newfound affluence by joining a country club, building a new home, and owning two cars. After several years of practice, Larry began to notice that he was stumbling, becoming awkward with his instruments, and tiring quickly. He privately consulted a doctor in another community without revealing his profession or identity. The doctor told him that he had multiple sclerosis. Larry's immediate concern was for his family. Knowing that his disease might eventually be fatal, he asked his local insurance agent to double his policy coverage, without revealing that he had multiple sclerosis. The insurance application was his undoing. A routine credit check revealed that no doctor by that name was licensed in the state. At first he tried to lie his way out by claiming that he had been licensed in a different state and that he simply had not had the time to take out a new license. However, when asked to produce evidence, he realized his scheme had been uncovered and confessed to the entire hoax.

Patients and friends immediately came to his defense. Many wanted to give him money for his defense, while others wrote or phoned the prosecutor, urging him to drop the charges. At Larry's church, one of the ministers reminded the congregation of the biblical injunction to "judge not, lest ye be judged" and suggested that its members pray for the young doctor, their friend, who was "in a little trouble." One member of the congregation even wrote to the President of the United States, asking for special dispensation for Larry. Larry was charged with practicing medicine without a license and illegal possession of barbiturates and narcotics. He was sentenced to one year in prison. At his sentencing, the judge stated, "Maybe you helped people. I am not sure. But it is also possible you might have hurt people." The pre-sentence evaluation completed by a probation officer stated that Larry had shown no remorse and had freely admitted, "I'd do it all over again."

Characteristics

Hervey Cleckley listed sixteen characteristics of the psychopath (Cleckley, 1976).

Psychologist Robert Hare has developed a new scale of twenty-two items describing the characteristics of the criminal psychopath (1985). Subsequent statistical analyses indicate that the twenty-item scale, reproduced below, could effectively make clinical judgment.

Items in the Revised (20-Item) Psychopathy Checklist

1. Glibness/Superficial Charm
2. Grandiose Sense of Self Worth
3. Need for Stimulation/Proneness to Boredom
4. Pathological Lying
5. Conning/Manipulative
6. Lack of Remorse or Guilt
7. Shallow Affect
8. Callous/Lack of Empathy
9. Parasitic Life-style
10. Poor Behavioral Controls
11. Promiscuous Sexual Behavior
12. Early Behavioral Problems
13. Lack of Realistic, Long-Term Plans
14. Impulsivity
15. Irresponsibility
16. Failure to Accept Responsibility for Own Actions
17. Many Short-Term Marital Relationships
18. Juvenile Delinquency
19. Revocation of Conditional Release
20. Criminal Versatility

Although there is a demonstrable diagnostic value in Hare's scale, the following thirteen diagnostic characteristics are sufficient for police officers to make a preliminary judgment as to the type of person they may be dealing with.

Manipulation of People

Psychopaths manipulate people like objects to gain their own ends. Ellen Spector Person (1986) has this to say about manipulation:

Manipulation is a specific kind of interpersonal interaction. Initiated by one individual to influence the feelings and behavior of another, it may serve intrapsychic purposes or goal-oriented aims or both. The manipulator is determined to get what he wants, to have things his way. Acutely sensitive to interpersonal cues, he intuitively knows how to use the emotions, needs, and weaknesses revealed to him for his own ends. He rarely responds with empathy or exhibits a sincere desire to help.

The kind of manipulation utilized by the psychopath, however, is generally based on charm. The manipulator appears to be helpful, charming, even ingratiating or seductive, but is covertly hostile, domineering, or, at best, neutral in interaction with another individual (object). The object is perceived as an aggressor, a competitor, or merely as an instrument to be used. (pp. 256–257)

Billy Dalton used people to get what he wanted; when their usefulness was ended, he left them stranded. In this way, and through similar behavior, psychopaths not only end up with no friends but also do not seem to want any. Psychopaths are generally self-centered, with little or no regard for the welfare of others, even though they may be good con artists and inspire confidence and faith. Like Billy Dalton, they can motivate people with whom they come in contact to do things they might not do for anyone else under normal circumstances. Unfortunately, much of the faith and confidence they inspire ends only in grief and misery.

This ability to manipulate people also can lead psychopaths to remarkable success in almost any role they assume. Without a formal education, Larry Lindgren was able to manipulate people and inspire confidence in himself, becoming remarkably successful in his masquerade as a physician.

Unexplained Failure

Although many psychopaths are above average in intelligence and have periods in their life when they succeed at almost whatever they choose, sooner or later they usually fail.

We have one near certainty; sooner or later, when the classic psychopath comes on stage,

things will go wrong . . . patterns of temporary success or at least stability are followed by strangely brutal and irresponsible behavior with accompanying stupid and unnecessary falls from grace for which there can be no rational explanation. (Harrington, 1971, p. 201)

Person has noted this pattern of failure in pointing out differences between psychopaths and other manipulators. While entrepreneurs' manipulation often produces a successful life pattern, a downward drift in the lives of psychopaths is inevitable (Person, 1986). Single, unexplained failures are often not enough to unmask psychopaths. Only after many failures do people begin to realize that something is indeed wrong. Prior to this, they are more apt to look for shortcomings or mistakes in themselves rather than see the situation for what it is – shrewd manipulation by a psychopath.

Absence of Anxiety

Psychopaths are rarely plagued by anxieties, phobias, or psychosomatic symptoms. They are most often at ease and poised in situations where a normal person would be tense and upset. Robert D. Hare (1982) suggests that there may be a physiological coping mechanism in psychopaths that enables them to be so emotionally detached and poised. How many normal individuals could successfully carry off a masquerade for almost six years and eventually achieve the success of "graduation" from medical school, as did Larry Lindgren? However, it is equally important to recognize that if psychopathic personalities are deprived of the opportunity to act out their abnormal behavior, situational anxiety may occur. When Michael Crawford was taken to the stockade to await a court-martial for setting the fire, he became so unmanageable that he had to be transferred to a hospital and admitted to a locked ward. Furthermore, after admission to this ward, where opportunities to act out were more limited, he made many dramatic suicidal gestures as a further result of his situational anxiety. In contrast to neurotics, whose anxieties are often unrelenting, psychopaths lose their anxiety when the pressure is relieved – thus the term *situational.*

Absence of Psychosis

Well-integrated and functioning psychopaths are not psychotic. Their behavior is not divorced from reality, nor do they have delusions or hallucinations. However, like Michael Crawford, they can act crazy to escape an unpleasant situation. The ability to act crazy can present a difficult diagnostic problem to anyone called upon to evaluate psychopaths.

> These people are regarded as mentally ill because there are paradoxes that at first seem so strange: sentimentality and brutality reside with this individual – these people do things that are bizarre – it is others' instinctive response to assume they're sick – you can imagine what the most frequent diagnosis was – some form of schizophrenia or another. (Samenow, 1986, p. 370)

Samenow goes on to say that psychopaths are "test-wise, psychologically sophisticated – able to ferret out what the examiner wants." R. Rogers' (1988) recent text on malingering and deception is of great assistance in evaluating psychopaths who are trying to manipulate the judicial system.

Persistence of Self-Defeating Antisocial Behavior

Although psychopaths are capable of plotting and executing very clever crimes to attain a material goal (such as money), they also may follow a pattern of criminal activity that is self-defeating to all personal goals they claim are important. Even after he had the support of the Red Cross volunteers to go to college, Michael Crawford set fire to a portion of the hospital, losing the support that they had previously offered.

Inability to Distinguish Truth from Falsehood

Cleckley (1955) commented on the psychopath's remarkable capacity to disregard the truth. As the "physician," Larry Lindgren appeared confident and wholly at ease in situations where the average person would feel embarrassed. It is not enough to realize that psychopaths may lie. It is equally important to know that these lies are not trivial and that psychopaths have a remarkable capacity to live as if they were true.

Inability to Accept Blame

When Larry Lindgren was interviewed during his pre-sentence evaluation, he demonstrated no remorse for his masquerade activities. Similarly, after Billy Dalton was caught, he did not appear conscience-stricken to the psychologist who evaluated him prior to sentencing. Albert DeSalvo (the Boston Strangler) blamed his need to sexually assault and kill other women on his wife's sexual hang-ups and lack of affection for him. It is characteristic of psychopaths to not accept blame.

Incapacity for Love and Closeness

Although psychopaths may possess an astonishing ability to engender and receive devotion from many, these persons have no real capacity for love. They are unable to form mature relationships with others and find it difficult to tolerate closeness. If a friendship is developing, they will generally take steps to alienate that person to avoid closeness.

Lack of Insight

Because of their intelligence, it often appears to the casual observer that psychopaths have a remarkable capacity for insight. This is strengthened by the impression that they are always ready to reassess their position, identify misbehavior, and plan for change. However, their subsequent actions demonstrate not true insight but rather, as Cleckley (1955) has called it, "a mimicry of insight." They resolve to do better without any real understanding of the behavior that led to the particular situation.

Shallow and Impersonal Responses to Sexual Life

As a corollary to their incapacity for love and closeness, psychopaths are also unable to achieve any deep response in a sexual relationship. This is true despite the notorious promiscuity of many psychopaths of both sexes. On close examination, it is apparent that these sexual activities are shallow, impersonal, and very self-centered.

Callousness and Sadism

Although we will devote greater attention to these topics in the next chapter on aberrant sexual behavior, it is important to note that callousness and sadism are often important characteristics of psychopathic behavior (McGinnis, 1983; Rule, 1986; Stevens, 1982).

Suicide Rarely Carried Out

Michael Crawford's suicidal behavior is typical of psychopaths. They frequently threaten suicide or even make sham suicidal attempts with a high degree of dramatic content.

These gestures, designed to gain attention, are often staged with stunning authenticity. On one of the many occasions when Michael attempted suicide, he staggered dramatically down the hospital corridor, dripping blood from the "slashes" in his chest. In reality, these were only superficial cuts that he had made with a small piece of glass. He had been very careful to cut nothing but small capillaries on the skin's surface. However, before this could be discovered, Michael had created quite a stir by collapsing in a moaning heap at the feet of the nurse whose sympathy he was trying to obtain.

When the rare suicide occurs, it is common for psychopaths to die with a surprised look on their faces, probably a result of poor judgment in overstepping the bounds of "safe" suicidal behavior.

Periods of Marked Creativity

Because of the psychopaths' pattern of self-defeat, repeated failures, criminal activity, and even hospitalization, it is easy to overlook periods of extensive creativity, industriousness, and effectiveness. One of the problems in helping psychopaths is how to convert brief periods of creativity into a stable pattern of behavior, thus avoiding the pattern of self-defeat.

Underlying Factors

Specific factors underlying psychopathic behavior are not understood. However, the difficulties psychopaths encounter in all forms of interpersonal relationships suggest the importance of a careful examination of early childhood development. In their study of the families of those people who eventually developed psychopathic behavior, P. O'Neal and her coworkers (1960) determined from their data that parental rejection in early childhood, a high frequency of broken homes, alcoholism, and low socioeconomic status were important underlying factors. They also found that those who developed psychopathic behavior have usually encountered a specific form of parental rejection, characterized by either the complete absence of parental discipline or its presence in a very inconsistent or lenient form. From this, it may be hypothesized that the absence or inconsistency of parental discipline deprives children of an important mechanism for obtaining feedback about behavior. This mechanism helps normal children develop their own internalized system (the superego) for controlling behavior during adult life. Furthermore, as they have not experienced early parental relationships based on positive interactions, psychopaths do not develop a capacity for engaging in compatible adult relationships. This view presents psychopathic behavior as acting-out against society that, in adulthood, represents the early rejecting parents. Furthermore, psychopaths' absence of anxiety about this behavior is another reflection of the absence or inconsistency of parental discipline in childhood. Without it, the children have not been able to assess what behavior or situations should make them anxious.

More recent studies have consistently shown that many familial factors are associated with an antisocial personality (Anolik, 1983; Fisher, 1983, 1984). As mentioned earlier, many have thought that psychopathic behavior may have some underlying organic roots. Some have suggested that the psychopath is constitutionally inferior. Recent research, especially, has looked for evidence of either brain injury or brain damage. However, despite many studies that show high rates of abnormality in the brain-wave patterns of adult criminals, there has been no positive proof that this abnormality is a precondition to development of psychopathic behavior. Ham's view is that "the psychopath's social insensitivities and core attributes are more the result of constitutional (perhaps genetic) factors than the result of experience" (Reid et al. 1986, p. 12). This view regarding possible genetic factors is supported by data from the Texas Adoption project. James M. Horn (1988) states that previous investigators found that mothers (but not fathers) of antisocial children had elevated Minnesota Multiphasic Inventory (MMPI) scores, especially on the Psychopathic Deviance (Pd) scale. They also tend to be irritable, easily angered, and often depressed. Horn remarks that it is not surprising that these mothers are poor parents. But are they poor parents because of difficulties in raising an antisocial child, or are the children antisocial because of some genetic inheritance from the mothers? The answer may lie in the study of adopted children who have been separated from their biological parents at birth. "If the correlation between biological parents and their adopted-away

children is not diminished by the separation, the influence of shared environment in the personality of both parents and children can be ruled out. In addition, if the adopted children resemble their own biological parents on psychopathic deviancy more than they resemble their adoptive parents, the evidence for the operation of genetic influence becomes stronger" (Hare, McPherson, & Forth, 1988, pp. 710–714).

The Texas Adoption Project studied three hundred adoptive families. Taken as a whole, the results support the view that there is:

> A significant tendency for high Pd children to come from Pd mothers, even when the children were reared by adoptive parents whose Pd scores were near average. Living together under the rearing conditions provided by the same adopted parents did not produce the slightest resemblance in Pd among unrelated children. Finally, the adopted children resembled the biological mothers they had never seen more than they resembled the parents who had reared them from birth. (Horn, 1988, p. 227)

It should also be noted that unwed mothers and their adopted-away children also showed significant correlation on the Schizophrenia and Depression scales of the MMPI. There were no significant correlations on any of the MMPI scales for adoptive parent/adopted child combinations. A ten-year follow-up study is currently under way (Horn, 1988). Finally, José Sanchez, a noted political scientist, has observed that the classic psychopath does not internalize external authority. He has, in effect, no "policeman from within." He professes an adherence to the rules and morals of the society but conforms only when it is useful to him. "His conformity is situational and superficial; he betrays his 'principles' at the slightest opportunity" (1986, p. 81). Sanchez states that modern American society makes heroes out of psychopaths. Further, the relative adaptability of this type of character structure makes the psychopath likely to emerge in increasing numbers. The modern world provides fertile ground for the rise of the psychopathic personality. In a related observation, Harrington notes that the psychopaths' ideal of acting out desires for immediate gratification has become an acceptable philosophy among many people – "even among people who are not psychopaths" (Harrington, 1972, p. 45).

In a world facing the ever-present threat of nuclear holocaust, declining faith in the authority of family, government, and the church, Vietnam, Watergate, and the Iran-Contra scandal have all proved the wrongdoing of top government and business officials. Marked cynicism has developed, as well as insecurity about personal and social survival. In such a world, the phrases "look out for number one" and "every man for himself" have a certain face validity. This psychopath philosophy could account, in large measure, for the increasing adaptability to the psychopathic life-style in today's society. Media exposure reinforces this. *Thou Shalt Not Kill,* a special television report by NBC, presents an interview with two death-row criminals, Lance and Kelbach. These men murdered numerous people for no apparent reason. They talk about these murders freely and with no remorse. They remark, with macabre humor, that their victims were going to die anyway; they were just speeding up the end a little. Kelbach chills the interviewer when he states that not only wouldn't it bother him if someone were to have a heart attack right in front of him, but his preference would be for the person to have an attack, crawl to the phone for help, then to "keel over" and die (Reese, 1987). Sanchez sees a bleak future.

> Psychopathy is distributed throughout the class structure of American society. Given the opportunities available to well-to-do psychopaths, the likelihood that they will engage in street criminal violence is extremely low. However, these individuals may continue to use white-collar crime to pursue their desires. Such activities may demand guiltless and loveless, but charming and manipulative personalities. Psychopaths who lack the economic means to satisfy their impulses may not think twice about engaging in armed robbery, and may injure or kill a victim who resists (or even one who does not resist but who is perceived as a means of experiencing excitement or for breaking up the monotony of everyday life). (Sanchez, 1986, p. 92)

HELPFUL HINTS TO LAW ENFORCEMENT OFFICERS

There are several important signs to help police officers recognize the possibility that they are dealing with a psychopath.

1. **Review the arrest record.** Psychopaths' rap sheets will reflect a variety of crimes. Because of their immature need for immediate gratification, these persons' crimes are extremely unpredictable. Unlike other criminals, who tend to develop a specialty and stick with it, psychopaths may commit a variety of crimes that range from sodomy to armed robbery and murder. Further, when they commit a crime they may not hesitate to kill non-resisting victims or witnesses just to experience the sensation of killing.

2. **Police officers must develop the ability to recognize con men's glib style of conversation.** Coupled with psychopaths' inability to follow through or engage in any behavior that is not self-seeking, this should tip off police officers to the kind of person they are dealing with.

3. **If police officers find themselves excessively liking or hating a suspect who is being interviewed, that person might be a psychopath.** From training and experience, most professionals will develop a professional attitude toward those with whom they come in contact. Generally, there are those whom they like, those whom they do not like, and

even some toward whom they are indifferent. However, a person who gets them so irritated that they tend to lose their professionalism, or who stimulates them to rescue him or her, is possibly a psychopath.

4. **Police officers should very carefully consider as a possible psychopath the criminal who is able to involve many people in his or her behavior, crimes, and rescue.** Cases presented in this chapter did not involve the psychopath alone.

5. **Well-integrated and functioning psychopaths can usually beat a lie detector (polygraph), or at least produce an inconclusive result (Reese, 1987).** The polygraph measures certain physiological correlates of anxiety and guilt, such as skin response, blood pressure, pulse, and respiration; it is an "emotional detective." If the test subject feels guilty or anxious about certain questions, there will be disturbances in the polygraphic pattern. However, since psychopaths are often immune to feelings of guilt and anxiety unless placed under severe stress, these physiological disturbances are not likely to appear, even when they respond to questions that might make the normal person feel guilt or anxiety.

6. **Speech is often used to conceal thoughts. This is certainly true of psychopaths.** They are completely capable of responding to vague questions with vague answers and to concrete questions with concrete answers. In this way, they are often able to persuade themselves that they are telling the truth. For example, if an officer asks a psychopathic suspect a vague question such as "What did you do after leaving Los Angeles?" he may reply that he took a plane to Denver. He conveniently omits his stopover in Las Vegas, where he participated in three armed robberies, or in Tucson, where he committed two rapes. As another example,

if the officer asks him if he has ever been in jail before, he may answer "No!" since he can rationalize that the officer is talking about this particular jail. However, he may have been in several other jails and/or a state or federal penitentiary. Unless specifically asked, he will conclude, with proper justification to himself, that he has not lied in answering the question. Consequently, it is easy to become discouraged when interviewing psychopaths. It may often be necessary to repeat the question several times and formulate it in different ways. Only persistent and careful questioning will elicit the necessary information. However, if this procedure is done with hostility, psychopaths are likely to clam up and not respond to further questioning.

7. **It is important not to bluff psychopaths.** They are masters of bluffing and are certainly better than most officers. The best way to interview psychopaths is to prepare carefully by knowing every detail of the case.

8. **It is important to be firm and clear with suspected psychopaths.** Police officers should say exactly what they mean and set appropriate limits on a subject's actions. These tactics are critical to effective handling of psychopaths. Although psychopaths can be very charming, they can also make officers very angry and may maneuver officers into a situation in which they violate the suspects' rights. Avoid this possibility.

Differences Between Lawbreakers and Psychopaths

While it is true that many criminals show some evidence of psychopathic behavior, there are important differences between ordinary lawbreakers and psychopaths.

1. **Ordinary lawbreakers are most often motivated by what their crime will**

net them, whether it is $25,000 from a bank robbery or another profitable venture. Psychopaths, on the other hand, often steal things for which they have no particular use. They may forge a check for a small amount when they have more than that in their pockets.

2. **Ordinary lawbreakers seek to avoid detection and apprehension.** Psychopaths do likewise for a period of time, but if they go undetected for too long, they may commit foolish crimes and leave telltale clues behind that tend to ensure apprehension.

3. **Ordinary lawbreakers will avoid the police and not volunteer to help them solve crimes.** On the other hand, psychopaths often see their criminal activities as a game between themselves and the police and are often detected in this way. For example, journalist Ann Rule (1986) wrote about Ted Bundy: "His cunning jousts with police were always akin to Dungeons and Dragons, and he so delighted in outwitting them, watching them scurry around to do what he considered his bidding."

4. **Ordinary lawbreakers generally maintain some creed of loyalty to friends, family, or even to their opposition to society.** However, psychopaths are uncommitted, with loyalty to no one and no sincerely held attitudes for or against anything.

Those wishing to understand the thinking process of psychopaths would do well to read Yochelson and Samenow's three-volume treatise, *The Criminal Personality* (1976, 1977, 1986). Samenow discusses some of the most important aspects of his own thinking about psychopaths in an article "The Nexus of Criminal Behavior."

It is interesting and worthy of mention that, as this chapter was being written, the following news story appeared in the July 22, 2003, edition of the *Arizona Daily Star:*

Film Phony Having "Nice Vacation" Conning Florida Firms

Orlando, Fla. (AP) – He's not exactly puttin' on the Ritz, but this phony Hollywood filmmaker is having a good time on the cuff, leaving hotels, restaurants and nightspots stuck with the bills. "He's having a hell of a nice vacation is what he's having," said Cathy Savino, director of the Orlando office of the Economic Development Commission of Mid-Florida. The bogus mogul has seen the whales at Sea World, toured the sound stages at Universal Studios, lounged at two hotels and seen the sights from a helicopter and the back of a burgundy-colored stretch limousine. He's taken women dancing and dining at a fancy Chinese restaurant. He's told people from Sanford to Orlando that he is with Warner Brothers, Lorimar Studios, Spielberg Productions, or his own JFT Productions. His tab has run into the thousands, but this man calling himself John Frank has never spent a dime. He's asked businessmen to send the bills to nonexistent companies. Frank's victims have described him as short, dark-haired and dumpy, dressed in a sloppy fashion. The Orange County Sheriff's Department is looking for him, spokesman Jim Solomons said yesterday. Savino has warned film offices statewide to be on the lookout.

The Disney-MGM Studios theme park and Universal Studios Florida have begun movie and television production in the Orlando area in the last year, bringing an influx of film people, technicians and executives. Frank told clerks and others that he was making a movie called *Runaways,* starring Judd Hirsch, Amy Irving, Dan Aykroyd and River Phoenix.

SUMMARY

Because of their persistent involvement in antisocial behavior, psychopaths are very likely to come into contact with law enforcement officers. Because of their unique psychological features, they present specific problems in detection, handling, and care following arrest. Psychopaths are potentially very dangerous because they do not require a reason to kill anyone – including police officers.

BIBLIOGRAPHY

Anolik, S. A. (1983). Family influences upon delinquency: Biosocial and psychosocial perspectives. *Adolescence, 18*(71), 489–498.

The antisocial personality – Part I. (1985). *Harvard Medical School Mental Health Letter, 2*(1), 1–4.

The antisocial personality disorder – Part II. (1985). *Harvard Medical School Mental Health Letter, 2*(2), 2–5.

Cleckley, H. M. (1955). *The mask of sanity.* St. Louis: C. V. Mosby.

Film phony having 'nice vacation' conning Florida firms. 22 July, 2003. *Arizona Daily Star.*

Fisher, D. (1983). Parental supervision and delinquency. *Perception and Motor Skills, 56,* 635–640.

_____. (1984). Family size and delinquents. *Perception and Motor Skills, 58,* 527–534.

Hare, R. D. (1985). Psychopathy and physiological activity during the anticipation of an aversive stimulus in a distraction paralysis. *Psychophysiology, 19,* 266–271.

_____. (1985). A checklist for the assessment of psychopathy. In *Clinical criminology,* ed. M. H. Ben-Aron, S. J. Hucker, & C. D. Webster. Toronto: M & M Graphics.

_____. (1986). In *Unmasking the psychopath,* ed. W. H. Reid, D. Dorr, J. I. Walker, & J. T. Bonner III. New York: W. W. Norton.

Hare, R. D., & McPherson, L. M. (1984). Violent and aggressive behavior by criminal psychopaths. Special Issue: Empirical approaches to law and psychiatry. *International Journal of Law and Psychiatry, 7*(1), 35–50.

Hare, R. D., McPherson, L. M., & Forth, A. E. (1988). Male psychopaths and their criminal careers. *Journal of Consulting Clinical Psychology, 56*(5), 710–714.

Harrington, A. (1972). *Psychopaths,* 44. New York: Simon & Schuster.

Holmes, R. M., & Deburger, J. E. (1985). Profiles of terror. *Federal Probation, 49*(3), 29–34.

Horn, J. M. (1988). Psychopathic deviancy and genetics: A preliminary report from the Texas adoption project. In *Police psychology: Operational assistance,* by J. T. Reese & J. M. Horn, pp. 225–228. Quantico, VA: U.S. Department of Justice, FBI.

McGinnis, J. (1983). *Fatal vision.* New York: G. P. Putnam's Sons.

O'Neal, P., Bergman, J., Schafer, J., & Robins, L. (1960). The relation of childhood behavior problems to adult psychiatric status. In *Scientific Papers and Discussions,* ed. J. Gottlieb & G. Tourney. American Psychiatric Association.

Person, E. S. (1986). Manipulativeness in entrepreneurs and psychopaths. In *Unmasking the psychopath,* ed. W. H. Reid et al., pp. 256–259. New York: W. W. Norton.

Reese, J. T. May, 1980. Thou shalt not kill – Motivations of criminal informants. *FBI Law Enforcement Bulletin 17.*

_____. (1987). *Behavioral science in law enforcement.* Quantico, VA: U.S. Department of Justice, FBI Academy.

Reid, W. H. (1985). The antisocial personality: A review. *Hospital and Community Psychiatry, 36*(8), 831–837.

Reid, W. H., Dorr, D., Walker, J. I., & Bonner J. T. III, eds. (1986). *Unmasking the psychopath.* New York: W. W. Norton.

Rogers, R., ed. (1988). *Clinical assessment of malingering and deception.* New York: Guilford Press.

Rule, A. (1986). *Stranger beside me.* New York: Signet.

Samenow, S. (1988). The nexus of criminal behavior. In *Police psychology: Operational assistance,* by J. T. Reese & J. M. Horn, pp. 330, 363–377. Quantico, VA: U.S. Department of Justice, FBI.

Sanchez, J. (1986). Social crisis and psychopathy: Toward a sociology of the psychopath. In *Unmasking the psychopath*, ed. W. H. Reid et al., pp. 78–96. New York: W. W. Norton.

Stevens, W. R. (1982). *Deadly intentions.* New York: Penguin.

Williamson, S., Hare, R. D., & Wong, S. (1987).

Violence: Criminal psychopaths and their victims. Special Issue: Forensic psychology. Canadian Journal of Behavioural Science, 19(4), 454–462.

Yochelson, S., & Samenow, S. (1976, 1977, 1986). *The criminal personality.* 3 vols. Northvale, NJ: Jason Aronson.

Chapter 10

ABERRANT SEXUAL BEHAVIOR

Aberrant sexual behavior represents an important category of abnormal behavior with which police officers frequently come in contact. Officers who encounter sex crimes, such as rape, child molesting, and exhibitionism, or crimes that often have an underlying sexual component, such as arson, shoplifting, and homicide, will be able to carry out their work more effectively if they have a basic understanding of the psychological concepts associated with these crimes. The community, because of the threats to its welfare posed by those who engage in aberrant sexual behavior, often places great pressure on law enforcement, challenging its competency if apprehension of the criminal is delayed. The public often does not realize the many obstacles that frequently impede investigation of sexual crimes, such as scanty evidence, lack of witnesses, and the reluctance of victims to file complaints. Sexually aberrant behavior can arouse feelings of disgust and indignation in average people; police officers are no exception. This personal reaction may decrease officers' effectiveness in performing their duties. A better understanding of sexually aberrant behavior may help officers handle their personal reactions more effectively, thereby allowing them to deal with this behavior from a broader and more professional frame of reference.

General Definitions and Concepts

Before examining specific types of sexually aberrant behavior, it is important to understand some general concepts relating to normal and abnormal sexual behavior. We have relied heavily on the work of psychiatrist R. J. Stoller (1975) in this discussion because we believe it has particular relevance for police officers.

Sexuality

Sexuality may be defined as all behavior associated with relations between the sexes and reproductive functions. In the theories of Sigmund Freud, discussed in Chapter 3, normal sexuality depends on the successful completion of a sequence of early childhood events between birth and age five. During this time, the person's involvement with and reactions to the various reproductive, receptive, and eliminative organs primarily determine the direction of personality growth. Relations with parents and peers further serve to shape individual identity and personality.

Normal development leads to a mature, adjusted person who is capable, during adolescence or adulthood, of entering into sexual relationships that are both physically and emotionally stable and satisfying. Adult sexual relations should be goal directed and designed to achieve satisfaction without excessive fear or guilt. Although these relations may not be free from conflict, they are generally based on a core of emotional stability that allows for a resolution of any conflicts that may occur. Consequently, those who have

94

attained normal sexual behavior patterns possess an awareness of their own physical and emotional needs and have the judgment necessary to fulfill them realistically within their environment.

Aberration

Just as it is difficult to define *normalcy*, it is equally hard to define *aberration*. Generally, aberration is behavior set apart from common behavior by its infrequent occurrence. In our society, sexual "aberration means an erotic technique that one uses for completion of the sexual act and that differs from the culture's traditional definition of normality, in our case gratification by heterosexual, genital intercourse" (Stoller, 1975, p. 3). Stoller divides aberrations into two types: deviations and perversions. Deviations are aberrations that are not primarily a result of forbidden fantasies, especially fantasies of harming others. Included in this category is sexual experimentation, which is carried out primarily as a result of curiosity and is not exciting enough to repeat.

In contrast, perversions, which will be the major subject of this chapter, are "erotic forms of hatred" (Stoller, 1975, p. 4). Through them, a person acts out fantasies in a habitual manner to achieve complete sexual satisfaction. In perversions, the core of hostility is the fantasy of revenge. This is hidden in the actions that constitute the perversion and usually serves to convert a childhood trauma to a situation of adult triumph. The perversion also contains a strong element of risk-taking, which enhances excitement. Perverse sexual behavior usually reflects the past history of the person's sexual development, especially the dynamics of the early family setting. Through the perversion, the person turns the earlier childhood trauma into a victory. The need to repeat it is derived not only from the inability to get completely rid of the earlier trauma, but also to gain revenge against the object that the person perceives as the cause of the trauma.

Aberrant Sexual Behavior and Criminality

Just as all aberrant sexual behavior does not indicate mental illness, all of it should not be considered criminal. While mental health professionals are interested in sexually aberrant behavior to determine if it is a sign of mental illness, police officers are interested in it for the primary purpose of determining its legality or illegality.

Many of the sexual behaviors between two people that are considered criminal revolve around the issue of consent. Is the "victim" capable of consent – able to make responsible independent decisions – and does the "victim" freely consent – without force or coercion? These are the considerations that distinguish criminal sexual behavior from personal preference, which is not criminal. Certain sex crimes, although generally considered "nuisance crimes" and classified as misdemeanors, may be indicative of a more general pattern of ritualization. In this case, the possibility of much more serious sex crimes must be considered. How they are to be prevented while ensuring individual rights is another matter. It is not our purpose to resolve these complex legal issues, but simply to point out to police officers that the confusion surrounding many laws in this area allows some flexibility of judgment in determining a course of action. Since they have this opportunity for discretion, it becomes even more important that they understand the underlying psychological principles associated with the varieties of sexually aberrant behavior. This will help them to choose a course of action consistent with individual needs and with the laws of our society.

The Varieties of Aberrant Sexual Behavior

In describing the aberrant forms of sexual behavior, we will focus on their basic characteristics, underlying factors in their development, and problems that they present to law enforcement.

The DSM-IV-TR describes people with "paraphilias" (loosely translated as "abnormal" love) or paraphilic disorders (aberrant sexual behavior) as people who are sexually aroused by things or situations that are not part of:

> Normative arousal-activity patterns and that in varying degrees may interfere with the capacity for reciprocal, affectionate activity. . . . The essential feature of [this type of] disorder is recurrent intense sexual urges and sexually arousing fantasies generally involving either (1) nonhuman objects, (2) the suffering or humiliation of oneself or one's partner (not merely simulated), or (3) children or other nonconsenting persons. (DSM–IV–TR, 2000)

People are considered to have such a disorder only if they have *acted* on these urges or fantasies. In most cases (with some notable exceptions, such as the serial or lust murderer to be described), there is no necessary connection between the urge or fantasy and the acting-out behavior. It is only the acting out of these fantasies or urges that constitutes a crime.

Two different patterns characterize people with paraphilias. Some can be aroused only if they fantasize about or are exposed to their specific arousal stimuli. On the other hand, some may act out only episodically; for example, during periods of stress. "At other times the person is able to function sexually without paraphilic fantasies or stimuli" (DSM-IV-TR, 2000). These are persons who have resolved the conflict or trauma to some extent, but not sufficiently to ensure that they will function at a more mature level regardless of the level of stress in their lives. Under severe pressure they revert to earlier, more immature patterns of behavior.

Fetishism

Fetishists achieve sexual excitement and gratification by substituting an inanimate object or a part of the body for the human love object. The range of fetishistic behavior is great and can include many activities, some of which are normal and others of which are highly abnormal. For example, nearly everyone who preserves mementos from a loved friend or relative is engaging in fetishistic behavior. Similarly, choosing sexual partners on the basis of their conformity to certain preferences of hair color, body shape, or other physical features is also a form of fetishistic behavior.

Some episodes of shoplifting are associated with fetishistic behavior. The objects sought have significant value through the sexual feelings that they arouse. In these cases, shoplifting becomes a fetishistic experience and exemplifies how aberrant sexual behavior can lead indirectly to crime. If it is not suspected, it may be missed as an underlying factor in the crime.

The fetishistic behavior that usually comes to police attention is associated with an inability to achieve sexual satisfaction through contact with the whole person and the displacement of the potential sexual response to an object or anatomical part that represents the person and is more safe to interact with (less likely to be rejecting). In benign forms of fetishism, the revenge and risk-taking associated with this behavior are minimal. For example, the hair fetishist may go about the city snipping off a piece of hair from unsuspecting women. However, in other cases, it is not possible for the fetishist to control the hostile impulses and the object must be truly, not symbolically, harmed or even destroyed. In these instances fetishistic behavior may be dangerous. Finally, fetishism occasionally results in violent behavior if the person is aggressively pursuing a particular part of another's body or an object belonging to someone who is unwilling to give it up.

Transvestitism

Transvestitism can be considered a type of fetishism – a fetish that focuses on wearing clothes of the opposite sex. The transvestite achieves sexual excitement and gratification through them, at times even enacting the role of the opposite sex. (This is in contrast to the transsexual, who completely assumes the identity of the opposite sex through behavior and/or a sex change operation.) The essential feature of this disorder is a recurring, intense sexual urge and sexually arousing fantasy of cross-dressing. While cross-dressed, he usually masturbates, fantasizing that other males are attracted to him because he is a woman in his female attire (DSM-IV-TR, 2000). When cross-dressing is done for purposes of sexual arousal (that is, to be sexually aroused by the clothing itself and by wearing the clothing) transvestitism occurs almost exclusively in heterosexual males. Homosexual males also cross-dress but as part of their sex role behavior and/or courtship practices, not for arousal itself. Female impersonators are most often homosexual males. The stealing of women's panties, a nuisance crime sometimes committed by transvestites, is strictly a heterosexual crime.

Since parental attitudes are key factors in the child's development of a proper sexual identity, it is not surprising that confusion of sexual identity in early childhood can be an underlying factor in the later development of transvestite behavior. For example, if the male child is subjected to behavior that attacks his masculinity, one possible refuge from this attack is to deny masculinity through cross-dressing, which is commonly associated with transvestites. Alternatively, many transvestites have an early childhood history that includes being forced into an unmasculine role by being cross-dressed. At these times, the child feels extremely threatened and may resort to fantasy as a way of controlling the threat. It is the fantasy that converts the trauma of the experience into a triumph. As the child grows older and becomes sexually active, this fantasy can become associated with sexual satisfaction; traumatic aspects of cross-dressing can be converted into a pleasurable experience. However, the underlying hostility associated with the earlier traumatic event does not disappear. If not properly controlled

through the triumphant fantasy, this hostility can lead to perverse behavior that may come to the attention of law enforcement officers. To some extent, transvestitism focuses on both nonhuman objects and self-humiliation to provide sexual arousal and satisfaction. We will now turn our attention to the group of paraphilias concerned with deriving sexual pleasure from the suffering or humiliation of oneself or one's partners. (This does *not* include people who engage in sexual activity in which they merely *pretend* or imagine that they are suffering or fantasize that they or their partner is being humiliated.)

Sadism and Masochism

When someone with a perversion cannot control their hostility, sadism and masochism often result. Sadists obtain sexual gratification by inflicting pain upon others, while masochists achieve the same level of sexual gratification by enduring pain inflicted upon themselves. Sadists may achieve this sexual satisfaction by engaging in serious criminal acts, such as torture, rape, and homicide. In other instances such as arson, the underlying sadistic sexual impulses may not be clearly evident to the police; but officers should keep the underlying sexual aspect of this behavior in mind as they conduct the investigation.

While masochists may not pose as great a danger to the community as sadists because their impulses lead to self-victimization, it is important to recognize that their behavior may still involve others. For example, in *bondage*, masochists place themselves under the power of a person of the opposite sex or, if a homosexual, under a person of the same sex. They then encourage this person to tie, chain, or beat them in order to achieve sexual excitement. Fantasy, both during and after the bondage, is an important component in achieving sexual satisfaction and for stimulating continuation of the behavior.

According to the DSM-IV-TR, sexual masochism can include sexual arousal by oxygen deprivation. This is a type of masochism that police officers are more likely to encounter in the course of their duties. Death resulting from this form of masochism is frequently mistaken for suicide or homicide. The fact that these autoerotic fatalities share common characteristics with suicide has led many investigators initially to classify an autoerotic death as a suicide. The death is caused "by means of a noose, ligature, plastic bag, mask, chemical . . . or chest compression. People in such behavior report that the activity is accompanied by sexual fantasies in which they asphyxiate or harm others, others asphyxiate or harm them, or they escape near brushes with death" (DSM-IV-TR, 2000). Other features, such as a blindfold, gag, or physical restraints, have led to mistaken suspicions of homicide (Reese, 1981). People who engage in such activity (almost invariably male) almost always provide an escape mechanism in the scenario that allows them to approach death and yet escape. Deaths occur when the escape mechanism fails (for example, such as a slip knot in the noose). This usually occurs as a result of unforeseen circumstances. Suicide is not the goal.

In sexual sadism, sadists experience sexual arousal by inflicting pain and humiliation on their victims. The look of terror in their victims' eyes is a source of arousal. The following example is an illustration of a sadistic homicide.

Case Example. Mary Sullivan, killed shortly after Christmas by the Boston Strangler, was described as a cheerful, friendly person who worked as a nurse's aide in a Cape Cod hospital. She had moved into a third-floor apartment with two other women her age. On a Saturday, the two women came home from work, opened the door, and found Mary murdered. The following police photographer's report described the body:

> . . . on the bed in propped position, buttocks on pillow, back against headboard, head on right shoulder, knees up, eyes closed, vitreous liquid, probably semen, dripping from mouth to right breast. Breasts and lower

extremities exposed, broomstick handle inserted in the vagina, steak knife on bed, seminal stains on blanket. Knotted about her neck was a charcoal colored stocking, over that a pink silk scarf tied with a huge bow under the chin, and over that, tied loosely, almost rakishly so that one could admit one's hand between it and her neck, a bright, pink and white flowered scarf. A gaily colored New Year's card reading "Happy New Year" had been placed against the toes of her left foot. (Frank, 1971)

Both sadism and masochism also can represent an acting-out of subconscious or unconscious feelings of guilt derived from the repeated fantasy. Associated with these guilt feelings is a need for punishment, which sadists direct against others and masochists take upon themselves. A variation of sadistic behavior is its association with psychopathic behavior (Chapter 9). This may seem paradoxical since psychopaths operate with a lack of guilt while sadists are usually motivated by excessive guilt. However, it is important to remember that the psychopath's absence of guilt may be in reality a severe repression of guilt dating back to the developmental years. Sadistic behavior, which directs aggressive feelings toward others, also helps keep guilty feelings repressed.

Exhibitionism

Exhibitionism is a "nuisance" sex crime that accounts for about one-third of all reported sex crimes in the United States, Canada, and Europe (Reese, 1989). Exhibitionists triumph over an early childhood trauma by the impulsive exposure of their genitals. To the police, this usually harmless form of sexual aberration often presents problems because of community reactions rather than the reality of any harmful threat. Exhibitionism therefore provides a good example of the confused situation that can arise from legal restrictions that vary in different locales — because of different standards of community mores — rather than from the behavior itself.

In our own society, although public exhibitionism of the genitals is usually prohibited by law, many acceptable forms and forums for exhibitionism have been sanctioned, including beauty contests, movies, and magazines, including, of course, soft- and hard-core pornographic material. Exhibitionists are not oversexed; the opposite is true. Most exhibitionists lack overt aggressiveness and self-confidence and feel markedly inferior to others. Furthermore, exhibitionists often show an indifferent attitude toward the opposite sex. Whatever power exhibitionists possess is achieved through their unusual behavior.

This is an important consideration in understanding why exhibitionists always act as if they wish to be caught. As R. J. Stoller (1975) points out, most exhibitionistic behavior of men occurs following a humiliation, sometimes at work, or from a woman – often the exhibitionist's wife. The exhibitionist then takes to the street, searching out a woman to whom he can exhibit himself. Overwhelmed by tension, the exhibitionist carries out his compulsive behavior, unaware of why he needs to, but clearly preoccupied with the desire to experience the risk rather than a concern about being caught. In fact, most police officers note that exhibitionists are often easily caught because they are reluctant to get away. To a normal person, this behavior is often incomprehensible. Further, officers are often confused by exhibitionists' behavior after they are caught, as they appear peaceful and pleasant.

Stoller's theory of perversion (1975) helps us to understand the male exhibitionist's unusual behavior. At the conclusion of the exhibitionistic behavior, the risk has been run and surmounted; the trauma has been converted to triumph. The police are not the risk, nor is being caught the risk the exhibitionist is attempting to overcome. Rather, the police became the agents of the triumph. The real risk for the exhibitionist arises from the humiliation that occurred earlier in the day, usually a repeat of some earlier childhood humiliation that left him feeling impotent and

less masculine – not that he will be caught. Displaying himself is a demonstration that he has not been humiliated or defeated by women. The woman who is the victim of this behavior and who becomes shocked, angry, frightened, and calls the police prove to the exhibitionist that he has reversed the childhood situation. She is now complying with a necessary part of his fantasy in that she becomes the attacked one and he is the attacker. When he is arrested, he is content because the arrest proves, however briefly, that he is potent – potent enough to create a disturbance that involves not only a victim, but also the official agency of society: the police. Thus, exhibitionism clearly reverses the feeling of humiliation associated with the original childhood trauma and turns this trauma into revenge and triumph.

Voyeurism

Voyeurs achieve sexual gratification by watching a nude woman or man in some form of the sexual act. "Peeping Toms," as they are popularly known, are usually but not always harmless, and more of a nuisance than a serious threat to the community. They are less frequently apprehended than others because the triumph over trauma contained in the fantasy is associated with the secretiveness of the behavior. Voyeurism may be associated with a wide variety of deviant sexual behavior. While some may only look, others may employ voyeurism as a prelude to further sexual activity that may be aggressive and violent. Simple voyeurs engage in immature sexual behavior, more appropriate to a very early stage of development. Normally, this curiosity about anatomical differences and the manner in which sexual organs function reaches a peak between ages three and five. During this time there is considerable peeping and displaying behavior by children. Parents often make many demands in their attempts to divert this curiosity into more acceptable forms of behavior, while at the same time allowing their children to satisfy their desire to know more about sex. A too-prudish attitude may instill in children a morbid curiosity that may later result in an irresistible desire to peep. Likewise, very strict prohibitions and overly severe punishment may make children fearful of normal sexual activity.

Data collected by FBI agents from their interviews with convicted serial rapists indicate that 68 percent of the respondents reported they engaged in window peeping in childhood or adolescence (Hazelwood & Warren, 1989). Based on an examination of the nuisance offender, Reese (1987) contends that:

> Many crimes which appear to be sexually related have their origins in obsessive-compulsive behavior. Many times felonious sex crimes have been preceded by a history of nuisance crimes . . . exhibitionism, voyeurism, and obscene phone calls, for example . . . which demonstrate a ritualistic pattern characteristic of obsessive-compulsive behavior. A study of these crimes reveals sexual inadequacy, anxiety and repeated stereotypic patterns of behavior or rituals on the part of the perpetrators. It is these ritualistic patterns . . . which provide the "key" to solving many crimes. (p. 6)

Those who commit "nuisance" sex crimes do not always (even perhaps usually) progress to the more serious crimes of rape and assault. However, the reverse side of the coin is that most offenders who do commit rape and assault have a history of nuisance crimes in their juvenile records and/or on their adult rap sheet.

Rape

Although rape is a universal crime, rape rates vary tremendously from one culture to another. The rape rate in the United States is thirteen times as high as that in England and Wales. In a review of anthropological research on rape, West (1987) reports:

> Cross-cultural anthropological comparisons have revealed consistent contrasts between societies in which many rapes are reported

and those where rapes are relatively rare. . . . Noteworthy features in rape-prone societies include an ideology of masculine aggressiveness, a high incidence of violence in general, restrictive attitudes towards premarital sexuality and a subservient role for women economically and in decision-making. Less rape-prone societies are generally less violent and enjoy great equality between the sexes.

For average police officers, the profile of rapists is critical. The important point is that sexual desire and/or sexual activity is not the primary motive of rapists – anger, violence, and control are. Some police officers assume that all rapists are sadists, but this oversimplifies a complex subject and merits separate attention. A. Nicholas Groth, a noted psychologist (1979), has distinguished three types of rape: anger rape, power rape, and sadistic rape. In each, it is important to assess the nature of the aggression, type of assault, offender's mood, pattern of offenses, use of language, underlying dynamics, nature of the assault, and impact on the victim. These differ in each of the three types.

In *anger rape*, the aggression is more physical than necessary and the victim is often battered. The assault is usually impulsive and spontaneous, and the offender is generally angry and depressed. Offenses are more often episodic and are accompanied by the use of abusive language. The underlying dynamics concern retribution for perceived wrongs or injustices, or a put-down experienced by the offender from a specific victim. The assault is of short duration and the victim usually suffers physical trauma to all areas of the body.

In *power rape*, the rapist generally uses only the amount of force or threat necessary to gain control of the victim and overcome the resistance. In these situations, the assault is premeditated and preceded by persistent rape fantasies. The offender's mood state is one of anxiety, in contrast to anger and depression. The offenses tend to be repetitive and may show an increase in aggression over time. The language of the rapist is more often instructional and inquisitive, frequently giving orders, asking personal questions, and inquiring of the victim's responses. In this instance, the underlying dynamics involve compensation for deep-seated insecurities and feelings of inadequacy. The assault may be carried out over an extended time, with the victim held captive throughout. The victim may be otherwise physically unharmed. Bodily injury is generally inadvertent rather than intentional.

In contrast to these two patterns of rape, *sadistic rape* involves an erotic use of physical force. The assault is calculated and pre-planned, and the offender's mood is usually one of intense excitement. The pattern of the offenses is often ritualistic, involving bondage, torture, and bizarre acts. The offender's use of language is commanding and degrading. The actions are characteristic of perversion, as they feature symbolic destruction and elimination. The assault may be extended, and the victim may often be kidnapped and occasionally killed. The victim suffers extreme physical trauma to the sexual areas of the body, and in some cases may be mutilated or murdered.

Many myths surround rapists. To describe these persons as oversexed is not only inaccurate but oversimplified. Rape is not an expression of sexual desire as much as it is an expression of other nonsexual needs. Rape is never simply the result of sexual arousal with no other opportunity for gratification. In fact, a significant percentage of rape offenders are married and sexually active at the time of their assaults. Rape is always a symptom of some type of psychological dysfunction, either temporary and transient or chronic and repetitive. It is usually a desperate act that results from an emotionally weak and insecure person's inability to handle the stresses and demands of life. Although rape may cut across all diagnostic categories of psychiatric disorders, most offenders are neither insane nor simply healthy and aggressive. The most prominent defect in rapists is the absence of close, emotionally intimate relationships with other persons – male or female. Rapists have little inner capacity for warmth, compassion,

or empathy. Although the judgment of rapists may be poor under stress, there is generally no problem with intellectual functioning. Rapists often commit this irrational act as a desperate attempt to deal with stresses that they are unable to otherwise contain and that they believe will destroy them.

Date Rape

Recently the attention of law enforcement personnel and rape counselors has been directed to the phenomenon of date rape. This offense occurs within the context of dating and typically involves the use of force by males in attempting sexual intercourse with their dates. The couple may have known each other and been dating for some time, or it may be a first date. In any event, the male refuses to accept a "no" answer from his date and proceeds to have intercourse (or some other sexual act) without her consent. Many factors are probably involved (that is, the belief that when a woman says no she really means yes, that she really wants sex just as much as he does, the conquering macho male image, and so on). The perpetrator often feels no sense of guilt and expresses no remorse for the attack. However, the fact that he may not see his actions as rape does not lessen the victim's trauma. Victims are likely to suffer even more trauma, as their trust was betrayed and they are now experiencing a great deal of personal guilt and self-image loss because of what they may perceive as poor judgment in getting involved with this man in the first place. Date rapes are often unreported and inadequately investigated for a number of reasons.

Serial Rape

A leading rape researcher, nurse Ann W. Burgess, and her associates (1986) define serial sexual killings as "motiveless killings, usually serial in nature, carried out by a single individual over a period of time" (p. 275). This definition would seem appropriate to describe the nonhomicidal serial rapist as well.

Serial rape is a crime that, along with sexual homicide or lust murder, has been the object of intensive study by the FBI's National Center for the Analysis of Violent Crime. By interviewing imprisoned serial rapists, a profile has emerged. They are most frequently white and begin to rape in their early twenties. They are married or in a consensual sexual relationship. Many serial rapists have been institutionalized in a correctional center or mental facility at least once prior to arrest for the most current offense. The vast majority of those interviewed had previously committed a rape, sexual nuisance crime, or some combination of the two.

The psychological profile of these men included a high incidence of childhood sexual abuse. A high percentage had a history of childhood behavior problems, including fighting, truancy, stealing, and so on. Many were identified at an early age as being either delinquent or emotionally disturbed. Hazellwood and Warren (1989) state:

> Many characteristics of the rapist appear relatively "normal." Rather than being an isolated, ineffectual individual, the serial rapist more often than not comes from an average or advantaged home, and as an adult, is a wellgroomed, intelligent, employed individual who is living with others in a family context. The greatest pathology is reflected in the serial rapist's developmental history. Few of the men described close relationships with either their mother or their father, a significant number of them had been institutionalized at some point in their adolescence, and an exceedingly high proportion reported sexual abuse as children or adolescents. (p. 25)

Serial rapists' criteria for selecting their victims seem to focus on availability rather than whether a victim reminds an offender of a significant other in his life, or because of some specific or symbolic consideration. Hazelwood and Warren (1988) also present the findings of the FBI's serial rapist research regarding the rapist's behavior during and after commission of his crimes. This research has

indicated that most serial rapist attacks were intentional and premeditated. Less than one-quarter was impulsive or opportunistic. "It is probable that the premeditation involved in these crimes is particularly characteristic of the serial rapist, is reflective of their preferential interest in this type of crime, and is largely accountable for their ability to avoid detection" (p. 25).

In an earlier article, Hazelwood and Burgess (1987) describe three styles of approach frequently used by serial rapists: the con, the blitz, and the surprise. The con involves offering assistance and requesting directions, and so on, thus enticing the victim to come near enough for the rapist to gain control. Examples include pretending to be a police officer, providing transportation to hitchhikers, or picking up women in singles' bars. The blitz employs direct physical assault to subdue the victim. This approach usually produces more physical injury and may be sexually arousing to the rapist. The surprise approach involves targeting the victim, preselecting her through unobserved contact, and finding out when she will be alone. This is the most frequently used approach, especially by men who lack confidence in their ability to subdue the victim physically or through subterfuge.

Most serial rapists use verbal threats backed by a "threatening physical presence" to control their victims. Most use minimal or no force, and most rapists in this study did not increase the amount of force used as they committed additional rapes. However, ten of the forty-one rapists did significantly increase the amount of force used over time (termed "increasers"). Hazelwood and Warren (1988) report that "they used progressively greater force over successive rapes, raped on average twice as many women in half the amount of time, and by the time of the last assault, were inflicting moderate to fatal injuries" (p. 6). Victims resisted the rapists in some manner (physically, verbally, or passively) in over half the cases. Researchers found no relationship between victim resistance and the amount of victim injury sustained. However, they did find that resistance seemed to increase the degree of the rapist's pleasure and tended to prolong the duration of the rape itself. Slightly over one-third of serial offenders experienced sexual dysfunction during the rape. Hazelwood and Burgess (1987) note that the occurrence of offender sexual dysfunction and an understanding thereof may provide valuable information to investigators in associating different offenses with a single offender, since the nature of the dysfunction and the means used to overcome it are likely to remain constant over a number of rapes. For example, one serial rapist always told his victim that he had trouble "getting it up" and that she would have to "lick my dick" to help him achieve erection.

The preferred sexual acts were fellatio and vaginal rape, although researchers found a tendency for the rapist's interest in oral sex to increase as his interest in vaginal sex decreased. Rapists generally reported low levels of pleasure from the sexual acts, a finding that lends support to the notion that rape is not truly a "sex crime" wherein the sexual activity is the main motivation or goal. Serial rapists do not undertake any specific precautions to avoid identification. However, the fact that most tend to rape strangers in their own homes probably helps them to avoid detection. The most frequent behavioral changes reported after committing the rape were (1) feeling remorse and guilt (44%–51%); (2) following the case in the media (28%); (3) an increase in alcohol and drug consumption (20%–27%); and (4) an "overall" change in behavior (20%–24%). Alcohol was involved in only one-third of the cases, and slightly less than one-third reported using some other drug prior to the rape. Twelve to fifteen percent of the rapists reported revisiting the crime scene, while another eight to thirteen percent communicated with their victim. Reasons given for doing so were to determine the progress of the police investigation, to engage in further sexual behavior, or to relive the offense.

Sexual Homicide

Sexual homicide results from one person killing another in the context of power, control, sexuality, and aggressive brutality. The psychiatric diagnosis of sexual sadism, sometimes applied to the victimizer, states that the essential feature of this deviant behavior (i.e., paraphilia) is the infliction of physical or psychological suffering on another person in order to achieve sexual excitement." (Burgess et al. 1986, p. 276)

In an eight-year period (1976–1984), the FBI Uniform Crime Report has shown a 160 percent increase in such crimes. Although most serial rapists do not indulge in sexual homicide, it is interesting to note that nearly 25 percent of 41 serial rapists studied by the FBI in the research previously discussed (the "increasers") progressed to inflicting serious injury and/or death upon their victims – thus becoming cases of sexual homicide. In a study exploring the role of fantasy and thinking patterns in the behavior of sexual killers, Ann W. Burgess and associates (1986) studied 36 sexual murderers. In analyzing the interview data, the killers themselves admitted to "long-standing, aggressive thoughts and fantasies directed toward sexualized death. The findings suggest that these thought patterns were established early and existed in a context of social isolation" (p. 277). It was further determined that the killers were consciously aware of the central role that fantasy played in their lives and of their preference for fantasy over reality. "Even those men unaware of this reported that their thoughts become retaliatory or vengeful when they perceived themselves as being slighted, rejected, frustrated, or betrayed" (p. 258). The researchers concluded that such thinking becomes an important component in maintaining sexually aggressive behavior.

The Lust Murderer

Robert R. Hazelwood and John E. Douglas (1980) contend that lust murderers are "unique and distinguished from the sadistic homicide by the involvement of a mutilating attack on the breasts, rectum, or genitals. Further, while there are always exceptions, two types of individuals commit the lust murder: the organized nonsocial and the disorganized asocial personalities" (p. 18). The organized nonsocial personality is equivalent to the DSM-IV-TR (2000) category "anti-social personality disorder" (psychopath); the disorganized asocial is similar to DSM-IV-TR's paranoid schizophrenia. Hazelwood and Douglas (1980) believe that a psychological study of the crime scene and victim will tell if investigators may be dealing with a lust murder, and that psychological clues present at the crime scene will reveal the personality of the perpetrator. The following list, based on the work of these FBI agents, may help the investigator distinguish between these two alternatives:

Organized Nonsocial (Psychopath)

1. Personality traits of the psychopath.
2. Generally lives some distance from crime scene; cruises seeking victim.
3. Excited by cruelty.
4. Commits crime in a secluded/isolated location and may transport the body to area where it is likely to be found.
5. Wants excitement regarding discovery of body, publicity, and so on.
6. Murder committed in brutally sadistic manner (such as overkill, mutilation, and so on).
7. Victim usually heterosexual and intraracial.
8. Evidence of mutilation or torture *prior* to death.
9. Strangulation, beating, knifing.
10. Carries weapon with him; takes it with him to use again.
11. Victim bitten in genital area, breasts.
12. Dissection of body to be rid of evidence and/or hinder identification.
13. Cannibalism rare.
14. Taunting message for police left in blood.
15. Penis penetration.
16. Necrophilia possible but rare, and rarely (if ever) repeated.
17. Foreign objects inserted into anus and vagina in a derogatory, defiant, taunting manner (example: Boston Strangler and Mary Sullivan case).
18. Semen found *in* victim (mouth, anus, vagina).
19. Seldom takes fetish reminder (souvenir) of victim.
20. Less physical evidence (cunning and methodical).
21. Returns to scene of crime to see if body discovered and to check on progress of investigation.
22. Taunts police, offers help, hangs out in police bars, and so on, to find out how investigation is going. Like a "game" between killer and police (as with Ted Bundy).
23. Rap sheet extensive; many different types of crimes.
24. Feels rejection and hatred for society. Hostile feelings expressed openly, and murder is final expression of this hostility.
25. Victim generally not known to killer; chosen at random when feeling strikes him. If known, usually very casually (neighbor, bar acquaintance, and so on).

Disorganized Asocial (Paranoid Schizophrenic)

1. Personality traits of the schizoid/paranoid schizophrenic.
2. Crime likely to be committed close to his residence or neighborhood.
3. Cruelty part of ritual.
4. Leaves body at scene of death; no real attempt to conceal body.
5. Not interested in this at all.
6. Murder may be brutal but some ritualistic element present.
7. Victim chosen because fits into delusional thinking.

8. This can be true also of asocial, but more likely nonsocial.
9. Death by sharp instrument, suffocation, poison.
10. Weapon of opportunity; may leave at the scene. Weapon may be symbolic to killer and he may place it in a particular position near victim.
11. Not likely.
12. No attempt to hide identification; killer may "curiously" explore body (to see what's there and so on) or leave evidence of some fetishism or ritualism in dissection of body.
13. Cannibalism not uncommon.
14. Blood smeared on victim, surroundings, self, showing frenzy of act.
15. Penis penetration possible, but not probable.
16. *Ritualistic* necrophilia possible and may be repeated with successive victims.
17. Foreign objects inserted in a probing, curiosity-motivated manner.
18. Semen found on/near victim.
19. Takes souvenir of victim to relive fantasy and crime.
20. More frenzy; more evidence.
21. Returns to scene for further mutilation or to relive incident.
22. None of this in asocial.
23. Usually no rap sheet of any significance.
24. Feels rejection and hatred but withdraws into fantasy and loneliness.
25. Victim has symbolic significance and fits into delusional thinking. May be known to killer.

Child Molestation or Pedophilia

Reporting of child sexual abuse continues to increase at an alarming rate. Considering that 85 percent of these children are abused by someone known to them, and given that professionals in legal, medical, and social service fields feel that sexual abuse is probably the most unreported and under-diagnosed type of child abuse, one can only assume that this problem will reach an unprecedented and even epidemic proportion in coming years. (Etherington & Stephens, 1984, p. 44)

In the 1980s, the crime of statutory rape, which had been defined as rape in spite of consent because the female involved was underage, has been defined primarily as child molestation or, under special circumstances, incest. Child molestation, or *pedophilia*, is illegal and prosecuted because immaturity and the dependency of children on adults for material and emotional security make free consent impossible. "The children involved are, by definition, victims. They are used to satisfy the adults' needs, not their own. They lack the capacity to decide matters of long-range consequence; there is no such thing as a consenting child" (Caplan, 1982, p. 47). A pedophile whose sexual object is a child of the opposite sex is a heterosexual pedophile; one who is attracted to a child of the same sex is a homosexual pedophile. The overwhelming majority of pedophiles may also be assessed in relation to their ability to interact with women and children. One type of pedophile is unable to interact socially with women because of anxiety but can be sexually aroused by them. These people experience less sexual anxiety with children. Another type of pedophile may interact socially with adult women but is unable to become sexually aroused by them. Only children sexually arouse this type. Finally, the last category can neither interact socially with women nor be sexually aroused by them. Only children sexually arouse them.

A. Nicholas Groth (1979) has described two types of pedophilia pathology – the *fixated* pedophile and the *regressed* pedophile. The primary sexual orientation of the fixated pedophile is to children. This interest usually begins in adolescence without an identifiable precipitating stress or feeling of distress. The behavior is more persistent and compulsive, and the offenses are usually preplanned. In this group, male victims tend to be the primary targets (homosexual). Offenders generally have little contact with women of their age and are usually single. Alcohol and drug abuse are usually not associated with the offense. In contrast, the primary sexual orientation of regressed pedophiles is to women their own age. Their pedophilic interests emerge in adulthood and are generally identified with a precipitating stress. The pedophilic involvements tend to be episodic, and the initial offense may be impulsive rather than premeditated. In contrast to fixated pedophiles, regressed pedophiles usually replace a conflictual adult relationship by involvement with a child; the child is therefore an adult substitute. Female victims are most often the target of this pedophilic behavior. Regressed pedophiles are usually able to have sexual contact with adult women. In many instances, their offense may be alcohol related and is clearly an attempt, although maladaptive, to cope with specific stresses in life.

It is important to note that violent behavior toward children may occur in either category and depends on the nature of the fantasy associated with pedophilic behavior. Therefore, police officers should always be alert to the underlying importance of fantasy and should endeavor, sometimes with professional assistance, to determine what the fantasy is as a way of determining whether the pedophile is likely to commit actual physical violence. This distinction between fixated and regressed pedophites is probably the most crucial factor in constructing a profile of the offender. Donald J. West (1987) reports "the tendency to turn to children when frustrated in contacts with adults seems to be a reaction commoner among heterosexuals than homosexuals. . . . This contradicts the common assumption that homosexuals pose a greater threat to children than heterosexuals" (p. 49).

Unlike rapists, child molesters are frequently reported to be socially shy, timid, unassertive, and lacking in self-esteem, with feelings of inadequacy, insecurity and alienation (West, 1987). In general, seduction is the tactic of the child molester – not force. However, this is not always the case. "A small minority of child molesters resemble aggressive

rapists both in personality and in their bullying and brutality to child victims" (West, 1987, p. 50).

Incest

Incest is a specific form of pedophilia or child molesting that involves an adult relative and a child. Specifically, it is the practice of sexual intercourse between closely related persons whose marriage is prohibited by law. Prohibition against incestuous relations is practically universal, but laws against it and the prescribed punishments vary considerably. The young son or daughter who is forced or enticed into incest by either mother or father will be thrown into a severe conflict. Resulting guilt and anxiety may lead to profound regression and mental illness. Sociologically, incest is viewed as a threat to the basic fabric of society and its principal unit, the family. However, the prohibition against incest does not prevent the development of strong erotic interests between family members. Consequently, many family activities are designed to sublimate these erotic interests into normal and acceptable behaviors. Failure in this process may often be an underlying factor in family disputes and should be taken into account by police officers when intervention becomes necessary. In *Techniques for Dealing with Child Sexual Abuse*, A. Baxter (1986) presents a list of the common myths and realities about sexual assault involving children:

1. *Myth*: Child abusers are dangerous strangers.
   Reality: The offender is usually a person the child knows, often a relative or friend of the family. Eighty percent of offenders are known to the child. In 50 percent of reported cases, it is the father figure.
2. *Myth*: Sexual abuse or incest is a single isolated incident.
   Reality: Sexual assault and incest are frequently repeated and may be ongoing.
3. *Myth*: Sexual assault and incest happen only to people in the lower classes.

Reality: The problem is not limited to economically disadvantaged families nor to certain ethnic groups.

4. *Myth*: Child victims will immediately disclose an incident of abuse.
   Reality: In about half the cases reported to the American Humane Association, the child did not reveal the incident until more than a week after the event.

5. *Myth*: Children invent stories of sexual abuse and are unreliable sources of information.
   Reality: Young children have few if any sexual experiences and are reliable sources of information.

6. *Myth*: Parents react with rage at disclosure.
   Reality: Parents often react with disbelief and may reprimand a child for talking about an alleged incident.

7. *Myth*: Adolescent girls are most often the victims of incest.
   Reality: The average age of the onset of sexual abuse is three years. Most sexual assault cases involve children under six years old.

8. *Myth*: Sexual abuse and incest are not very common.
   Reality: Child sexual abuse is not rare; studies reveal that one in five girls and

one in eleven boys are sexually assaulted before age eighteen. A child is sexually abused every two minutes in the United States. The problem is much greater than current statistics would indicate because only five to six percent of actual cases are reported.

9. *Myth*: A bad mother is responsible for incest between her husband and daughter.
   Reality: The offender and victim use all possible means to keep the abuse a secret. The offender uses his position of authority, the child's trust, and bribes and/or threats to maintain the child's cooperation and silence.

It is important to note that although violent behavior is not the rule in child molestation cases, violence toward children may occur in either general pedophilia or incest. This depends on the nature of the perpetrator's fantasy associated with the pedophilic behavior. Therefore, as a way of determining whether pedophiles are likely to commit actual physical violence, police officers should always be alert to the underlying importance of fantasy and should endeavor, sometimes with professional assistance, to determine what the fantasy is.

HELPFUL HINTS TO LAW ENFORCEMENT OFFICERS

From this discussion, it is apparent that law enforcement officers who handle sex crimes must know enough about sexual aberrations to be able to make appropriate judgments about each sexual criminal as an individual. This is true not only for specialists in sex crimes, who are usually trained and experienced, but also for beat patrol officers, especially those in small departments that do not have specialized personnel readily available. Common misconceptions about sexual criminals include the beliefs that there is a high correlation between brain damage and sexual deviance and that sexual offenders usually suffer from severe mental illness. Furthermore, while hard drugs are rarely a factor in sexual crimes, there ap-

pears to be a strong connection between the use of alcohol and deviant sexual behavior, since excess alcohol leads to the lowering of inhibitions. Although overt aggression is associated with sexual aberration relatively infrequently, hostile fantasies are common. For this reason, police officers should *always* be alert to the potential for dangerous behavior. In questioning those with sexual aberrations, officers should go beyond the actual behavior and try to find out more about the person's fantasies to determine if perversions and erotic hatred are present. By doing so, officers can better determine the person's potential dangerousness.

Police officers should examine their own attitudes toward sexual aberrations and recognize that these offenses result from motives and impulses that are often not understood or controllable, rather than from "moral perversity." This does not lessen the seriousness of crimes associated with sexual aberrations, but should increase officers' ability to act professionally and responsibly. This professionalism also should carry over into contacts with the victims. If they are not treated respectfully and courteously, they may be unwilling to divulge information that could be helpful in identifying and apprehending the offender.

SUMMARY

This chapter has outlined several varieties of aberrant sexual behavior, their characteristics, and their importance to police officers. The criminality of aberrant sexual behavior can vary considerably. Not all forms are criminal, nor are all sexual aberrant criminals. Only by understanding the characteristics of the individual sexual aberrant will officers be able to maintain a professional attitude. This attitude should include recognition that while sexual criminals are not necessarily monsters, they are also not simply unfortunate persons. They should neither be treated inhumanely nor be allowed to involve others in their aberration to the detriment of others' welfare and freedom of choice.

BIBLIOGRAPHY

Asel, G. G., et al. Identifying dangerous child molesters. In *Violent behavior: Social learning approaches to prediction, management, and treatment*, ed. R. B. Stuart. New York: Brunner/Mazel.

American Psychiatric Association. (2000). *Diagnostic and statistical manual of mental disorders*, 4th ed. revised. Washington, D.C.

Axthelm, P., and Ryan, M. 6 February, 1989. A condemned man's last bequest (Ted Bundy). *People 44*(8).

Baxter, A. (1986). *Techniques for dealing with child sexual abuse*. Springfield, IL: Charles C Thomas.

Burgess, A. W. (1985). Dangerous sexual offenders: Commentary. *Medical Aspects of Sexuality, 19*(2), 119–123.

Burgess, A. W., et al. (1978). *Sexual assault of children and adolescents*. Lexington, MA: Lexington Books.

Burgess, A. W., et al. (1984). Children and adolescents exploited through sex rings and pornography. *American Journal of Psychiatry, 41*(5), 656–662.

BURGESS, A. W., et al. (1986). Sexual homicide: A motivational model. *Journal of Interpersonal Violence, 1*(3), 273–287.

Burgess, A. W., et al. (1989). Serial rapists and their victims: Reenactment and repetition. In *Human sexual aggression: Current perspectives*, ed. R. A. Prentky & V. L. Quinsey , vol. 528, pp. 277–295. New York: Annals of the New York Academy of Sciences.

Butler, S. (1985). *Conspiracy of silence: The trauma of incest*. San Francisco, CA: Volcano Press.

Caplan, G. M. January, 1982. Sexual exploitation of children: The conspiracy of silence. *Police Magazine*, 46–51.

De M. Young (1982). *The sexual victimization of children*. Jefferson, NC: McFarland and Company.

Dietz, P. E., Hazelwood, R. R., & Warren, J. In press. *The psychopathic sexual sadist*.

Etherington, C. A., & Stephens, K. S. February, 1984. The police officer and the sexually abused child: Developing an approach to a critical problem. *Police Chief*, 44–47.

Everstine, D. S., & Everstine, L. (1989). *Sexual trauma in children and adolescents*. New York: Brunner/Mazel.

Faller, K. C. (1988). *Child sexual abuse (An interdisciplinary manual for diagnosis, case management and treatment)*. New York: Columbia University Press.

Federal Bureau of Investigation. August, 1985. The men who murdered: Violent crime (Special Issue). *FBI Law Enforcement Bulletin*.

_____. August, 1985. The split reality of murder. Violent crime (Special Issue). *FBI Law Enforcement Bulletin*.

Finkelhor, D. (1986). *A sourcebook on child sexual abuse.* Beverly Hills, CA: Sage Publications.

———. (1987). The sexual abuse of children: Current research reviewed. *Psychiatric Annals, 17*(4), 233–241.

Frank, G. (1971). *The Boston strangler.* New York: New American Libraries.

Goleman, D. 3 September, 1989. Double standard cited as contributing factor in rapes. *Arizona Daily Star,* 1E.

Groth, A. N. (1979). *Men who rape: The psychology of the offender.* New York: Plenum Press.

Groth, A. N., & Loredo, C. M. (1981). Juvenile sex offenders: Guidelines for assessment. *International Journal of Offender Therapy and Comparative Criminology, 25,* 31–39.

Hazelwood, R. R. (1983). The behavioral-oriented interview of rape vVictims: The key to profiling. *FBI Law Enforcement Bulletin, 52*(9), 8–15.

———. (1987). Analyzing the rape and profiling the offender. In *Practical aspects of rape investigation,* ed. R. R. Hazelwood & A. W. Burgess. New York: Elsevier.

Hazelwood, R. R., & Burgess, A. W. 9 April, 1986. An introduction to serial rapist research by the FBI. Presented in testimony before the Subcommittee of the Committee on Government Operations.

———. (1987). An introduction to the serial rapist: Research by the FBI. *FBI Law Enforcement Bulletin, 58*(9), 16–24.

Hazelwood, R. R., Dietz, P. E., & Burgess, A. W. (1981). The investigation of autoerotic fatalities. *Journal of Police Science and Administration, 9*(4), 404–411.

———. (1982). Sexual fatalities: Behavioral reconstruction in equivocal cases. *Journal of Forensic Science, 27*(4), 763–773.

Hazelwood, R. R., & Douglas, J. E. April, 1980. The lust murderer. *FBI Law Enforcement Bulletin,* 18–22.

Hazelwood, R. R., & Horpold, J. A. June, 1986. Rape: The dangers of providing confrontational advice. *FBI Law Enforcement Bulletin,* 1-S.

Hazelwood, R. R., Reboussin, R., & Warren, J. I. In press. Serial rape: Correlates of increased aggression and the relationship of offender pleasure to victim resistance. *Journal of Interpersonal Violence.*

Hazelwood, R. R., & Warren, J. February, 1989. The serial rapist: His characteristics and victims (conclusion). *FBI Law Enforcement Bulletin,* 11–25.

———. (1988) The crime behavior of the serial rapist. *FBI Law Enforcement Bulletin,* 1–10.

Hellman, D. S., & Blackman, N. (1966). Enuresis, fire-setting and cruelty to animals: A triad predictive of adult crime. *American Journal of Psychiatry, 122,* 1431–1435.

Herman, J. (1982). *Father-daughter incest.* Cambridge, MA: Harvard University Press.

Herrmann, K. J., & Jupp, M. J. (1985). Commercial child pornography and pedophile organizations: An international report. *Response to the Victimization of Women and Children, 8*(2), 7–10.

Holmes, R. M. (1983). *The sex offender and the criminal justice system.* Springfield, IL: Charles C Thomas.

Holmes, R. M., & Deburger, J. E. (1985). Profiles in terror: The serial murderer. *Federal Probation, 49*(3), 29–34.

Jansen, M. R. February, 1984. Incest: Exploitative child abuse. *Police Chief,* 46–50.

Kempe, R. S., & Kempe, C. H. (1984). *The common secret: Sexual abuse of children and adolescents.* New York: W. H. Freeman and Co.

Liebert, J. A. (1985). Contributions of psychiatric consultation in the investigation of serial murder. *International Journal of Offender Therapy and Comparative Criminology, 29*(3), 187–200.

Lowery, S. A., & Wetli, C. V. (1982). Sexual asphyxia: A neglected area of study. *Deviant Behavior, 4*(1), 19–39.

Michaud, S. G. 26 October, 1986. The F.B.I.'s new psyche squad. National center for the analysis of violent crime. *New York Times Magazine,* 40.

Morneu, R. H., Jr. (1983). *Sex crimes investigation: A major case approach.* Springfield, IL: Charles C Thomas.

O'Brien, D. (1985). *Two of a kind: The Hillside Strangler.* New York: Signet.

O'Brien, S. J. (1986). *Why they did it: Stories of eight convicted child molesters.* Springfield, IL: Charles C Thomas.

Pierce, R. L., & Pierce, L. H. (1985). Analysis of sexual abuse hotline reports. *Child Abuse and Neglect, 9*(1), 37–45.

Prentky, R. A., & Quinsey, V. L., eds. (1989). *Human sexual aggression: Current perspectives.* New York: Annals of the New York Academy of Sciences.

Reese, J. T. (1987). Obsessive compulsive behavior: The nuisance offender. In *Behavioral science in law enforcement* by J. T. Reese, pp. 6–12. Quantico, VA: U.S. Department of Justice, FBI.

Ressler, R., Burgess, A., & Douglas, J. (1988). *Sexual homicide – patterns and motives.* Lexington, MA: Lexington Books.

Ressler, R. K., et al. (1986). Murderers who rape and mutilate. *Journal of Interpersonal Violence, 1*(3), 273–287.

Seng, M. J. (1986). Sexual behavior between adults and children: Some issues of definition. *Journal of Offender Counseling Services and Rehabilitation, 11*(1), 47–61.

Sheehan, W., & Garfinkel, B. D. (1988). Adolescent autoerotic deaths. *Journal of the American Academy of Child and Adolescent Psychiatry, 27*(3), 367–370.

Stoller, R. J. (1975). *Perversion: The erotic form of hatred.* New York: Pantheon Books.

Stone, L. E., Tyler, R. P., & Mead, J. J. (1984). Law enforcement officers as investigators and therapists in child sexual abuse: A training model. *Child Abuse and Neglect, 8*(1), 75–82.

Tyler, R. P., & Stone, L. E. (1985). Child pornography: Perpetuating the sexual victimization of children. *Child Abuse and Neglect, 9*(3), 313–318.

Warren, J. I., Reboussin, R., & Hazelwood, R. R. In press. Prediction of rapist type and violence from verbal, physical, and sexual scales.

West, D. J. (1987). *Sexual crimes and confrontations.* Aldershot, England: Gower Publishing Co.

Wilson, G. D., ed. (1987). *Variant sexuality: Research and theory.* London: Croom Helm.

Chapter 11

DELINQUENT BEHAVIOR

Up to this point our discussion of abnormal behavior has focused on adults. However, the abnormal behavior of juvenile offenders also poses significant problems for law enforcement officers.

GENERAL CONSIDERATIONS

Most police officers come into contact with juveniles only when they have indulged or are indulging in antisocial behavior. Because of this limited range of contacts, officers may perceive most children as either delinquent or potentially delinquent. Although common sense tells us this is not true, it is sometimes easy for police officers to develop negative attitudes toward those juveniles they must encounter. The line between *delinquent behavior* and *delinquent criminal behavior* is not always clear. For example, many offenses for which juveniles may be arrested, and therefore labeled criminals, are not those for which adults could be detained. Running away from home, violation of curfew, and possession of alcohol are not adult offenses. This is not to suggest that officers should ignore or condone these actions; rather, referral to another community agency might be more helpful to children than referral to juvenile court.

The fact that officers can be flexible in their decisions when dealing with juveniles makes it even more important for them to understand delinquent behavior. The appropriate use of this flexibility may not only prevent a child from ending up with the stigma associated with a juvenile criminal record, but also may help prevent delinquent behavior from progressing to the point where it becomes a fixed life-style, continuing into adulthood and leading to an adult criminal record. Before presenting some helpful hints to law enforcement officers, it is important to discuss some specific underlying factors involved in the onset of delinquent behavior.

Underlying Factors

Broken homes, neglect, poverty, low intelligence, brain damage, mental illness, and other factors have been proposed at one time or another as the "causes" of delinquency. However, none, in isolation, has stood the test of time or scientific scrutiny. Rather, juvenile delinquency is a series of behavior patterns involving many factors that have complex relationships with each other. It is often tempting to look for simple answers to complex problems. Oversimplifications, such as "Delinquency is caused by parents being too easy on their kids," or "All delinquents are suffering from emotional confusion and an identity crisis," should be avoided. To know more about factors that underlie delinquent behavior, it is important to be aware of important stresses during childhood and adolescence. The stress situations to be discussed are not exhaustive but are intended as examples of situations that can lead to delinquent behavior.

Childhood

When children experience rejection, it is not unusual for them to disappear. Feeling that no one wants them, they may show their anger by running away. In response to the rejection, the children are saying "I don't want you." Alternately, the children may decide to test their parents to find out if they really care. These tests may include accidental arson, in which the child lights a match to see what might happen. The death of a loved one, particularly a parent, also may lead to antisocial behavior. Instead of expressing depression and grief, children may demonstrate hostility against the society they blame for taking the parent away.

Sometimes children are labeled troublemakers by teachers and parents with little basis in fact. Once labeled, however, children may begin to act as others see them. For example, if you are going to be blamed every time something is missing, you might as well take it and enjoy it. Or if you are going to be blamed for starting a fight no matter what happens, probably the best way to handle things is to hit the other guy first and at least obtain an advantage. Delinquent behavior also may result from conflicts with parents. Some parents are overprotective and overindulgent, while others are too strict. Some may set standards of conduct and/or achievement that no child can possibly attain, while others do not set any goals for their children. Many parents are so busy trying to maintain their own marginal adjustment that they are unable to help their children handle their problems. Through their behavior, these parents may indirectly encourage children to act out as a way of blaming the children for the parents' own failures.

Adolescence

Adolescents can be affected by the same stresses of childhood just described, but they are also subject to other stresses unique to this period of life. For example, as children grow older, they may begin to feel stressed with regard to school, particularly whether to go to college. Difficulties with parents may increase because, as children grow older, they are able to be more independent. Or conversely, they may want to remain children and not grow up. This difficult choice between independence and dependence often leads to conflict with the parents, who also have mixed feelings about acknowledging their children's growth. As teenagers search for their identity, they may have trouble with self-image and worry about popularity. A girl may have difficulty finding an acceptable moral code; a boy may feel uncertain as he begins to relate socially to girls. Anxiety and other feelings may lead to delinquent behavior – an inadequate means of resolving them. Adolescents' ability to handle these stresses will depend on the strengths they developed while growing up. If their self-image is adequate, adolescents will be better able to withstand these stresses, and it is less likely that they will resort to delinquent behavior to deal with these situations. The development of stress tolerance depends primarily on the presence of a warm, praising family. Healthy, positive relationships with parents lead to greater emotional resiliency (Weissberg, 1983). If adolescents are unable to handle these stresses except by developing a pattern of delinquent behavior, they are likely to come into contact with the police. Through their actions, officers may inadvertently support the continuation of acting-out behavior, or they may be able to offer help before more serious trouble occurs. Consequently, it is important for officers to recognize what they should and should not do when confronted with aggressive juvenile behaviors.

MORE HELPFUL HINTS TO LAW ENFORCEMENT OFFICERS

In the opinion of many juveniles, police officers have two strikes against them even before contact occurs. First, to some they are a symbol of all bad experiences with other authority figures, including fathers, mothers, teachers, and older siblings. As a result, officers may become a target of displacement as angry feelings that juveniles have for other authority figures are directed toward the officers. In addition, the norms of juveniles' specific peer groups may dictate that the police be viewed as enemies and that toughness be demonstrated by "not letting the cops shove you around" or by "clamming up" whenever an officer asks questions. It is therefore important that officers recognize that any relationship formed with a juvenile will depend on the manner in which they approach him or her, the methods used, and their ability to communicate.

Avoid Negative Approaches

Regardless of what abusive language juveniles may use, officers should never respond in kind. They must remain professional at all times and treat youths with courtesy and respect – at least until a juvenile's conduct clearly shows that he or she does not merit this treatment. Officers should never make fun of juveniles or their predicaments. A deputy recently stopped two boys riding their motorcycles along the side of a country dirt road. While he was writing out a citation for this illegal activity, another deputy who had arrived on the scene sat in his car and smiled. What he was actually smiling about was never determined, but the boys interpreted it as being directed at them. They later told their friends that the sheriff's department "stunk" and that the deputies had nothing better to do but drive around and hassle teenagers who were riding bikes too close to the road. This indicates that perhaps the juveniles never really understood what they were being cited for. The event certainly did nothing to improve the officers' image.

Police officers should avoid using excessive authority. Although officers should be firm, they should not be overbearing. Juveniles will not respond positively to an approach that implies "I'm a cop, and you kids have to do what I say." Officers who are unduly afraid of losing control of a situation are in trouble from the beginning. Children are very sensitive to adult insecurities, and such officers run the risk of being tuned out. While nothing will make average officers angrier than the awareness that the person to whom they are speaking is not listening, police often do this themselves, especially toward juveniles. A local judge reported that this is a frequent complaint of those brought to the juvenile court center. For example, if officers have found a juvenile who is out after curfew, they should listen to the adolescent and learn the circumstances. This will let the juvenile know that the officers are interested in what he or she is saying.

Although traffic laws should be enforced, many juveniles complain that officers don't give them a second chance on questionable offenses. Too-rigid enforcement of minor traffic laws against juveniles may be related to officers' unwillingness to listen to the reasons juveniles give for their actions. For example, juveniles may not interpret certain traffic control procedures in the same way as adults. Adults who get a speeding ticket are more likely to dismiss it as bad luck, or concede, after reflection, that they deserved it. However, because juveniles are usually more insecure, they are more likely to feel that the officer was unfair because someone else down the street "speeds all over the neighborhood and never gets caught." In these minor traffic offenses, justice may be better served if officers are somewhat lenient. A warning, administered firmly but with respect for the juvenile as a person, may give him or her a good feeling about the interaction with the officer. Giving a citation, even if technically justified, may turn the juvenile off and leave him or her with the impression that the police's main goal in life is to harass kids. It is important, however, to remember officer safety. Do not make assumptions about whom you are dealing with just because they appear to be "kids." Use proper safety procedures at all times when making traffic stops.

Managing Teenage Crowds

During adolescent development, teenagers acquire much of their personal identity from peer groups. In fact, peer groups are often more influential in shaping adolescents' behavior than parents, teachers, and other adults (LETIN, 1986). They also tend to prefer their own company and often hang out in large groups around businesses, shopping centers, and so on, causing problems that lead to citizen complaints. Police spend many hours breaking up minor disturbances and dealing with obnoxious behavior. Police officers should realize that immaturity combined with alcohol and/or other drugs may produce bizarre, infuriating, and often dangerous, violent behavior. Teenagers who are "under the influence" may be acting out deep-seated emotional problems unrelated to the immediate event. In cases of extreme intoxication, officers should remember that the immediate problem is medical, and that without proper treatment the subject may die. Officers should also remember "teenage or young adult males are the highest risk category for in-custody suicide or death from overdose! Be careful!" (LETIN, 1986, pp. 1–7). Some useful techniques for handling boisterous teenage crowds include:

1. Decide whether backup or medical assistance should be called for before leaving the patrol car.
2. One officer should "hang back" in a protected position with a good view of scene.
3. One officer should approach within eight to ten feet of the crowd's edge.
4. Ignore youngsters who are doing the most talking; ignore ringleaders.

5. Tip the balance of power by calling two or three youngsters at random, separating them from the crowd, and engage them in a separate conversation or interview.
6. Maintain eye contact with two or three youngsters when addressing the crowd, and always:
   a. Be direct and brief.
   b. Avoid judgmental remarks.
   c. Avoid reference to the citizen complaint.
   d. Make 'I' statements, such as "I expect you to disperse in one minute."
   e. Make fact-based descriptive statements, such as "I see about twenty-four people and that's too many."
7. Establish some degree of one-to-one trust and communication. Say what you expect the crowd to do without describing the consequences of failure to do so. If there is no response, describe what you intend to do and be fully prepared to back up what you have said. Never make empty threats. (LETIN, 1986)

Some officers refuse to help juveniles in situations where they would normally offer assistance to adults. When this occurs, juveniles can sense discrimination. Officers should not talk about juveniles or their actions as if they were not present. Reciting a person's offenses, especially in a way that causes embarrassment or shame, is inadvisable. Officers should avoid lecturing or sermonizing and confine their communication to either advice or clear admonishment. Finally, it is important for officers never to lie to juveniles. If an officer gives a juvenile the impression that certain actions will or will not be taken and then does not follow through, the juvenile will feel betrayed and angry. Deception and a failure to keep promises are doubtful policies with anyone; with juveniles, they are never advisable. If the youthful offender develops an early mistrust of law enforcement, it is unlikely that trust will ever be regained.

Positive Approaches

Officers should respect juveniles as they would adults. Even if a juvenile is wrong, officers should be patient. They should remember that children test limits, not only with parents and teachers but also with police. Officers should be firm, not grim. Humor and a relaxed manner can reduce tension, dispel hostility, and help resolve the situation. This approach will help a juvenile to see that police officers are human, compassionate, and that they can understand how another person feels. Officers should explain their actions and answer the juvenile's questions. They should recognize that explanation is different from justification. Justification may not be necessary, but an explanation is always useful. While it may be appropriate in some situations for officers to criticize a juvenile's behavior, they should never attack the youth's personality or character. In treating a child, a therapist tries to help a child understand that it is certain aspects of his or her behavior that are not acceptable, not his or her personality. This principle also applies to interactions between police and juveniles. Focus should always be on the offending behavior and should not attack the juvenile's worth as a person (say "that behavior was stupid" rather than "you are stupid").

Officers should become familiar with those community agencies and programs that are concerned with the welfare of children and adolescents, including their programs, eligibility, and referral policies. In larger communities, a handbook is usually available that lists those sources offering programs for juveniles. All officers should be familiar with this information. Those assigned to juvenile work should have a copy readily available. Finally, law enforcement officers should become involved with the community's youth through activities that may include police department tours, athletic and other school programs, university courses, and visits to juvenile court centers and detention homes.

SUMMARY

In this chapter the author has discussed some of the more important issues for law enforcement officers who work with juveniles. Officers should recognize that juveniles are people and that knowledge and understanding of child and adolescent behavior will enhance officers' ability to deal with delinquent behavior. Effective officers may avoid unnecessary placement of many juveniles into the criminal justice system through referrals to other appropriate agencies. The author has also suggested that there is no single cause or cure for juveniles' complex behavior but that stress situations in childhood and adolescence are important indicators. We have discussed some useful techniques for dealing with teenage crowds. Finally, we have discussed some kinds of police behavior that turn juveniles off and have suggested more desirable approaches that improve communication. Officer safety also has been emphasized. By following these prescriptions, professional officers can carry out their law enforcement responsibilities and also perform an important community service by helping guide and direct the growth of young people. Information relative to juvenile drug addiction, violent behavior, and suicidal behavior will be discussed in later chapters.

BIBLIOGRAPHY

Aichorn, A. (1935). *Wayward youth.* New York: Viking Press.

Ferdinand, T. N., & Luchterhand, E. G. (1970). Inner-city youth, the police, the juvenile court and justice. *Social Problems, 17,* 510–527.

Hagan, J. L. (1972). The labelling perspective, the delinquent, the police: A review of the literature. *Canadian Journal of Criminology and Corrections, 14,* 150–165.

Law Enforcement Training and Information Network (LETIN). (1986). *Training Guide, Dealing with Adolescents,* vol. 2, cassette lo.

McCord, W. (1956). *Psychopathy and delinquency.* New York: Grune & Stratton.

Malmquist, C. P. (1978). *Handbook of adolescence: psychopathology, antisocial development, psychotherapy.* New York: Jason Aronson.

Pursuit, D. (1972). *Police programs for preventing crime and delinquency.* Springfield, IL: Charles C Thomas.

Rusinko, W. T., Johnson, K. W., & Hornung, C. A. (1978). The importance of police contact in the formulation of youths' attitude toward police. *Journal of Criminal Justice, 6,* 53–67.

Weissberg, M. (1983). *Dangerous secrets, maladaptive responses to stress.* New York: W. W. Norton.

Chapter 12

DRUG-DEPENDENT BEHAVIOR

Drug-dependent behavior usually occurs along with more basic patterns of maladaptive behavior. It appears not only in people with personality disorders but also in those with neuroses and psychoses. In addition, the drug epidemic that has swept the United States in the last fifteen or twenty years, particularly the epidemic of cocaine and "crack" use, has brought with it drug-induced symptoms of personality and psychotic disorders. Before proceeding to a more detailed discussion of specific forms of drug-dependent behavior, its underlying factors, and behavioral manifestations, we will present some general considerations to assist law enforcement officers in developing a comprehensive perspective on this critical police problem.

General Considerations

Drugs that produce behaviors with which police officers come in contact can be called "drugs of abuse," which in turn can be defined as substances, taken through any route of administration, that alter the mood, the level of perception, or brain functioning. Such drugs include substances ranging from prescribed medication to alcohol to solvents (Schuckit, 1979). Because of the impact of drugs on their behavior, drug abusers often come to police attention. Approximately half of all incidents the police encounter are related to the use or abuse of alcohol and other drugs. These may include a traffic accident involving a drunken driver, a heroin overdose brought to the emergency room, or a homicide occurring during a drug rip-off. Since police officers frequently see the most sordid effects of drug abuse, they should beware of the tendency to classify all abusers as drunks, junkies, acid freaks, and potheads, with all the moral condemnation that these terms imply. By becoming thoroughly familiar with the behavioral aspects of drug use and abuse, officers can approach this aspect of their job in a professional and nonjudgmental manner.

Definitions

The point at which drug use is transformed into abuse is largely determined by one's point of view. *Medically*, doctors consider the use of aspirin to relieve headache and reduce fever as legitimate. However, they would consider it a case of aspirin abuse if a patient had swallowed dozens of aspirin tablets in a suicide attempt, arriving at the hospital unconscious. Likewise, physicians may legitimately prescribe morphine, an opiate, to ease the suffering of a terminal cancer patient. This use of an opiate is appropriate when nothing else will alleviate the severe pain. From these examples, it is clear that physicians consider a drug to be abused if it does not contribute to the person's ultimate health and well-being. Drug use and abuse can also be viewed *behaviorally*. For example, LSD was originally synthesized to be used under carefully controlled experimental conditions in the treatment of certain personality disorders. However, when abused through indiscriminate use without expert supervision, it produces abnormal behavior that may be dangerous to the user and to others. Drug use and abuse can also be defined *legally*. For instance, while it is legal to sell and use alcohol, it is illegal to drive an automobile while intoxicated, a condition defined in most states as a blood alcohol concentration of greater than 0.10. Even though people may not have actually reached this level of blood alcohol, they may still be abusing alcohol if they stop at their favorite bar on the way home from work to have several highballs, knowing full well that they must drive after drinking. However, other drugs, regardless of their impact on behavior, are considered as having been abused simply because their possession is illegal. From these examples, it is apparent that the precise understanding of drug abuse depends on the circumstances of the user and the viewpoint of the observer. In addition to the various definitions of drug abuse, there are some terms that are commonly used to describe individual reactions to drugs. It is important to become familiar with these terms.

Intoxication

Intoxication is the state or condition induced through excessive use of any drug, although it most commonly refers to alcohol. In defining intoxication, the critical issue is not how much of the drug has been taken into the body, but rather how much of it is there at any one time and for how long. For example, it is not the quantity of alcohol a person consumes that governs the impact, but how much is in the bloodstream at a specific time.

This is a function of how much has been consumed over what period of time and how sensitive that individual is to the drug in question — how quickly his or her body absorbs the drug and how intensely it responds to the drug. However, since most officers do not have immediate access to blood samples or any information about an individual's sensitivity to drugs, we generally conclude that a person is intoxicated when his or her behavior changes. Common indices are loud or slurred speech, uncoordinated movements, and/or overaggressive behavior.

Drug Dependence

In the early stages of drug dependence, symptoms occur only when the drug is currently being used. Depending on the drug, the individual, and the society, there are differences in the proportion of those who become dependent. Historically *drug dependence* has been a general term describing the compulsive use of a drug for whatever reason. Early signs that drug dependence is beginning include the individual's beginning to think about and anticipate the next drug-using experience. Drug use becomes an end in itself, and the person begins to organize his or her life around drug use: planning the next time and making sure ahead of time that there will be enough of the drug available. Such persons may begin to feel that drug use is an indispensible part of enjoying social or recreational events. Later in the development of the dependence, the individual becomes unable to *consistently* or *predictably* control the amount or frequency of drug use.

Addiction

In earlier editions of this book, addicts were defined as people who cannot abstain from the use of a drug *without suffering severe physical symptoms*. This withdrawal syndrome was defined as a combination of painful and debilitating *physical* reactions that occur after an addictive drug is withdrawn. It was thought that addicts often continued taking drugs to avoid the discomfort of the physical symptoms of withdrawal and not to seek a new high. By this definition, drugs such as amphetamines, cocaine, and marijuana were thought to produce tolerance (getting "used to" the drug and needing more and more to get high) and/or habituation (psychological dependence) but not addiction. But with the acceleration of the cocaine abuse problem and subsequent research, it has become clear that the lines between physical and psychological addiction are less clear than previously thought. Both cocaine and amphetamines include acute depression as a "psychological" symptom that comes with abstaining from use after dependence is developed. It is not uncommon for suicide or suicide attempts to occur during this depression. Abusers of these drugs frequently are unable to function in their daily lives when they discontinue use. Certainly these are physical symptoms of withdrawal, even though they may not be "physical." In addition, as discussed in greater detail below, cocaine has been found in animal research to produce a *high-seeking* behavior that is limited only by death or unconsciousness. There is never "enough." Cocaine does not produce what is conventionally thought of as "tolerance," which builds over time and with increasing use. These changes in understanding have led to a change in the way drug abuse is viewed. Drugs are no longer compared so much in terms of their tendency to produce physical symptoms of withdrawal, but rather on the acuteness of the dependence they produce and the physical *and social* consequences of their continued abuse.

In 1981, a World Health Organization working group proposed that the focus be placed on elements of a "drug-dependence syndrome" rather than on physical dependence or addiction. In 1987 that organization, in describing Mental and Behavioral Disorders Due to Psychoactive Substance Use, named "acute intoxication, harmful use, dependency syndrome, withdrawal state with delirium, psychotic disorder, drug- or alcohol-induced amnesia, and flashbacks" as some of the indicators of such disorders (Arif & Westermeyer, 1988, p. 6).

Tolerance

All drugs that are addictive – capable of producing the withdrawal syndrome – also produce *tolerance*. This term refers to the inability of the individual to experience the same effects from the same dose of a drug over a period of time. If the effect is to remain the same, the user must constantly increase the dose. It is important to recognize that not all drugs that produce tolerance are addictive, because they do not all produce a withdrawal syndrome.

Habituation

In contrast to addiction and tolerance, which are physiological terms associated with drug abuse, *habituation* refers to a psychological aspect of drug abuse. All drugs that affect behavior are habit forming, to some extent. The degree to which they are habit forming is a combination of their capacity to produce tolerance, the behavioral changes they produce, and the personality characteristics of the user. Although physical dependence is the primary consequence, psychological dependence is a factor. In habituation, it is the psychological dependence that is important because there is no physical dependence.

Polydrug Abuse

Although for simplicity we have chosen to describe the distinct characteristics of the abuse of specific drugs, the combination of drugs has become more and more commonplace. Abusers of most drugs other than alcohol frequently abuse alcohol as well as their primary drug, in combination with it, and often when they don't have the money or for other reasons don't have access to their preferred drug. The combining of drugs or combining of alcohol and drugs often produces unpredictable physical and behavioral reactions.

Alcohol

Alcohol is the most commonly abused substance in the United States, as evidenced by the frequency with which police officers find behavior influenced by alcohol. More than 50 percent of arrests are related to alcohol. There is a very good chance that fatal road accidents will involve a drunken driver. It is therefore important for the police to be aware of alcohol and the behavior it engenders.

Characteristics of Alcohol Abuse

Many theories have been developed to explain the causes of excessive drinking. Some theories hold that people drink because they are depressed; others point out that excessive alcohol use is often associated with feelings of guilt. Feelings of inadequacy, failure, and low self-esteem, as well as poor interpersonal relationships, are also characteristics of people who use alcohol excessively.

Alcoholics Anonymous, begun in the 1930s and thus far proven to be the most successful model for the treatment of drug and alcohol abuse, proposes that alcoholism (and drug abuse) are *diseases* that are physical, emotional, and spiritual. Research begun by Jellinek (1964) developed a model of alcoholism that included four phases in the course of alcohol dependence: the pre-alcoholic phase, the prodromal phase, the crucial phase, and the chronic phase. The three main symptoms that were viewed as markers of the latter three phases were: (1) the onset of amnesia while drinking (that is, blackouts), which was considered to signal the beginning of the prodromal phase; (2) the inability to control the amount of alcohol consumed or the period of time one drinks (from this perspective, thought to mark the beginning of the crucial phase). It is important to note that loss of control could be partial or intermittent; (3) the chronic phase, thought to be indicated by the

onset of prolonged periods of intoxication (Arif & Westermeyer, 1988). This is one of many systems describing the developmental course of alcoholism from the disease perspective. Yet not every alcohol-dependent person has all these symptoms, nor do they necessarily occur in this order. There are many different patterns of alcohol use and abuse. In the alcohol-dependent person a variety of patterns of drinking may occur over time and sometimes in combination. Because it is so pervasive, it has been particularly difficult to identify the specific and universal characteristics of alcohol dependence. However, there is no difficulty in identifying the personal, medical, social, and law enforcement problems that result from this dependence.

It is important to note that according to the National Institute of Drug and Alcohol Abuse, 18 million people in this country suffer from serious alcohol abuse problems. In his September 6, 1989, speech announcing a new attack in the war on cocaine and crack, President Bush estimated that 8 million people are frequent users of cocaine. Alcohol is still the most serious and pervasive drug problem in the United States.

Characteristics of alcohol abusers that police officers should be aware of include an extremely low frustration point toward any wish, request, desire, or demand made of them. If any demands that they make are not granted, they may react with anger or even violence. "Alcohol's direct relation to violence and violent crime is considered far greater than that of any other drug" (Solomon & Keeley, 1982). Police officers should also be alert to the possible presence of deep depression and suicidal behavior in alcohol abusers.

HELPFUL HINTS TO LAW ENFORCEMENT OFFICERS

The signs of acute alcohol intoxication can include varying degrees of exhilaration and excitement, loss of inhibition and restraint, bizarre behavior, slurred speech, and lack of coordination. When encountering someone

who is intoxicated, officers might remember the last time they were in a similar state. Acknowledging their own feelings, including a sense of power and a glib tongue, will help them relate better to alcohol abusers. Officers should be patient but firm. They should remember that the abusers involved are not their normal selves and probably won't remember how obnoxious they were. If they are belligerent, officers should ignore this behavior as much as possible unless they are in danger of hurting themselves or others. If officers can keep them talking while they are working, their job will be easier. When alcohol intoxication has been especially severe, drowsiness, stupor, and possibly unconsciousness may occur. It is important for officers to recognize that unconsciousness may mask other physical disorders that have either resulted from acute alcohol intake or are coincident with it. The former category may include head injuries, pneumonia, fractures, and bleeding from the stomach, while the latter may include such conditions as diabetic coma and the stupor following an epileptic seizure. In a few cases, even small amounts of alcohol can result in markedly abnormal behavior. This is called *pathological intoxication* and refers to cases in which an extremely small amount of alcohol, which in most individuals would have only minimal effects, can cause an outburst of markedly irrational, combative, and destructive behavior. Officers also may encounter alcoholics who have stopped drinking either because of illness or lack of access to alcohol. This cessation may lead to a number of symptoms of which officers should be aware so they can help bring proper medical attention to alcoholics. (These symptoms are unlikely to occur in the person who uses alcohol in response to stressful life events.) The symptoms may not occur until after the person has been arrested and jailed, since confinement automatically bars access to alcohol.

The most common sign of alcohol withdrawal in chronic alcohol abusers is tremulousness (shakes or jitters). Most often visible in the hands, it is usually associated with irritability, nausea, and vomiting. All these symptoms will occur relatively quickly, and, in jail, they are often seen the morning after arrest. When they stop drinking, most chronic abusers

will experience nothing more than severe shakes. Some, however, may demonstrate more serious conditions, such as *alcoholic hallucinosis* or *delirium tremens*. In the former, abusers hear accusatory and threatening voices. These may occur even if the abusers otherwise look all right and know where they are and what time it is. The treatment is hospitalization, appropriate medication, adequate diet, and good nursing care. In delirium tremens, seeing and feeling objects that are not present is more common than hearing voices (auditory hallucinations). Persons may perceive bugs crawling on them or see huge insects. In contrast to alcoholic hallucinosis, delirium tremens is associated with a loss of orientation to time and place. Delirium tremens may also be associated with epileptic seizures, which can be life-threatening. Good treatment requires prompt medical attention in a hospital, with appropriate medication, adequate diet, and good nursing care.

An important part of the police's past difficulties in handling alcohol abusers has been the neglect of the needs of alcoholics by other agencies, such as hospitals and clinics. However, the attitudes of society toward alcohol abusers have been changing. Most states have passed legislation removing public intoxication from the criminal code and defining it as a medico-social problem. Many hospitals and clinics are creating comprehensive alcohol treatment programs, including detoxification centers, or are affiliated with them. With the development of these treatment programs, police officers can now bring acutely intoxicated persons to an appropriate facility rather than ignoring them or placing them in the "drunk tank." Without the support of these programs, the criminal justice system incurs high costs in handling alcohol abusers. Police officers need to be familiar with these programs as both a referral source and a caregiver. Law enforcement officers should work closely with community groups; both medical and nonmedical, to encourage people who need help to use available programs. There is no question that police cooperation in such a community effort will free officers to attend to more serious crimes than public intoxication and chronic inebriation.

Other Forms of Drug Abuse

While alcohol is the most commonly abused drug, it is not the only one. There are numerous others to which individuals become addicted, tolerant, or habituated. They are also of concern to police officers for several reasons: they affect human behavior, their nonmedical sale or possession in many instances is legally prohibited, they are associated with public health epidemics such as AIDS, and, according to recent research, some drug abuse is associated with a high incidence of criminal activity. Consequently, police officers also should be familiar with the characteristics and behavioral effects of these other drugs.

In the following discussion, we have grouped these drugs into several general categories. As officers encounter specific drugs other than those mentioned, they can determine their category and deduce their general characteristics and effects.

Amphetamines

In contrast to illegal drugs such as psychedelics, marijuana, and cocaine, amphetamines (*speed*) were heavily prescribed in the past by physicians, especially to assist patients in weight reduction. Now, however, the legitimate use of amphetamines has been restricted, primarily because of a high incidence of abuse.

Most abusers take speed in the form of pills (*pep pills* or *goof balls*), but some use it intravenously in a synthetic form (Methedrine) to obtain a better high. This *mainlining* of speed is very dangerous because it can lead to a severe paranoid psychosis. Among users, the initial high from amphetamines becomes harder to achieve since a high level of tolerance occurs quickly. Over time, increasing amounts are required to produce the same effect. As with other drugs, psychological dependence or habituation results.

One of the most recent and potent developments of the drug cartels is a drug called "ice," which is a colorless, odorless form of crystal methamphetamine that is smoked to produce a euphoric high. Hawaii's U.S. attorney, Dan Bent, warned: "Only now are we learning that its high is many times more potent and longer than crack, that its low is deep, morbid and entrenched, and that its addiction is at least as great as crack and possibly far greater" (Holmes, 1989, p. 13). A puff of crack produces a high that lasts for about twenty minutes, but the high produced from smoking ice endures for twelve to twenty-four hours.

The acute paranoid psychosis that may result from amphetamines is often difficult to differentiate from functional paranoid psychosis. However, officers encountering anyone in an acute paranoid psychosis should take him or her to a medical facility for emergency treatment. Paranoid psychotics should be approached with extreme caution, since they have the potential of being dangerous (Chapter 14). They are also frightened, and officers should not do anything that will increase their fear, because increased fear is likely to lead to greater potential for violence.

Barbiturates

Because they are legally available through prescription, barbiturates are probably the most frequently abused drugs after alcohol. Their abuse is particularly dangerous because they produce habituation, tolerance, and addiction. Furthermore, they can increase the effects of other drugs (principally alcohol) when taken in combination. This type of combination abuse accounts for a high number of accidental deaths.

Police officers often can identify a chronic barbiturate abuser by a degree of mental confusion, some impairment of intellectual ability, and a staggering gait. Individuals suspected of chronic barbiturate intoxication should also be taken to the emergency room for medical evaluation. In contrast to narcotic addicts, who are likely to overestimate the amount they have been taking, barbiturate abusers may grossly underestimate the amount they are taking because they are reluctant to reveal the cause of their physical symptoms. This is extremely serious because underestimation can lead doctors to place abusers on an inadequate amount of the drug prior to beginning withdrawal.

Mild Tranquilizers

Mild tranquilizers, such as Valium and Librium, have an effect similar to barbiturates. This is not surprising since many "tranquilizers" are misnamed and actually sedate more than tranquilize. Although they do not produce an actual withdrawal syndrome as barbiturates do, tranquilizer withdrawal may present similar problems and should be accomplished in a hospital. Because there is a cross-tolerance between many tranquilizers and barbiturates, abusers may increase the impact of these drugs by taking several kinds.

Narcotic Drugs (Opiates)

Narcotics are derivatives of opium and include both natural forms (morphine, heroin, and codeine) as well as synthetics (Demerol, methadone, and Numorphan). Tolerance and habituation occur rapidly. Abstinence results in a withdrawal syndrome, characteristic of addictive drugs. Narcotics may be taken either intravenously (*mainlining*), by subcutaneous injection (*skin popping*), or by nasal inhalation (*snorting*). This last use is effective only with a very high-grade opiate, such as that experienced in Vietnam by American servicemen.

Studies that have attempted to demonstrate personality differences between opiate and alcohol addicts have not yielded conclusive results. The choice of the addicting drug appears to be determined by social and cultural factors. Many young users commonly abuse both opiates and alcohol, either at the same time or in rapid succession.

Hallucinogens

Hallucinogens, otherwise known as psychedelics, have been used for centuries in their natural state as part of the religious rites of many ancient civilizations. Only recently have they been abused in both their natural and synthetic states. Common among the natural hallucinogens is mescaline, derived from the peyote (cactus) plant; common among the synthetics is lysergic acid diethylamide (LSD), first synthesized in 1938. More recently, PCP (phencyclidine) has become popular.

The acute toxic reactions of hallucinogens include disorganized thinking and an altered state of perception of the environment. These reactions are greatly influenced by the social setting and the person's expectations prior to taking the drug. These altered perceptions can lead to heightened experiences in each of the five senses (hearing, seeing, smelling, touching, and tasting). In contrast to alcohol and the opiates, hallucinogens are neither addictive nor tolerance producing. They may be habituating for some people, depending on personality. The serious problems associated with hallucinogen abuse are secondary not only to the acute psychotic symptoms of a toxic reaction but also to the possible acting-out of violent impulses directed either against others or the users themselves. Chronic users may have uncontrolled and overwhelming panic reactions in association with flashbacks, in which the effects of hallucinogens are reproduced, although none have been taken. These episodes are extremely frightening and can result in severe panic, which may make users a potential danger to themselves or others. Because of the acute panic often associated with a bad reaction to hallucinogens, emergency measures should include efforts to prevent users from hurting themselves or others. These precautions can include restricting movement, either by placing the person in a closed room or by using restraints.

Other efforts to reduce the input of external stimuli may include placing the person in a quiet, nonstimulating environment. Police who come in contact with persons under the effects of a hallucinogen should lower their voices and talk calmly to them (the *talk-down cure*). It also helps to reduce external stimuli.

Marijuana

While classified by some as a psychedelic, marijuana (*pot*) is probably best considered by itself not only because of its frequent and widespread use, but also because, in its milder forms, it does not produce hallucinogenic experiences approaching those associated with psychedelic drugs. However, in its strongest form (hashish), it can produce symptoms similar to those of psychedelic substances. Like psychedelics, but unlike alcohol and opiates, marijuana use does not lead to addiction or tolerance. Habituation and dependence can occur in some users, depending on their previous psychological state and underlying pattern of behavior. However, many are able to use marijuana without becoming psychologically dependent or habituated. Although marijuana usually is regarded as having lower abuse potential than most other drugs we will discuss in this chapter, the percentage of THC (tetrahydrocannabinol, the major psychoactive ingredient found in marijuana) in illicit marijuana has increased from an average of one to five percent in the late 1960s to as much as ten to 15 percent by the mid-1980s. "The greater potency of current marijuana supplies may be contributing to an increasing prevalence of Cannabis Dependence and associated disorders" (DSM-IV-TR, 2000). The regular use of this illegal drug seems to lower psychological resistance to the idea of using other illegal drugs. Hence, although marijuana use does not necessarily lead to using more addictive drugs, marijuana users are likely to combine its use with alcohol or illegal "supplemental" drugs. A pattern of chronic marijuana use is typical in the history of those who use cocaine and heroin compulsively or abusively.

Cocaine and "Crack"

The 1980s saw cocaine use and abuse in the United States rise to epidemic proportions. Cocaine is derived from the leaves of the coca shrub, which is found in portions of South America and Southeast Asia. Like natural psychedelic substances, it has a long history of use, primarily by the Indians of the Andes. It was first isolated for medicinal purposes in 1855. In the early 1900s, this country saw an epidemic of cocaine use, manifested principally in the use of cocaine in cola drinks, patent medicines, and liqueurs. In 1914 cocaine was made illegal. Between 1920 and 1970 cocaine was limited primarily to specific subgroups of the population, such as jazz musicians and artists. But after the advent of the "drug culture" in the late 1960s, cocaine began to be viewed as the "champagne" of drugs and was thought to have surprisingly few harmful side effects or characteristics.

In the last ten to twenty years, cocaine production has increased dramatically in the countries of South America that were the natural home of the coca plant, such as Bolivia and Peru. Colombia, Argentina, Brazil, and Ecuador have seen the development of a newly thriving business in coca production. This multinational business has led to a law enforcement problem of monumental proportions, primarily focused around the importation and distribution of cocaine in the United States. "In the United States recent flooding of the marketplace with crack – ready-to-use free base in $10 or $20 packages – has resulted in an upsurge of new consumers" (Washton & Gold, 1987). In a 1982 National Survey on Drug Abuse, it was found that "of all persons in the household population in the United States who were 12 years old or older, 22 million persons had used cocaine at some time during their life" (Kozel & Adams, 1985). This number is undoubtedly much higher in today's society.

Cocaine can be sniffed, injected, or smoked (as "crack," a "freebase," or cocaine alkaloid). Crack is sold in the form of tiny pellets, or "rocks," which can be smoked with no further chemical processing. Because of the intense exhilaration that it produces, cocaine is often used with other drugs. For example, barbiturate abusers may use it to counteract the down of sedatives. It is not unusual for crack smokers to use alcohol in conjunction with it to "cool down" their lungs and body temperature. Injectable cocaine is sometimes combined with heroin in the same syringe, yielding a drug combination known as a "speedball." This mixture is particularly dangerous since cocaine and heroin act together to depress respiration. A variety of depressive drugs, such as Valium, Librium, barbiturates, Quaaludes, and alcohol, are often used to counter the severe "jittery" nerves that accompany cocaine addiction (Washton & Gold, 1987). The consumer-oriented approach of multinational drug cartels operating from their base in Latin America has led to the development of more and more refinements in the cocaine/crack market. "Designer" drugs are now available that combine cocaine or crack with heroin.

Withdrawal from and tolerance to cocaine is quite different from that of other drugs. Cocaine abuse is associated with either an episodic or binging pattern of use, or a more chronic daily or almost daily use. "'Binging' is a common form of episodic use consisting of compressed time periods of continuous high-dose use, e.g., consumption of several grams or more of cocaine during a single 48-hour period. . . . Binges are generally followed by an extremely intense and unpleasant 'crash' requiring at least two or more days of recuperation. In some cases the 'crash' may extend into cocaine withdrawal . . . lasting several days." Withdrawal symptoms characteristic of the cessation of cocaine binging or daily use include severe depression, exhaustion, sleep disorders, and agitation (DSM-IV-TR, 2000).

Cocaine tolerance is also unique among the commonly abused drugs. Laboratory studies of animals show that "animals given unlimited access to cocaine will keep using it until they

pass out from exhaustion or convulsions or until they die from overdose" (Kozel & Adams, 1985). The unique factor in cocaine tolerance is that there is no ceiling to one's desire for more cocaine; there is never "enough."

> After approximately five to twenty minutes, this state of arousal is rapidly replaced by a restless irritability often accompanied by dysphoria [depression]. It is this dysphoric state that appears to prompt the user to continue smoking in an effort to recapture the initial rush. Since tolerance develops rapidly to the rewarding sensations, concomitant with sensitization to irritability and dysphoria, the intoxication can capture the user in a cycle of repeating use. (Washton & Gold, 1987)

Crime and public health problems associated with cocaine and crack abuse have escalated in the last decade. In drug testing, federal probationers who were closely supervised were shown to have a very high (55%) incidence of cocaine use (Wish, Cuadrado, & Martorana, 1986). Several studies have indicated that cocaine abuse is highly correlated with criminal activity of many types (Incidardi, 1981; Sanchez & Johnson, 1987; Hunt et al. 1986; "Arrestee Drug Use" 1986). Cocaine (and heroin) intravenous use has become significantly linked to the spread of AIDS. Crack houses in major cities have been associated with a dramatic increase in syphilis as a result of frequent promiscuous sex on the premises and have become a hotbed of AIDS transmission, often through open genital sores. Hospitals in the major cities, particularly those that serve inner-city areas, have seen a flood of crack-related emergencies: overdoses, sudden unexpected deaths from minor doses, and so on. There are no treatment facilities with beds to handle these cases. Further, cocaine- and crack-related psychosis and delirium have led to a dramatic rise in violence in the corridors and emergency rooms of county hospitals. Medical personnel have become emotionally burned out by the babies born to crack-addicted mothers who have nowhere to go, and by crack addicts whom they must put back on the streets because there are not enough treatment facilities. With the advent of crack, the inexpensive, accessible form of cocaine, addiction has become available to people in all social/economic strata. The economic and social changes that have resulted from the influx of crack and massive amounts of money produced by its sale are destroying not just individuals and families but whole neighborhoods. Vigilante groups have formed in many cities, producing complex problems for law enforcement officers and officials. The sudden increase in youthful crack dealers, especially in the ghettos of major cities, has led to an acute breakdown in the existing family structure. Often

children have become the breadwinners of the family. With the crack epidemic has come an epidemic of violence, touching even affluent communities.

The vast amounts of money involved in crack distribution threaten law enforcement agencies and officers as never before. Dealers carry very large amounts of cash, offering unequaled temptation to officers. The importation and distribution of cocaine in general, and crack in particular, has created such public concern that the federal government has committed millions of dollars to this fight. International negotiations to stop the flow of cocaine into the United States frequently headline the nation's newspapers.

HELPFUL HINTS TO LAW ENFORCEMENT OFFICERS

A person who has overdosed should be treated as a medical emergency, and police officers must be able to recognize the symptoms. Acute opiate overdose is characterized by a marked unresponsiveness, in the presence of very slow or labored breathing. Needle marks and/or *tracks* will be noted. The pupils are pinpoints, and both pulse and heartbeat are extremely slow. If the overdose has been severe and the individual is still alive, body temperature will have fallen. When breathing is poor, it is important immediately to create an air passage and to supply artificial respiration while in transit to the hospital emergency room. In contrast to acute overdose, neither chronic intoxication from opiates nor withdrawal from them are generally medical emergencies. Because of the drugs' tolerance-producing effects, addicts will require rapidly increasing amounts of an opiate to obtain the same result. However, this process is self-limiting. Once addicts' habits have reached a certain level, their primary motivation for continuing to use an opiate is to avoid withdrawal rather than to reach a new high. Addicts dread withdrawal because it is extremely uncomfortable. Runny nose, excessive tearing, sweating, as well as

severe nausea and vomiting occur within eight to sixteen hours after the last dose if no further opiate is taken. Later effects include severe muscle cramps and spasms, marked sleeplessness, and an increase in nausea and vomiting. If untreated, the addict is in a state of *cold turkey*, and the withdrawal syndrome will reach its peak within forty-eight and seventy-two hours. Most addicts are not able to go cold turkey unless they are in jail, where opiates are unavailable. Otherwise, the temptation to relieve withdrawal symptoms by another fix is too great to resist. Heroin addicts who cannot get into a treatment program will sometimes approach a police officer and ask to be booked for some offense that will draw ten days in jail if they are convicted. The addicts plead guilty in order to withdraw in jail because their tolerance level has reached the point where they can no longer steal enough to support their habit. They arrange to go to jail not to quit drugs but to lower the amount they need. Difficulties associated with withdrawal and the history of re-addiction in many addicts, even after successful withdrawal, have led to the use of a synthetic opiate, methadone, for both withdrawal and maintenance. Methadone is useful in withdrawal because its administration can be controlled more carefully than heroin, since it is long acting and can be taken orally. It is useful in maintenance of chronic heroin addicts, even though it substitutes one addiction for another, because it appears to enable addicts to function more successfully than when they are on heroin.

The criminal aspects of heroin addiction have been well publicized and are related primarily to addicts' need to obtain finances to support the high cost of the addiction. However, some addicts exhibited criminal behavior before their addiction, and heroin merely increases their need to engage in that behavior.

SUMMARY

In this chapter the author has discussed alcoholism and other forms of drug abuse, including their characteristics, underlying factors, and physical and psychological effects. Abuse of these drugs results in abnormal behavior, and therefore police officers frequently become involved. The role of officers in handling problems associated with drug abuse is a difficult one at best. But in dealing with drug abusers, officers must maintain a professional attitude toward those against whom most of society prefers to turn its back. They must have sufficient knowledge of the characteristics of commonly abused drugs and their effects so that they can give first aid to people who are suffering severe symptoms from their use, ensure that they receive necessary emergency medical care, and, if necessary, act as a liaison between them and available treatment facilities.

BIBLIOGRAPHY

American Psychiatric Association. (2000). *Diagnostic and statistical manual,* 4th ed. revised. Washington, D.C.: American Psychiatric Association.

Arif, A., ed. (1987). *Adverse health consequences of cocaine abuse.* Geneva: World Health Organization.

Arif, A., and Westermeyer, J., eds. (1988). *Manual of drug and alcohol abuse.* New York: Plenum Medical Book Co.

Arrestee drug use. (1986). *NIDA Notes, 3,* 10–11.

Brooke, J. 13 August, 1989. Tucson bust is big; coke trade bigger. Peru: vital rain forest being sacrificed for illegal coca crops." *Arizona Daily Star,* 1.

Browker, K. J., & Anglin, M. D. (1987). Adolescent cocaine use: Epidemiology, risk factors, and prevention. *Journal of Drug Education, 17*(2), 163–180.

Burchell, J. 13 August, 1989. Tucson bust is big; coke trade bigger. Tucson: Deputy confiscates 842 pounds of coke worth $8.5 million. *Arizona Daily Star,* 1.

Burke, J. 25 March, 1989. Crack bigwigs in Detroit get prison, fines. *Arizona Daily Star,* 41.

Can cocaine conquer America? January, 1987. *Readers' Digest,* 30–38.

Chafetz, M. E. (1959). Practical and theoretical considerations in the psychotherapy of alcoholism. *Quarterly Journal of Studies on Alcohol, 20,* 281–294.

Church, G. J. 30 May, 1988. Thinking the unthinkable. *Time,* 12–19.

Densen-Gerber, J., & Baden, M. M. (1981). *The doctor talks to you about cocaine, angel dust (PCP), and other drugs.* A discussion by Judianne Densen-Gerber and Michael Baden (sound recording). Bayside, N.Y.: Soundwords.

Erickson, P. G., et al. (1987). *The steel drug: Cocaine in perspective.* Lexington, MA: Lexington Books.

Gordon, B. (1979). *I'm dancing as fast as I can.* New York: Harper & Row.

Gottschalk, L. A., et al. (1977). *Guide to the investigation and reporting of drug-abuse deaths: Problems and methods.* Rockville, MD: Psychosocial Branch, Division of Research, National Institute of Drug Abuse (NIDA).

Grabowski, J., ed. (1984). *Cocaine, pharmacology, effects and treatment of abuse.* Rockville, MD: Department of Health and Human Services, Public Health Service, Alcohol, Drug Abuse and Mental Health Administration, NIDA.

Holmes, E. II. 3 September, 1989. New narcotic, 'ice,' threatens to freeze out crack as drug of choice. *Arizona Daily Star*, 13A.

Hunt, D., et al. (1986). The costly bonus: cocaine-related crime among methadone treatment clients. *Advances in Alcohol and Substance Abuse*, *6*(2), 107–122.

Hunt, T. 6 September, 1989. Bush calls drugs gravest threat. *Arizona Daily Star*, 1.

Incidardi, J. A. (1981). Crime and alternative patterns of substance abuse. In *Drug and alcohol abuse: Implications for treatment*, ed. S. E. Gardner, pp. 95–115. Washington, D.C.: NIDA.

Kerr, P. 20 August,1989. Crack, syphilis creating new avenues for AIDS, experts say. *Arizona Daily Star*, 15A.

Kolata, G. 13 August, 1989. Tucson bust is big; coke trade bigger. New York City: Crack's lure upends family structure in poor neighborhoods. *Arizona Daily Star*, 1.

Kozel, N. J., & Adams, E. H., eds. (1985). *Cocaine use in America: Epidemiologic and clinical perspectives*. NIDA Research Monograph 61. Rockville, MD: NIDA.

Madden, J. S. (1984). *A guide to alcohol and drug dependence*. Bristol, England: Wright & Sons.

Meyer, R. E., ed. (1986). *Psychopathology and addictive disorders*. New York: Guilford Press.

Mullaly, R. W. (1986). *Cocaine fact sheets*. Intuition Press.

Newcomb, J. D., & Bentler, P. M. (1986). Cocaine use among young adults. *Advances in Alcohol and Substance Abuse*, *6*(2), 73–96.

Robinson, M. 1 September, 1989. New forms of narcotics invading streets, panel told. *Arizona Daily Star*, 5A.

Sanchez, J. E., & Johnson, B. D. (1987). Women and the drugs-crime connection: Crime rates among drug abusing women at Rikers Island. *Journal of Psychoactive Drugs, 19*(2), 205–216.

Schuckit, M. A. (1979). *Drug and alcohol abuse: A clinical guide to diagnosis and treatment*. New York: Plenum Medical Book Co.

Shaffer, H., & Burclass, M. E., eds. (1981). *Classic contributions in the addictions*. New York: Brunner/Mazel.

Solomon, J., & Keeley, K. A. (1982). *Perspectives in alcohol and drug abuse: Similarities and differences*. Boston: John Wright/PSG Inc.

Spitz, H. I., & Rosecan, J. S. (1987). *Cocaine abuse: New directions in treatment and research*. New York: Brunner/Mazel.

Turner, C. E., et al. (1988). *Cocaine: An annotated bibliography*. Jackson, Miss.: Research Institute of Pharmaceutical Sciences, University of Mississippi and University Press of Mississippi.

Vereby, K., & Gold, M. S. (1988). From coca leaves to crack: The effects of dose and routes of administration in abuse liability. *Psychiatric Annals, 18*(9), 513–520.

Washton, A. M. (1986). Crack: The newest lethal addiction. *Medical Aspects of Human Sexuality, 20*(9), 49–55.

Washton, A. M., & Gold, M. S., eds. (1987). *Cocaine: A clinician's handbook*. New York: Guilford Press.

Wish, E. D., Cuadrado, M., & Martorana, J. A. (1986). Estimates of drug use in intensive supervision probationers: Results from a pilot study. *Federal Probation, 50*(4), 4–16.

Chapter 13

PARANOID BEHAVIOR

Paranoid behavior is always associated with a high level of anxiety – the feeling that one is not safe. Suspiciousness, distrust, and a disproportionate amount of concern with the thoughts, feelings, and/or actions of another person or persons are the core elements of paranoids' relationships with the world around them. Paranoid persons perceive the world to be dangerous and believe they always must be on guard against the possibility of attack from others. They believe that other people's thoughts and feelings are focused on them and that those thoughts and feelings are negative in some way. Consequently, they live with an endless series of tensions arising from frequent misunderstandings and misinterpretations. They find it difficult to confide in others. If they do, they expect to be betrayed. They devote much of their attention, time, and energy to detecting an anticipated betrayal or attack, and/or actively defending themselves against the perceived danger. Any close relationships such persons might have are likely to be limited to a very few people and to have difficulty surviving any stress. People with paranoia resulting from psychological states, disorders, or schizophrenia usually have had a lifelong tendency toward secretiveness, seclusion, and solitary rumination, although these may be concealed behind a façade of superficial give and take. Paranoid delusions can also result from deafness, reactions to legal or illegal drugs, and from the dementia that accompanies some illnesses, such as AIDS.

Three diagnoses of paranoid behavior that are psychological in origin in the person with a paranoid personality disorder, someone with a delusional or paranoid disorder, and the paranoid schizophrenic – may be clearly differentiated, as the following table illustrates.

Table 13-1. Three Diagnoses of Paranoid Behavior			
	Paranoid Personality	Paranoid Disorder	Paranoid Schizophrenia
Thinking Disturbance	Yes	Yes	Yes
Delusions	No	Yes	Yes
Hallucinations	No	No	Yes
Regression	No	No	Yes

The Progression of Paranoid Behavior

Paranoid behavior becomes more severe when generalized suspiciousness and distrust begin to merge with the people's increasing withdrawal. As they isolate themselves (or, in the case of elderly persons who are losing their hearing, become more and more isolated from others), they become more preoccupied with their inner world and experience strange feelings of alienation and uneasiness. They think other people are as preoccupied with their inner world as they are. They begin to scrutinize their surroundings with even more suspicion and search for hidden meanings and motives in all the events around them. Those with paranoid disorders are likely to develop delusions that are not especially bizarre (that is, delusions that involve situations from real life, such as having a disease, being deceived by a spouse, being loved at a distance by a famous person, or being followed or persecuted in some way).

Recent research indicates that some families have a general attitude of suspiciousness and distrust toward the outside world, are generally isolated, or foster negative attitudes in dealing with the world in general, and with authority figures in particular. Individuals from such families expect that the world is "out to get them" and constantly look for evidence to confirm this expectation. These people have a particularly difficult time trusting authority, strangers, public officials – even friends and relatives. Here's how the paranoid process develops. Hypervigilant persons may begin to watch the little things people do and note with increasing wariness their posture, gestures, glances, and movements. They demonstrate a readiness to react to any situation as potentially threatening, whether or not an actual threat is present. What is important is that they *feel* threatened. In this preoccupied state, they begin to believe that everything is somehow related to them, although they may not know why. As this process continues, their anxiety increases and their defensive use of

projection begins. For example, they may feel that their desk has become disarranged. First they may feel only annoyance, but later they may begin to wonder about it. If they cannot find something in a desk drawer or notice that other things have been disturbed, they grow more anxious. They begin to examine other personal possessions and are concerned that these have also been disarranged. When jostled or crowded in the street, they begin to feel angry. They hear remarks and immediately assume they are about them. If there is laughter, they feel it is directed at them (Cameron, 1959). Paranoid persons use projection to transfer many of their own unconscious wishes and feelings onto others. For example, they are able to avoid looking at their own hostile feelings by perceiving them, through projection, as the hostile attacks of others. They also use denial to avoid any reality that would argue against their beliefs. Denial also protects them from the stresses they would feel if faced by their own weaknesses and failures. Instead of perceiving them as their own shortcomings, they become the fantasied shortcomings, evil intentions, and/or misdeeds of others. The more the paranoid persons can defensively belittle others, the further they remove themselves from looking at their own weaknesses. The more they point out others' mistakes and sins, the less attention they must pay to their own. Even though the thoughts of paranoid people may be delusional, the thoughts still may have some core of truth (Kaffman, 1984; Thompson-Pope & Turkat, 1988). In fact, the hypervigilant characteristic of paranoid persons makes it likely that they have picked up subtle nonverbal cues of hostility and/or rejection in others who are not aware of having communicated such feelings. This misdirected focus increases their anxiety, which must then be reduced. To accomplish this, they form endless hypotheses about what is happening. Seeking to find a plausible explanation, they fail to recognize their own underlying feelings and their contribution to the situation. Since paranoid people's reality testing is defective, all their hypotheses are doomed to failure because they are likely to contain distortions of reality.

To this point, the projections have no specific focus. If paranoids have spoken openly of persecution, they have referred only to "they" or "people" who are doing or planning things, without being able to specify who "they" are or what the exact plan is. However, this situation cannot endure because its vagueness is too anxiety producing. To reduce this anxiety, paranoid persons begin to conceptualize these dangerous "others" into a specific group, or the plan into a specific plot, of which they are the intended victim. They may conceive of this group as an organized gang of criminals, a group of international spies, a secret police force, or a racial or religious group. They may identify some of the members as people they know and to whom they attach an important role in this organization. Their thinking crystallizes around a specific plot that this group is formulating, of which they are the center. When this focusing of delusions occurs, their anxiety is reduced. However, they soon discover that they have a new problem. They must now defend themselves against this attack or plot. As they mobilize their own aggression to defend themselves, their tactics alienate others and may lead to counter-aggression. Once they have experienced this counter-aggression, they can complain that people are "really" against them – that they are being interfered with, discriminated against, or persecuted. They now can point to real events in the world that justify their original unreal, delusional complaints.

In chronic cases, some paranoids may appear to have no more than a nonspecific resentful or aggressive attitude toward the world, behind which their delusions are more or less successfully concealed (paranoid personality disorder). Persons with "delusional or paranoid disorder" (DSM-IV-TR, 2000) have a very specific focus to their delusion: their spouse, a lover at a distance, "doctors," and so on. In still others, the paranoid beliefs are not so well hidden. They are either open about their delusional beliefs in a particular area, or they are more outspoken about their feeling that they are being interfered with, discriminated against, or persecuted. They may show outbursts of hostility toward others or make unfounded accusations against them, particularly if their beliefs are challenged. These outbursts cause people to avoid close contact with them, pushing them further into social isolation.

Some paranoids, a minority, are driven to even more aggressive action. They abandon the role of passive observer and begin to plan actively against their "enemies." This may include an attempt to escape by sudden flight, often with elaborate precautions to cover up their trail. Others, instead of fleeing, may attack to catch the "enemy" unaware and take revenge for what they have suffered or to forestall what they fear may happen.

Case Example. This case was adapted and revised from a lengthy presentation in Cameron (1959). Joe Dodge is an unmarried thirty-two-year-old man who was brought to the hospital by police after a suicide attempt. Although he gave the impression of being friendly, polite, and cooperative during their initial interview, it was also apparent that he was very frightened and that behind his friendly politeness, he was on his guard. Upon further questioning, he told this story, without any recognition of its delusional character. For several years he had been living alone in a cheap hotel on a modest but steady income from investments. Despite his youth and good health, he lived as if he were an elderly retired businessman. Occasionally he would look into new business prospects, but he never found anything that attracted him. He preferred to sit around the hotel lobby and think. When asked what he thought about, he would not say. He stated that he conversed with other men, played cards with them, read newspapers, and, following the custom of the hotel, placed a dozen small bets with bookies on racehorses each day.

His first acute paranoid attack came a day after he had been in a violent quarrel with his bookies over a bet. He had placed a number of bets, and one of his horses had come in first and paid good odds. He went for his money, only to be told that he had not bet on the winning horse in that race. He was enraged but did not say anything initially, and instead went to a nearby bar, where he had a few drinks. As he thought more about it, he realized that he had been deliberately cheated. His anger increased, and he returned to the bookies and demanded his payoff. When they refused to give it to him, he began to shout insults and threatened to call the police. They threw him out. For a while he paced up and down the sidewalk until he cooled off a little and returned to his hotel. Although still furious, he was able to sit down and think about the situation. It suddenly occurred to him that, since bookies were notorious for having gangster protection, he might be in danger because he had threatened them. The more he thought about it, the more endangered he felt. He fantasized about the gangsters who would come to kill him. The next morning, when he came down to the lobby, he noticed some rough-looking strangers hanging around. He thought they were watching him closely and waving signals to each other. At one time during the morning, when an automobile filled with men stopped in front of the hotel entrance, he became convinced that they were gangsters who had come to kidnap and kill him. Although this did not happen, his vigilance grew and with it so did the evidence that he was in deadly peril. He began to see strangers everywhere, all of whom seemed to be watching and shadowing him wherever he went and whatever he did. He felt there was no escape and was convinced that he was marked for execution. After several days, he retreated in near panic to his hotel room, where he barricaded himself against the coming attack. From his room, he telephoned a relative and told him the whole story. The relative, who was aware of Joe's intelligence and business skills, accepted everything that he said as truth and agreed that Joe must somehow escape. This relative, who

had unwittingly entered into Joe's delusional system, made a plan with him to leave secretly the next day.

During a sleepless night, in anticipation of his escape the next morning, Joe realized that the gangsters had probably tapped the telephone and heard the entire plan. In panic, he packed his bag, slipped out of the hotel, and drove off alone without daring to notify his relative who was coming to help him in the morning. In his automobile, he began to head west toward the home of another relative one thousand miles away. As he fled across the country, it became more obvious to him that escape was impossible. When he stopped for gas, casual comments by strangers helped him believe that he was caught in a great net that was slowly closing around him. In one city, he came out of a restaurant to find a policeman looking at his auto license plate. To Joe, this meant without question that the police were in league with the gangsters and keeping them informed of his movements. In another town, where he stopped to eat, the counterman eyed him as he worked. He immediately felt panic. As he became more certain that death was inevitable, he took precautions against having to live through the horrible torture that he anticipated they had in store for him. He stopped to purchase razor blades, which he hid in his suit, and to forge a prescription for a lethal dose of a sedative, which he carefully took out of the capsules and placed in a chewing-gum wrapper. At night, he avoided motels and slept in his locked automobile, hiding under his coat. Eventually he reached the home of his relative. However, by this time his anxiety and terror were overwhelming. Consequently, he wrote a suicide note, describing his terror. He then swallowed the sedative from the chewing-gum wrapper and lay down. Fortunately, the note was discovered in time and the police were called. They took him to the hospital, where his stomach was pumped. This acute paranoid reaction was the first that Joe had experienced. Unfortunately, it was not the last. His delusions persisted, and he eventually became a chronic paranoid schizophrenic.

HELPFUL HINTS TO LAW ENFORCEMENT OFFICERS

As indicated previously, basic distrust is the core characteristic of paranoid behavior. Recognition of this is critical to police officers who must respond to it. Because paranoid persons consider significant people in their lives to have been undependable or rejecting, they are apt to view any authority figure or representative of "the system," including officers, as undependable and hostile. Consequently, officers should expect that paranoid persons would be suspicious of anything they say and will regard officers with dislike and resentment when approached. This attitude and behavior can be characteristic not only of people with paranoid disorders, but also of people who feel isolated from the larger society (such as the homeless, minorities, immigrants, and so on). Three other groups of people may evidence paranoid behavior when approached by officers: people who are having a paranoid reaction to drugs, legal or illegal; people suffering from post-traumatic stress syndrome, such as combat veterans (described in Chapter 8); and people on certain drugs, such as cocaine, amphetamines, and in some cases marijuana and hashish (Dalby & Duncan, 1987), which can all produce symptoms of severe paranoia. How do officers approach paranoid people? How do they counter this basic distrust?

First, what paranoids need most is understanding and acceptance without condescension. Because they are hypervigilant, they are likely to be particularly sensitive to an attitude of disbelief. When they have delusions, they require someone who will listen with courtesy to their beliefs and make no judgment about whether they are true or false. Offer no argument to the paranoid; convey no impression that he or she is crazy. They require attention and acknowledgment (not of the content of their beliefs, but of their feelings). Usually the safest way to approach paranoid persons is by assuming a friendly but distant neutrality.

Second, officers must remember that paranoid people are usually extremely anxious.

Consequently, they must be approached in a way that does not heighten these anxieties further. If paranoids' anxiety increases, their vigilance also will increase, as will the possibility of a violent reaction.

Third, officers should be aware that because paranoids sometimes misinterpret reality, they may misinterpret officers' intentions. Officers should proceed slowly and with caution, constantly reassuring paranoid persons that they are there to assist and protect them.

In situations where officers have continuous contact with paranoid people, it is important to be alert to any changes in the people's thinking that indicates an increasing severity in their condition and a possible eruption of violence. Officers should look for focusing of delusional content. For example, if a paranoid who regularly makes complaints to the police begins to change her statements from vague "theys" to specific individuals or groups, this is a danger sign that she may feel forced to take action to protect herself. If it is necessary to take paranoids into custody, officers should not order them around. Officers must not frighten them with mace or other weapons, for paranoid persons may panic and react violently. However, while attempting to gain paranoid people's trust, officers must never let down their guard. They must remain alert while guarding against the communication of any hostility, fear, or suspiciousness. Paranoid individuals are very sensitive to others' feelings toward them. Officers must also remember that paranoids can be suicidal (Chapter 15) as well as homicidal (Chapters 10 and 14). In Chapter 10 we discussed in detail the characteristics of the homicidal paranoid schizophrenic.

In a study that investigated the arrest records of paranoid schizophrenic psychiatric patients who attempted to see the U.S. president or other highly visible political figures because of delusional beliefs, it was found that one in seven had been arrested for murder or aggravated assault during the nine to twelve years following their discharge from mental hospitals where they had been committed (Shore, Filson, & Johnson, 1988). The potential for homicidal violence is always present in paranoid individuals.

SUMMARY

In this chapter the author has reviewed several diagnostic classifications in which paranoid behavior is a core element. The chapter described the developing and ongoing process of paranoid behavior. The author has advised officers how paranoid people can best be approached. The next chapter will discuss violent behavior and how it can be handled by police officers.

BIBLIOGRAPHY

American Psychiatric Association. (2000). *Diagnostic and statistical manual of mental disorders*, 4th ed. revised. Washington, D.C.: American Psychiatric Association.

Aural root of paranoia. January, 1983. *Science Digest, 91*, 90.

Cameron, N. (1959). Paranoid conditions and paranoia. In *American handbook of psychiatry*, ed. S. Arieti, vol. 1, pp. 508–539. New York: Basic Books.

Dalby, J. T., & Duncan, B. J. (1987). Shared paranoid disorder preceded by cannabis abuse: Case report. *Canadian Journal of Psychiatry, 32*(1), 64–65.

Hesbert, W. 19 March, 1988. Paranoia: Fearful delusions (body and mind). *New York Times Magazine*, 62.

Kaffman, M. (1981). Paranoid disorders: The interpersonal perspective. *Journal of Family Therapy, 3*(1), 21–30.

_____. (1984). Paranoid disorder: The core truth behind the delusional system. Special Issue: Family psychiatry in the kibbutz. *International Journal of Family Therapy, 6*(40), 220–232.

Khouri, P. J. (1988). AIDS: The brain on fire: Cerebral manifestations of HIV infection. *Carrier Foundation Letter*, no. 130:1–2.

Menuck, M. (1983). Clinical aspects of dangerous behavior. *Journal of Psychiatry and Law, 11*(3), 277–304.

Munro, A. (1988). Delusional (paranoid) disorders. *Canadian Journal of Psychiatry, 33*(5), 399–404.

Shore, D., Filson, C. R., & Johnson, W. E. (1988). Violent crime arrests and paranoid schizophrenia: The White House case studies. *Schizophrenia Bulletin, 14*(2), 279–281.

Thompson-Pope, S. K., & Tvrkat, I. D. (1988). Reactions to ambiguous stimuli among paranoid personalities. *Journal of Psychopathology and Behavioral Assessment, 10*(1), 21–32.

Winokur, G. (1985). Familial psychopathology in delusional disorder. *Comprehensive Psychiatry, 26*(3), 241–248.

Chapter 14

VIOLENT BEHAVIOR

Because of the implied and actual danger of violent behavior, an understanding of its causes, characteristics, and management is extremely critical to law enforcement officers.

> E. I. Megargee (1969) wrote: No definition of violence has ever proved to be completely successful. Although everyone 'knows what violence is' no one has ever been able to define it adequately so that every possible instance of violent behavior is included within the definition while all the excluded behavior is clearly nonviolent."

S. A. Shah (1981) equates violence to dangerousness and defines it as a propensity (an increased probability as compared to others) to engage in dangerous behaviors. Dangerous behaviors are acts that are characterized by the application or overt threat of force and are likely to result in injury to other persons; they are considered synonymous with violent behaviors. (p. 152)

DEFINITIONS AND CONCEPTS

Webster's New World Dictionary defines violence as "the exertion of physical force so as to injure or abuse," or "intense, furious, often destructive action." This association of destructive action with the intent to abuse or injure the self or others implies that feelings of aggression or hostility are present at some level in connection with almost all violent acts. However, the reverse is not always true, since aggressive and hostile feelings are not necessarily accompanied by violent behavior. Later in this chapter we shall describe some critical factors that may contribute to the transformation of aggressive behavior into violent behavior. Violent behavior may be categorized into three broad areas: (1) *individual violent behavior*, in which psychological factors predominate; (2) *social violent behavior*, in which violence is a direct outgrowth of group behavior and the actions of the society itself;

and (3) *"mixed" violent behavior*, in which both individual psychological factors and group social factors operate.

Individual Violence

In individual violence, the violent behavior evolves principally from psychological forces within each person. Violent behavior is multidetermined; that is, each violent incident is caused by a combination of factors rather than any single factor operating in isolation. This violent behavior may be normal and socially approved or may be labeled as abnormal and socially condemned. There is a certain amount of violent behavior, or potential for it, present in all of us. However, as long as it is controlled or expressed in socially approved forms, the person does not get into trouble. For example, a boxer may inflict mayhem on his opponent and be rewarded by cheers and the victor's share of the purse; the matador will be applauded as he spears the bull; or the soldier is taught in basic training that the spirit of the bayonet is to kill. In each case, society approves and the person does not suffer a penalty. Other types of individual violent behavior are not approved by society and, in most instances, are labeled criminal. If perpetrators are discovered, they must answer to society through its courts and prison system. However, society may make exceptions. For example, if violent behavior is associated with mental illness, the person may be held responsible to a lesser degree or not at all.

Later in this chapter we will discuss attempts that have been made to predict the potential for individual violent behavior based on an understanding of some of those factors that may influence its presence. However, at this time we should point out other important aspects of individual violent behavior. For example, studies have indicated that the consumption of alcohol increases proneness to aggressive acts such as rape, homicide, and assault. According to M. Weissberg (1983), "alcohol 'heats up' the atmosphere and acts as a catalyst for all kinds of destructive activity" (p. 22). Alcohol also is involved in many domestic violence situations (Neidig & Friedman, 1984).

The correlation between self-destructive acts of violence, such as suicide (Chapter 15), and destructive acts against others is well recognized. Both authors have had many experiences with those who were depressed and wanted to kill themselves but did not have the guts to do it. Unable to carry out these wishes actively, they began to consider acts that might lead to their being killed, such as being shot while holding up a bank or killing someone, then confessing in order to be executed. Case histories of mass murderers such as Charles Whitman, Richard Speck, and Albert DeSalvo demonstrate the existence of suicidal ideation and/or suicide attempts prior to the occurrence of their infamous crimes.

Research has suggested that some people who are violent may have an associated brain disturbance and that this condition may be partially or wholly responsible for their behavior (Bell, 1982; Bell and Barth, 1983; Monroe, 1978; Reed, 1988; Spellacy, 1977). Epileptic patients sometimes show marked mental and emotional changes, especially those patients whose condition is poorly controlled by medication. Disorientation, hallucinations, excitement, incoherent speech, erratic behavior, and automatisms (complex acts, movements, lip smacking, chewing movements) may occur (Chusid, 1982). For many years, temporal lobe epilepsy was referred to as "murderer's epilepsy," possibly because it sometimes offered an impressive defense for persons accused of certain violent crimes. B. T. Reed (1988) has even urged that certain neuropsychological factors be kept in mind when dealing with hostage-takers or barricaded subjects.

Social Violence

Just as society allows some forms of individual violence such as boxing, so it does not necessarily disapprove of all social violence. For example, in sports it is difficult to think of a more violent group activity than hockey or lacrosse. Also, society may not necessarily disapprove of a riot or civil disturbance before it first has made the judgment about which side it ethically or morally supports. Further, a society may be divided in its approval or condemnation of some types of social violence. For instance, in contrast to the feelings of many others, a number of Irish-Americans agree with the goals of the Irish Republican Army (IRA) and have lent that organization both direct and indirect support.

Public support also may be a double-edged sword. While initially encouraging some to take more aggressive or violent steps, it also may determine the limits within which demonstrators must remain if they are not to completely alienate themselves from their initial societal support. Again, in the case of the

IRA, recent terrorist activities have led to the loss of support from many Irish-Americans who earlier approved of their goals. (Some destructive forms of social or collective violence will be considered in more detail in Chapters 16 and 17 when we talk about disasters and riots.)

Mixed Violence

Mixed violence is a category of violent or aggressive behavior in which both individual psychological factors and social factors play a role. Examples are prison riots, strikes, and civil disturbances by minority groups. In these situations, a particular population or subgroup, such as the inmates of a jail or prison, in combination with a social condition such as bad food, cramped quarters, or alleged discrimination, may lead to aggressive or violent behavior. However, every person who is a member of the subgroup may not become involved, since the person's psychological predisposition also will be a determining factor.

The Problem of Violence in Our Society

J. G. Stratton (1984) notes that violence has been a constant theme since the beginning of history. Perhaps the first reported act of violence occurred early in the Bible when Cain slew his brother, Abel. Throughout recorded history there are accounts of wars, slavery, and man's brutality toward his fellow man.

America began in violence. Many early settlers were criminal refugees from England and Europe. The colonies became independent through armed revolution, and the westward expansion was marked by war and violence.

To this day, the United States continues to embrace violence as a desirable approach in many situations. As Ramsey Clark, former attorney general for the United States, stated in an address to a symposia held at the Texas Research Institute of Mental Sciences:

America, an affluent society, is particularly afflicted by materialism. Success is money. . . . Poverty rations health, food, housing, family stability, personal safety, education, opportunity, comfort, justice itself. . . . Finally, America glorifies the power of violence and ignores its pity. Nonviolence is seen as cowardly. . . . We respect force, and it is very human to want respect. . . . Few Americans are strong enough to adhere to nonviolence under pressure. "Winning" is everything and force is the way. (Clark, 1981, p. 19)

"Violence is every bit a public health issue for me and my successors in this century as smallpox, tuberculosis, and syphilis were for my predecessors in the last two centuries." So said U.S. Surgeon General C. Everett Koop in an address to the American Academy of Pediatrics (Koop, 1982, p. 613). Public health professionals define an epidemic as a condition occurring at a rate exceeding its natural occurrence. Certainly homicide meets that qualification. "Homicide has doubled in this country and is now claiming more than 20,000 lives a year" (Meredith, 1984, pp. 43–48). Public health officials at the Federal Center for Disease Control have established a Violence Epidemiology Branch and anticipate that a public health approach to the problem of violence will yield more positive results than prior approaches. This approach looks at the occurrence and distribution of disease in a population over time. Disease is considered to be a function of the relationship among host, agent, and environment. Applied to homicide research, the host would be the murderer and the victim; the agent, the weapon used in the homicide; and the environment, all the circumstances surrounding the killing. Public health officials know they have a long way to go before being able to fill in all the specifics the epidemiological method requires, but they are optimistic that this approach will eventually yield valuable, practical information having a bearing on the problem. For example, an epidemiological study of killings in New York City reveals that a thirteen-year-old is one-seventh as likely to kill during a robbery as a fourteen-year-old (Meredith, 1984).

The homicide epidemic continues to increase in magnitude. An article in a recent edition of *Time* magazine states: "With a month left before year's end, all-time murder records have already been set in several cities, and the bloody pace shows no signs of slowing down. In New York City homicides are up 18 percent, in Houston 44 percent, and in the nation's capital an appalling 65 percent" (*Sudden Death* 1988, p. 22). New York City police attribute this tragic rise in killings to the spread of crack, the cheap, readily available derivative of cocaine. Police say that crack dealers and abusers seem comfortable with the use of deadly force and that the profit margin makes it worthwhile to kill. The deadly arsenal possessed by street gangs make drug wars more lethal. Rival dealers and witnesses are killed with little, if any, attempt to conceal the identity of the killers. The article concludes "overburdened police forces have had little success in breaking the power of the drug gang even when they adopted systematic buy-and-bust tactics or resorted to the dragnet-style crackdowns pioneered by the Los Angeles police."

Not only is the United States experiencing a homicide and crack epidemic, but according to a Department of Justice survey, the percentage of violent crime victims (rape, robbery, and assault) who were injured during an attack increased from 1982 to 1986. The percentage of victims who were injured during attack was 27.5 percent in 1973 and dropped to 26.9 percent in 1982 before climbing to 30.3 percent in 1986 (Harlow, 1989). The latest figures indicate that the number of violent crimes reported nationwide in 1988 increased 5.5 percent from 1987, to a new high of 1.5 million. Uniform Crime Reports for 1988 showed that homicides rose 2.9 percent to a total of 20,675. The previous high for violent crimes had been 1.48 million in 1987. Rapes increased 1.5 percent over 1987; robberies were up 4.9 percent and aggravated assaults up 6.4 percent (Violent

Crime Rose 5.5 Percent in '88, FBI Says, *Arizona Daily Star*, 7 August 1989).

Wolfgang's Subculture of Violence

In 1967, M. E. Wolfgang and F. Ferracuti first presented the concept of a subculture of violence. This referred to the existence, within our broader cultural context, of a set of values, attitudes, and beliefs that support the use of physical aggression as a worthwhile approach to solving personal and interpersonal problems.

> In this subculture, generated primarily in a lower socioeconomic class disadvantaged in all the traditionally known ways, the use of violence is either tolerated or permitted or specifically encouraged from infancy through adulthood. From child-rearing practices that commonly use physical punishment and that contain elements of abuse, to childhood and adolescent play, street gang and group behavior, domestic quarrels and barroom brawls, physically assaultive conduct is condoned and even an expected response to many interpersonal relationships. Machismo, but more than this, is involved in the value system that promotes the steady resort to violence upon the appearance of relatively weak provoking stimuli. The repertoire of response to frustration or to certain kinds of stimuli (including name-calling and challenges to the ego) is limited often to a physically aggressive one, and the capacity to withdraw or to articulate a verbal response is minimal. (Wolfgang, 1981, p. 97)

Wolfgang's subculture of violence may well be on its way to becoming the dominant characteristic of the main American culture. The recent Supreme Court decision allowing the imposition of the death penalty for murderers who committed their crimes as young as sixteen years of age and for mentally retarded killers lends substance to this hypothesis.

Social learning theory holds that aggressive or violent behavior is learned or acquired just as all other behavior is learned or acquired; by imitation and by direct experience. In learning by imitation, the major sources are familial influences, subcultural influences, and symbolic modeling. Simply stated, this means that aggressive children tend to come from families that display aggressive behavior and encourage aggression as a major problem solver. A subculture that encourages and offers live modeling of aggressive behavior promotes such aggressive behavior, as does symbolic modeling (that is, television, movies) in which words and pictures convey the aggressive message. The "direct experience" method of learning aggressive behavior involves concepts such as positive and negative reinforcement, punishment, aversive conditioning, and extinction. Social learning theory says that behaviors that are positively reinforced are likely to occur again; behaviors negatively reinforced are likely to disappear. Social learning teaches the child that aggression can satisfy a number of needs. As domestic violence specialist Dr. Peter Neidig (1989) remarked in a recent seminar on spouse abuse, "Violence Works!"

The Role of TV in Violent/Aggressive Behavior

In reviewing the impact of television on violence and violent behavior, a controversy has existed over the definition of violence on television. The definition most often cited is "the overt expression of physical force against others or self, or compelling action against one's will on pain of being hurt or killed, or actually hurting or killing" (Gerbner, 1972). Results of studies of the effect of television on violent behavior also have been quite controversial (Surgeon General's Committee, 1972; Andison, 1977; Belson, 1977; Kaplan & Singer, 1976; Milavsky, 1977; Rubenstein, et al. 1977). The intensity of the controversy is increased by recognition that television exerts a powerful influence on viewers' purchasing behaviors. A recent newspaper story stated that there has been a near sellout of TV prime time for the fall season. "Spurred by increased automobile advertising and renewed confidence in television's ability to sell, the networks

have sold more commercial time for next season than ever before" (*Arizona Daily Star* 26 July, 1989). If TV has such a powerful effect on people's product preferences, it seems logical to extend such an influence to other behaviors, including violent/aggressive behavior. Testifying before the House Committee on the Judiciary's Subcommittee on Economic and Commercial Law, Brian Wilcox of the American Psychological Association said: "One firmly established effect on viewing television violence, is its ability to shape attitudes and values. Children who watch repeated acts of violence on television become desensitized to the effects of violence when they witness it in the real world beyond television. They become less likely to empathize with or help victims of actual violence" (Landers, 1989, p. 34). Wilcox also stated that TV violence affects adults as well as children. "The value-shaping effect of televised violence is especially pervasive, and holds true for persons of all ages, not just children." Another by-product of viewing TV violence is "copycat violence" (Wilcox, 1989). Children learn specific ways to commit a violent act, and while most never act on this newly acquired information, some do. A case in point is taken from a recent news story headlined "Boy charged in slaying of cousin, 12" (the boy was fourteen). The shooting occurred after the two children finished watching a movie (*Biloxi Blues*) in which "an army drill instructor gets drunk and puts a .45 caliber gun to the head of a private and pulls the trigger. All you hear is a click," said police Sergeant Hallums (Duarte, 1989, p. 1A, 2A). Apparently there may have been "copycat violence" in this incident, with tragic results. Wilcox further testified that viewing violence on TV can remove or relax the normal inhibitions most children have that prevent aggressive behavior. The effect would be most pronounced on children who are already predisposed to violent behavior. Children (and adults) who watch a great deal of violence on TV become supersensitive to possible violence in their world and have an exaggerated fear of violence (Landers, 1989). Wilcox concludes that research linking TV violence with aggression has been "fairly well accepted."

J. G. Stratton (1984) discusses the effects of TV viewing upon the police image. Through highly dramatic presentations, the public gains the impression that "violence, shots fired and people getting killed are everyday events for almost every officer on patrol, despite the fact that about 50 percent of officers never fire their weapon on duty. Media presentations of police activity can even shape the police officer's self-image. He comes to feel that he should be as invincible or tough as any fictionalized TV or movie cop" (p. 9).

Violence and the Police

Domestic Violence

A result of a national survey on violence in American homes indicates that the incidence of husband beating is actually slightly higher than that of wife beating. Another study of couples surveyed one month prior to marriage revealed that 34 percent of the males and 40 percent of the females reported engaging in at least one episode of violence directed against their partner in the previous year.

Dr. Peter Neidig, who for years has run a very successful domestic violence containment program for the U.S. military, offers some interesting observations based on his work with military families (Neidig, 1988, 1989). In military families, Neidig found no difference in terms of overall frequency of violent acts by husbands and wives. He did, however, find significant differences in specific violent behaviors. Husbands admit to more pushing, grabbing, shoving, and more incidents of beating their spouse. Wives admit to more throwing of objects and threatening with and/or using a knife/gun on their mates. Injuries requiring medical attention are relatively rare in military families, but when they do occur they are much more likely to be sustained by the wife. When violence escalates

to homicide, wives are about as likely to kill their husbands, as husbands are to kill their wives. If untreated, domestic violence generally increases in frequency and severity. Violence begets violence. Individuals who themselves were victims of domestic violence in their upbringing tend to use violence in their own family setting. They may tend to see such treatment as normal and/or deserved. With repeated episodes, there is a tendency for violence to change from what can be described as "mutual combat" to violence in which the roles of perpetrator and victim become fixed. When roles become fixed, violence changes from "expressive" (violence as a result of frustration and anger, with no real intent to injure anyone, followed by remorse) to "instrumental" (where there is an intent to hurt someone and where expressions of remorse, if offered at all, are insincere and meaningless).

It is common to protect one's self-esteem by laying the blame (projecting) onto the spouse – "She made me do it," "He started it," "He/she deserved it," and so on. However, evidence indicates that both are involved in the escalation to violence. Violent couples learn to sense when tensions are nearing the breaking point and know which button to push to trigger the explosion. They may do this in order to get the violence over with or to feel that they are more in control as to when and how the violence starts. The question is often asked (especially by police and other emergency workers) "Why do they stay together?" or "Why doesn't she/he leave the abusive spouse?" Abusive couples often elect *not* to stay together. However, most abusive couples say they would rather stay in the relationship and end the violence than terminate the relationship.

Domestic violence is usually intermittent in nature. Even the most violent relationships are not violent all the time, and there may be many positive qualities in the relationship. Added to this is the fact that a violent episode is usually followed by remorse and sincere apologies, with promises to change. This lends hope to the wish (of both) that this will be the last violent episode. Shelters for women serve a useful purpose in providing an emergency refuge when needed, by heightening a community's awareness of domestic violence, by providing a woman with other options, and by providing a means for a permanent break in the relationship if that is desired. Nonetheless, violence is an interpersonal pattern that couples can control once they learn to detect certain cues and acquire the necessary skills. In a later chapter on stress, we will discuss in greater detail the problem of domestic violence in police families, a problem, like alcohol, that is well hidden from public and even from police view (Neidig & Friedman, 1984).

A Police Foundation study of family homicides and aggravated assaults in Kansas City, Missouri, indicates that there are some warning signs of which police should be aware.

> In one-fourth of the homicides and one-third of the aggravated assault cases, either the victim or the suspect had an arrest for a disturbance or an assault within two years previous to the homicide or assault in question. Even more striking is the fact that about 90 percent of the homicide victims and suspects had previous disturbance calls to their address, with about 50 percent of them having five or more calls. The same was true for assault victims and suspects. (Wolfgang, 1981, p. 109)

Frequent calls to the same address involving the same subjects should be red-tagged for possible homicidal violence. The best predictors of future domestic killings are the presence of a gun, a history of previous calls (especially if violence seems to be increasing with each disturbance), and alcohol use (Wolfgang, 1981).

Front-Page Violence – Sudden Murder

At approximately 4 P.M. July 18, 1984, in Ysidro, California, James O. Huberty, a forty-one-year-old white male, dressed himself in a dark shirt and camouflage trousers, took his weapons – a 9-mm Browning automatic pistol, a 12-gauge pump shotgun, and a 9-mm

Uzi semiautomatic rifle – and told his wife that he was "going hunting – hunting for humans" (Sudden Death, 1984). He proceeded approximately 200 yards from his apartment to a nearby McDonald's, where he opened fire, killing twenty-one people and wounding nineteen – the largest mass murder in U.S. history up to that time. Huberty had no history of violence, although he did have a history of not relating well to other people. He was described as a loner who was always angry, who did not communicate with others (his bumper sticker read "I'm not deaf, I'm just ignoring you"), and who carried a grudge. His neighbors said he was a "sour man" who regularly exploded in towering rages against his wife and their two daughters (ages fourteen and ten). Surprisingly, he had a degree in sociology from a small college in Ohio. He had become a mortician's assistant, where he was described as good at embalming but not good at relating to the living ("When Rage Turns Into Mass Murder" 30 July 1984). He then became a welder for thirteen years but was laid off. He moved to California in order to get a fresh start, obtained a job as a security guard, but was fired two weeks before the shooting.

His wife said he had threatened suicide in Ohio by putting a gun to his head, but she had talked him out of it. She had continued urging him to seek professional help, and on the day before the shooting, she said he had made a telephone call to a local mental health center. Apparently the center was busy and promised to return his call. They never did (the center denies a record of the call). On the morning of the shooting, when he was at the San Diego Zoo with his wife and children, he told her "society had its chance," apparently referring to the unreturned call ("Murder at McDonald's" 30 July, 1984).

The Overcontrolled Personality

Fred Cowan was described by his sister-in-law as "a very gentle man who loved children." His parochial-school principal remembered him fondly as a boy with an "extremely exemplary character." He received A's in courtesy, cooperation, religion, and attendance. "There was nothing to indicate that he was anything but a very fine young man." However, Fred Cowan was a loser, without special friends.

A coworker at the New Rochelle, New York, moving company where Cowan was employed agreed with all the "good boy" comments. "Basically he was a nice, quiet guy who seldom, if ever, talked. He was someone you could push around." But Fred Cowan, a hulking man, six feet tall, weighing 250 pounds, would not be pushed around forever. Two weeks after he was suspended from his job as a furniture mover for refusing to move a refrigerator, he returned to the company office, vowing to get even with the supervisor who had disciplined him. Failing to find the man, he killed four coworkers and a policeman before taking his own life (Lee, Zimbardo, & Bertholf, 1977). Lee and his colleagues observed:

> What terrifies us most about such brutal incidents is their unpredictability and senselessness. How can you defend yourself against aggression that is masked by passivity, against crimes of violence by fine young men of exemplary character? And their lethal reaction is usually inappropriate to whatever instigated it. The crime exceeds the cause: a person is battered to death for taking another driver's intended parking space; an employer is murdered for refusing to give an undeserved promotion; a man is killed for unknowingly taking someone else's seat at the bar. (p. 69)

Lee categorizes such sudden, explosive, no-prior-history killers as "shy murderers" and describes their evolution from "overcontrolled" to "undercontrolled" personalities (Megargee, 1966). According to Lee, "shy" people treated at the Shyness Clinic at Stanford University demonstrated the following characteristics. They were so fearful of the ridicule and rejection they see lurking in the most casual contacts with people that they tried to avoid or escape all potentially threatening interactions. "When they have to interact with others, it is often a perfunctory, ritualized simulation of a human relationship" (Lee, Zimbardo, & Bertholf, 1977). They present a façade of coolness and detachment that serves to protect them from any real closeness with others. Some complain of being "bored" by loud-mouthed characters who know nothing but who get all the attention and social rewards.

> With some therapeutic probing, the anger beneath the boredom begins to emerge. Put upon by these bigmouths, forced to comply with the wishes of domineering people, with the endless dos and don'ts of parents and teachers, extremely shy individuals take the path of least resistance . . . they give in, give out, give up, and do what is expected of them – albeit reluctantly. . . .

> On occasion, the shy person does confront others, but . . . unable to negotiate in a dispute or pose a plan for conciliation, he is powerless to effect a peaceful, mutually acceptable solution. Instead he yields, a cycle that occurs again and again. Resentment builds but is held in check by powerful restraints that deny expression of virtually all strong emotions. Then one day, the rage and resentment become too strong; a minor provocation pushes the pent-up hostility over the threshold, and the impulse is carried into action. (Lee, Zimbardo, & Bertholf, 1977)

There are four common features in an overcontrolled personality: (1) overwhelming emotional tension, (2) inability to perceive any alternative to violence, (3) time distortion, and (4) dissociation of self from the person taking the deadly action. The scene starts as follows. The shy, overcontrolled person faces a situation in which he is frustrated and belittled in a way that has happened many times before. The instigation to anger may be mild: a minor right is violated, an insignificant privilege denied. He feels the usual anguish welling up, but for some reason he does not walk away from the situation as he usually does or accept it without protest. Feelings of anguish and anger keep growing and growing until they overwhelm him. The emotional tension makes it hard for the man to breathe or even to talk; his chest and throat are constricted. This inner turmoil is reflected in his perception of the outside world: everyone seems to be moving faster and faster, while for him time slows down. He sees his movements as languid, his thinking as sluggish. The past and future become vague concepts, irrelevant to the focused present. He feels caught up in events that carry him along without conscious volition. The thought surfaces, "There is no way out." It quickly changes to "There is no other way out." A sense of detachment develops that separates the man's observing self from the emotions, thoughts, behavior, and sense of responsibility of his acting self. He attacks, and the observer is helpless to stop the murder. Though triggered by minor irritation or frustration, the attack has been fueled by a lifetime of all too many major ones. Innocent victims die not so much for what they did, but for what society did not do: respect the dignity of this individual and reach out to encourage him to make a human connection, despite his withdrawn manner.

In many cases, the frenzied assault is terminated only when the murderer "notices" his arm is so tired – from repeatedly firing the gun or stabbing his victim – that he can't move it. In some instances there is a blackout, amnesia for some or all of the events. Just as those who know the sudden murderer cannot believe he could have been responsible for such violence, the ego of the sudden murderer cannot accept the alien deed as being of its own doing. With the violence discharged, calm returns. Internalized inhibitions take command again. In a matter of minutes, the overcontrolled, feminine, shy man once again becomes his good old self (Lee, Zimbardo, & Bertholf, 1977).

The Undercontrolled Personality

The *nonshy* murderers typically report a "much simpler, very different scenario." They

feel cheated or betrayed; they are not getting their fair share. The emotion is strongly felt but is not overwhelming. It is quite consciously experienced as being caused by a particular person or a specific group. There is no time distortion, but since these murderers usually have a poorly developed sense of the future, they don't think about possible punishment. The murder may be planned, or it may happen suddenly when push comes to shove. Resentment builds but is held in check. Then one day a minor provocation pushes it over the threshold. Impulse turns into action.

These murderers do not consider that there may be a reasonable explanation for the behavior of their intended victims or that there may be another means of remedying their grievances. But they have no feeling of inevitability, of being swept away involuntarily. In fact, in some cases the murderer takes pride in the deed; he is acting like a strong person and not a sissy (Lee, Zimbardo, & Bertholf, 1977).

Front-Page Violence – Celebrity Murder

Case Example. "On the afternoon of March 30, 1981, John Hinckley, Jr., proved to America that security measures are rarely impregnable. As President Reagan left the Washington Hilton, waving to onlookers and members of the press corps, Hinckley fired six bullets with a .22 caliber 'Saturday Night Special' revolver that he had purchased at a Dallas pawn shop. The president, his press secretary James Brady, a Secret Service agent, and a Washington, D.C. policeman sustained serious injuries" (*Behavioral Medicine*, May 1981). Hinckley had become obsessed with the movie star Jodie Foster. In one of his letters to the actress, he reportedly said, "In order for me to prove myself worthy of your love, I have to do something spectacular." "You'll be proud of me, Jodie. Millions of Americans will know me – us" (*People* July, 1989).

Case Example. "Rebecca Schaeffer was living every young actress's dream – until, police say, a deluded fan with a gun took it all away" (*People* July, 1989). Schaeffer, twenty-one, was the co-star of the television series *My Sister Sam*. On Tuesday, July 18, 1989, Schaeffer was shot once in the chest when she answered the door of her Los Angeles apartment. She was pronounced dead on arrival at a hospital. The next day Tucson, Arizona police received a report of a possible 96 (mental case) who was behaving dangerously and bizarrely on a freeway. They found Robert John Bardo running on the freeway, screaming that he had killed the actress. L.A. police stated that they had been informed that Bardo was obsessed with Schaeffer and had written love letters to her and threatened to hurt her. Tucson PD faxed Bardo's picture to the LAPD. Schaeffer's neighbors identified him as the man who had been hanging around her apartment the morning of the murder.

Violence against celebrities has reportedly been on the rise and has become a topic of increasing concern. Dr. Jack Pott, assistant director of psychiatric services in Maricopa County, Arizona, believes that the increase in celebrity attacks stems from "an increasingly narcissistic society or maybe the fantasy life we see on television" (*Arizona Daily Star* 21 July, 1989). Dr. Barry Morenz, professor of psychiatry at the University of Arizona College of Medicine, states: "These people become obsessed with someone, usually famous, and they believe they will eventually have a love relationship. . . . Such people create an identity for themselves that is based solely on the fame of the person they are pursuing. . . . They borrow from the famous person's identity because they have none of their own." Dr. Lawrence Cronin of Palo Verde Hospital, Tucson, adds: "The fact that love has been unrequited is almost irrelevant. People invent ingenious confabulations about why the person isn't making more direct contact ("$1 Million Bond Set for Suspect," *Arizona Daily Star* 21 July, 1989, p. 2A).

It seems obvious that association with celebrities can lead to a certain amount of

fame – a "basking in their light." This association may be a fact or it may be pure fantasy. With some individuals who have no identity of their own and no positive self-image, fantasy can replace fact. We all have heard "If you really want something and you wish hard enough, it will come true." Most of us are aware of the realistic limitations that govern wishing, but the people who become obsessed with a celebrity really begin to believe that their fantasies about the object of their obsessions are real. They construct a pseudoreality for themselves and the celebrity as they wish reality to be. That the celebrity does not share this "reality" they have constructed is, Dr. Cronin remarks, quite immaterial. Their actions are governed by their pseudoworld, not the real world that the celebrity inhabits. For example, John Hinckley wrote to his fantasy figure, Jodie Foster, "You didn't wear your plaid skirt today. You have no right to disrupt our relationship in such a manner" (*People* July, 1989).

Another factor that may be of some importance in understanding those individuals who attack or murder celebrities is the fact that no one likes to be a nobody. Sirhan Sirhan is reported to have told a psychiatrist that in the few seconds it had taken him to pull the trigger, he had achieved the fame of Robert Kennedy. From that moment on, no one could think of Kennedy without thinking of the man who killed him. In the eyes of such people, it is perhaps better to be wanted by the police than not to be wanted at all.

In considering the reasons for such violence against celebrities, psychologist Marilyn Marx has commented: "The cult of celebrity provides archetypes and icons with which alienated souls can identify. On top of that, this country has been embarking for a long time on a field experiment in the use of violence on TV. It is commonplace to watch people getting blown away. We've given the losers in life and sex a rare chance to express their dominance" (*People* July, 1989).

Juvenile Violence

"Violence among children, adolescents, and young adults has been steadily and rapidly increasing, and increasing more significantly than in any other age grouping, thus contributing to the overall increase of crimes of violence in society" (Wolfgang, 1981). If this was true in 1981, it became even truer in the final years of the 1980s. Gang wars in the cities, drive-by shootings, and "wildings" (juveniles looking for violence) have become major, seemingly unsolvable problems.

José Sanchez (1986) notes that the "baby boom" of the 1960s made America a young society. This demographic overload led to a breakdown in the traditional channels of socialization as the divorce rate increased. The young turned to each other for guidance. Since much of this youth culture also had access to a large proportion of what economists call "discretionary income," they became an important market. This tremendous market potential was targeted by advertisers – increasing juveniles' wants, raising their aspirations, and creating an atmosphere of frustrating, individual comparison among lower-class youths.

According to Silberman (1980), "increased wants" combined with lack of adult controls led to the creation of a "lethal criminogenic force," especially among those youths who did not possess the buying power of more affluent youths. Many turned to crime (especially robbery and drug dealing) as an easy way to obtain money. In fact, drug dealing has become so widespread and easy that police routinely find hundreds, even thousands of dollars on the children and adolescents they arrest.

The most ominous aspect of the violent youths of the 1980s is their lack of affect. In the past, juveniles who "exploded in violence tended to feel considerable guilt or remorse afterward. However, the new criminals have been so brutalized in their own upbringing that they seem incapable of viewing their victims as human beings or in realizing they have killed another person. Increasingly, psychiatric reports on juveniles arrested for murder are filled with phrases such as 'shows no feeling,' 'shows no remorse,' 'demonstrates no relationship'" (Silberman, 1980, p. 83). For example, in the spring of 1989, the nation was horrified by the gang rape of a young female stockbroker who was assaulted in New York City's Central Park by a juvenile gang out on a "wilding." She was severely beaten, raped, and left for dead. When arrested, the youths were said to have been unremorseful. Some even "giggled" when telling how they set upon her and left her to die.

Recently the term *unattached children* has emerged to describe children who are "pawns of circumstance, their disorder the result of any number of factors – abuse, divorce, a parent's death or absence, their own premature birth or early illness, inadequate day care – that may have separated them in infancy from the precious bonding and nurturing that is essential to normal development" (Fichtner, 1989, p. 4B). Dr. Terry Levy of the Miami Psychotherapy Institute says: "The term 'unattached' is somewhat new. The theories on bonding are age-old. We've known about the bonding issues for a long time, but it's only recently that we're starting to appreciate what it's doing to our society" (Fichtner, 1989, p. 6B). This "lack of bonding" theme seems to run consistently through all discussions of troubled children, juveniles, and adults. As Hartog states, "The weak links in our society – those individuals who have an underlying rage and are *disconnected emotionally* from others – are fed by the general violence which now concerns our society. If such people are surrounded, inundated by destructive and violent behavior, then such models only serve as stimuli for acting out inner turmoils" (*Behavioral Medicine* 1981, p. 35).

Hate Crimes against Lesbians and Gay Men

"*Hate crimes* are words or actions intended to harm or intimidate an individual because of her or his membership in a minority group; they include violent assaults, murder, rape, and property crimes motivated by prejudice, as well as threats of violence or other acts of intimidation" (Finn & McNeil, 1987). "Hate crimes, which are also called *bias crimes*, are especially serious because they potentially victimize an entire class of people. Based on an individual's minority status, they assail the victim's identity and intimidate other group members" (Herek, 1989, p. 940). The frequency of hate crimes against lesbians and gays has increased in the last few years. Recent surveys indicate that as many as 92 percent of lesbians and gays have been the target of verbal abuse and/or threats. Many such incidents go unreported for a variety of reasons. Homosexuals always have experienced discrimination and hate crimes because of their sexual orientation and life-style, but now a new element is involved: the fear of AIDS. This fear is also present in many police, paramedics, and other emergency workers. Officers should be aware of their own feelings about such hate crimes and should keep up to date on current first aid procedures when dealing with AIDS victims. Officers should remember that all citizens are entitled to police protection and assistance.

Violence in Health Care Facilities

"Hospitals and other health care facilities are not immune from the violence that has become part of our everyday lives. Shootings, assaults, and robberies are becoming facts of daily life in hospital environments" (Turner, 1986). In 1982, a patient held his family members and a nurse hostage in a Maryland hospital. In 1984, a man with a rifle entered a Wyoming hospital through the emergency room and demanded to see his ex-wife (who was not there). That same year a man held the people in a hospital cafeteria hostage. He wanted to know the medical condition of his son. In 1987 a patient intent on suicide barricaded himself inside a Tucson psychiatric hospital and made a nurse furnish him with

drugs. He planned to get high then kill himself but was persuaded to surrender by a police negotiator.

Hospital personnel are sometimes told not to document such incidents for fear of lawsuits, staff confrontations, and negative publicity. Turner (1986) states that hospital staff members are under a great deal of pressure because of patient demands and unrealistic demands from the administration at the same time they are concerned about layoffs due to shortened hospital stays. An increase in anger and tension among hospital staff occurs and may be displaced onto patients and/or other staff members.

Protection from violence in the workplace can become an issue worthy of strike action, work slowdowns, or stoppages. Again, the finger of blame is pointed at our violent society, which seems to accept and even encourage this method of coping.

> Violent and aggressive behavior is becoming a primary and, frighteningly, an acceptable form of communication in society. The public seems to accept this mode of action when other more socially accepted methods do not seem to be working or are working too slowly. In the larger society, health care is seen as something everyone is entitled to, and the legitimacy of aggressive behavior to gain what you need is growing. Among the factors responsible for this acceptance of violence is the violent content of films and television. (Turner, 1986)

Violent episodes occurring in medical settings present special problems to responding police. Most hospital personnel have had little if any training in handling such behavior; the fact that they are physicians, nurses, psychologists, or other kinds of professional workers does not make them immune to the stress of the violence (especially if it is a hostage situation), nor does it endow them with any special expertise in dealing with such "nonscheduled" violence. The police may find such an environment extremely difficult to work in, especially if the medical staff tries to assume some responsibility for handling the problem. Police also have to be aware of the possible negative publicity they may receive if patients are killed or injured, regardless of whose fault it is. One proactive measure that police might consider is to offer the services of a police negotiator to acquaint the hospital with police procedures during a barricaded subject or hostage situation. Police also may meet with administrative and/or security staff to set up standard operating procedures (SOPS), to be employed in other incidents of violence. This would include a number(s) that hospital personnel may call for police help, especially if that help must be summoned without the usual lights and sirens of an emergency response.

Violence Against Police Officers

Assaults on police officers have increased dramatically in the 1980s. FBI statistics indicate that over 60,000 police officers were victims of assault in 1984. In a recent issue of *Police Stress* (1989), the names of 159 officers killed in the line of duty in 1988 were listed. In a unique study of violence against police, Toch (1977) conceptualized violent behavior as a "clue, a symptom, a calling card which, if properly read, could expose the central motives and concerns of violent men." Contrary to the popular belief that most violent behavior is senseless, Toch found that it is usually purposive and that its occurrence often indicates hidden meanings. Toch's subjects were thirty-two Oakland Police Department officers who had been assaulted at least once; nineteen men who had assaulted police officers (in many instances the officers they assaulted were part of the officer study group); forty-four inmates in the California Medical Facility at Vacaville; twenty-nine prisoners at San Quentin; and thirty-three parolees with violent behavior records. To test the validity of their findings, researchers also secured permission to analyze 344 incidents of assaultive behavior on San Francisco police officers.

From their data, Toch and his colleagues identified the following motives for assaults on police. The two motives most frequently encountered were reactions against perceived tampering with the person by the officer, either verbally or physically, and the desire to rescue or defend a person who is receiving an officer's attention. In over half the sample, the sequence of events leading to the assault on an officer starts with a person's negative reaction to an officer's verbal approach. Typically the officer approaches a civilian with a request, a question, or an order. No serious crime has been committed, and the contact could be considered as preventive police work or coping with a nuisance. Violence may occur immediately, but most often does not happen until after the civilian has first expressed displeasure at the officer's words. Then after the officer has made additional moves, the civilian attacks.

Binder and Scharf (1980) have elucidated the process that often leads to violent police-citizen encounters by delineating four phases. The first is the phase of *anticipation*, in which police officers react emotionally and intellectually on the basis of a dispatch by radio, direct observation, or information from another person who requests assistance. The response to a radio call stating that a child is having difficulty retrieving a cat from the top of a telephone pole would be expected to be different from the initial reaction to a call asking police officers to go to a location where there is alleged to be an insane, violent man with a knife. In addition to the content of the initial information received, the manner in which it is communicated can also affect the emotional and intellectual response of officers and their preliminary consideration of alternative actions.

After the anticipation phase, officers enter the *entry* phase. When officers arrive at the scene of the encounter, they must immediately determine the extent of any danger, establish their authority, clarify their expectation for the citizen, and gather information to supplement their general knowledge and the clues they received by radio or from an initiating person. The potential for physical force may increase or decrease according to decisions officers make early in the encounter.

Following the entry phase there is the *information exchange* phase, which may range from a few seconds, in which officers may shout "Police. Don't move," to a longer period. Clearly, the longer the period, the less likelihood the incident will lead to a violent police-citizen encounter. At the end comes the *final decision* phase.

Case Example. Two detectives from burglary were patrolling late one night in an unmarked car when they encountered, in an isolated, poorly lighted shopping center, one white male, about forty years old, standing beside a phone booth (darkened) and a white-paneled pickup truck (anticipation phase). Since the shopping center had recently been hit by a number of burglaries, the detectives left their car, showed their badges, and asked the man for identification (entry phase). He refused to give any identification, stating that "anyone could buy a badge in a dime store, anyone could carry a gun, and besides, people other than policemen have police radios in their car" (information exchange phase).

Even at this early point, this situation had the potential to escalate into violence. However, the next action of the officers successfully defused the situation. Rather than engaging in further confrontations, they chose another approach. They asked him if he would show identification to a marked patrol unit. He replied that he would (final decision phase). Within five minutes a marked unit arrived, identification was made, and the citizen, who turned out to be a reputable telephone company employee, wrote a letter to the police department, complimenting the detectives for treating him "like a man" rather than trying to "strong-arm" him. In contrast to this situation, Toch discovered others in which the phases are collapsed through "one step games" and police officers have little chance of avoiding violence. In these cases, the suspect has often been drinking, and the

mere approach of an officer is sufficient to trigger violence. Assaults on police officers are associated with high alcoholic intake. Toch also reports another group of sequences that frequently lead to assaults. In these situations, violence exists prior to officers' arrival. Family disturbances are typical examples. The officers' intervention is seen as a source of annoyance or frustration, a possible ally of the opposition, an intrusion, or simply a new problem to be dealt with. Violence, a coping device for frustration, is already in force when officers arrive, and simply continues, with the additional participants — the officers — being assigned one of the above roles.

A study by Horstman (1973) points out how the personality and the actions of officers often contribute to assault. He describes situations in which an officer's overbearing attitude apparently goaded a suspect into attacking him or her. Although unable to identify a single precipitating event for the onset of violent behavior, Horstman did describe a "process of escalation, building on each experience between officer and suspect until the 'hair trigger' is honed and pulled to the execution of a critical event such as grabbing a suspect's arm to consummate an arrest."

Other dangerous situations with a high degree of associated violent behavior include the arrest of someone in a group and while conducting a search. The humiliation of these acts, particularly when they take place in front of friends, may lead a violence-prone person to strike out in frustration. If possible, officers should get suspects out of sight of friends and onlookers before patting them down. Due to potential dangers associated with the arrest procedure, officers should keep in mind several attitudes and types of behavior when making an arrest. Officers should indirectly guide the arrested person into the wagon or car by "talking them in" rather than grabbing their arm and escorting them. They should carry this out with a calm voice and manner. Once a person's last name is known, it should be used together with his or her correct title.

Using other forms of address, such as first or last names only or nicknames, should be avoided unless suspects are personally known to officers and willingly accept this. Officers should be careful not to convey dislike for those they are arresting and should not treat the situation as a personal matter. When they encounter suspects who refuse to comply with directions, officers should clearly indicate that they are acting only as required by law. They might further mention that resistance to arrest only makes the situation more difficult and may result in additional charges. Finally, they may point out that the question of guilt or innocence is up to the court.

In arresting intoxicated persons, it is important to remember that they may not fully comprehend the situation. Influenced by alcohol and in an unclear state of mind, they are more likely to resist arrest. Therefore, it becomes even more important for officers to avoid provocative and antagonizing comments and actions. When officers confront extremely excited persons, they should realize that many people need an opportunity to yell, scream, or threaten for a period of time before quieting down. Officers who employ discretionary patience will find that persons will often rapidly calm down without the risk of physical injury to self or the officer.

Horstman (1973) describes an interesting complication of the old Mutt and Jeff routine. In this situation, one cop plays Mr. Good Guy and the partner plays Mr. Bastard. The bad cop gives the suspect a rough time and is then interrupted by the good cop, who openly disagrees with the techniques and philosophy of the partner and attempts to convince the subject that the good cop will protect and help him or her if only the suspect will trust the good cop and tell the truth. In assault cases, Horstman found a high incidence of Mutt and Jeff routines in which the bad cop carried his actions too far and violence resulted. Supervisors should watch out for this situation so that those who need additional training in how to handle people can acquire it.

Police Violence Against Citizens

Nielsen (1988) calls attention to a pressing issue facing police administrators: the problem officer. Problem officers can be categorized into two types. The first are the "drone" officers, who do just enough to get by. (We will discuss these officers in a later chapter.) The second type are the officers who overreact, either with their mouths or with their fists, baton, Kel light, etc.

According to Schmidt (1984), approximately 27 percent of all civil suits filed in a five-year period against police officers and police agencies alleged excessive use of force; 6 percent claimed misuse of firearms. "Alleged police misconduct suits now exceed 6000 per year. The typical suit consumes 111 hours of defense time plus another 97 hours of investigative time . . . [police] administrators become personally vulnerable when officers lose control and act impulsively" (Nielsen, 1988). Among the various liability theories used in the past to bring police agencies and administrators into civil court are negligent appointment, negligent retention, and negligent entrustment. Now two new theories are being employed: failure to supervise properly and failure to train. Failure to train is being used increasingly in firearms cases and in the use of other types of force (Nielson, 1988).

Certain officers have a knack for turning a routine nonviolent situation into a battle royal. Readers familiar with the fictional L.A. cop Roscoe Rules in Joseph Wambaugh's *Choirboys* (1975) will remember how Roscoe turned a neighborhood disturbance that was already beginning to fade away into a violent confrontation that ended with two policemen injured and four citizens going to jail.

Nielsen and his associates have developed a program of anger management, which is designed to address the problem of the overreacting cop. This program emphasizes self-awareness of officers' own feelings of hostility and anger while increasing their competency in managing the hostility and aggression of others they may encounter in patrol activities. Nielsen states that this program has been in use in the Salt Lake City Police Department for some time and has gained the acceptance of line officers. It is also useful in mitigating the administration's liability in cases of negligent training and failure to supervise (Nielsen, 1988).

The Prediction of Dangerousness

"Acts that threaten and actually inflict serious harm on the lives and physical welfare of other members of the community have been of long-standing concern to all societies" (Shah, 1981). This is particularly true of the criminal justice and mental health systems. An individual's propensity to engage in dangerous behavior is of special concern at many decision points in both systems. Shah (1981) lists sixteen such decision points, including such decisions as granting bail or releasing on personal recognizance, trying juveniles accused of serious crimes in adult court, releasing prisoners on parole, removing a child from the home, committing a mentally ill person for involuntary treatment, and so on.

Psychologists and psychiatrists are frequently asked to testify as to whether an individual is potentially dangerous. The difficulty is that such a question usually cannot be answered by a flat yes or no. Too many complex factors are involved. Studies have shown that mental health professionals display poor predictive ability and that they tend to markedly over predict dangerousness (Monahan 1978; Steadman & Cocozza, 1974). This is not to say that the accurate prediction of dangerousness is impossible under all circumstances or that psychiatrists and psychologists' will always over predict its occurrence (Monahan, 1978).

Shah (1981) admits that the prediction of dangerousness results in high rates of false positives when the group for which the dangerousness is predicted has a low occurrence base rate (that is, as with the mentally ill). However, when dealing with groups that have much higher rates for dangerous behavior (repeat criminal offenders with three or more previous convictions for violent crimes), the predictive task is easier. A research project called PROMIS (Prosecutor's Management Information System) studied all District of Columbia arrests for nonfederal crimes between January 1, 1971, and August 31, 1975. The study involved 72,610 arrests and 45,575 defendants and provided data concerning the frequency with which individuals were rearrested, reprosecuted, and reconvicted during that fifty-six-month period. The study found that persons who were repeatedly arrested, prosecuted, and convicted accounted for a disproportionately large share of street crime. For example, persons who had been arrested four or more times in the period studied represented only seven percent of the arrestees but they accounted for fully 24 percent of all arrests. Thus the extensiveness of criminal history (regardless of whether it is expressed in terms of arrests, prosecutions, or convictions) seems to be a good predictor of future criminality (Shah, 1981). With this type of empirical data about career criminals, especially considering the size of the sample (45,575 defendants), Shah (1981) asks if it is really accurate to say that dangerousness cannot be predicted. "Although there will certainly be public policy and moral dilemmas pertaining to the actual use of such predictive judgments, the technical predictive task is not as difficult for groups who have high base rates for serious and violent criminal behavior." Fortunately, police officers (and police agencies) do not have to assume responsibility for predicting dangerousness – just the responsibility of handling and containing it whenever and wherever it occurs.

Hotline for Violent Men

In the 1980s, the FBI National Center for the Analysis of Violent Crimes joined Dr. Ann Burgess and her team from the University of Pennsylvania's School of Nursing in a research project designed to learn more about serial rapists. Forty-one incarcerated rapists were interviewed. These men were responsible for 837 rapes and more than 400 attempted rapes. During one interview, a subject was asked what, if anything, the criminal justice system could have done to cause him to turn himself in. He surprised the interviewer by saying "Have you thought of a hotline? You've got hotlines for runaways, drug abusers, rape victims, and suicidal individuals. Why not one for people who have committed or are contemplating committing deviant criminal sexual acts? You know, I didn't just start raping. I have had sexual fantasies about kidnapping a woman and making her my slave since I was a teenager. I knew it wasn't normal at the time, but who could I talk to about it? Not my parents or friends, or anyone else. They would have thought I was crazy or sick" (Hazelwood & Burgess, 1988). From that point on, all rapists interviewed were asked about a hotline for offenders, and many reacted quite favorably to the idea.

It is interesting to note that there now is a group called MEN, an acronym for Men Evolving Nonviolently. MEN is described as a companion group to others such as the Oakland Men's Project and the Los Angeles group, Men Against Rape. Two of MEN's members say that violence is a cry for help from a segment of our society that is sick. The group is directed mainly toward men involved in family violence, but apparently does not exclude men whose violence lies in other areas.

The Future of Violence

Many people cope with stress in maladaptive and dangerous ways. . . . Alcoholism, child abuse, incest, spousal violence, and suicide are prime examples of maladaptive responses to stress. Why people resort to maladaptive responses under stress is a highly complex and personal issue. However, it is safe to say that the ability to adapt to stress is associated with childhood experiences, the development of a sense of security and self-esteem and the availability of empathic parental figures in early life. (Weissberg, 1983)

Ramsey Clark (1981) has said that healthy children raised in decent conditions among loving people in a gentle and just society where freedom and equality are valued will rarely commit violent acts toward others. The capacity for interpersonal violence will increase as a society varies from these. (p. 2)

Many years ago, in the 1950s, the senior author recalls Dr. Gerald Caplan saying that America is most wasteful of its major resource: its children. America has not gone forward in the succeeding years and appears to have gone backward. One need only look at the latchkey kids, poor (and unequal) schools, cuts in social and human welfare programs, the lack of adequate day care facilities to at least partially meet the needs of families where both parents must work, the less-than-minimum wage often paid to young workers, the crack and alcohol epidemic, the decline of the traditional family . . . the list goes on and on. The chances for stress-resistant adults to emerge from such a background seem almost nil. The complexity of the problem of violence boggles the mind. Seeking any singular, simple solution is fruitless. Meredith (1984) quotes a passage from Sufi writer Idries Shah concerning the prophet Nasrudin. In a parable about fate, Nasrudin illustrates the many culprits of violence:

"What is Fate?" Nasrudin was asked by a scholar.

"An endless succession of intertwined events, each influencing the other."

"That is hardly a satisfactory answer. I believe in cause and effect."

"Very well," said the Mullah, look at that." He pointed to a procession passing in the street.

"That man is being taken to be hanged. Is that because someone gave him a silver piece and enabled him to buy the knife with which he committed the murder; or because someone saw him do it; or because nobody stopped him?"

HELPFUL HINTS TO LAW ENFORCEMENT OFFICERS

In addressing the Tenth Annual Update in Neuroscience, Dr. William Dubin, clinical director of the Pennsylvania Psychiatric Center, focused on problems of potential violence faced by psychiatrists. His insight may be of value to police officers. People become violent, said the doctor, when they feel "helpless . . . castrated, humiliated, or cornered." They then begin to display the following signs of increasing tension and anxiety:

1. Tense posture, clenching and unclenching of fist or jaw, or, for instance, a tight grip on a table or chair.
2. They may become verbally abusive. Verbal abuse is a symptom of psychic pain. Do not overreact. It is a mistake, explains Dubin, to get "caught up in the decibels" when confronted with strident or abusive behavior. He also cautions that counterthreats and anger should be avoided because they are likely to provoke physical confrontation.
3. Despite the presence of loud and menacing speech, physical clues may signal that the individual is not going to act out – as, for instance, when arms are folded or held behind the back. A willingness to cooperate may also subdue a belligerent person. This can be shown, for example, by allowing the officer to perform some concrete task, such as inspecting the individual for injuries.
4. Hyperactivity is another "red flag" of impending violence that should not be ignored. Dubin gives the example of a street woman who was brought by police to a clinic for treatment. The woman was ignored by the staff and allowed to pace for thirty-five minutes. When a nurse finally approached her and asked "May I be of help?" her answer was a physical assault.

New officers often pick up violent methods from old-timers. Recruits, just out of the academy and new to the streets, are faced with problems of human behavior that defy solution, make them anxious, frightened, and sometimes threaten their lives. Under such conditions, young troopers often listen intently to violence-prone solutions given with confidence by seasoned officers ("That's how it really is out here on the streets, kid"). Whether they become involved in violence will depend on their personality, their sense of right and wrong, and their disposition toward violence or nonviolence. It will also depend on their knowledge and understanding of violent behavior. The following principles regarding their ability to enter interpersonal situations in a nonthreatening manner will increase their ability to act effectively. These may be summarized in the following code of behavior:

1. When you approach a situation, try to analyze what is going on. Before you become involved, a few seconds of reflection will enable you to size up the situation more effectively and reduce the possibility of precipitating violence.
2. Do not "play games" with violence-prone persons. Because of their experience, they will be better players. The result of game playing is more likely to be the onset rather than the prevention of violent behavior.
3. Learn to listen not only to what persons are saying but also to the feelings with which they express themselves.
4. A display of personal involvement will escalate a situation and increase the potential for violent behavior.
5. Excited persons should be given time to cool down. Many loud-mouthed people will calm down after a while, especially if they are not given further reason to put on a show by officers.
6. Remember that persons who resort to violent behavior are often suffering from either a long-term or short-term loss of self-esteem. Therefore, do everything

possible to preserve people's self-esteem and avoid actions that contribute to its further loss. Leave them a way out so their self-esteem is not further destroyed.

7. Never threaten. Any proposed action that you verbalize should be carried out. On the other hand, if you verbalize something you are not prepared to carry out, you may talk yourself into a corner and end up taking an action you did not really intend.

8. Treat each individual you encounter with respect, patience, and tact, unless

the immediate dangerousness of the situation merits another attitude.

9. Although you should not become personally involved, do not act like an automaton. Relax, use humor if appropriate, and recognize that your authority will not vanish if you smile.

10. If you are not sure of department policies, such as those regarding the use of reasonable force, you should ask your supervisor. You should not rely on your peers because their policy interpretations may have been wrong for years.

SUMMARY

In this chapter the author has discussed a subject of great importance to law enforcement officers – violent behavior and the handling of the violent person. The chapter presented a catalog of violent causes along with the characteristics of those individuals who commit them. While the ability to predict a person's dangerousness is at best uncertain, there is much knowledge about violence and many immediate behavioral clues that can enable officers to heighten their understanding of the dangerousness of a person in a specific situation. The author has noted how officer-citizen contacts can sometimes get out of hand, resulting in injuries to either the citizen, the officer, or both, leading to citizens' complaints that can threaten an officer's career and open a department to civil suits. Finally, the author has offered hints to officers that may reduce the possibility of friction and subsequent violent behavior in contacts with criminals and citizens.

BIBLIOGRAPHY

Agee, V. L. (1979). *Treatment of the violent incorrigible adolescent.* Lexington, MA: Lexington Books.

Andison, F. S. (1977). TV violence and viewer aggression: A cumulation of study results, 1956–76. *Public Opinion Quarterly, 41*, 314–331.

Arizona Daily Star. 21 July, 1989. $1 million bond set for suspect.

Axthelm, P. 31 July, 1989. An innocent life, a heartbreaking death. *People*, 60–66.

Bell, T. J. (1982). Behavioral sequelae of head injury. In *Head injury*, ed. P. R. Cooper. Baltimore: Williams & Wilkins.

Bell, T. J., & Barth, J. (1983). Mild head injury. *Psychiatric Developments, 3*, 263–275.

Belson, W. 6 September, 1977. *Television violence and the adolescent boy*. Paper delivered at meeting of

British Association for the Advancement of Science, London, England.

Berh, S. F., & Loseke, D. R. (1980). Handling family violence: Situational determinants of police arrests in domestic disturbances. *Law and Society Review, 15*, 317.

Binder, A., & Scharf, P. (1980). The violent police-citizen encounter. *Annals of the American Academy of Police Science, 452*, 111–121.

Brodsky, S. L., & Williamson, G. D. (1985). Attitudes of police toward violence. *Psychological Reports, 57*(3, Pt. 2), 1179–1180.

Chusid, J. G. (1982). *Correlative neuroanatomy and functional neurology*, 18th ed. Los Altos, CA: Lange Medical Publications.

Clark, R. (1981). A few modest proposals to reduce

individual violence in America. In *Violence and the violent individual,* by J. R. Hays, T. K. Roberts, & K. S. Soloway. New York: SP Medical and Scientific Books.

Cocozza, J. J., & Steadman, H. J. (1974). Some refinements in the measurement and prediction of dangerous behavior. *American Journal of Psychiatry, 131,* 1012–1014.

Cohen, M. L., Groth, A. N., & Siegel, R. (1978). The clinical prediction of dangerousness. *Crime and Delinquency, 24,* 28–39.

Duarte, C. 25 July, 1989. Boy charged in slaying of cousin, 12. *Arizona Daily Star,* pp. 1A and 2A.

Fichtner, M. 11 May, 1989. Unattached children terrorize parents, society. *Arizona Daily Star.*

Finn, P. and McNeil, T. (1987). Cited by Herek, Hate crimes versus lesbians and gay men: Issues for research and policy. *American Psychologist, 44*(6), 948–955.

Gelles, R., & Straus, M. (1989). *Intimate violence.* New York: Simon & Schuster.

Gelman, D., & Elan, R. 12 December, 1988. Prisoners of pain. *Newsweek,* 65.

Gerbner, G. (1972). Violence in television drama: Trends and symbolic functions. In *Television and social behavior, Vol. 1: Media and control,* ed. G. A. Comstock & E. A. Rubenstein. Washington, D.C.: U.S. Government Printing Office.

Gerbner, G., et al. (1977). TV violence profile no. 8: The highlights. *Journal of Communications, 27,* 171–180.

Gunman kills 21 in California restaurant. 1984. *Facts on File,* 548.

Harlow, C. W. 8 May, 1989. Injuries rising in violent crimes. *Arizona Daily Star.*

Hazelwood, R. R., & Burgess, A. W. (1988). An introduction to serial rapist research by the FBI. In *Police psychology: Operational assistance,* ed. J. T. Reese & J. M. Horn , p. 197. Quantico, VA: Behavioral Science Unit, FBI Academy.

Herek, G. M. (1989). Hate crimes against lesbians and gay men: Issues for research and policy. *American Psychologist, 44*(6), 948–955.

Heyman, M. N. (1984). A study of presidential assassins. *Behavioral Sciences and the Law, 2*(2), 131–149.

Horstman, P. L. December, 1973. Assaults on police officers. *Police Chief.*

Kaplan, R. M., & Singer, R. D. (1976). Television violence and viewer aggression: A re-examination of the evidence. *Journal of Social Issues, 32,* 35–70.

Kochnower, J. M., et al. (1978). *Television viewing behaviors of emotionally disturbed children: An interview study.* New York: Brookdale International Institute.

Koop, C. E. October, 1982. *Violence and public health.* Paper presented at the annual meeting of the American Academy of Pediatricians, New York City.

Kozol, H. L., Boucher, R. S., & Garofalo, R. F. (1972). The diagnosis and treatment of dangerousness. *Journal of Crime and Delinquency, 18,* 378–392.

Landers, S. July, 1989. Watching TV violence shapes people's values. *APA Monitor,* 33.

Lee, M., Zimbardo, P. E., & Bertholf, M. November, 1977. Shy murderers. *Psychology Today,* 69ff.

Lester, D. (1978). Assaults on police officers in American cities. *Psychological Reports, 42,* 946.

Megargee, E. I. (1966). Undercontrolled and overcontrolled personality types in extreme antisocial aggression. *Psychological Monographs, 80.*

_____. (1969). The psychology of violence: A critical review of theories of violence. In *Crimes of violence: A staff report to the National Commission on the Causes and Prevention of Violence,* ed. D. J. Mubihill & M. M. Tumin, vol. 13. Washington, D.C.: U.S. Government Printing Office.

Meredith, N. December, 1984. The murder epidemic. *Science,* 43–48.

Milavsky, W. R. 19 August, 1977. *TV and aggressive behavior of elementary school boys.* Paper presented at the annual meeting of American Psychological Association, San Francisco.

Monahan, J. (1978). Prediction, research and the emergency commitment of dangerous mentally ill persons: A reconsideration. *American Journal of Psychiatry, 135,* 198–201.

_____. (1981). *The clinical prediction of violent behavior.* Washington, D.C.: National Institute of Mental Health.

Monroe, R. R. (1978). *Brain dysfunction in aggressive criminals.* Lexington, MA: D.C. Heath and Co.

Murder at McDonald's. 30 July, 1984. *Newsweek,* 30–31.

Neidig, P. H. (1988). Spouse abuse; Issues and attitudes: A guide for family advocacy. In *Public Information Presentations in the Military, 10.* Behavioral Science Associates.

_____. April, 1989. *Seminar on spouse abuse,* sponsored by Tucson Psychiatric Institute, Tucson, Arizona.

Neidig, P. H., & Friedman, D. H. (1984). *Spouse abuse: A treatment program for couples.* Champaign, IL: Research Press.

Nielsen, E. (1988). Anger management: A training program for reducing incidents of police misconduct. In *Police psychology: Operational assistance,* ed. J. T. Reese & J. M. Horn, pp. 319–325. Quantico, VA: Behavioral Science Unit, FBI Academy.

O'Leary, K. D., & Arias, I. In press. Prevalence, correlates and development of spouse abuse. In *Marriage and families: Behavioral treatments and processes,* ed. R. Peters . Champaign, IL: Research Press.

O'Leary, K. D., & Curley, A. D. (1986). Assertion and family violence: Correlates of spouse abuse. *Journal of Marital and Family Therapy, 12*(3), 281–289.

Police Stress. (1989). *9,* 2.

Reed, B. T. (1988). Neurological considerations in hostage negotiations: Introductory concepts. In *Police psychology: Operational assistance,* ed. J. T. Reese & J. M. Horn , pp. 339–346. Quantico, VA: Behavioral Science Unit, FBI Academy.

Reese, J. T. (1986). Policing the violent society: The American experience. *Stress Medicine, 2,* 233–240.

Reiser, M. (1982). *Police psychology: Collected papers.* Los Angeles: LEHI Publishing Co.

Rubenstein, E. A., et al. (1977). *Television viewing behaviors of mental patients: A survey of psychiatric centers in New York State.* New York: Brookdale International Institute.

Sanchez, J. (1986). Social crisis and psychopathology: Toward a sociology of the psychopath. In *Unmasking the psychopath,* ed. Reid et al., pp. 78–97. New York: W. W. Norton.

Schmidt, W. (1984). Recent developments in police civil liability." In *Police civil liability,* ed. L. Tenito. Columbia, MD: Hanron Press.

Shah, S. A. (1981). Dangerousness: Conceptual, prediction and public policy issues. In *Violence and the violent individual,* ed. J. R. Hays, T. K. Roberts, & K. S. Soleway, pp. 151–178. New York: SP Medical and Scientific Books.

Silberman, C. (1980). *Criminal violence and criminal justice.* New York: Vintage Books.

Social Science Research Council. (1975). *A profile of televised violence.* New York.

Spellacy, F. (1977). Neuropsychological differences between violent and non-violent adolescents. *Journal of Clinical Psychology, 33,* 966–969.

Steadman, H. J., & Cocozza, J. J. (1974). *Careers of the criminally insane: Excessive social control of deviance.* Lexington, MA: D.C. Heath.

Stratton, J. G. (1984). *Police passages.* Manhattan Beach, CA: Glennon Publishing Co.

Stratton, M. A., Gelles, R. H., & Steinmetz, S. K. (1980). *Behind closed doors: Violence in the American family.* New York: Doubleday/Anchor.

Sudden death. 30 July, 1984. *Time Magazine* 90–91.

Swartz, S. 12 June, 1989. Let men be more human. *Arizona Daily Star,* p. 7.

Toch, H. (1977). *Police, prisons and the problem of violence.* Rockville, MD: National Institute of Mental Health.

Turner, J. T. March, 1986. Is violence holding our health care hostage?" *Security Management,* 26–32.

Walker, L. E. A. (1989). Psychology and violence against women. *Journal of the American Psychological Association, 44*(4), 695.

Wambaugh, J. (1975). *The choirboys.* New York: Delacorte Press.

Weissberg, M. (1983). *Dangerous secrets: Maladaptive responses to stress.* New York: W. W. Norton.

When rage turns into mass murder. 30 July, 1984. *U.S. News and World Report,* 14.

Wilcox, B. July, 1989. Watching TV violence shapes people's values. *APA Monitor,* 33.

Wolfgang, M. E. (1981). Sociocultural overview of criminal violence. In *Violence and the violent individual,* ed. J. R. Jays, T. K. Roberts, & K. S. Soleway, pp. 97–115. New York: SP Medical and Scientific Books.

Wolfgang, M. E., & Ferracuti, F. (1967). *The subculture of violence.* New York: Barnes & Noble.

Worden, R. E., & Pollitz, A. A. (1984). Police arrests in domestic disturbances: A further look. *Law and Society Review, 18,* 105–120.

Chapter 15

SUICIDAL BEHAVIOR

Contact with suicidal behavior is a common part of police officers' work. Not only will they be called after a suicide occurs, but they also may be the first to discover the body while on patrol. If suicide is threatened, they often are asked to come to the rescue.

In recent years suicidal behavior has been recognized as a major public health and mental health problem. At least 25,000 successful suicides take place in the United States annually, and the number of attempts is much higher. Various studies range from eight to fifty unsuccessful attempts for every successful one.

If we also consider that officers may encounter suicide attempts disguised as homicidal behavior (Chapter 14) or disguised in auto or other accidents, it becomes clear why it is important for officers to know more about and to understand suicidal behavior. In this chapter, after reviewing the historical background of the field of suicidology, we will examine the suicidal person, clues presented to suicidal intentions, and some helpful hints to the officer in handling suicidal behavior.

HISTORICAL BACKGROUND

Although it has recently attained more visibility and popularity, the field of suicidology – the study of suicidal or self-destructive behavior – is not new. Throughout history every society and culture has demonstrated concern with death and has devised methods to cope with the fear and trauma associated with it. As early as the ancient Greeks, philosophers argued whether a man had a right to take his own life. At various times since, societies have either condemned or approved of suicidal behavior.

Suicide prevention, an important aspect of suicidology, also has deep roots. In 1621 Robert Burton, in his famous *Anatomy of Melancholy*, spoke of the "prognostics of melancholy or signs of things to come." He described how these prognostic signs (called *prodromal clues* by today's suicidologists) typically exist for a few days to a few weeks before the suicide attempt is made. Further, he pointed out that recognition of these signs could save lives.

In his 1897 treatise *Le Suicide*, the famous sociologist Emile Durkheim advanced the theory of social causation as an important factor in determining suicidal behavior. He believed that a person's responses to the environment, including suicidal behavior, were more explainable in terms of social forces rather than psychological factors. However, early attention to suicidal behavior was not limited to theorists such as Durkheim. For example, in the early 1900s the Vienna, Austria,

156

police department established a welfare division that handled all suicides and suicide attempts. Following an attempt, a summons was served on the attempter. If it was ignored, a second summons was issued. If this also went unanswered, a social worker was sent to investigate and prepare an evaluation. In 1928, this division handled 2,373 cases. Over 1,000 were hospitalized for treatment, and an additional 544 were seen as outpatients. Considered a public service function, the program also provided employment, housing, and financial counseling – problem areas closely associated with suicidal behavior.

Other historical perspectives include those of the ancient Greeks. While most believed that taking one's life was improper, some felt it could be justified in certain circumstances. For example, the Epicureans, a notable group of early Greek philosophers, believed that life was to be enjoyed, but recognized that when it became impossible to achieve this goal, suicide was an appropriate way to hasten the inevitable. Similarly, in early Roman times suicide was considered an offense only if one took one's life to avoid trial or caused another party to suffer by one's death. With the advent of Christianity, viewpoints on suicidal behavior began to change. In A.D. 693 the Council of Toledo imposed excommunication upon suicides and denied them a Christian burial. By the eleventh century, suicide had become a recognized public problem, and laws were passed to control it. Guided by Christian values, courts regarded suicide as "murder of oneself," and therefore viewed suicide or a suicide attempt as a criminal act for which not only the one committing suicide, but also his or her entire family could be punished. These views have continued to exist in one form or another into modern times. For example, laws against suicidal behavior existed in England until 1961. Between 1946 and 1955, nearly 6,000 suicide attempters were arrested and over 5,000 were found guilty and sentenced to either jail or prison. The United States also had laws against suicide and suicide attempts until the

1960s. As late as 1964, nine states still declared attempted suicide a crime, and eighteen others had laws against "aiding and abetting" a suicide attempter. Not only did these laws label suicidal behavior as criminal, but more important, they also prevented observers from obtaining accurate statistics. In most jurisdictions where suicide was regarded as criminal behavior, the admissibility of evidence at a coroner's inquest followed the rules of criminal evidence (such as prohibition against hearsay); this prevented an accurate accounting of suicide attempts. Today, in cases of questionable deaths (suicide, homicide, or accident), some form of "psychological autopsy" will probably be used. Detailed postmortem mental histories are compiled, and interviews with significant others are conducted to assess more accurately the manner of death (Schneidman, 1987).

In the past, financial penalties also were associated with suicide. For many years' insurance companies included suicide clauses in their policies that called for the return of premiums paid rather than the face value of the policy, as in other deaths. However, current policies specify full payment, but only if the insurance has been in force for a sufficient time. Another reason for the stigma associated with suicidal behavior is the myth that suicide is a psychotic act. Therefore, many families prefer to cover up anything that might point to suicide, as if to say "we have to admit that he is dead, but we don't have to admit that he was crazy."

Until the 1950s these legal, financial, and ethical prohibitions, as well as the associated stigma, greatly retarded a realistic study of suicidal behavior. In the United States three psychologists, N. L. Farberow, Edwin S. Schneidman, and R. E. Litman, became interested in suicide notes found on file in the Los Angeles County Coroner's office. Their study of these notes and the circumstances surrounding the deaths of those who had written them convinced them that suicide was a major public health and mental health problem deserving of further study. They also became convinced that suicide was an individual matter that could be prevented in most cases if warning clues had been recognized (Schneidman, Farberow, & Litman, 1970). As a result of their efforts, in 1960 the first suicide prevention center was opened on the grounds of Los Angeles County Hospital. Gradually aware ness of its existence spread, and referrals of people who were giving either verbal or behavioral clues of suicidal intent began to come in. The telephone became a popular means of contact. By 1970 over 99 percent of first contacts were by phone. By the mid-sixties, the concept of the suicide prevention center had gained popularity. Funding was made available from many sources, including the National Institute of Mental Health, to establish more suicide prevention centers in other cities. Eventually most centers discovered that they were receiving phone calls concerning all kinds of crises; consequently they broadened their services to *crisis intervention* and eliminated the single focus on suicide prevention.

Suicide Attempters

Schneidman has divided those who attempt suicide into four groups, based on the manner in which they approach the attempt.

Those in the first group do not intend to die. Their gestures are often dramatic, maybe recurring, with the principal aim of conveying a message about what is happening and that they want something done about it immediately. These persons may take a quantity of aspirin, then immediately tell someone so they can be rushed to a hospital; or they may climb to the top of a water tower and threaten to jump unless a condition is met.

Because these kinds of attempts are often attention getting, there is danger that those who deal with them may ignore their seriousness or even make fun of them. For example, emergency room personnel often regard those who make this type of suicide attempt as intruding into their "real" lifesaving activities. However, if this type of suicidal behavior is not taken seriously, people may be goaded into more serious attempts to convince others that they are not kidding.

Another reason for taking these attempts seriously is that these are the people who, if they die, often have a surprised look on their faces. Prisoners who tie a sheet around their necks and jump from their cell bunks when they hear the jailer approaching may underestimate the time required for the jailer to reach them. Jumpers maneuvering on a water tower may misjudge the tower's slipperiness and fall to their deaths. Although police officers may judge an act's potential lethality as low, it is important to refer these people to mental health professionals so that intervention into the pattern of suicidal behavior can begin.

The second group is the "gamblers." These people have reached the point at which they are willing to let fate or some other person determine whether they live or die. Examples include those who play Russian roulette. Although these people may have given up some control to outside persons or situations, they remain uncertain as to whether they wish to live or die and often wish to do both at the same time.

In these cases, suicide prevention depends on recognizing the coexistence of the wishes to live and die and throwing support onto the side of life. It is important to help troubled persons realize that there are more satisfying alternatives to suicide, and that even though they may feel intolerably miserable at this time, things will change, and with help they will be able to overcome these feelings. One technique that the authors have found useful is to confront attempters with what their contemplated suicide may mean to those they love, especially any children they may have. Sometimes they will claim that "the kids will be better off without me." They then should be told emphatically that the children will not be better off; that they need them. It is interesting to note that there is a noticeable correlation between emerging suicidal feelings in adolescents and the prior death of a parent through suicide (Joan, 1986). It is also helpful to point out underlying anger by asking, "Do you really hate them that much?" This approach firmly closes the door on the use of rationalizations by suicide attempters and gives them time to find other ways of handling their problems.

The third group includes those who seriously intend to die, but unforeseen factors intervene and save their lives. One of the authors recalls a retired sergeant who became very depressed and decided to commit suicide. When his wife and son left one morning, he connected a hose to the car exhaust, closed the garage door, and started the car. However, his son had used the car the night before and it soon ran out of gas. He then went back in the house to look for his son's rifle, but upon locating it, discovered that there was no ammunition. He then proceeded to the kitchen, where he found some poisonous liquid under the sink. When he tried to drink it, he became sick and vomited. At this point, his married daughter arrived. Knowing that she usually left the keys in her car, he hid while she entered the front door then sneaked out the back, started the car, and sped away. Down the road, he ran the auto into a concrete abutment at a speed estimated at ninety miles an hour. The car was a total wreck, but he only had broken a leg. There is no question that this man was trying very hard to die but that fate had intervened. Despite the seriousness of their attempts, these people often welcome rescue and are later grateful that they were saved.

The fourth group consists of the successful attempters. These persons also might have been saved if someone had been alert enough to detect some of their early clues to their contemplated behavior. Recently a young professor at a local university bought a gun, went into the desert, and shot himself. From later talks with his graduate students and faculty colleagues, it became apparent that he had given many clues to his intention.

Yet, as Schneidman has pointed out, we often are loathe to suspect suicidal intentions in those with whom we are close or who possess some type of status. For example, N. L. Farberow (1980) has noted that many physicians who commit suicide could have been saved if they had been treated like ordinary citizens in distress and hospitalized or referred to other appropriate treatment centers. The same situation exists in suicides by police officers. Officers are often reluctant to admit the possibility of suicidal behavior and are even more hesitant to broach the matter to the officer experiencing these thoughts and feelings or to a supervisor. Each of these groups of suicide attempters presents prior clues. Whether or not the suicide is successful, later investigation usually reveals that these clues were present.

Clues to Suicidal Behavior

Schneidman (1987) has classified clues to contemplated suicidal behavior into three broad categories: verbal, behavioral, and situational.

Verbal Clues

Verbal clues can be direct or indirect. For example, a direct verbal clue is the statement "I'm going to kill myself," or "I'm going to take my car up the mountain and run it and me off the cliff." Less clear are indirect verbal clues, or "coded" messages. A depressed young man appeared in our clinic one day and asked, "How does one leave his body to the medical school?" Other examples include: "Well, I'll never have to worry about that anymore," or "You won't have to put up with my complaining much longer." Vague statements by a person that she might "do something" or complaints about "getting out of control" also can suggest suicidal intent.

When people give verbal clues, officers should not be afraid to bring the question of suicide into the open. Some may hesitate because they are afraid that their questions might suggest this act to someone who has not yet considered it. However, this is unlikely. If suicide hasn't been on people's minds, inquiring about it is not going to trigger the behavior. Posing a direct question about suicidal thoughts will often play a role in forming a trusting relationship because persons contemplating suicide will be relieved to find that someone is able to understand what they have been thinking.

Behavioral Clues

Behavioral clues also may be direct or indirect. Direct clues include a history of a prior attempt. Officers should be especially alert if the prior attempt was almost lethal, or if there has been more than one attempt. However, any history of past attempts, regardless of their potential lethality, should be viewed as calling attention to a suicidal risk.

Indirect behavioral clues to suicidal intent may include suddenly making a will, the giving away of prized possessions, or sending home clothing and other things needed for daily living. A few years ago road crews working on an army reservation found a young man's skeleton. Investigation revealed that the skeleton was that of a young lieutenant who had vanished from the base fifteen years earlier and had been listed as a deserter. Investigators managed to reconstruct the last few days of his life, even though many years had passed. Several days before his disappearance he had withdrawn all of his money from a local bank. Some he had lent, without security, to a friend who wanted to purchase a new car. He had sent the rest home to his father, along with a footlocker containing his best clothes and prized possessions. He then had bought a revolver from a pawnshop, gone out in the desert, and shot himself. The rusted gun was found with his skeleton. Although he had no history of depression or suicidal behavior and had given no direct verbal clues, he had displayed warning signs that might have saved his life if someone had correctly interpreted them.

Situational Communications

In addition to verbal and behavioral clues, situational communications often indicate

contemplated suicidal behavior. Some situations are so stressful that they may lead to desperate attempts to escape them through suicidal behavior. For example, although most prisoners manage to do time without cracking up, others find it intolerable and will try to get out of jail or prison through suicide attempts. Although most of these attempts are clearly manipulative and are usually not fatal, they should not be ignored.

In a study of suicidal behavior in jails, the authors found that six out of eight prisoners transferred from the county jail to the psychiatric service of the county hospital because of suicidal behavior admitted that the motivation for their behavior had been to get out of jail and into the hospital. While all six stated that they did not intend to kill themselves, all emphatically threatened to "do a better job next time" if forced to return to jail. After being returned to jail, four of the six made additional suicide attempts (Beigel & Russell, 1972).

Other situations that may constitute serious emotional emergencies leading to suicide attempts include hospitalization, the possibility of major surgery, discovery of a malignancy or terminal illness, loss of a job or loved one, and being arrested for certain crimes, such as child molestation or rape. If the arrestee has a reputation as a community leader, teacher, or minister, the subject becomes a high risk for in-custody suicide.

Syndromatic Communications

The category of syndromatic communications was presented as the fourth group of prodromal indicators (Schneidman, Farberow, & Litman, 1970). We have retained this category because, in our opinion, it includes a number of "signs" that police officers can take note of, especially in evaluating the suicidal intent of a friend, family member, or fellow officer – people they are familiar with. These are a group of symptoms that, if they appeared singly, would not lead to concern. However, as the number seen in a single individual increases, concern about possible suicidal behavior also increases.

Loss of Sleep

In nearly every study of suicidal patients, loss of sleep is prominently mentioned. The problem may be difficulty in falling asleep, or if the people fall asleep readily, they may awaken in the middle of the night and be unable to go back to sleep. They may experience frequent and horrible nightmares as they sleep fitfully and may awaken at the slightest sound.

Loss of Weight

Any appreciable loss of weight over a short time, in the absence of a known physical cause such as dieting or severe illness, may be significant.

Loss of Appetite

All foods, even favorites, lose their appeal. Individuals find eating a task that they would just as soon ignore. These first three signs (loss of sleep, loss of weight, and loss of appetite) constitute the "triad of depression." This is not surprising since depression is the most common mental state underlying suicidal behavior.

Fearfulness

Persons who are contemplating suicide may express vague fears of losing control. If these persons had a previous depression that included a suicide attempt, they might say, "I don't want to end up that way again."

Fatigue

Complaints of always being tired may be accompanied by a slumping posture and movements that communicate a feeling of great effort.

Loss of Interest

These may include loss of interest in hobbies, work, social contacts, and/or sex. The more general the loss of interest, the more serious the depression and the more likely a possible suicide attempt.

Irritability

Continuing irritability, particularly in the absence of provocation, is directed toward those whom individuals ostensibly love.

Feelings of Self-Deprecation

People who begin to describe themselves as "worthless, bad, evil, and a failure" and who resist attempts to convince them that the opposite is true may be suicide risks.

Feelings of Hopelessness and of Being Trapped

When individuals regard their situation as a trap and see themselves as "hopeless," it is possible that they are not far from feeling that there is no way out other than their own death. Schneidman (1987) says that suicidal people often have a particular logic, a style of thinking that brings them to the conclusion that death is the only solution to their problems.

Changes in Drinking Patterns

When drinking patterns begin to change, either through increased drinking, drinking alone, or drinking at odd times, an acute state of depression may be present. Accidental suicides are often associated with changes in drinking patterns, since increased alcohol use combined with pill taking can be a lethal combination, even though the person did not intend to die.

> Over half of the people who commit suicide visit their medical doctor in the month before they kill themselves: 80 percent of

those who die of an overdose do so with one prescription that they have recently obtained. . . . Much has been made of "automatic" drug-taking behavior, cases in which people become confused and inadvertently take an overdose . . . this explanation usually conceals a bona fide suicide attempt. (Weissberg,, 1983, p. 22)

Teenage Suicide

At present, suicide is said to be the number-three cause of death among adolescents. It is widely accepted that suicide, like rape, is greatly underreported. The number-one cause of death among teenagers is car accidents. Many of these are single-car crashes, leading to the suspicion that they are not really accidents but planned or impulsive suicides. "Many accidents are, in fact, intentional, the result of suicidal and homicidal behavior. Others are due to unconscious factors: accident 'proneness' is often the result of psychological disequilibrium" (Weissberg, 1983).

Causes of Teenage Suicide

Like other complex problems, there is no single answer to why teenagers kill themselves. When asked the reasons for the high rate of suicide among their age group, teenagers usually cite four reasons: (1) increased pressure not to fail; (2) special hassles involved in being a teenager; (3) rejection or sense of loss within the family; and (4) disillusionment with planning a career (Joan, 1986). Less frequently mentioned is a family history of alcoholism or other substance abuse, domestic violence, and/or sexual abuse. Teenagers from such families do not have a consistent model for love, sharing, or other positive experiences. They often do not go for help because they fear retaliation from parents and that they will not be believed. They feel trapped; they have nowhere to go; their situation is hopeless; they can't take it any more. Suicide becomes

a deliberate and desperate attempt to end the hurt and pain.

Sometimes "copycat" suicides will occur in adolescent populations, where one teenage suicide will seem to spawn a rash of imitative behavior. Troubled adolescents who have not resolved their own problems appear the most likely victims (Mitchell, 1987). Teen suicides are especially upsetting to the community, and local mental health resources should be enlisted immediately in a debriefing effort to reassure the community (especially other teenagers) and to present educational information that will reduce the likelihood of further incidents.

Warning Signs

In general, the same warning signs that apply to adults apply as well to teenagers. But because teenagers (and younger children) are not adults, there are certain other signs. A significant drop in school grades may sometimes justifiably cause concern. If youngsters are depressed, it is harder to meet school requirements and their grades may drop. Teenagers' emotional swings and immaturity can cause their world to be wonderful one minute and horrible the next. A breakup in a relationship may seem like the end of the world. A recent loss may lead to memories of other losses, thus increasing the suffering to unmanageable proportions (Joan, 1986). If teenagers have made a previous attempt, the risk for another attempt will be high. Each unsuccessful attempt (each cry for help) may trigger another, more lethal attempt until someone responds appropriately or the adolescents die.

Officers responding to the scene should use the techniques presented in Chapter 20 on crisis intervention and should urge the subject and the family to obtain immediate professional help. Do not permit the subject or the family to gloss over the incident, since experience indicates that teens who do not receive competent help usually continue on the road to self-destruction and may eventually kill themselves.

Suicide Among the Elderly

Reversing a half-century trend, the suicide rate among elderly Americans steadily increased in the 1980s, according to government records (*Arizona Daily Star* 19 July, 1989). Statistics compiled by the National Center for Health Statistics, Department of Health and Human Services, show a 25 percent increase in the suicide rate of those sixty-five years and older from 1981 to 1986. As with suicides in the general population, many elderly suicides do not get reported; this reported 25 percent increase is probably an underestimate. Also, since the elderly are supposed to die, there often is not as much concern with ascertaining the true circumstances surrounding the death of a senior citizen. (Tolchin, 1989)

M. Reiser (1982) notes that:

in recent years, rumor has been perpetuated to the effect that police officers have the highest suicide rate of any occupational group. . . . However, inquiries made to federal, state and local agencies, insurance companies and suicide prevention centers reveal that data on suicide rates an not kept by occupation. [A check with the local health department in September 1989 reveals this is still true.] These figures were also unavailable from the National Center for Health Statistics for years beyond 1950.

In the absence of any hard statistics on suicide rates by occupation, one may question whether police officers do have significantly higher rates for suicide than other occupations. The national average rate of suicide was 12.8 per 100,000 for 1986 (the last year for which statistics are available). Various police suicide rates have been reported: 80 per 100,000 for the New York Police Department (Friedman, 1968); 203 per 100,000 for the state of Wyoming (Nelson & Smith, 1970); 17.9 per 100,000 for the St. Louis Police Department; and 0 per 100,000 for the Denver Police Department (Heiman, 1975). Reiser's study of Los Angeles PD suicides for the years 1970 to 1977 lists a rate of 8.1 per 100,000. This is a low figure when compared

with the national average and the suicide rates for Los Angeles males and females compiled by the Los Angeles Suicide Prevention Center for the years 1972 (16.7 per 100,000) and 1973 (15.3 per 100,000) (Reiser, 1982).

The authors of this text are aware of only one suicide by a police officer in the state of Arizona during the nineteen-year period beginning in 1970. Investigation revealed that this officer had been informed of an incurable disease and attempted to disguise his suicide as an on-duty homicide to protect his family financially. Regardless of whether the suicide rate for police officers is high or low, many officers become depressed enough to seriously consider suicide. The availability of their service weapon imbues this situation with a high lethal potential. When there is such a high suicide risk, there is no alternative but to hospitalize officers for their own safety. Although officers may be very angry and resist, most, like other potential suicides, will eventually be grateful for this rescue.

The real victims of a police officer's suicide, and for that matter anyone's suicide, are the spouse and family. John G. Stratton (1984) speaks of police widows as the "forgotten ones." Police wives, he states, get caught up in the police life-style. They often are immersed in their husband's job and have altered their own lives to accommodate the police world. They have become part of the police family, sharing not only their husband's trials and tribulations, but also his successes. They are generally proud of being a police officer's spouse and are proud of the department. They value the friendship and closeness of other police families. Then the officer commits suicide. Suddenly their loved one is gone — gone in a way that deprives the family of whatever support they could expect from fellow officers and their families. A police officer's suicide makes fellow officers very uncomfortable because it reminds them of their own mortality and also causes anxiety about their own potential for such an act. After all, if the pressures of the job drove that person to suicide (and that is what most of them think), maybe some day the pressures will get too much for them and they will end up "eating their gun." Police administrators, officers, and families should be very concerned that the family survivors of a suicidal officer are given whatever help is needed and are not neglected or, even worse, shunned after his or her death.

In an article on suicidal behavior among police officers, Scott W. Allen (1986) observes that suicide is an infrequent behavior in any population, but there is a tendency for certain individuals toward self-injury, self-defeat, and self-destruction. Farberow (1980) calls such negative behavior "indirect self-destructive behavior" (ISDB) and states that it occurs when the desire for excitement and degree of risk-taking exceed the safe boundaries of survival. Allen believes that the risk of developing ISDB is great in police officers because risk-taking and excitement play such an important role in the development of their identity. It has probably already played a role in their selection of law enforcement as a vocation.

In the positive sense, risk-taking allows officers to begin mastering fear-provoking situations and facilitates their ambition to succeed. But when risk taking becomes combined with depression, feelings of hopelessness and helplessness, and a poor self-image, it becomes ISDB and can jeopardize the safety of the officers and those with whom they serve. "Adding to the danger of ISDB is a lack of awareness on the individual's part to either realize or care about the effects of his behavior . . . a lack of awareness that his actions may, in fact, be suicidal" (Allen, 1986, p. 414).

A second pathogenic quality of ISDB is that, like stress, it may develop insidiously over a considerable period of time. Just as prolonged stress may lead, over a period of time, to high blood pressure and coronary heart disease, so the development of ISDB can span many years. Allen warns that work-related ISDB can occur in any officer, but those in high-stress specialized assignments (SWAT, narcotics, hostage negotiators, and others) may be at high risk. Their need for excitement may result in poor judgment and fatal decisions. Regular uniformed officers who are "hot dogs" (who tend to respond independently and with little regard for officer safety) may be exhibiting ISDB. A supervisor should suspect any officer who seems to collect more than his or her share of accidents, patrol car damage, and personal injuries over a relatively short period of time.

Another pathogenic trait of ISDB is that the need for excitement and personal risk can be compulsive and addictive. Supervisors should be alert for a trooper who seems to be on his or her way to becoming an "adrenalin junkie." Behavior that at first glance appears to be "good police work" may be, in fact, the early warning signs of addictive ISDB.

HELPFUL HINTS TO LAW ENFORCEMENT OFFICERS

Establishing a relationship with the possible suicide attempter, identification and clarification of this person's focal problem, evaluation of suicide potential, assessment of the strengths and resources available to the individual, implementation of rescue operations if necessary, and referral to appropriate agencies are the critical aspects of suicide prevention that may occur in this or any other sequence or at the same time. Law enforcement officers who come in contact with a potential suicide attempter should have a basic knowledge of these important aspects of suicide prevention.

The Relationship

When officers come in contact with suicidal ideation, they should be patient, interested, self-assured, optimistic, and knowledgeable. By assuming this attitude and behavior, they communicate to potential suicide attempters that they have done the right thing by letting officers know they are contemplating suicide. Potential attempters should be accepted without challenge or criticism and allowed to tell their story in their own way while officers listen. If potential attempters make contact through a telephone call, certain clear approaches should be followed. First, the officer answering the call should clearly identify the agency and give his or her name. As soon as it is known that callers are suicidal, the officer should request a name and telephone number. If callers refuse to give a name, the officer should calmly accept this refusal for the moment and proceed with the conversation. However, at some later appropriate time, the names and phone numbers of interested persons, such as family members, physicians, or close friends who might be possible resources, should be obtained. Since the immediate goal is to gather information to be used in evaluating suicide potential, getting into a discussion or argument about whether callers are going to reveal their name will be counterproductive.

Identification and Clarification of the Problem

In conversations with officers, suicide attempters often may display a profound sense of confusion, chaos, and disorganization. Because they are often unclear about their main problems and get lost in details, one of the most important services officers can perform is to help them recognize what their principal problems are and to place them in proper perspective. For example, a woman called the police department and voiced many complaints, including feelings of worthlessness, despair, and inadequacy. She said that she was not a good mother because she could not manage her housework and that her family would be better off without her. Careful initial listening by the officer, followed by some specific questioning, helped him learn that her main problem was her relationship with her husband. When the officer reflected this back to her with authority, she was able to

organize herself better and to address this specific problem more effectively.

Evaluation of Suicide Potential

"Suicide potential" refers to the probability that a person might kill him- or herself in the immediate or relatively near future. As soon as officers begin talking with someone who is contemplating suicide, it is extremely important that they start to evaluate the suicide potential in order to make an accurate assessment of the immediate lethal risk. Officers' plans of action will depend upon this evaluation.

Statistics indicate that the suicide rate rises with increasing age and that men are more likely to kill themselves than women. Other things being equal, a communication from an older male indicates more danger than one from a young female. However, young people do kill themselves, even though their original aim may have been to manipulate others rather than to die. Therefore, age and sex offer only a general framework for evaluating suicide potential. Each case must be further appraised according to other criteria. One of them is the suicide plan. Three main elements should be considered in appraising the plan: lethality of the proposed method, availability of the means, and specificity of the plan's details. Methods involving a gun, jumping, or hanging are more lethal than pills or wrist cutting. Further, if the gun is at hand, the threat must be taken more seriously than when people talk about shooting themselves but do not have a gun. If people describe specific details, indicating that they have spent time making preparations, such as changing a will, writing suicide notes, collecting pills, buying a gun, and setting a time, seriousness increases markedly. In addition, if the plan is bizarre and the details are apparently irrational, it is quite possible that officers are dealing with a psychotic person; this also increases potential lethality.

Information about precipitating stressors also is useful in evaluating potential. Typical precipitating stresses include losses, such as a loved one by death, divorce, or separation; loss of a job, money, prestige, or status; loss of health through sickness, surgery, or an accident; or threat of prosecution for criminal involvement or exposure for some misdeed. Occasionally, increased anxiety and tension may be associated with success, such as a job promotion with increased responsibilities. Officers must evaluate stress from the callers' point of view and not from their own or society's. What officers might consider minimal stress may be felt as especially severe by callers.

The specific clues to suicidal behavior described in the previous section also serve as criteria in evaluating suicide potential. Officers should keep in mind how these symptoms compare to the stress that they have found out about. For example, if the symptoms are severe but the stress precipitating them appears to be minor, then either the story may be incomplete or the individual may be chronically unstable, with a history of prior crises similar to this one. Stress and symptoms also must be evaluated in relation to the individual's life-style. For example, officers should evaluate whether the suicidal behavior is acute or chronic. If officers discover that serious attempts have been made in the past, the current situation must be rated as potentially more dangerous. On the other hand, if undergoing severe stress, a person with no prior history of suicide attempts also may be at high risk.

In forming a plan of action, officers should assess the available relationships of potential suicide attempters. If they discover that the suicidal person has severed all communications with others, then potential danger is increased. Finally, it is also useful for officers to inquire tactfully into the medical status of potential suicide attempters. For example, if the person is suffering from a chronic illness that has changed his or her self-image, suicide potential may be greater.

In summary, no single suicide criterion need be alarming by itself, with the possible exception of the person who has a very lethal and specific plan. Rather, the evaluation of suicide potential should be based on the general pattern that develops after an examination of all the criteria in the context of a specific person. For example, feelings of exhaustion and loss of resources will have different implications in two persons of different ages. A twenty-five-year-old married man stated that he was tired, depressed, and was having vague ideas of committing suicide by driving into a freeway abutment. There was no history of prior suicidal behavior. He reported difficulty in his marriage and talked of separation but was still in contact with his wife and working at his job, which he had had for many years. This case was considered a low suicide risk. In contrast, at high risk was a sixty-four-year-old man with a history of alcoholism who reported that he had made a serious suicide attempt one year ago and was saved when someone unexpectedly walked in and found him unconscious. He had a history of three failed marriages and many job changes. Further, he said that his physical health had been failing, that he had no family left, and that he was thinking of killing himself with the gun he had in the house.

Assessment of Resources

In handling persons who are contemplating suicide, it is as important to assess their environmental resources, as it is to evaluate specific aspects of their thinking and behavior. For example, although individuals may have many negative feelings and do things that indicate suicidal intent, this intent may be offset by positive factors, such as a continued relationship with a loved one or even a positive reaction to officers with whom they first come in contact. The knowledge that people are already in touch with a treatment agency or therapist also may lessen concern about suicide potential. Finally, the presence of loved ones; particularly family and relatives, and their willingness to stand by the troubled person will also decrease suicide potential.

Rescue Operations and Referral Procedures

Officers' response to a specific situation will be determined by their evaluation of the suicide risk and the information they have obtained about available resources. In general, those situations that officers rate as having a high suicide potential because of few resources will require immediate intervention. If the person is on the telephone, the officer should attempt to keep him or her on the line until a police unit arrives at the scene. This person should be taken immediately to a hospital for a professional evaluation unless family or close friends are present who will help bring the situation under control and who will accept responsibility for the potential attempter's welfare. In either case, those in control should be instructed not to leave the person alone and be advised to help them seek professional help.

Some situations encountered by police are of low or medium risk, and initially can be handled satisfactorily by a sympathetic and understanding listener who provides telephone counseling. However, an attempt also should be made to refer this person to an agency for appropriate continuing care. Consequently, officers should be familiar with agencies in the community and know their hours of operation and telephone numbers. They should offer to make an appointment and should follow up by so informing the person, if possible, while he or she is still on the line. Although the call may not be judged serious in terms of immediate suicide potential, the caller still has serious life problems that require help. A failure to respond may eventually lead to a more serious cry for help.

In the rare situation in which someone calls 911 in the midst of a suicide attempt, police and medical personnel should be dispatched immediately. If an individual is calling about another person, the informant should be instructed to take the suicide attempter to a nearby emergency room, or that 911 personnel will call an ambulance. The following are suggestions about general and community resources that are usually available in these situations. Officers should consider one or more of these possibilities.

The family is often a neglected resource in this crisis. Attempters should be encouraged to discuss their problems with their family. If it is important that someone be with attempters during the crisis, family members should be called and told of the situation, even though attempters may express reluctance. However, they should first be informed that their family will be called. *Close friends* may be used in the same way as families. For example, callers or attempters can be encouraged to have a friend stay with them during a difficult period. The friend also may be helpful in talking things out and giving them support. People often turn to their *family doctors* for help because physicians are seen as supportive authority figures. If potential suicide attempters have a good relationship with their physician, they should be encouraged to discuss their problems with him or her. Physicians also can be helpful when medication or hospitalization is required. If the potential attempter is religious, the involvement of a *clergyman* may be helpful. In addition to people, the resources of *the community and its agencies* may be useful. The hospital emergency room, suicide prevention center, community mental health center or social work agency, private therapist, and/or psychiatric hospital can be appropriate resources. When officers consider using one of them, they should recognize that their responsibility does not end until they have made certain that attempters have been turned over to its care. The following are examples of typical calls handled by a police station in which suicidal behavior or suicidal ideation was prominent. Following a description of the phone call, we will suggest how the problem might be handled. These examples have been chosen for teaching purposes. Not all calls fall within such well-defined areas.

Case Example. A woman between thirty and forty years old calls one night saying that she doesn't understand why she feels so depressed. She says she is alone, complains of not being able to sleep and of having troubled thoughts and feelings. She mentions she had thoughts about killing herself but that she didn't really want to, even though she had been having these thoughts for years. She sounds agitated, depressed, and somewhat hysterical. She is demanding and asks what could be done for her right now because she feels that she would not be able to make it through the night. On further questioning, the officer is able to determine that many such episodes had occurred.

In such a situation, it is best for officers to listen patiently and wait for an opportunity to point out that things often look worse at night, but that it is not the best time to get help. The woman should be advised to call her doctor, a social service agency, or a mental health clinic in the morning to make an appointment. Officers should take her number and call her back the next morning to reinforce their suggestion. At the same time, they can suggest that she call a close friend or relative to come over and spend the night with her.

Case Example. A woman who sounds between twenty-five and thirty-five calls the police station but will not identify herself. She asks the officer what anyone can do for a person who doesn't want to live any more. Although she sounds in control, she vaguely alludes to a long-standing problem. She demands that the officer do something about her problem.

Officers should point out to her that she has a responsibility to cooperate if she really wants help. They should tell her that it is important for them to know more about her situation and who she is before they can help. If she mentions that she has a therapist and gives his or her name, she should be referred back to the therapist. Officers also can tell the woman that they will notify the therapist that the woman has called. Although she may initially express resistance, it is likely she will accept officers' direction.

Case Example. A woman, perhaps in her early fifties, calls one evening to complain that she is very depressed and feels that no one is interested in her. She talks about her many physical problems and complains that her doctor is not helping her enough and that her husband is not giving her enough attention. She states that she feels her life is over and there is no point in continuing to live.

She should be encouraged to talk with her husband and tell him how she is feeling. If this is not feasible, either because he is not at home or because she is unwilling, she should be encouraged to call her family physician and talk to him or her. Officers may offer to call her physician. If none of these resources is immediately available, she should be referred to a suicide prevention center or to an appropriate mental health facility.

Case Example. A young man, probably in his early twenties, calls the police station. He is evasive and reluctant to give his name. He talks about a problem that he does not identify, but states that he is calling for help because he has reached the point where the only solution is to kill himself. He describes impulsive suicide plans, such as smashing his car on the freeway or cutting himself with a razor blade.

In this situation, it is important for officers to be supportive. They may tell the young man that he did the right thing in calling as a first step toward getting help. Officers should give the young man a list of resources. In this discussion, it is important to talk with him about which resource he might feel most comfortable contacting. Any assistance that officers can give him in making this contact will be helpful.

Case Example. A young man in his early thirties calls one evening to complain that his life is a mess because of his bungling. He explains that he has gotten himself in such a jam, financially and with his family, that he feels the only solution is to kill himself.

Officers often will be able to identify a specific recent setback in the person's life. Once officers have uncovered this recent stress, they should tell the caller that he is reacting to this specific stress and that he needs help with this special problem. The caller should be reminded that he was able to function well before this setback and that he is probably suffering from temporary depression, for which he needs professional help.

Case Example. A man, age sixty, calls one evening and sounds very depressed and discouraged. He is apologetic about calling and troubling the officers. He complains about a physical problem that has prevented him from working and states that he now feels this problem are beyond help. He expresses many sad feelings about being old and a burden upon others. When asked about his suicidal thoughts, he reveals a specific plan for killing himself.

A police unit should be dispatched and contact maintained with the individual until the unit arrives. Family, friends, and other resources should be mobilized and involved.

Case Example. A family member or friend calls the police one evening about someone who is depressed and withdrawn. The caller is concerned about having just learned of a friend's plan to kill himself. The caller is asking how serious the situation is and what to do.

This caller should be advised to contact the potential suicide attempter immediately and explain that he or she is concerned and trying to get help. The caller should be told to encourage the potential suicide attempter to call a suicide prevention center or another appropriate agency. The initial caller should keep in contact and be asked to continue to inform officers about what is happening.

Case Example. This caller is a neighbor who is concerned about someone but is reluctant to be identified or to assume any responsibility. Instead, officers are asked to do something and take over the problem. Further, the caller is vague about the nature of the disturbing situation. In these cases, officers should get as much information as possible and tell the caller that it is important to take some steps, such as letting the potential suicide attempter know of his or her concern.

It should also be pointed out to the caller that it is unrealistic for officers to contact the person about whom the caller is concerned without being able to state who notified the police. If the caller is still reluctant to be identified, it is even more important for the officers to emphasize that it is the caller's responsibility to become involved.

Case Example. A physician, minister, or mental health professional in a position of responsibility calls about someone who needs immediate rescue to prevent a suicide. Officers should get only as much information as is needed before quickly dispatching a unit. They should ask the professional's opinion about what should be done after the potential suicide attempter is taken into protective custody.

Case Example. A caller informs the police that a neighbor or family member is being physically restrained from attempting suicide at that very moment and cannot be left unattended. This caller should be advised to take the person to the nearest hospital immediately. If the caller cannot manage alone, a unit should be dispatched. In the meantime, officers should emphasize that any harmful drugs or objects should be removed from the scene and that someone should always remain with the potential suicide.

In each of these examples, officers have a responsibility to obtain as much information as possible and to maintain contact with the situation until it has been resolved. They must avoid empty reassurance and superficial platitudes that will only convey to the person seeking help that the officers do not understand the problem and do not have real empathy. If officers convey this impression, it is likely that the person who is contemplating suicide will not be able to form a trusting relationship with them. He or she may then break off communication and attempt suicide.

Police Response to an Ongoing Suicide Call

Police officers responding to an ongoing suicide call should keep the following in mind. These suggestions are similar to those that officers may find helpful in other crisis situations.

1. **Assume the proper mental attitude.** It is often difficult for police officers to have an appropriate mental attitude since they may see the behavior of the person attempting suicide as manipulative. Perhaps officers have been called to assist this person before and feel the person does not really want to commit suicide. However, every suicide threat or attempt should be taken seriously. Achieve the proper mental attitude by reminding yourself that every human life has dignity and that your responsibility is to help this person regardless of his or her behavior.

2. **Secure the scene and assess the threat to your own safety, the safety of others, and the safety of the suicide attempter. In securing the scene, try to keep as many people as possible away from the immediate action.** Ongoing suicide scenes frequently resemble a three-ring circus, with squad cars, an ambulance, a fire department truck, and neighbors in close proximity. Dispense with all that is unneeded and try to keep other people clear of the immediate area. Do not be surprised when onlookers try to thwart your efforts either by making fun of the attempter or by urging him or her to go ahead with the attempt. Officers should approach the scene using all officer-safety procedures. Many suicide

attempters, lacking whatever it takes to end their own life, attempt to place police officers in the role of executioner. Some suicidal subjects are perfectly willing to threaten, injure, or even kill a police officer to force police to kill them.

3. **Introduce yourself and your organization, using name and title ("I am Officer Smith of the City Police Department").** This is important because it assists attempters in relating to you. Ask what they like to be called. Do not assume that because a man's name is Kenneth, he likes to be called Kenny or even Ken. This may be the name by which the person with whom he is angry or disappointed addresses him; using it will create an unnecessary obstacle. This is especially true when dealing with juveniles, since they may interpret your use of a nickname or even a first name as a "putdown." You might say "Your name is Richard Smith. Do you mind if I call you Richard? What do your friends call you?" or "What would you like me to call you?"

4. **Give plenty of reassurance.** Continually emphasize that you are there to help, that you can help, that there is hope, and that there are other alternatives to suicide. Many times it is useful to say something such as "In my experience as a police officer, I have seen people who have been as unhappy as you, and yet down the road they're glad that they didn't do it." Remember that suicide prevention consists of helping people find alternatives to the suicidal act. Attempters are in this situation because they have not found alternatives and see life as hopeless.

5. **Try to determine the main theme.** One of two major themes will usually predominate. Either attempters are angry at someone and want that person to pay for whatever they feel was done to them, or they see life as hopeless. You can deal more directly with the

problem if you know which of these themes predominates. For example, if attempters are angry at a specific person and want that individual to pay for whatever has been done to them, you might point out that there is no magic replay of the suicide act. If they have guessed wrong and the individual really is not going to feel sorry, they missed the boat. Many people in this stressful situation show magical thinking. For example, a suicide attempter may talk about making her husband pay for all the harm that he has done as if she were going to be around at her own funeral to see how sorry he is going to feel. With diplomacy, you should point out that she won't be around and that he may not feel this way at all.

If people are feeling hopeless, helpless, unworthy, and inadequate, it is sometimes helpful to point out that they can always kill themselves if talking with you doesn't work. "But just talk to me and let's see if we can work something out. You can always commit suicide just like right now, but let's see if we can come up with an alternative first." Sometimes these approaches will be successful, but at other times you may have to confront the person with the true consequences of the proposed act. For example, a mother or father may say, "The children will be better off without me." You can say once again "In my experiences as a police officer, this is not true. . . . I have seen children whose parents committed suicide and they are left with deep emotional scars. Children whose parent(s) commits suicide often think about committing suicide themselves and sometimes do." Then, judging the ability of the person to handle the guilt, you might say to him or her, "Do you really hate the children that much?"

Remember that if one thing doesn't work, try another. If your attempt doesn't work or seems to aggravate the situation, quickly back off. It is amazing what will solve the problem and what won't. For example, in New Orleans a man jumped into one of the canals. People threw him lifelines but he refused to grab them. He weakened as he dogpaddled to keep to the surface, while shouting that he was going to drown and life wasn't worth living. Suddenly a rookie cop arriving on the scene drew his revolver, aimed at the man in the water, and shouted, "Come out of there or I'll blow your goddam head off," whereupon the man grasped the line and allowed himself to be pulled ashore. You never know what will work. Be flexible.

6. **Comply with any requests if at all possible.** For example, the person attempting suicide may say "Get that damn SWAT guy off the roof" or "Get those officers away from my front door." Grant the request. This does not mean that officers should give up trying to maneuver into more advantageous positions should quick action become necessary. But if something is annoying attempters, or if they want a soda or a glass of water, grant their wish. Try to show that you understand where they are coming from and that nothing they have done so far cannot be undone.

Many times people in this situation feel they have gone too far and must go through with the act. Some even fear that they may go to jail if they don't kill themselves. Do not deceive them but, if possible, frequently reinforce the idea that nothing has happened that cannot be undone. If they have done something that can't be undone (for example, if they have killed somebody), point out that at least they can stop from doing any more harm or making the situation worse.

7. **Remember that the person attempting suicide is in control.** Attempters

have seized ultimate control over their lives. If you threaten this control directly or indirectly, you may precipitate completion of the act. Someone with a gun to his head, or on the edge of a roof ready to jump, is in full command of the situation. Also remember that if attempters have a hostage and are threatening that hostage, they have control. Your job is to take control from these people in an unobtrusive way by showing your sincere desire to help them out of the situation.

8. **After the crisis is over, reassure the attempters.** Tell them that they did the right thing. If they surrender the gun, come down from the roof, or otherwise neutralize the situation, be quick to praise them for a wise decision. They may disagree with you, but the fact that they allowed you to convince them otherwise shows that they are probably relieved at the outcome.

Response to a Suicide Scene that has been Interrupted Before Police Arrival

If police officers responding to a suicide scene find that the attempt has been aborted, either voluntarily or through the use of force, officers should introduce themselves by name, rank, and organization, reassuring people that they are there to help, and make certain that the necessary medical facilities are available to help if needed. If the person has to go to the hospital, officers should tell the family where the person is going and that it probably will be best if one of them follows in their own car or rides in a police car because hospital personnel will have questions that only they can answer. It may also be necessary (according to statutes of the particular state) for an eyewitness to sign a petition for involuntary commitment. At the very least, the hospital will welcome the opportunity to obtain background information on the subject. Officers should also inquire about precipitating events, whether there

was a previous history, and what the family sees in terms of the future. This will enable them to complete their report more fully and accurately.

Response to a Successful Suicide

If officers respond to a successful suicide, they must secure the scene. In larger departments, they will call homicide and they will take over the investigation. In smaller departments, the officers may have to do the investigation. Officers should remember that suicide is a stigma to many people — an act that brings disgrace to the family. Even though most suicides leave suicide notes, the note may have been withheld from the police or even destroyed. There are many reasons for this, including social stigma, financial penalties in insurance policies, or perhaps a desire to keep the true nature of the act from other members of the family. Officers always should be alert for suicidal acts in which there has been an attempt to conceal the nature of the act. For example, in a southwestern city some years ago, a body was found in a deserted shack in an isolated area. There was no furniture in the shack, and the body was hanging from a rope tied to a beam in the ceiling. The beam was too high for the individual to have reached it without standing on something. The case might have been labeled homicide except an alert detective noted that the dirt floor under the body was still a little damp. Further investigation revealed that the suicide had ingeniously managed to hang himself by standing on two big blocks of ice. He intended that his body would be found after the ice had thoroughly melted, leaving no trace as to how the body became suspended from the beam. The motivation for the disguised act was his desire to leave a considerable amount of insurance to his wife and children. Another caution for officers investigating a strangulation or hanging is to remember that it may have been an act of sexual bondage, not suicide.

SUMMARY

Suicidal behavior is a public health and mental health problem of major dimensions. It occurs among the rich and the poor, the young and the old, among members of all races and religious backgrounds, and within all professions and occupations – even police officers. At the same time, it is an individual matter that can be prevented if one is trained to recognize the clues that most potential attempters display before attempting or successfully completing the act.

Police responsibility involves understanding the personalities of those most likely to attempt suicide, knowing the various clues to contemplated suicidal behavior, and being aware of those principles of suicide prevention that will allow officers to respond appropriately to both telephone calls and emergency situations.

BIBLIOGRAPHY

Agren, H. (1983). Life at risk: Markers of suicidality in depression. *Psychiatric Developments, 1,* 87–104.

Allen, S.W. (1986). Suicide and indirect self-destructive behavior among police. In *Psychological services for law enforcement,* ed. J. T. Reese & H. A. Goldstein, pp. 412–417. Washington, D.C.: U.S. Government Printing Office.

Beigel, A., & Russell, L, H. E. (1972). Suicide attempts in jails: Prognostic considerations. *Hospital and Community Psychiatry, 23,* 361–363.

Burton, R. (1961). *The anatomy of melancholy,* ed. by F. Dell & P. Jourdan-Smith. London: J. M. Dent & Sons. Originally published 1621.

Farberow, N. L., ed. (1980). *The many faces of suicide.* New York: McGraw-Hill.

Farberow, N. L., & Schneidman, E. S. (1961). *The cry for help.* New York: McGrawHill.

Friedman, P. (1968). Suicide among police: A study of ninety-three suicides among New York City policemen, 1934–1940. In *Essay in self-destruction,* ed. E. Schneidman . New York: Science House.

Hatton, C. L., ed. (1977). *Suicide: Assessment and intervention.* New York: Appleton Century-Crofts.

Heiman, M. F. (1975). The police suicide. *Journal of Police Science and Administration, 3*(3), 267–273.

Joan, P. (1986). *Preventing teenage suicide: The living alternative handbook.* New York: Human Sciences Press.

Lester, D. May, 1983. The suicidal police officer: Recognition and helping. *Criminal Justice Career Digest,* 4-8.

Maris, R. W. (1981). *Pathways to suicide: A study of self-destructive behaviors.* Baltimore: Johns Hopkins University Press.

McIntosh, J. L. (1985). *Research on suicide: A bibliography.* Westport, Conn.: Greenwood Press.

_____. (1988). *Suicide among the elderly, 1984–1988.* Monticello, IL.: Vance Bibliographies.

Mitchell, J. T. January/February, 1987. By their own hand. *Chief Fire Executive, 48.*

Murphy, G. E., Clendenin, W. W., & Darrvish, H. S. (1972). The role of the police in suicide prevention. *Life-Threatening Behavior, 1,* 96–105.

Nelson, F. L. (1987). The chronically self-destructive patient versus the negligent provider. *American Journal of Forensic Psychology, 5*(2), 47–51.

Nelson, Z. P., & Smith, W. November, 1970. The law enforcement profession: An incidence of high suicide. *Omega,* 293–299.

Pfeffer, C. R., ed. (1989). *Suicide among youth: Perspectives on risk and prevention.* Washington, D.C.: American Psychiatric Press.

Reiser, M. (1982). *Police psychology: Collected papers.* Los Angeles: LEHI Publishing Co.

Schneidman, E. March, 1987. At the point of no return. *Psychology Today,* 55–58.

Schneidman, E. S., Farberow, N. L., & Litman, R. E. (1970). *The psychology of suicide.* New York: Science House.

Stratton, J. G. (1984). *Police passages.* Manhattan Beach, CA: Glennon Publishing Co.

Tolchin, M. 19 July, 1989. After long decline, suicide rate of elderly shows puzzling rise. *New York Times,* p. A-1.

Weissberg, M. (1983). *Dangerous secrets: Maladaptive responses to stress.* New York: W. W. Norton.

PART V

BEHAVIORAL ASPECTS OF
CRISIS SITUATIONS

Chapter 16

BEHAVIORAL ASPECTS OF DISASTERS

Sirporin (1976) defines a disaster as "an extreme social crisis situation in which individuals and their social systems become dysfunctional and disorganized, sustain personal, collective, and public hardships, and also become a 'community of sufferers.'"

Mitchell and Resnik (1981) point out that in a disaster there is a sudden, increased demand on community resources (police, fire, rescue, hospital, and government) under extremely stressful conditions. In most cases there are deaths and serious injuries as well as severe psychological damage and destruction of property. "Not only does a disaster elicit an immediate emotional response from all persons regardless of whether an injury is suffered, but it is also disturbing to and a cause of concern for an entire community" (Wilkinson & Enrique, 1985).

B. Raphael (1986) points out that we tend to think of disasters in terms of sudden and dramatic events, but disasters also may be gradual and prolonged, creeping on almost insignificantly, as in the case of drought and famine.

Examples

The town of Barneveld died suddenly on June 8, 1984, when a tornado struck without warning. Winds in excess of 300 miles per hour completely flattened or seriously damaged every building (approximately 200). Nine of the town's population of 579 was killed and 55 were hospitalized. Another 150 sustained minor injuries. Ninety percent of the townspeople were left homeless in the drenching rains and the darkness (Mitchell, 1986).

On January 13, 1982, Air Florida Flight 90 failed to achieve the necessary altitude and crashed into the 14th Street Bridge and the frozen Potomac River in Washington, D.C. In spite of extraordinary rescue efforts by emergency personnel, seventy-eight lives were lost (only five survivors were pulled from the icy waters) (Mitchell, 1983).

In Chapter 14 we presented the story of the San Ysidro mass execution. Dr. Michael Mantell, a San Diego police psychologist, writes: "The disaster scene tested San Diego's emergency personnel services, stretching human reactions to the limit. Coroner, cops, emergency medical technicians, firefighters, even news reporters, were faced with gripping images, associations, thoughts, feelings, smells, and mental anguish, the likes of which even the most 'macho' had difficulty confronting" (Mantell, 1986, p. 357).

These mass casualty incidents can produce maximum emotional distress in a minimum amount of time. In a country as large as the United States, the average emergency service worker can expect to encounter at least one such disaster in his or her professional lifetime (Mitchell, 1981).

The ability of police officers to deal effectively with the behavioral aspects of these disaster situations will depend on their understanding of the types of reactions that may occur, the factors that lead to the behavior associated with them, and the specific intervention tools available.

HISTORICAL BACKGROUND

Much of our knowledge about stress and its effects, particularly during disasters, has come from military experience. In the Civil War, medical personnel first observed and recorded the principle that environmental stresses may produce symptoms of abnormal behavior in soldiers. Surgeons of both the North and the South described a condition (*nostalgia*) that seemed responsible for considerable ineffectiveness. Soldiers afflicted with this disorder showed many symptoms of emotional instability, including nervousness, anxiety, discontent, and passive-aggressive behavior. In this group, there was a higher frequency of absent without leaves and other disciplinary problems. Medical personnel realized that these symptoms were a result of a pathological interaction between the soldier and his environment. They made note of this in their journals, but the war soon ended. The lesson they had learned was soon forgotten. When World War I began, the military again discovered soldiers with similar symptoms, especially in combat areas. This time the diagnosis was *shell shock*, a term coined by Lieutenant Colonel Mott, a British medical officer. He believed that the observed symptoms were a result of a brain concussion of varying severity secondary to the effects of exploding shells. However, later observers noted that not all soldiers exposed to combat developed these symptoms, and furthermore, some of those with shell shock had not been exposed to combat and had not been anywhere near an exploding shell. Consequently, this strictly physical explanation for their ineffectiveness was discarded. These individuals were considered emotional casualties of the war.

The British and the French noticed that when these casualties were evacuated to rear-echelon medical installations, only a few ever returned to combat duty. However, if they were treated on the front lines, a majority could be returned to full combat duty within twenty-four to forty-eight hours. The treatment was relatively simple and emphasized food, rest, and emotional support, along with a firm expectation from the treating officer, repeatedly conveyed to the soldier, that the soldier would be all right in a few hours and able to return to his group.

These well-documented experiences from World War I were quickly forgotten. At the start of World War II, the military was again found to be lacking in knowledge about the effects of battle stress. When the first full scale American battles resulted in a large number of unanticipated psychological casualties, these casualties were evacuated to rear-line medical installations, contrary to what experience in the later stages of World War I had taught. Many evacuated soldiers did not recover and ended up with medical discharges and diagnoses of psychoneurosis or psychosis. However, as the war continued, American psychiatrists became more skilled in treating war neuroses, using hypnosis and drug-induced interviews to relieve anxiety and restore health. The value of treatment on the front lines was rediscovered, and psychiatrists were again assigned to combat positions. The high level of psychological casualties decreased (Glass, 1953). From these and later wartime experiences, two basic principles of combat psychiatry emerged: treat victims as near the combat front as possible, and return them to duty as soon as possible. These principles have direct application to civilian disaster situations, including floods, tornadoes, fires, industrial accidents, and auto accidents.

THE FOUR PHASES OF DISASTER REACTIONS

Studies of disasters have led to a description of four distinct phases that can be anticipated in any reaction to a major stress situation. These are warning, impact, immediate reaction, and delayed response (American Psychiatric Association, 1964). Understanding of these four phases will enable police officers to effectively apply those principles and techniques of psychological first aid that we will describe later.

The Warning Period

Warning of an impending disaster is desirable. However, this warning might have a destructive or disorganizing effect on individual behavior. While some people function at a high level of effectiveness in the face of danger, others may respond to a warning signal as if a disaster had already occurred, becoming completely helpless. This latter group usually consists of two types of people: those who have experienced a previous or similar disaster in which they were helpless and for whom the warning signal rekindles earlier helpless feelings; and those who will always be helpless in the face of any danger or threat. These people are susceptible to panic and must not be left to their own devices or they will communicate their panic to others.

The Impact Period

When disaster strikes, people will experience many frightening feelings. Although patterns of behavior have been well established, the initial impact will almost always be stunned inactivity. It has generally been shown that for about the first fifteen minutes, no one will be able to act effectively. Approximately fifteen minutes after a disaster has occurred, about 25 percent of the people will be able to resume effective behavior; and within one hour, another 60 percent will be capable of effective functioning. Dr. Jeffrey Mitchell

(1986a), an expert on the psychological aspects of disaster situations, states that about 50 percent of any population involved in a major event is "adequately functioning." He gives no time limits, so it appears that his figures and ours are not too dissimilar. Most of the remaining 15 percent will take several hours to several weeks before they will be able to function effectively. A few may never recover.

Immediate Reaction After Impact

The period immediately following a disaster or stress situation is critical because this is when the ineffective behavior of survivors and rescue workers is most costly. In contrast, effective behavior can save lives, relieve suffering, and decrease confusion.

Period of Delayed Response

When the community or the person is no longer in immediate danger, the situation can be evaluated and action taken to meet needs. However, although the immediate danger is over, some people may have a delayed reaction. Persons who were observed to be functioning effectively immediately after the disaster may no longer be doing so. Instead, they now may demonstrate signs of emotional disturbance, including anxiety or depression. Therefore, some people may require continued observation to ensure that they do not have a delayed reaction to a disaster.

Normal and Abnormal Behavioral Reactions

Police officers often may have to set priorities as to whom they give psychological first aid most immediately. It is therefore important for them to distinguish between normal behavioral reactions to stress or disasters and abnormal reactions. They should first recognize that fear, anxiety, indecisiveness, confusion, and even temporary disorientation can be normal reactions. Their presence does not necessarily mean that an abnormal reaction is occurring. Abnormal reactions are more complex and can be divided into four general categories.

First, there is the individual who is in complete *panic.* In addition to the symptoms and signs just listed, judgment and reasoning have completely disappeared. However, the person who simply tries to escape a dangerous situation is not necessarily in a state of panic. Rather, the panicked individual attempts to leave, often in an unreasonable manner and without any indication of good judgment. It is important that this person be immediately identified and isolated from others before they are affected by his or her reaction.

C. Nylen and D. Hultaker (1984), in an article describing Sweden's approach to public evacuation in a nuclear emergency, state that panic and other irrational behavior are relatively uncommon in disaster and emergency situations. Most people do not panic; instead, it is often very difficult to persuade them that a dangerous situation truly exists. This is especially true when the presenting danger is radioactive emission from a nuclear generating plant rather than a fire, flood, or tornado, with which they may have some familiarity. However, it would be a mistake to ignore the risk of panic entirely, since the potential for such a reaction does lurk in every disaster situation. Most panics have been reported from fires and other incidents where large numbers of people are gathered in a restricted area and everyone is forced to use the few escape routes that may be available. It also must be remembered that panic is a contagious condition. It is necessary to identify those experiencing panic attacks quickly in order to remove them before the contagion spreads and infects others.

The second category of abnormal behavioral reactions is the *depressed group.* These people are slowed down, numbed, and dazed. The individual with a depressed reaction may sit in the midst of utter chaos, gazing vacantly into space, unable to respond. This is

probably the most frequent abnormal behavioral reaction. People suffering from it usually respond quickly to psychological first aid. This group seems to correspond to Mitchell's "second group" (his first group is the 50 percent he describes as "adequately functioning"), which he describes as "stunned and shocked. . . . The people in this group are typically inactive, withdrawn, and obviously overwhelmed" (Mitchell, 1986a).

The third category is the *overactive reaction.* At first this may look like panic, but the critical difference is that affected persons do not try to leave the situation, but rather begin markedly increased physical activity. They may talk rapidly, joke inappropriately, or make endless suggestions of little value. If their hyperactivity can be controlled, they may eventually prove very helpful in dealing with the disaster. Consequently, anything they are given to do that will work off their excess activity is helpful. After they have settled down, they can be assigned to constructive tasks. This group seems to resemble Mitchell's "hysterical group." Victims in this group may display agitation, random movements, pacing, running, screaming, and a general out-of-control demeanor. They differ from the panic group in that their behavior is not primarily oriented to hasty escape. They are obviously overwhelmed by the incident. They also may endanger themselves because they are not able to think clearly in the emergency and may behave in a manner that brings them closer to danger (Mitchell, 1986).

Finally, the last category of abnormal behavioral reactions to stress or disaster situations includes the *abnormal body reactions.* In these cases, physical reactions to stress are incapacitating and may include severe nausea and vomiting that will not stop or hysterical blindness or paralysis. These individuals should be made as comfortable as possible and tagged for early evacuation and medical treatment.

It should be noted, however, that most people, though they may be somewhat overwhelmed initially, do manage to perform adequately after the first hour after impact. In fact, recent studies of over one hundred disaster situations by the Disaster Research Center identified six disaster myths regarded as truth by the public, mass media, and public officials (Michelson, 1984).

MYTH	*FACT*
People will panic.	They do *not* panic. In fact, getting them to evacuate is a bigger problem.
People are unable to cope.	People react in an active, helpful manner.
Local organizations are overwhelmed and unable to perform effectively.	The destruction in relation to total resources is quite low.
Antisocial behavior (that is, looting) is commonplace.	Looting and so on are rare in disaster situations.
Community morale is low in stricken areas.	Community morale is generally high.
Firm measures are needed to prevent personal and social chaos.	Coordination is more essential than firm measures.

Mitchell (1986c) suggests that police and other emergency workers can use a simple scan to assess the victim's psychological state. He refers to the "SEA-3 scan": *S*: speech; *E*: emotional status; *A*-3: alertness – awareness – actions (behavior).

If behavior in each category appears appropriate, the individual is probably functioning adequately and does not require further assistance from an emergency worker. If disturbances in the various categories are noted, the victim is most likely in need of psychological first aid.

Psychological First Aid

Just as officers can administer physical first aid to someone who has been injured in an auto accident, they also can apply psychological first aid to those with acute emotional reactions to disasters. The officers' principal goal is to return the greatest number of people to effective functioning in the shortest time. In responding to stress or disaster situations, officers should keep in mind the following principles:

1. **They should respect every person's right to his or her own feelings.** Just because officers have responded appropriately, they should not expect that everyone else will. They should realize that there will be as many different reactions as there are different people because each person is unique. A psychological casualty is not an inferior or cowardly person.

2. **Officers should remember that emotional disability secondary to a disaster situation is as real as physical disability.** No one would expect a soldier who has had both of his legs shot off to buck up and go back into the fray. Similarly, police officers should not expect people who have had a severe emotional reaction to pull themselves together quickly and carry on.

3. **Every physically injured person will have some emotional reaction to the injury.** Furthermore, some people may have severe emotional reactions to minor injuries because of their personal significance. For example, an artist who has cut a finger may have a more severe reaction than a lawyer with the same injury. Occasionally, the major reason for a severe reaction is not obvious and may relate to a symbolic event or unconscious fear.

Because of this fear, people may distort the seriousness of the injury, consequently increasing their emotional reaction. Finally, it is important for police officers to recognize that there is often more strength in people than may initially appear. Although this may seem contradictory to the first principle, which states that a person's feelings should be recognized and accepted, it is not. Officers should direct their support to the individual's strength. If this strength can be mobilized, officers can significantly reduce the emotional reaction to a disaster.

4. **In handling a disaster situation, officers must remain calm if they are to be effective.** They must keep their wits about them so that they do not inadvertently compound the disaster and the emotional reactions to it. Consequently, they also should remember not to do the following when encountering people with acute emotional reactions to stress situations. They should not strike, slap, or hit anyone. They should remember that it will not do any good to tell someone to "snap out of it" or to "use their willpower." Such statements will only increase feelings of inadequacy, which may already be overwhelming. Finally, they must not upset anyone with pity, blame, or ridicule, since these also will increase feelings of inadequacy.

5. **Police officers should establish some form of communication with the person as soon as possible, either verbal or nonverbal.** In this regard, it is helpful to remember how a parent treats a hurt child who comes in crying from the playground. The good parent will take the child onto his or her lap, comfort the child, and ask what happened. As the child sobs out the story, the parent may put ice or some medicine on the bruise or scratch and get a bandage while continually reassuring the child that everything will be fine.

This is a good example, because many people regress to childlike behavior in disaster situations.

While officers may not take a person onto their laps, they can certainly put an arm around a person, ask what happened, and help the person ventilate feelings. In doing so, officers are not interested in the truth or falsehood of any statements, but rather are trying to get the person to talk about feelings.

6. **After establishing communication, the next important thing police officers can do is to get the person to engage in constructive activity.** This will reduce physical tension as well as divert the person from thinking about his or her own problems. By serving others, the person's feelings of adequacy can be restored. However, officers should not let these people help too much in rescue efforts, or they will be exposed to further stress. After this physical release has been achieved, the person should be encouraged to rest and pay attention to his or her own needs, such as hot food or dry clothing. Throughout, officers should firmly convey the expectation that the person will be all right soon.

7. **Remember that to suffer together is to suffer less.** Officers should try to get the person back to family and friends as soon as possible. For example, if there has been a tornado and people have been rushed to hospitals, officers should try to maintain a list of who went where in order to assist survivors in finding their loved ones.

8. **Finally, officers should always be aware of their own feelings.** It is natural to feel resentment, anger, and hostility toward those who seem to be physically uninjured and yet contribute nothing to resolving the situation. Officers must not allow these feelings to interfere with their ability to help others in a disaster.

The Israel National Police approach their disaster contingency planning with the realization that many police officers are "psychologically unprepared to handle the realities of a major fire or airline crash" (Levinson, 1989, p. 11). Numerous discussions with police officers indicate that many did not know how to cope with death and fatalities, even at homicide scenes. They seek tasks that remove them from the necessity of even looking at the deceased. Further, it is believed that when trained, experienced technicians poorly fingerprint bodies in the morgue, this is due to a reluctance to touch the dead person. After working a major disaster scene with many fatalities, one experienced officer wrote in a private letter, "I am a seasoned cop and a veteran of many murder scenes, but never have I seen anything like this. I will carry the scars of what I have seen for many years to come" (Levinson, 1989, p. 11).

Critical Incident Stress Debriefing

Mitchell (1986) points out that prior to the mid-1970s, there appeared to be little, if any, concern about the stress associated with handling search and rescue or any other emergency situations, not because it did not exist prior to that date but because "What has changed over the last two decades is knowledge and attitudes." It has taken many years for knowledge about the negative impact of work-related stress to filter down from researchers to administrators, supervisors, and trainers. Research has also shown that emergency service workers, including police, are not exempt from the adverse effects of stress — particularly the stressors inherent in disaster situations.

A dramatic change in attitudes also has occurred in the past few years. Police commanders and other personnel have begun to entertain the possibility that the "John Wayne" attitude ("I ain't hurtin' unless the bone is showing") is sometimes not only inappropriate but even harmful to those who adopt this method of handling stress. More and more it is being recognized that normal people (and this includes cops) are strongly affected when they have to deal with (or even just witness) violent death, brutality, or mass casualties and have a right to feelings of anger, depression, frustration, fear, and hostility. In disaster situations, such feelings have to be held in check so officers can do their job — but the feelings are still there. They don't just go away, even when the emergency is over, and they have the potential to undermine mental health and even physical welfare unless recognized and treated. The concept of critical incident stress debriefings (CISD) has evolved to meet this need.

The development of the CISD process began in 1974 when the originator of the concept, Jeffrey T. Mitchell, was a regional emergency medical services coordinator in Maryland. Mitchell presented the concept publicly in the January 1983 edition of the *Journal of Emergency Medical Services.* The first CISD team came into existence in 1983 in Arlington County/Alexandria, Virginia. It is still in operation. Since 1983 seventy-five teams have been established in twenty-five states. Teams now also exist in Canada, Australia, Norway, and West Germany. "In all, the teams have provided over 4,500 debriefings to thousands of emergency personnel in events ranging from single victim auto accidents and shootings to full scale disasters such as the recent Ramstein, Germany, air show catastrophe" (Mitchell, 1988). The main objectives of CISD are twofold: to mitigate the impact of a critical incident on emergency services personnel (police, fire, paramedical, and others) and to hasten the return of emergency personnel to routine duties after the incident. CISD teams are made up of mental health professionals with training (and, it is hoped, experience) in handling critical incidents. As defined by Mitchell, "critical incidents" are "any situation faced by emergency service personnel that causes them to experience unusually strong emotional reactions which have the potential to interfere with their ability to function either at the scene or later. . . . All that is necessary is that the incident, regardless of the type, generates unusually strong feelings in emergency workers" (Mitchell, 1989).

The team is made up of roughly one-third mental health professionals and two-thirds peer support personnel drawn from the volunteer ranks of emergency service personnel. The teams' function in three areas: pre-incident, incident, and post-incident. Pre-incident functions include educating emergency medical services (EMS) personnel, commanders, and administrators about critical incident stress, how it differs from nonemergency stress, and how to employ the CISD team to the best advantage in any incident. The incident phase centers mainly on providing *on-scene support services* to stressed-out emergency service workers. The team also advises command on related matters and lends indirect support to victims and government agencies that can provide necessary services. The on-site team also provides *defusings* for EMS workers immediately after the incident. Defusings are designed to provide a brief discussion of the event and an opportunity for the EMS workers directly involved to ventilate some of their feelings, thus significantly reducing the acute stress surrounding the incident. Not all workers from the scene attend – only those most directly involved. *Demobilizations* are provided for large-scale incidents only and take the place of defusings. As soon as emergency workers disengage from disaster operations, they gather in a large meeting hall, where mental health professional(s) provide a ten-minute presentation on the typical effects of critical incident stress and the signs and symptoms that may appear. Personnel are given suggestions for stress reduction and an opportunity to ask questions. The mental health professional(s) makes him or herself available for private discussions after the meeting. The EMS workers are given an opportunity to eat and relax before returning to duty or going home. The entire demobilization process takes about thirty minutes.

After the critical incident event is over, EMS personnel usually do not feel like talking, especially to outsiders. In this twenty-four-hour period, the workers' emotions are too intense to profit from a team debriefing. What is most important at this stage is to provide emotional and, if necessary, administrative support to those involved. EMS personnel usually prefer to talk only to other members of the unit who were involved. Within twenty-four to forty-eight hours after the conclusion of the incident, a formal critical incident stress debriefing is held. All workers from the scene are required to attend. A qualified mental health practitioner leads this debriefing. The structure follows this general format.

1. **Introductory phase.** The rules of the procedure are described. Emphasis is placed on complete confidentiality, and members pledge to remain silent about whatever goes on or is said.
2. **The fact phase.** Participants are asked to give some facts about themselves and their activities during the incident.
3. **The feeling phase.** People are encouraged to respond to "How did you feel when that happened?" "How are your feelings now?" and so on. This is the opportunity for EMS workers to get some strong feelings out in the open, where feelings can be shared and evaluated. However, no one is required to talk.
4. **The symptom phase.** People are asked such questions as "What unusual things did you experience at the time of the incident?" "What are you experiencing now?" "How has this changed your life?" and so on.
5. **The teaching phase.** The mental health professional presents information about stress, symptoms, reactions, and so on, with emphasis on how natural and normal it is for EMS workers to experience a variety of emotional and physical symptoms and signs.
6. **The reentry phase.** This final phase is the opportunity to wrap up loose ends, answer any outstanding questions, and give reassurances to individuals that

they will be able to put this incident behind them – they don't have to carry around unwanted emotional baggage because of the incident. Positive statements are made to the effect that they performed well during the emergency and that any feelings and symptoms they experienced were to be expected, are of a temporary nature, and should exert no long-range effect on their lives. This is not to say that the incident will ever be completely forgotten, but it will become one of their life's experiences, through which they have emerged wiser and more experienced. Finally, personnel are advised about getting additional professional help should they feel the need.

R. Robinson (1986) study of stress and emergency services (fire, police, and ambulance) concluded that most EMS personnel benefit from critical incident stress debriefings. The more serious the incident, the more helpful the debriefings were perceived. Further, most individuals felt that their unit benefited from the CISD process even though they expressed doubts that they themselves had received much benefit. Seventy-five percent of those who participated in Dr. Robinson's preliminary study mentioned three main benefits of a CISD: (1) the opportunity to express one's feelings and receive assurance that their reactions are normal; (2) the chance to learn from others and mobilize one's own coping behavior; and (3) the opportunity to gain a greater understanding of critical incident stress and its ramifications for EMS personnel. Many also reported a lessening of stress-related symptoms after debriefing.

Long-Term Effects of a Disaster

We have seen that there is a commonality of symptoms among disaster victims. Medical and mental health professionals differ as to the duration and meaning of these symptoms. Some consider the emotional effects to be of a temporary nature, with few, if any, long-range effects. Others state that posttraumatic effects can last a lifetime. Disaster trauma may affect other aspects of an individual's life. Wilkinson and Enrique (1985) note that marital and family problems may be exacerbated, as may be somatic complaints and actual susceptibility to disease. This latter finding comes as no surprise, as it is well known that stress adversely affects the body's immune system. Wilkinson also cautions "emotional problems arising from a disaster tend to escalate over time if early attention is not paid them." This is why it is so important that police officers be trained to administer psychological first aid to those victims requiring it and to encourage all disaster victims to seek professional counseling from qualified personnel if they feel that additional help is needed.

SUMMARY

This chapter has described reactions to acute stress and disaster situations. Emotional casualties are often more frequent than physical disabilities. By recognizing this, officers can have an important influence on reducing abnormal behavior reactions to disaster situations. Not only can they save lives and relieve suffering, but perhaps more important, they can also help people get back on their feet as quickly as possible so that they can assist officers in the many tasks brought about by the disaster situation. Finally, attention is directed to the vulnerability of officers during disaster duty. Utilization of CISD teams is recommended to mitigate the impact of a disaster on police and other emergency workers and to help all emergency service workers to return to duty in good emotional and physical condition following a critical incident.

BIBLIOGRAPHY

Adams, P. R., & Adams, G. R. (1984). Mount Saint Helens's ashfall. *American Psychologist, 39*(3), 252–260.

American Psychiatric Association. (1964). *First aid for psychological disasters.* Washington, D.C.: APA.

Baum, A. April, 1988. Disasters, natural and otherwise. *Psychology Today*, 57–60.

Cohe, R. E. (1980). *Handbook for mental health care of disaster victims.* Baltimore: Johns Hopkins University Press.

Frederick, C. J. (1986). Post-traumatic stress responses to victims of violent crime: Information for law enforcement officials. In *Psychological services for law enforcement*, ed. J. T. Reese & H. A. Goldstein, pp. 341–350. Washington, D.C.: U.S. Government Printing Office.

Glass, A. J. (1953). Psychotherapy in the combat zone. In *Proceedings of Symposium on Stress.* Washington, D.C.: Army Medical Graduate School, Walter Reed Medical Center.

Kerr, D. November, 1982. Police emergency operations: An airplane crash and the community relations function, *Police Chief*, 53–56.

Levinson, J. Summer, 1989. When disaster strikes. *Police Stress*, 11.

Mantell, M. R. (1986). San Ysidro: When the badge turns blue. In *Psychological services for law enforcement*, ed. J. T. Reese & H. A. Goldstein, pp. 357–360. Washington, D.C.: U.S. Government Printing Office.

Mathis, R., McKiddy, R. N., & Way, B. November, 1982. Police emergency operations: The management of crisis. *Police Chief*, 48–52.

Michelson, R. May, 1984. Disaster myths. *Police Chief*, 36.

Mitchell, J. T. January, 1983. When disaster strikes: The critical incident stress debriefing process. *Journal of Emergency Medical Services*, 36–39.

_____. May (1986a). Assessing and managing psychological impact, etc. *Emergency Care Quarterly*, 51–58.

_____. August, 1986b. Living dangerously: Why some firefighters take risks on the job. *Firehouse.*

_____. September/October, 1986c. Critical incident stress management. *Response*, 24.

_____. June, 1987. Effective stress control at major incidents. *Maryland Fire and Rescue Bulletin, 3*, 6.

_____. November, 1988. Stress: The history, status and future of critical incident stress debriefing. *Journal of Emergency Medical Services*, 43–46.

_____. (1989). *Seminar on critical incident stress debriefing*, presented at Tempe, Arizona, 23–24 August.

Mitchell, J. T., & Bray, G. (1989). *Emergency services stress.* Baltimore, MD: Chevron Publishing Co.

Mitchell, J. T., & Resnik, H. L. P. (1981). *Emergency response to crisis.* Bowie, MD: Robert J. Brady Co.

Nelson, E. (1986). Understanding and assessing traumatic stress reactions. In *Psychological services for law enforcement*, ed. J. T. Reese & H. A. Goldstein, pp. 369–374. Washington, D.C.: U.S. Government Printing Office.

Nylen, C., & Hultaker, O. May, 1984. Sweden's approach to public evaluation in a nuclear emergency. *Police Chief*, 46–50.

Raphael, B. (1986). *When disaster strikes: How individuals and communities cope with catastrophe.* New York: Basic Books.

Robinson, R., ed. (1986). *Proceedings from a conference on dealing with stress and trauma in emergencies*, 7–9 August, Social Biology Center, Melbourne, Australia.

Siporin, M. (1976). Altruism, disaster, and crisis intervention. In *Emergency and disaster management: A mental health source book*, ed. H. J. Parad et al. Bowie, MD: Charles Press Publishers.

Spitzer, C. 10 May, 1988. Stress: The invisible toll on rescue workers. *Washington Post.*

Wagner, M. (1986). Trauma debriefing in the Chicago Police Department. In *Psychological services for law enforcement*, ed. J. T. Reese & H. A. Goldstein, pp. 399–403. Washington, D.C.: U.S. Government Printing Office.

Wilkinson, C. B., & Enrique, V. 1985. The management and treatment of disaster victims. *Psychiatric Annals, 15*(3), 174–184.

Chapter 17

BEHAVIORAL ASPECTS OF CROWD AND RIOT CONTROL

Whenever a large number of people come together, such as at protest rallies, athletic events, strikes, parades, rock concerts, peaceful demonstrations, etc., the potential for crowd or mob discord is present. When disturbances do occur, it is the responsibility of the police to restore order, to protect life and property and to maintain the peace. Beyond this, the law enforcement officer must be able to quickly determine if a gathering will become uncontrollable and he must take immediate steps to prevent disorder. (Covey, 1987, p. 213)

Without knowledge of certain psychological principles associated with crowd and riot control, it will be difficult for officers to handle crowd behavior effectively. With knowledge, however, they will be able to plot a course of action that will have the best chance of preventing violence or panic, or of controlling such an outbreak if it has already begun.

In this chapter we will discuss characteristics of crowds and mobs; underlying factors that influence their behavior; countermeasures police officers can take to control it; techniques employed by agitators in mob action; various panic-producing situations that might occur and the actions that can be taken to prevent them; and the type of mental preparation required of police officers before undertaking crowd control duty. We will then discuss different kinds of crowd incidents: the "issueless," event-oriented crowd; the campus event crowd; and finally, the teen-age crowd.

During World War II and the 1950s, the police had no significant problems involving crowd control. This period of relative tranquility was shattered by the social unrest and riots of the 1960s, when cities were burning. According to Deputy Superintendent Riordan of the Chicago Police Department (1981), "Protest marches, parades, demonstrations, sit-ins, major disturbances, and riots – these were new experiences for all of us. The plans for handling large peaceful crowds which existed were not convertible for use in incidents involving hostile crowds" (p. 42). There was a dire need for training in how to handle such situations and the crowds involved. Police departments rushed command personnel into riot control and civil disturbance training, first conducted by the U.S. Army. In these command seminars, policies and procedures were formed regarding the training of police officers for such duty. The typical course for officers that evolved included a review of applicable laws, some information on crowd psychology (little was actually known), an emphasis on crowd and riot formations, baton positions and attack movements used in formation, techniques for the use of chemical agents, and arrest and booking procedures. Role-playing situations where officers had to put into practice the techniques taught them usually followed the academic portion of the course. Police recruits in today's academies are still being offered this type of training.

Characteristics of Crowds and Mobs

It is important to distinguish between a crowd and a mob, since the majority of gatherings do not present any special problems to the police. A crowd is a large number of people temporarily congregated without organization, who think and act as individuals. A crowd may be a *physical crowd* or a *psychological crowd.* An example of the former would be people in a shopping center who have gathered together accidentally without a specific organization or purpose other than shopping. In contrast, the psychological crowd exists when there is a common interest. This type of crowd can be further described as either *casual* or *intentional.* An example of the casual psychological crowd is a gathering at an accident or a fire. In contrast, the intentional psychological crowd might be found at a sporting event, political rally, or funeral. It is the intentional psychological crowd that is most susceptible to transformation into a mob. A mob is a crowd whose members, influenced by stimuli of intense excitement or agitation, lose their sense of reason and respect for law and follow leaders into lawless acts of violence and destruction. It is helpful to classify mobs according to the behavior and motivation of its members.

The *aggressive mob* riots and terrorizes (for example, race riots, lynching, and prison uprisings). The escape mob is in a state of panic or blind flight. Members of an *escape mob* lose their power of reasoning and may cause their own destruction. Finally, a *dispersed mob* may quickly join together, accomplish an act, then disperse again. This mob's objective is to create simultaneous disturbances as diversions from the actions of a principal mob (for example, setting fires to incite additional violence, or sniping).

The Riot Process

Having defined types of crowds, characterizing how a crowd may turn into a mob, and describing types of mobs, we now will turn to the riot process and describe it in detail.

Precipitating Incident

Almost anything can serve as the precipitating incident to a riot. It might be a forceful apprehension by an officer or a routine traffic stop. It may not be an act but only a rumor that leads people to pour into the streets in agitation and anger. It may not be a single event, but rather a series of incidents and/or rumors that set the stage for the final incident that triggers the riot. For example, in the summer of 1980 residents of Miami, Florida, engaged in several days of civil disturbance. The precipitating incident occurred when several police officers were acquitted in court of charges stemming from a case of alleged police brutality in which a black man had died. Although this was the immediate precipitating incident, the roots of this riot had actually been developing over several years and may have even dated back to the 1968 riots. For several days the weather had been unusually hot. For several months economic conditions had been worsening, with a resulting increase in black unemployment. More important, there had been several incidents of alleged police brutality toward blacks in recent years, with the growing belief that nothing would ever be done about it by either the police or local government. All of these events prior to the precipitating incident created an emotional climate conducive to the spontaneous eruption of violence after an incident that would not normally have provoked this extreme reaction.

Studies have shown that in many cases the riot process can be stopped at this point if the mayor or another important official visits the area immediately, talks to the people, and promises to listen and respond to their grievances.

Confrontation

During the second phase of the riot process, the police must avoid either overreaction or under reaction. Many confrontations exhaust the energy of riot participants and nothing further happens. However, in some situations a *keynoting process* may begin. This occurs when the angriest members of a crowd, or perhaps a single more militant individual, urge more violent action. To counter this, moderate community leaders may try to persuade the crowd to disband, promising that a committee will be formed to channel protest to city hall. If these leaders prevail, the crowd will disband and the riot will be over, but if militants or hostile keynoters win, the riot will escalate to the next stage.

Roman Holiday

The *Roman Holiday* phase usually involves young males who are angry, hostile, and impulsive. Although their actions may have been planned in advance, a spontaneous reaction is more likely. They may begin to break windows, overturn cars or set them afire, and engage in other destructive actions. During this stage it is again important for the police not to over- or underreact. If they respond with excessive force, interviews of victims by the news media will reach dissident communities and lead to further escalation. On the other hand, a permissive attitude may be construed as a go-ahead signal, and the result will be the same. When the Roman Holiday phase is not handled properly, more people, both adults and children, begin to take part in looting and stealing. Firebombs and guns may be brought into play, and the riot may escalate into open conflict.

Open Conflict

This phase turns into combat in the city. The police must now use force to contain the riot and restore order. Moderate to intense sniper fire can occur. Firebombing increases and is used as a selective weapon by rioters. The police respond by using weapons. The National Guard is often called in. A dissident community, especially if agitated by militants, may arm itself and assemble its own firepower. The establishment will eventually win, since the odds are in its favor because of its greater resources.

The Individual Rioter

Although rioting is mob action, the individual is still the mob's basic unit. We must ask: Why do individuals participate in mob action? What is it about a mob that leads people to lose control and commit acts that they would not do under other circumstances? To help answer these questions, we will discuss several underlying factors that affect individual behavior in a mob.

The first is *anonymity*. People tend to lose their identity in a mob since they feel that they will not be blamed for their actions. Because they see the things they do as only a small part of a larger picture of violence and destruction, their sense of anonymity is enhanced.

A second factor is the *impersonality of group behavior*. Recalling the football player who bears no personal grudges against his rival but will "do or die for old Notre Dame," or the soldier who has "no animosity" against the enemy soldier he may shoot may understand this better. The impersonality of mob behavior is also demonstrated when one member of a race or group is not seen as an individual but as a stereotype. Snipers who put a police officer in the crosshairs of their high-powered riflescope may hate; but they hate the police *symbol*, not the individual officer they are trying to kill. It does not matter to snipers that the officer in their sights may have a spouse and children or that the officer may be one of the fairest on the force. Neither would it matter if the officer were one of the most hated. Snipers stereotype the officer as a "pig" and kill with an impersonal attitude.

Because of the intense emotions present during a riot, members of the mob tend to suspend their own normally critical judgment and react impulsively to suggestions of a dominant member. Police officers can counter this kind of negative *suggestibility* by conveying an alternate course of action to the mob. For example, during one march on Washington, when agitators were trying to incite tired mob members to continue the disturbances at the Pentagon, undercover police officers infiltrated the crowd and encouraged people to take advantage of waiting buses to rest their tired feet. The mob responded positively to this countermeasure and left the area.

Closely allied to suggestibility is *contagion.* The reader is probably more familiar with this term in a medical sense, such as a contagious disease resulting from the transmission of a virus from the sick to the healthy. Similarly, ideas and feelings can be contagious. People become emotionally stimulated by the feelings and ideas of others, although they have not shared the experiences from which they originate.

Imitation is another factor. When large numbers of people gather, the urge to do what others are doing is very strong. Group identity grows and draws people psychologically closer. Contrary to popular belief, hostility is not eliminated or reduced by having a good fight or letting off steam through violent acts. This behavior merely solidifies hostile feelings and increases hatred within the mob. As open violence increases, more destruction is likely to follow.

Novelty also may encourage individual participation in a mob. Many who lead dull and uninteresting lives may view a riot as a break in their daily routine and react with enthusiasm. A riot gives these people an opportunity to do things they have always wanted to but did not dare.

The Riot-Prone Personality

From the personality disorders discussed in Chapter 6, it is evident that some people might be more apt than others to become involved in a riot. For example, passive-aggressive persons, with underlying feelings of

hostility and aggression, may need only a small provocation to release these feelings against others. Paranoid persons – chronically angry, hostile, and suspicious – will take advantage of an opportunity to act out these feelings. Psychopaths are not only riot-prone but are often instigators and leaders of riots, especially in jails and prisons. On the street, psychopaths may engage in riot behavior as a mask for criminal activity or for the attention they receive as militant leaders. Finally, emotionally immature persons may engage in riots because of a tendency toward immature acting-out behavior. They are suggestible and may be a follow-the-leader type, welcoming the opportunity to release hostility through destructive action. In a mob, they gain the courage to do things they would not do alone.

Agitation Techniques

To counter the behavior of rioters, it is important for police officers to understand the principal techniques agitators' use in inciting and sustaining incite mob action.

The Emotion-Producing Rumor

Police engaged in civil disturbance duty should have an intelligence unit established to identify and control rumors, since the adept agitator will use rumors to increase the tempo of a disorder or to transform an orderly demonstration into a violent one. Police must be aware of these rumors and put out factual information to defuse them.

Propaganda

Agitators use newspaper, radio, television, and magazine propaganda to aggravate existing prejudices and grievances. In this way they can bring a crowd together at a particular location or time and incite emotion by using propaganda to intensify real or imagined inequities. Aroused in this manner, the crowd is ripe for transformation into a violent mob. The police can effectively counter propaganda through up-to-date, factual information, especially about their own actions or those of other controlling forces, such as the National Guard. The local mayor may help by publishing proclamations that give the public concise information and instructions.

Forceful Harangue

As well-trained speakers, experienced agitators use emotionally loaded words and phrases to appeal to local needs, fears, and prejudices. Emphatic movements, such as waving arms, help influence people to abandon their critical reasoning and engage in actions that they would condemn under normal circumstances. Police may apprehend these speakers (running the risk of transforming them into martyrs) or disperse the crowd (which is sometimes quite difficult). The mayor of one large American city undermined the planned actions of an agitator by meeting him at the airport with a courtesy car and appearing on the platform to introduce him. This implied association with the establishment created distrust among those who were prepared to listen to and follow the militant.

The Appearance of an Irritating Person or Symbolic Object

A crowd may be brought to a fever pitch by the appearance of an object, such as a flag, or a particular person for whom the crowd has antipathy. This is sometimes difficult to combat, since it often occurs accidentally. If this happens, the object or person should be removed as quickly as possible, especially if it can be done without further exciting the crowd. When information is obtained ahead of time that the appearance of a particular individual might trigger a disturbance, the appearance should be canceled.

Acts of Violence

Agitators can successfully play upon acts of violence, when they occur, to begin a chain reaction leading to further violence. Although we have been discussing techniques by which trained agitators can incite crowds, amateur agitators who seize a spur-of-the moment opportunity trigger many disturbances. For example, a major riot erupted in Dallas, Texas, some years ago during a march to protest the police shooting of a Mexican American boy. A black female bystander grabbed a police microphone and began shouting "Kill the pigs — kill the pigs!" Forty-eight businesses were damaged in the resulting melee and five police officers were injured.

Panic also may occur when police begin to move in. The police must be prepared to size up panic-producing situations and take active steps to prevent a panic or control the mob's actions when panic starts. Panic has been described as *blind flight*. It develops when the mob perceives a threat to survival, and it spreads rapidly. This perceived threat may be physical and/or psychological, real or imagined. It is usually felt to be so imminent that the mob views flight as the only possible escape.

In a riot, the presence or threat of riot-control agents, such as tear gas, may be enough to spark a panic reaction. The mob becomes irrational and fearful, seeking only to get away from the danger. Escape routes become clogged, and the physical pressure of those in the back causes those in front to be crushed, smothered, or trampled. More panic results, and a vicious cycle ensues.

Police may counter panic reactions with the following techniques: (1) provide up-to-date, factual information to the community and keep it coming; (2) provide escape routes and inform the crowd or mob where these routes are; and (3) keep these routes open and make sure that front-to-rear communication is maintained. The importance of establishing escape routes, keeping them open, and making sure the crowd knows where they are cannot be overemphasized. Ninety-three soccer fans died inside a British stadium because they had no place to go when the crowd began pushing them into a steel mesh antiriot fence that soon collapsed. Two hundred other fans were seriously injured.

Sufficient communication equipment must be provided, and alternate means for backup should be at hand in case the primary communication equipment and/or personnel are ineffective. Despite the difficulties, police must be alert to prevent these incidents.

Helpful Hints to Law Enforcement Officers

Having described the types of behaviors and techniques associated with riot behavior, both group and individual, it is now important to discuss those techniques that law enforcement must employ if it is to successfully contain and control this behavior. Like the individual and group activities that are a part of riot behavior, riot control involves actions both by the individual police officer and the police as a whole.

Self-Control

Individual police officers and the police as a group must not lose self-control when dealing with riots. Professional, businesslike detachment, along with impartiality and the sharp execution of orders, will enhance the police image and contribute to orderly restoration of law and order. Only force that is necessary to control a situation should be used, since excessive force in a sensitive situation will destroy previous gains and seriously affect future accomplishments.

Alertness

Police officers, especially those in command positions, must be alert so they can detect rapid changes in the course of a disturbance. Just as soldiers prepare for the sounds and sights of battle through desensitizing techniques, such as infiltration courses and mock enemy villages, police personnel should be prepared for the sounds and sights of riots and other civil disturbances.

At the Arizona Law Enforcement Training Academy, two techniques have been useful in training officers and recruits to maintain their alertness. The first is a two-hour class on "maintaining your cool," in which the emotionality of certain words and their ability to provoke highly charged emotional reactions are presented. Recruits are told to look at the person on their right and think of the most insulting thing to call or say to that person. Then both are asked to stand, and the first recruit is asked to say it to the other's face using the nastiest tone possible. Then the second person is asked to respond in the nastiest way possible to that insult. This exercise dramatically points out the emotional power of words and makes recruits more alert to their own reactions to name-calling and verbal baiting. Developing an alertness to their own reactions will help officers maintain their cool during riots when they are called names or are insulted.

The second technique is an attempt to simulate the sights and sounds of battle. During this exercise, one recruit class is required to handle a disturbance staged by another recruit class. Depending on the actions of the "police," the disturbance becomes either aggravated or quieted down. After the exercise, a critique is held to discuss the actions of the "crowd" and "police" to determine which actions led to which results. A valuable part of the exercise is that recruits can see how both sides tend to get carried away by their emotions. Alerting officers to this aspect of riot behavior is important in increasing riot-control effectiveness.

Working as a Team

Police officers are trained to work individually and to deal with individuals. They think in terms of the individual rather than the group. But when dealing with crowd/mob control, officers have to work as a team member. They cannot deal with this group as individuals but must deal with it as part of a group themselves – the *controlling* group. The controlling group must be well organized and act with precision if it is to be effective. This change of attitude or approach is sometimes difficult for individual police officers to accept. Police officers need training to become proficient at crowd control (Covey, 1987).

Community Support

Acquiring and maintaining community support is an important factor in riot control. To maintain community support, police must act competently and professionally. They must protect and defend everyone in their jurisdiction, not just a select few.

The Use of Humor

Crowd control duty elicits tension in controlling personnel. This is especially true if officers expect the crowd to be hostile and/or violent. In response to this anticipation, officers tend to look grim and stern. This sets up a self-fulfilling prophesy: You expect trouble, you'll get trouble. Rather, officers should relax, be friendly, and initiate conversation with individuals in the crowd if possible. Officers should remember that a smile is contagious and will not completely destroy their authority.

Humor is often overlooked as an effective police tactic in crowd control. It can be used to help control sit-ins, marches, and other mobile demonstrations; in handling confrontations between mobs and control forces that have not yet reached a stage of violence; in dispersing groups to minimize animosity; in reducing hostility when it is necessary to make selected or mass arrests at a demonstration; or in the general prevention of hostility secondary to an issue that has led to a demonstration (Coates, 1972).

Where possible, police should direct humor against themselves to reduce some of the hostility demonstrators feel toward them. Humor should be verbal rather than visual. If the humor is effective, it tends to be contagious, with one laugh facilitating the next.

Although initial attempts to use a light touch on a crowd may not be well received, repeated attempts may have a cumulative effect. However, heavy-handed humor should be avoided; in most situations, ethnic humor is definitely out of place. Due to the positive benefits of humor in riot control, police departments might identify for crowd control duty those officers who demonstrate an ability to handle crowds with wit and humor.

Police Policy

Most law enforcement authorities have policies that guide the handling of crowds or mobs. These policies should be reexamined frequently to evaluate their effectiveness. For example, a common police practice during riots is to order all officers on twenty-four-hour alert and increase on-duty time to twelve hours or longer. However, the effectiveness of this practice is questionable. A tired officer is a poor officer, especially when faced with the stress of civil disorder. How long can a police officer stay on the street, facing a hostile and potentially violent crowd, without losing control? A police sergeant commented, "When my men are fresh, they toss off the insults and jeering with good humor. After an hour or two, their patience begins to wear thin. Give them another couple of hours and they're probably ready to bust heads."

Some other common practices seem equally ill advised. For example, in anticipation of trouble with student demonstrators, twenty or more deputies were brought to the scene in a school bus. They were confined on the bus in the hot sun for three to four hours, awaiting a possible call to action. Fortunately the call never came, and the deputies were driven back to the sheriff's office. One can speculate what frame of mind these officers were in after an hour on a hot bus. Had the call to action come, they might have used more force than necessary to control the demonstration.

Law enforcement authorities should plan policies that reduce the physical and emotional stress of riot duty. A place for officers to rest in comfort while on call should be set up immediately, with beverages and sandwiches available. If possible, this should be provided by a local civic organization. This will show officers that they have community support. A sense of group identity supports effective action. It is advisable for law enforcement authorities to arrange for officers who are coming off street duty during civil disturbances to spend time with other officers. This will enable them to share experiences, fostering an esprit de corps. As mentioned, since most officers are trained to work individually, more training must be provided to help them work as a team during civil disorders. Attainment of this goal requires constant practice. Police should plan regular team meetings, even if a riot is not imminent.

Competent Crowd Control

An example of police competence is found in the demonstration experience at Syracuse University as reported by Chief Thomas J. Sardino. In April, 1985 Syracuse University students began an antiapartheid demonstration that included a hunger strike by some students, marches, speeches, and an encampment on the lawn opposite the administration building. At times, up to one thousand demonstrators were involved. Chief Sardino (1985) writes:

> As the biggest campus demonstrations since the antiwar protests of the early '70s spread throughout the New York institutions of higher education, some onlookers were expecting the bloodshed and stench of tear gas that marked such occasions a decade-and-a-half earlier. The agonizing visions of students lying dead before the rifles of National Guardsmen raised the question of whether or not administration and government response would be less drastic this time.

Since the university is under the jurisdiction of the Syracuse City Police Department, Chief Sardino was confronted with the problem. He decided to employ a proactive rather than reactive approach. With this in mind, during the week preceding the demonstrations he met with the Coalition to End Racism and Apartheid (CERA) and with student protest leaders to discuss their plans and to explain to them their right to peaceful assembly and protest.

On the fifth day of the demonstration, he was absent from a coalition meeting with university officials during which demonstrators were ordered to remove their encampment by 1800 hours that day or face forceful eviction by campus security personnel. When the chief heard of the meeting, he immediately went to the chancellor's office and stated that in his opinion, the Constitution of the United States provided for both points of view (for the protest to continue and for the university to conduct its business as required). He then went to the crowd of demonstrators and asked to use their microphone so he could address the students. He told them that the police department would protect their right to demonstrate as forcefully as it would protect the right of the university to remain open. He further stated that no peaceful demonstrators would be arrested and that the only time the police department would do anything to anybody would be if the law was broken. Within days, and with no arrests, the university and the coalition reached an agreement to end the encampment and the demonstration.

In contrast, the nearby Cornell University campus received several bomb threats, experienced student occupation of university buildings, student suspensions, and a total of 1,065 arrests. The State University of New York at Albany, Colgate University at Hamilton, and Columbia University in New York City experienced some form of student occupation, blockades, interference with university business, and arrests (Sardino, 1985).

To be certain that the reader does not get the impression that Chief Sardino was simply being "too soft" with the demonstrators, let us quote the philosophy behind his actions:

> I hold a firm belief that our universities represent incubators of public opinion for today

as well as the future. Academic freedom, freedom of speech and assembly, and the right to dissent are precious commodities in a democratic society. They must be respected and protected! And, they must be exercised with a recognition that freedom from attacks upon other people and destruction of property are also rights to be respected and protected.

Assault is still assault whether committed in an ordinary street fight or during a political or social protest. The balance between dissent and anarchy, between academic freedom and sophistry, is at best precarious. And, it is precisely that balance in which law enforcement must find its proper role when intervening in conflicts of social expression. (Sardino, 1985)

Another example of police competence in handling demonstrations that have the potential of developing into mass disturbances is taken from a campus scene at the University of Kansas (KU). Again, the issue was South African apartheid, and the group working for its abolishment was the KU Committee on South Africa. Their demands were that the KU Endowment Association (KUEA) divests itself of holdings in any corporations doing business in South Africa. A mock "die-in" organized by the Committee on South Africa was to take place to protest the imminence of nuclear attack. The location selected for the demonstration was a large, grassy plot across from the administration building.

When university police received two bomb threats to the Military Science Building and the Kansas Union, events escalated rapidly. Members of the Committee on South Africa began a sit-in in the administration building, and were joined by about fifty members of the "die-in" crowd. The response of KU administrators and the KUPD was very low key. They decided that the students could remain in the building as long as their presence was not disruptive (they were confining themselves to the public area of the building) and that the building could remain open overnight. The director of police ordered one

officer to be on duty in the building near the area occupied by the protesters. Officers were rotated into this assignment so that nearly all uniformed officers drew a shift in the building. The establishment of informal contact with the demonstrators resulted in positive feelings on both sides. The protestors got a chance to see the officers as fellow human beings who were just doing their job, and the officers began to get a feeling for the protestors and their values. This rapport continued throughout the demonstration, even when arrests eventually had to be made. In an interview with a student demonstrator printed in a local paper, the demonstrator said: "the police officers were really nice . . . really supportive. . . . We've got mutual respect. . . . They're doing their job and we respect that." In summarizing the experience, Sergeant Brothers (1985) of the university police states:

In retrospect, a question well worth asking is how did KU Police manage to effect 65 arrests and control three moderate-sized demonstrations and several small ones with no injuries, no property damage and no necessity for the use of force. The answer is *communication* . . . there were excellent communications between police and KU administration, and between police and demonstrators throughout the entire protest period. Of particular importance was the excellent rapport established between KU police officers and members of the anti-apartheid group. Director Denney's decision to facilitate informal contact between officers and participants in the sit-in at Strong helped build a most effective working relationship between police and protestor. Because of this, both sides were able to recognize the humanity of their counterparts, a perception that kept forcible resistance from rearing its ugly head.

Another factor was a conscious effort on the part of the police to avoid falling into an adversary role as the agent of the university administration. Instead, they managed to project themselves as agents of the law. "Such minor points as not aggressively handing out citations for every perceived violation of the law, but instead waiting until complaints about the protestors' conduct were received before taking action, helped to establish the police in a neutral role" (Brothers, 1985).

Types of Crowds

The "Issueless," Event-Oriented Crowd

Spectator sports events, contested before large numbers of people, are an ever-present fact of contemporary social life. A week does not go by without the gathering of tens of thousands of people whose sole purpose is to witness a sporting event. These events are capable of exciting strong emotions, leading to violent outbursts by groups of spectators that may result in injury or death (Lewis, 1982). Mark (1970) refers to such sports riots as "issueless" in the sense that there is no underlying social problem (no hidden agenda) tied to the riot.

J. R. Brick (1982) describes these sports crowds as "expressive or revelous" crowds because its members are expressing their feelings and sentiments by releasing their energy through their movement. A crowd of this type is not aggressive or destructive. However, it is often mistaken for the aggressive crowd and is unwittingly treated as if it were dangerous. Brick warns that it is important to avoid this mistake. It is wiser to let the group continue to express itself if there is no serious breach of the peace. "Indeed, interrupting the release of energies in an expressive manner may divert the latent energies of such a crowd into aggressive and destructive behavior" (Brick, 1982). J. M. Lewis (1982) describes such a mistake in police strategy following the Pittsburgh Steelers' Super Bowl win:

> The Super Bowl win was the first title the Steelers had won in forty-two years. . . . After the Steelers won the game, people started moving toward Market Square, an area dotted with night clubs and after-hours places. . . .
>
> Within a half-hour after the end of the game, the crowd had grown to between 10 and

15,000. The majority of the people who gathered at Market Square to celebrate were young. The police permitted drinking and dope smoking. Four hundred extra police were added to the detail just in case things should get out of hand.

Police strategy was to stop matters early because they didn't want the crowd to swell to extremely large numbers. They began to force the people apart, pushing them down streets in an effort to break up the mob. As police began to force people apart, the character of a portion of the crowd changed from that of a carefree, celebrating mass to an ugly, nasty aggregate of people.

Full beer bottles and cans were thrown from the crowd and from some downtown buildings. Downtown store windows were destroyed and police started to use billy clubs on some of the fans. Four police dogs were used at some of the trouble spots and at one point, a dog was turned loose in the crowd and a rumor spread that someone's finger was bitten off. At least two back windows in police cars were broken and someone turned on a fire hydrant.

At one point, a police officer tried to arrest a young man, and was subsequently pelted by beer bottles and snowballs by an angry mob that crowded to within two feet of him. One policeman was hit in the face with a full can of beer and suffered a fractured skull.

At 9:30 P.M., the police made an announcement over a bullhorn that "anyone on the streets after ten o'clock will be arrested." Their "show of force" did convince the people that they were serious. The streets were clear by 11:30 P.M.

The Campus-Event Crowd

Another setting for the "issueless" crowd is the campuses of colleges and universities (and, to a lesser extent, in junior and senior high schools). Campus police and security forces must control crowds attending dances, rock concerts, athletic events, and graduations. If they have had any training at all, police and security personnel will have probably undergone the riot control training typically offered to basic police trainees. This seems hardly effective for the management of university crowds.

There are certain differences between events on campus and events occurring on private property (such as sports arenas) and government property (such as community centers, parks and other recreational activities). The university "invites" outsiders to come on campus for sporting events, rock concerts, and other musical events, as well as personal appearances by political figures and celebrities, who often discuss controversial and very emotional subjects. The university is therefore the "host" and campus police must see that their "guests" enjoy their visit by assuring their safety and well-being.

Campus police always must remember that students are the university's reason for being (Wensyel, 1987). Students have a right to enjoy activities in safety and security. Students also have the right to demonstrate peacefully, knowing that demonstration (especially if the media are present) is the most effective way to parade their cause(s) before thousands or even millions (Chandler, 1986). There is another difference in the campus setting. Parents often expect the university to protect their "children" – even if the "child" is a junior or senior, but especially if a freshman. Failure to control crowds may result in a student's injury or death and open the university (and police) to lawsuits.

Campus police must walk the line between being seen as "enforcers" and being the university's visible public relations people. They must protect the peaceful experience of visitors and prevent harassment by anyone. J. W. Wensyel (1987) states that good crowd control at campus events does not just happen. It involves three distinct operations: development of control plans, enforcement of those plans during the event, and after-action analysis and modification of the basic plan to correct weaknesses and improve the plan. Carl Franklin of the University of Oklahoma states that planning for a major event, such as the opening game of the

Sooner football season, starts almost a year before that first kick-off. "The staff of the Oklahoma University Police Department starts looking ahead to the next year before the dust settles from the just-finished season." Wensyel (1987) discusses in detail the specifics of crowd control at dances, rock concerts, and football games. He notes that the major problems at rock concerts are the huge, often unruly crowds they draw. The presence of drugs and alcoholic beverages and their effects on young users is as important as the need to control outsiders and gate crashers. Next to rock concerts, football games draw the biggest crowds, and they are the biggest source of problems. He also notes that police must be very sensitive to the fact that concerts and football games (and certain other athletic events) are big money makers for schools and that fervent fans may become quite vocal and punitive if they perceive unnecessary or inappropriate interference in their affairs by campus police.

Teenage Crowds

Police often have to deal with teenage crowds. Since peer approval is so important to almost all teens, and since they tend to prefer their own company, it is not surprising that they hang out in sizable groups and cause problems and provoke citizen complaints. Police officers may spend considerable time breaking up disturbances between rival schools, dealing with teenage vandalism, and coping with other unacceptable behavior (Law Enforcement Training and Information Network [LETIN] 1986).

Teenagers, especially those traveling in groups, may be under the influence of alcohol or other drugs. These drugs can produce bizarre, even psychotic like behavior. Teenagers may be acting out some deep-seated emotional problem unrelated to the reality at hand. Officers should remember that, as in the case of severely intoxicated adults, the immediate problem might be a medical one. Immediate referral to some medical facility could be advisable. Officers should also remember that teenagers and young adults are high-risk subjects for in-custody suicide. Regardless of teenagers' behavior, officers should retain their cool and ignore any insulting remarks. Attempts to communicate with an intoxicated subject are especially useless except simply to tell the individual exactly what you want him to do. Techniques of teenage crowd control include:

1. Before leaving the patrol car, decide whether or not backup or medical assistance should be called.
2. One officer should "hang back" in a protected position with a good view of scene.
3. One officer should approach within eight to ten feet of crowd's edge.
4. Ignore youngsters who are doing the most talking; ignore ringleaders.
5. Tip the balance of power by calling two or three youngsters at random. Separate them from the crowd and engage them in a pointedly separate conversation or interview.
6. When addressing the crowd, maintain eye contact with two or three youngsters, and always:
   a. Be direct and brief.
   b. Avoid judgmental remarks.
   c. Avoid reference to the citizen complaint.
   d. Make 'I' statements: "I expect you to disperse in one minute."
   e. Make fact-based descriptive statements: "I see about twenty-four people and that's too many."
7. Establish some degree of one-on-one trust and communication. Say what you expect the crowd to do without describing the consequences of its failure to do so. If there is no response, describe what you intend to do and be fully prepared to back up what you have said. Never make empty threats. (LETIN 1986, p. 10)

Police Officers' Code of Conduct

We suggest this code of conduct for police officers during civil disturbances and riots. This code can be a guide to professional behavior not only during these conflicts but in other stressful situations as well.

a. Remember that your most powerful weapons are psychological ones – patience, tolerance, good humor, tact, and the ability to set an example by your own conduct.
b. Remember that it is your uniform and your position as symbols of the establishment that cause some people to react negatively. Do not take threats, insults, or abuse personally.
c. Do not look on all situations as a challenge to your ability as police officers. No one expects you to take unnecessary chances or to prove something.
d. Try to learn all you can about how a person functions in a group, especially under stress conditions. The more you know about this type of behavior, the better you will be able to predict, control, and alter it.
e. Don't overestimate your endurance threshold. A tired police officer is a poor one, especially during civil disturbance duty.
f. Have faith in others. You are not alone. There is a whole system behind you, with local officials and other responsible citizens working to restore order.
g. Remember that all riots must end sometime and that then the task of restoring affected areas or people must begin. Therefore, do not do anything during the stress of the disturbance that jeopardizes either you or the department's position in carrying out this task.
h. Remember that you are a professional law enforcement officer. Take pride in your ability to act professionally under any and all conditions.

SUMMARY

In this chapter the author has presented many of the principles that influence the behavior of crowds and mobs. The chapter also discussed underlying factors that cause people to participate and the characteristics of those who emerge as leaders of mobs. The author has suggested techniques to help law enforcement officers control mobs and manage issueless, event-oriented crowds associated with private or university functions, and has discussed the management of teenage crowds and certain precautions police officers should employ when dealing with adolescent crowds. Finally, the author has provided a code of conduct for police officers.

BIBLIOGRAPHY

Advisory Commission on Civil Disorders. (1970). *Report of the National Advisory Commission on Civil Disorders.* Washington, D.C.: U.S. Government Printing Office.

Brick, J. R. March-April, 1982. Crowd management. *Campus Law Enforcement Journal,* 23–25.

Brothers, J. T. September-October, 1985. Communication is the key to small demonstration control. *Campus Law Enforcement Journal,* 13–16.

Chandler, C. L. October, 1986. The role of law enforcement in student confrontations. *Law and Order,* 74–75.

Coalter, F. (1985). Crowd behaviour at football matches: A study in Scotland. *Leisure Studies, 4*(1), 111–117.

Coates, J. F. (1972). Wit and humor: A neglected aid in crowd and mob control. *International Journal of Offender Therapy and Comparative Criminology, 16,* 184–191.

Covey, R. July, 1987. *Crowd and riot control.* Tucson, AZ: Arizona Law Enforcement Training Academy (lesson plan; 4-hour course).

Gaskell, G., 7 Benewick, R. (1987). Social scientific perspectives on the crowd in Britain. *Quarterly Journal of Social Affairs, 3*(1), 53–70.

Kreps, G. A. (1973). Change in crisis-relevant organizations: Police departments and civil disturbances. *American Behavioral Scientist, 16,* 356–367.

Law Enforcement Training and Information Network. (1986). *Dealing with adolescents: Training guide,* vol. 2, p. 10. Belleville, IL: LETIN.

Lewis, J. M. (1982). Fan violence: An American social problem. *Journal of Research in Social Problems and Public Policy, 2,* 175–206.

Mark, G. T. (1970). Issueless riots. *The Annals, 39,* 21–33.

Riordan, J. (1981). Managing crowd control problems. *Police Chief, 9,* 42–45.

Sardino, T. J. September-October, 1985. The demonstrations experience at Syracuse University. *Campus Law Enforcement Journal,* 33–34.

Spiegel, J. (1968). *Toward a theory of collective violence.* Waltham, MA: Brandeis University Press.

Swan, L. A. (1980). *The politics of riot behavior.* Washington, D.C.: University Press of America.

Wensyel, J. W. (1987). *Campus public safety and security with guidance as well for high school and private secondary schools.* Springfield, IL: Charles C Thomas.

Chapter 18

BEHAVIORAL ASPECTS OF HOSTAGE SITUATIONS

Law enforcement officers in the United States, as well as other countries, have been faced almost daily with the reality of the hostage/barricaded subject situation. The modern day negotiation process has been time-tested and refined by law enforcement in response to these situations. (Gilmartin & Gibson, 1985, p. 46)

For police officers, this means that no matter where they work, their chances of confronting a hostage situation in today's violent and unstable world are mounting daily. This chapter will explain why this subject is important to police officers. It will also provide definition of pertinent terms; suggest a philosophy for conducting hostage negotiations; describe various types of hostage negotiations; review the psychological characteristics of those engaged in hostage taking; and review hostage negotiation techniques and strategies, including moral dilemmas presented to police in certain negotiation situations, the effect of the incident on hostage victims, and the impact of the hostage negotiation process on the hostage negotiation team, including special weapons and tactic teams (SWAT) members. Special stress factors associated with hostage/barricaded situations where the perpetrator is a police officer will be noted.

Importance to Police Officers

Since the early 1970s, hostage taking by criminals and political extremists has increased,

and every indication is that the frequency of hostage incidents will continue to rise. In 1976 in the United States there were 207 cases involving 291 hostages. In the last few years, the New York City Police Department has averaged one hostage situation a day (Schlossberg, 1981). Over a three-year period, the Houston Police Department has been involved in 168 incidents, and the San Antonio Police Department has had 110 incidents over a ten-year period (McMains, 1988).

None of these involved political terrorism. But this is not to suggest that incidents involving political terrorism have not also been on the increase. In 1979 there were fifty-two proven terrorist incidents that resulted in eight dead and twenty-four injured (Quainton, 1980). In September 1984, the U.S. Department of State reported: "Events in 1983 presaged what may be the beginning of a more deadly trend – high casualty strikes against lower level targets. We noted 1925 casualties (652 killed, 1273 injured) resulting from 116 international terrorist incidents, the highest casualty figure we have recorded since we began keeping records in 1968 – the lethality of terrorism in 1983 increased significantly" (Office for Combatting Terrorism, 1984).

This increase has continued unabated to this writing and reinforces the need for police officers to be familiar with political terrorist tactics. Further, terrorist methods are being employed more frequently by criminals and others in situations where local police are responsible for intervention. Therefore, while political terrorism is still not an everyday occurrence, local police must handle, with distressing regularity, armed robbery attempts where hostages are seized to aid flight; respond to jail and prison riots where hostages are taken to ensure compliance with prisoner demands; and react to family fights and other crisis situations where victims are seized for no other reason than to prove a point or gather increased attention.

In addition to the influence of political terrorism, the increase in hostage taking also may result from a number of other factors. First, there has been a sharp increase in the number of felonies. Twenty years ago only 10 percent of all murders happened during another crime; today almost 30 percent of murder victims die in this fashion (Lunde, 1975). This increase in felonies is partially a result of an increase in shopping centers, jewelry stores, and other lucrative targets for criminal activities. When the growing number of holdups of these targets is coupled with the increasing speed of police response, the opportunities grow for hostage situations to develop at almost any time.

With the development of federal, state, and county computerized record systems, patrol officers can identify wanted persons through routine checks. This often can lead to a surprise confrontation that is likely to increase the chance of dealing with a barricaded subject or hostage situation. Another factor may be the increase in the number of previously violent people who are released to the community because prisons, jails, and mental health facilities no longer have the space or programs to handle them. Finally, deteriorating economic conditions, associated with high unemployment, may cause the increase in hostage taking. Those who find themselves without jobs and are thus incapable of supporting their families often become desperate as their feeling of being trapped increases. Faced with a seemingly hopeless situation,

they often resort to hostage taking as a last desperate attempt to fight their way out.

Definition of Terms

- A *hostage situation* exists when a person seizes another person against the latter's will and holds him or her to enforce certain demands. This can be done with a few or many people.
- *Barricaded subjects* are persons who barricade themselves in defiance of law enforcement authorities. At one time or another, all hostage situations can include barricaded subjects. However, all barricaded subjects cannot be considered hostage situations, because in most cases barricaded subjects have not taken any hostages. Police tactics and techniques in handling both these incidents are similar.
- *Negotiation* is the bargaining process between principals. In this case, the principals are the hostage takers and the law enforcement authorities.
- *Negotiators*, if used, are the persons who mediate between principals. Negotiators do not have decision-making power. This often allows them to buy time, since the demands of the hostage taker and responses of police authorities must be relayed back and forth. The absence of decision-making authority also relieves negotiators from the responsibility of negative or unfavorable decisions by police authorities that have to be relayed to the hostage-takers.

The U.S. State Department defines *terrorism* as premeditated, politically motivated violence perpetrated against noncombatant targets by subnational groups or clandestine state agents. *International terrorism* is terrorism involving citizens or territory of more than one country (U.S. Department of State, 1984).

The Philosophy of Hostage Negotiation

Prior to the '70s, the typical police response to hostage situations and barricaded subjects was to assemble all available personnel and firepower, deliver an ultimatum to surrender to the hostage-taker or barricaded subject, and then, after an interval of time (the length generally depended on the patience of the commander at the scene), issue an order for a full-scale assault. The criminal was sure to be overcome in this unequal contest, but unfortunately one or more hostages, innocent bystanders, and sometimes even police officers would be killed or injured. These casualties, while mourned, were considered the necessary price of the mission (Pierson, 1980).

Today, police departments have a very different approach to barricaded subjects and hostage situations. The method involves handling these potentially explosive situations by bargaining rather than force – with logic and common sense instead of bullets and tear gas. Hostage negotiation has been called law enforcement's most effective nonlethal weapon (Soskis & Van Zandt, 1986). Whenever a barricaded subject or hostage situation exists, the police may respond by (1) containing and attempting to negotiate; (2) containing and demanding surrender; (3) using chemical agents to force surrender; (4) using snipers or sharpshooters to neutralize the subjects; or (5) assault. If responses (3), (4), or (5) are tried and fail, it is impossible to go back to responses (1) and (2). Therefore, attempting to contain and negotiate the release of hostages or surrender of the barricaded subject is the preferred method. Optimally, police try to return the hostage or hostages unharmed and to take the criminal or criminals into custody (Fuselier, 1981).

Harvey Schlossberg (1989), the New York Police Department cop psychologist who originated the hostage negotiation approach, states that the primary objective of the hostage negotiation team is to (1) protect the lives of the hostages, (2) protect the lives of the bystanders, (3) protect the lives of the police, and (4) protect the life of the criminal (hostage taker). The release of hostages and arrest of the criminal are secondary.

Confronting Hostage Situations

Types of Hostage Situations

Hostage situations may occur under the following conditions:

1. **Criminals may plan from the outset to use hostages as part of their criminal act to ensure their escape, gain ransom money, or for some other purpose.**
2. **Criminals may not plan to take hostages but become trapped inside an establishment they intended to rob.** A quick response precludes escape, and they seize hostages as their way out. (This is probably the most common situation faced by law enforcement officers.)
3. **In jails or prisons, prisoners seize hostages to highlight their demands for change (better food, more visits) or to assist in an escape.** Sometimes a mentally disturbed prisoner may seize hostages for reasons associated with his or her particular mental disturbance. Prisoners often seize hostages to espouse a particular point of view (as did the Symbionese Liberation Army) (Alexander & Gleason, 1981).
4. **A psychotic person may seize hostages in response to delusional thinking (to right a perceived wrong or carry out a secret mission).** A severely depressed person may conclude that the only logical answer to life's pain is murder-suicide, usually involving family members. An individual with an explosive personality may hold his or her family hostage after destroying the contents of the house in a rage reaction.
5. **Normal people who are under severe stress and become intoxicated may take a hostage.** A parent may take a child hostage in a custody dispute, believing that the other parent is unfit and that this is the only way he or she can gain custody.

6. **Political terrorists may take hostages, usually to achieve publicity, force the release of political prisoners, or gain revenge.** Their demands go far beyond the authority of local police departments and usually cannot be handled by them. The likelihood of hostages being killed is much higher in this situation, since the terrorists have probably discussed the possibility or even the desirability of killing the hostages and may be prepared to die as martyrs.

Personalities Involved in Different Hostage Situations

All hostage takers have some kind of emotional problem. Bolz notes the resemblance that hostage takers have to suicide attempters. Each often is fearful, desperate, depressed, impulsive, and angry. It was this assumption that allowed the New York Police Department hostage negotiation team to believe it could talk its way out of almost any seige because "just as every suicide attempt could be successful if the subject had really wanted death, every hostage holder could have killed his captives before the police even arrived to negotiate" (Bolz & Hershey, 1979). The following illustrate different hostage situations.

Criminals Who Plan to Take Hostages

Since psychopaths (antisocial personality disorder) are so often found among criminals, it is not surprising that they sometimes plan to take hostages as part of their criminal activity, most often for ransom or to enhance bargaining power. Familiarity with the characteristics of psychopaths (Chapter 9) should assist negotiators in hostage situations involving this type of personality. Psychopaths are classic manipulators and con artists, and they may be adept in eliciting the *Stockholm syndrome* in the hostages (sympathy for the hostage taker). However, even more

important is their lack of real feelings for people. This insensitivity, coupled with their sometimes sadistic and impulsive behavior, may make the situation very dangerous for hostages. It is best to appeal to psychopaths in terms of what profits them the most. It also is important to remember that psychopaths can't tolerate success. Even when things are going well for them, they need to stir up trouble. It follows that they need frequent stimulation, which negotiators should provide through frequent contacts and challenging, problem-solving situations. Without these, psychopaths may turn their attention to the hostages. It is possible that if one or more of the hostages are women, they will be raped.

While some criminals may not be diagnosed as antisocial personality disorders, the majority of them still fall into one of the other diagnostic categories listed under personality disorders. This means that they are not psychotic and generally do not suffer from the neurotic symptoms of tension and anxiety except under very stressful conditions. Therefore, since they are in touch with reality, it is probable that police negotiators can convince them that their own best interests lie in surrender rather than in harming the hostages or prolonging the hostage situation.

Criminals Who Don't Plan to Take Hostages

Criminals engaged in a felony who seize hostages when things go sour and the police arrive too soon are usually preoccupied with escape. If escape is blocked, they become concerned primarily with their own safety. With hostages, they may be fearful of terminating the situation, since the police may shoot them. These criminals are usually not psychotic. They are probably familiar with the police and know what to expect. In these cases negotiations should be oriented toward helping the hostage takers see the advisability of surrendering so that they do not further jeopardize themselves by additional charges.

Their personal safety upon surrender should be assured.

Prisoners

It is an unfortunate fact in our society that some prisons tend to be the garbage heaps into which the worst and most violent among us are discarded (Hassel, 1975). When a riot or hostage situation occurs in jails or prisons, a psychopath is almost always one of the leaders. Hostages are most often correctional personnel or volunteers who happen to be in the prison at the time the riot begins. In some cases, the seizure of volunteers or professionals is a part of the riot plan.

Since prisoners are desperate and feelings may run high, particularly against guards, the threat to hostages of injury or death is great. The situation is further complicated because prisoners usually demand freedom. Many correctional institutions have a firm policy that no inmate will leave the institution by taking hostages. Thus the primary demand cannot be met under any circumstances. Demands for better food, living conditions, or amnesty for rioters can be negotiated. In contrast to civilian police action in other hostage situations where early confrontation is avoided, authorities in correctional institutions believe that quick, forceful action on the part of corrections and other law enforcement personnel is advisable so that the disturbance can be quelled before rioting prisoners can organize and strong leaders emerge to direct the riot. If early intervention is impossible, the disturbance should be contained in the smallest possible area.

Efforts should be made to identify jail and prison inmates who are known psychopaths. These inmates can then be monitored whenever tensions are running high so they can be promptly removed at the first hint of a disturbance. This is critical since they are often the instigators of the disturbance or add fuel to the situation once the riot begins. Finally, they are likely to be chosen by inmates as their spokesmen in any negotiations, thus complicating the proceedings.

Mentally Disturbed Hostage Takers

In this case, hostage takers are psychotic or borderline. If they are paranoid schizophrenics, they may have seized hostages to right a perceived wrong or to carry out a delusion. If psychotically depressed, they can be very dangerous because of the presence of inadequate, unworthy, and hopeless feelings that convince them that they are unfit to live. Not only is their potential for suicide extremely high, but such hostage takers may decide to take some or all of the hostages with them. They also may kill any police officers who offer them the opportunity. In such situations, hostages are often members of the person's own family or persons well known to him or her. Such hostage takers may believe that they are actually doing these people a favor by saving them from a sinful or terrible life. Delusional thinking will often have a strong religious component, such as the case of a recent murder-suicide in Tucson in which a wife killed her husband and their three children so they could leave this world and meet their Sun God.

Negotiating with these disturbed people is difficult. Although it is generally recommended that department psychologists not be involved as negotiators in hostage situations, psychologists must be considered as negotiators when hostage takers are mentally disturbed. Psychologists' clinical experience may allow them to respond more effectively to the many nuances of behavior and emotions characteristic of these people.

While the author is trained in hostage negotiations and has often been a negotiator, other police psychologists have been reluctant or opposed to direct involvement in negotiations. The author does not share their concern. Sometimes barricaded subjects do not wish to speak to police officers; sometimes they are quite willing to speak to a doctor, especially if the doctor discloses his or her identity in a nonthreatening way. Just as police officers represent safety and protection to many people, a doctor, for many people including hostage takers, represents someone who is concerned for the welfare of others and who would not allow police actions (or anybody else's) to be harmful to the hostage taker. Further, police mental health professionals may be able to offer hospitalization or some direct relief, other than jail, to barricaded subjects or hostage takers.

Those with Severe Stress Reactions

All of us have a breaking point, and all of us sometimes display stupid, impulsive, and ineffective behavior under sufficient stress. For example, a person who has been a good husband, father, provider, and citizen may lose his job. More things go wrong. He becomes depressed, irritable, and perhaps begins to drink a little too much. One day, after going to an interview with high expectations of finally getting work, the job does not materialize. He comes home that night and is met by a wife who also is stressed by his unemployment and financial insecurity, as well as her own problems. An argument ensues, he has a couple more drinks, throws a beer bottle through the window in a fit of anger, then grabs a gun. He yells at her to "get the hell out," that he's "going to take care of everything." She won't have to worry any more about it. She hastily leaves as he begins to smash the furniture. She calls the police. All of a sudden he looks out his window and finds he has started World War III. SWAT is there, police cruisers are parked all over, along with fire and rescue, all the neighbors are outside – everything has gone to hell.

The negotiator should realize that what is needed is time for the person to cool down. Sometimes it is advisable to do nothing and let him sleep it off. There is always a risk in this decision, especially if the person has made some veiled or actual suicidal or homicidal threats. However, some officers feel compelled to take action, thus starting a chain of unnecessary events that increase the potential for violence, injury, or even death.

Police officers should never take action just because they think action is called for.

Political Terrorists

Many terrorists and terrorist organizations, both in the United States and in foreign countries, adhere to a variation of a religious philosophy. All significant acts of terrorism must be measured against the only moral reality that matters – that their action contributes to the revolution. "The conventional mores such as truth, honesty, and the values reflected in the Ten Commandments are dismissed as bourgeois morality and are considered merely imperialistic devices to maintain the status quo" (Conrad V. Hassel, 1975).

In the 1970s and 1980s, the major threats to Americans have been from Arab terrorists. According to Caram (1987), Arab terrorists are usually "very emotional, ignorant, and volatile. . . . They have a tendency toward mob violence. If one of them is hurt or killed, you can be sure that retaliation will follow, probably against the hostages. They say 'Blood demands blood!'" Caram believes that in hostage situations involving Arab hostage takers, the need is to *mediate*, not negotiate. "They may not be willing to budge, and may present nonnegotiable demands. Try to bring in a neutral mediator, from a higher social class if possible" (Caram, 1987).

In discussing the threat of terrorism in the United States, B. Jenkins (1985) states that many people, including police and private security personnel, do not realize that terrorism exists in this country. They believe it happens only overseas. Jenkins cites three reasons for this impression: (1) there have been few spectacular terrorist incidents in recent years (bank robberies and bombings go largely unnoticed in this country); (2) there is a high violence rate in the United States, making the actions of terrorists seem insignificant; and (3) so far terrorism in the United States has mainly been directed at property rather than at people. Jenkins cites several examples of terrorist acts in this country (bank robberies and police killings committed by the Black Liberation army; the Weather Underground attack on an armored car in Nyack, New York, in 1981; the 1983 explosion in the Capitol Building; placement of a bomb outside the Army War College at Fort McNair; and "numerous other bombings of federal buildings and installations"). He further points out that several of these incidents involved terrorist groups working together. He also cautions that it would be foolhardy to exclude transnational terrorists in any discussion of domestic terrorism. The very structure of transnational terrorist groups is conducive to joint operations.

According to T. Strentz (1987), the *leaders* of terrorist groups usually exhibit some type of paranoia. It is futile to argue or use logic with such persons. Any questioning of their beliefs indicates that the questioner does not understand, is one of the enemies plotting against them, or is seeking to discredit their ideas. Often their paranoia is well hidden. On the surface they appear self-confident and very commanding; thus they are likely to emerge as leaders. Police involvement with terrorist leaders is infrequent because they usually operate behind the scenes.

Another type of persons involved in terrorist organizations are the *activist-operators*, who usually have antisocial, psychopathic personalities. They are frequently former or current soldiers-of-fortune or ex-convicts with a long and varied rap sheet. They are opportunists. A wily leader, who then allows the opportunists to take the spotlight while he or she remains the power behind the throne, may have recruited them from a prison population. In turn, activist-operators see this situation as an opportunity to lead a hedonistic life with the support of the leader and the organization, which they view as naive and completely within their own control. They thus become the muscle and field commander for the terrorist group. A third personality type in most terrorist organizations is the *idealist*, who is dedicated to a better world. Such persons are usually assigned gofer duties. They are the desperate, dependent youths who are seeking

the truth and have fallen victim to a leader's rhetoric and the opportunist's deceit (Alexander & Gleason, 1981). While such types are the least psychologically disturbed, "he's a guilt ridden hitchhiker who thumbs a ride on every cause from Christianity to Communism. He's a fanatic, needing a Stalin (or a Christ) to worship and die for. He's a mortal enemy of things as they are, and he insists on sacrificing himself for a dream impossible to obtain" (Hoffer, 1963). Leaders and idealists are almost impossible to negotiate with. Negotiators should focus attention on activist-operators. They are the psychopathic opportunists, loyal only to themselves and their self-interests. They want what is best for them and will sell out their companions to further their own well-being. Additionally, without their criminal expertise and daring, the terrorist group is reduced to a hate group.

Since terrorists often take hostages to gain publicity, hostages are better protected if the media are kept away, depriving the terrorists of the publicity required for martyrdom. The terrorist view is that a sacrifice without the cooperation of the press is useless. Experience indicates that if terrorists know that the media will not present their deaths as an act of sacrifice but rather as the act of deranged criminals, they may modify their demands, thus allowing the psychological advantage to revert to the law enforcement negotiator.

Responding to the Hostage Situation

Patrol officers are often the first to encounter the hostage situation, since most develop impulsively during the commission of a felony, in the setting of a family dispute, or from a deranged person's phone call. Patrol officers should consider immediate intervention if the hostage taker has not gained physical control of the crime scene and victims (IACP Training Key 234, 1976). In these cases, officers must exercise caution for the safety of the hostages. Immediate intervention by patrol officers is not appropriate if the suspect controls the crime area and the hostages. Patrol action would needlessly endanger the lives of hostages, the hostage taker, and possibly the officers themselves. The officers' objective is to analyze and stabilize the incident and notify the appropriate supervisor that a hostage incident has developed. In these situations some officers may develop attitudinal problems. "Put a cop on the job for a number of years, give him some success, and then put a bulletproof vest on him, and he sometimes begins to think he cannot be hurt. And that can be a deadly misjudgment" (Bolz & Hershey, 1979). Pierson (1980) refers to this attitude as "tombstone courage," noting that many officers feel pressured to act in an emergency, even if they are not sure of the proper action. The officer who fails to exhaust every other alternative before unnecessarily confronting armed subjects who are posing no immediate threat to their or another's life is a good example of "tombstone courage." Such officers are frequently called heroes – and are often decorated posthumously. If trained negotiators are available, they should be brought to the scene. However, in many small departments or in cases where negotiators cannot arrive on the scene for some time, patrol officers and their supervisor may have to establish negotiations and carry out the process.

Establishing Hostage Negotiations

For many police officers, negotiation principles are not easy to learn. Typically, officers have been trained to assist those in danger by eliminating the threat as quickly as possible. However, in a hostage situation they are confronted by a situation where they cannot quickly direct the outcome. Their primary job is to preserve the status quo until a trained negotiator becomes available. Their initial goals are to establish a working relationship with the hostage taker, obtain information about the incident, set the stage for further negotiations, and fill up time (IACP Training Key 235, 1976).

The essential ingredient in all hostage negotiations is the establishment of effective communication between the negotiator and the hostage taker. First, police officers must elicit enough information so that they and their superiors can understand the situation fully and thus work with the hostage taker. Three essential questions regarding hostage takers must be answered in the initial stage: "Who are they? "What do they want?" and "What will they take?" Effective communication between the hostage taker and police officers requires a common language. The hostage taker will carefully consider every word that officers say. If officers do not remember what they said or do not express themselves with clarity, there may be room for misinterpretation by the hostage taker, which could be disastrous. Police officers or negotiators should frame questions to discourage hostage takers from replying merely yes or no. Asking questions in a way that encourages conversation permits the buying of time and increases the likelihood of establishing rapport with the hostage taker.

Officers must be very attentive at all times. This is difficult because the officers are naturally apprehensive, fearing for their own lives and the lives of the hostages. They also are trying to observe everything they can about the details of the incident. Officers should remember that the hostage taker will judge the attentiveness and sincerity of the negotiating officer through his or her actions. Nonverbal communication may be even more important than verbal. Why should hostage takers be willing to talk to the police? They need somebody to relate to. They will accept the police officer if they are convinced of an officer's sincerity and that the officer won't set them up. They recognize that they need the officer's assistance to obtain an agreeable settlement, especially in those cases where they did not intend to take hostages. In all probability they are frightened and confused. They know they need help if they have any hope of getting out of the situation.

Negotiation procedures will differ in each situation, depending on the purpose of the hostage taking, whether the hostages are in immediate danger of injury or death, how many suspects are involved, what type of weapons they have, and the location of the incident. However, regardless of the specifics, there are general guidelines that can be followed in most hostage situations.

Access to the Hostage Taker

After the situation has somewhat stabilized, the one police officer who is acting as temporary negotiator should make initial contact with the suspect by phone, bullhorn, or the patrol car loudspeaker. Contact by a wire phone (not cellular) is best. The officer should identify him- or herself by name, rank, and department, and ask if anybody requires medical assistance. No attempt should be made to disguise the true identity of the police officer or the department mental health professional (if he or she is involved in direct negotiations). Any deception at this point is likely to fail and seriously impair the development of the trust required in negotiations, which could needlessly endanger the lives of the hostages, the negotiator, and perhaps other police officers. Particularly if the matter arose from a family dispute, the same hostage taker may be involved in another hostage-taking situation a few months later. One hostage taker, deceived into negotiating his surrender, told the sergeant afterward, "You better hope I never get into this situation again, because the next time I won't trust any of you bastard cops and I'll blow the first one away that sets foot on my property." After police gain access to the hostage taker, the next step is to establish a dialogue. What does the hostage taker want? What does he or she have in mind? How can the situation be resolved? (Fitzpatrick, 1980).

Many specialized problems can arise in establishing contact with the hostage takers. B. T. Reed (1988) points out that certain language disorders associated with mild head trauma can be mistaken for psychological thought disorders. Fowler, Devivo, and Fowler (1985) present an adaptation of Flanders and Amisir's verbal interactional analysis techniques for use in hostage negotiations. R. Nielson and G. Shea (1982) have offered suggestions for officer training to enhance creativity in negotiations. M. Reiser (1982) describes the use of indirect suggestions in hostage negotiations. L. Froman and J. Glorioso (1984) have applied communications theory to hostage negotiations. Olin and Born (1983) offer a behavioral approach to hostage negotiations. J. M. Arcaya (1988) has presented a psychoanalytic theory of intervention. It is also important to know everything you can about hostage takers' personalities. Are they normal, abnormal, or depressed? Depressed hostage takers in particular are powder kegs and may present the greatest threat, not only to hostages but also to the negotiator and other police. They may be willing to commit suicide by using murder as a strategy to force police to kill them.

What Not to Do

Negotiating officers must avoid three common mistakes. The first is to lose patience. Based on an analysis of twenty-nine hostage incidents reported by twenty-three law enforcement negotiators, Mirabella and Trudeau concluded that the average time span for hostage negotiation is twelve hours. H. Schlossberg (1989) states that the average time for a professional criminal hostage situation is five to six hours; for a "psycho" case, seventeen hours; and for prison-terrorist groups, two weeks. Prior knowledge and acceptance of these averages will help law enforcement personnel reduce anxiety, prevent the premature use of force, and assist logistical planning and management. The second mistake is taking precipitous action. Despite outside pressure on the police to resolve the situation quickly, and the natural tendency for hostage situations to create impatience because they are stressful, police must resist the tendency to act prematurely even if negotiations seem to have fallen apart. There may be ups and downs in the negotiating process. These should not be seen as a signal (or an excuse) to break off further attempts to negotiate. A third critical mistake is for the negotiator to make value judgments about hostage takers. Successful negotiation requires that the negotiator remain objective and concentrate on maintaining a dialogue with the hostage takers that will eventually resolve the incident without violence (IACP Training Key 235, 1976). Although no two hostage situations are alike, and although flexibility in negotiation is the major requirement of an effective negotiator, there are certain set rules that should be followed.

1. **Do not give weapons or ammunition to hostage takers.**
2. **Never provide additional hostages or exchange hostages.** Above all, never exchange a police officer for a hostage. This is not because of any special premium placed on the officer relative to other hostages, but simply because the introduction of a police officer as a hostage can create unneeded complexities and problems in an already problematic situation (for example, how fellow officers will feel knowing that one of their own is a hostage, or perhaps the hostage takers have special hostility toward police officers).
3. **Never give anything without getting something.** When demands are met, exchange something (for example, food or cigarettes for one of the hostages).
4. **In the early years of hostage negotiation, negotiation was carried on face to face.** However, a few years of experience suggested this was too dangerous (some nineteen negotiators were killed or injured in these early days). Now, wherever possible, negotiations are conducted by phone. If circumstances beyond their control force negotiators to go face to face with hostage takers, negotiators should be promised that they will not be harmed, according

to Bolz. "If the perpetrators say they will not hurt you, our experience indicates you can count on it" (Hershey, 1979). However, given today's drug-related violence, we are not sure this is still valid advice.
5. **If there is more than one captor, try to reach agreement at the start on who will represent the group so that the negotiator does not speak to more than one perpetrator at a time.**

Deception and Lying

As stated earlier, the negotiator should avoid lying to deceive the hostage taker. However, if it is possible to lull the perpetrator into a sense of security that enables members of the tactical force to step in quickly and neutralize him, this should be done. We agree with Bolz and Hershey (1979) that "there is no honor owed to anyone holding an innocent party against his will." In other situations, the commanding officer at the scene may deem it best not to inform the negotiator of tactical plans so that he or she can maintain integrity in dealing with the hostage taker without making deliberately false statements. This also enables the negotiator to disclaim responsibility in case something goes wrong. For example, if the negotiator has told a hostage taker that the money demanded is on the way and later this is proven false, the negotiator can claim that he or she was only relaying information. He or she didn't lie; the police did.

Mobile Situations

If at all possible, hostage takers and hostages should not be permitted to leave the contained area and become mobile. However, to obtain freedom the hostage taker may demand to leave the area – sometimes in a police car, plane, or helicopter. Even though authorities may wish to close this door, it is quite possible that, without any hope of escape, hostage takers may be more likely to kill their victims and themselves. This is particularly true of political terrorists. Tactical advantages may accrue to authorities by allowing suspects and hostages to leave the scene (for example, sharpshooters may get a chance to neutralize hostage takers, particularly if there is only one; or hostages may have an opportunity to escape during the mobile phase). Law enforcement agencies should have contingency plans in the event that the hostage situation enters a mobile stage.

What If a Hostage Is Killed?

Schlossberg (1989) states that the "only excuse for going tactical is if the hostage taker kills a hostage when a deadline expires. If he shoots someone before the hostage situation happens, it doesn't count – he still hasn't killed anyone since you made the containment." It also is possible that hostage takers did not mean to take a life. Even if they did, the goal of the hostage negotiator is to save the lives of the hostages still remaining. Therefore, while the death of a hostage complicates the picture, it does not necessarily rule out further negotiations.

If it seems appropriate, the negotiator may tell hostage takers that even though there has been an injury or death, they only can worsen the situation by continuing in this manner and that the only chance they have of resolving the situation in their favor is to show evidence of good faith from this moment on. In most hostage situations, the most problematic time for the safety of hostages is the first half hour after the incident begins. This is when hostage takers are more likely to be emotionally unstable. From their point of view, everything is deteriorating rapidly. They may panic when they see converging all the forces they have unwittingly set in motion. In an attempt to diffuse this panic, the negotiator's approach must be low key. The negotiator should reassure hostage takers that nobody is going to rush in after them. Calm conversation can serve not only to stabilize hostage takers but also to wear them down. As Taylor (1979) points out, "wearing a man down means giving him enough time to become physically tired and emotionally subdued, so that he sees clearly that his best chance to resolve his crisis is to let his hostages go and, finally, to surrender." Schlossberg reminds negotiators that the primary goal is not simply to calm down hostage takers but to utterly exhaust them – physically and mentally.

Communication with Hostages

Although negotiators usually intentionally downplay the importance of the hostages when dealing with hostage takers, in many situations there are contacts with the hostages. Hostages may question police competence, interfere with negotiations, and/or take control of communication between the suspect and police (Mirabella & Trudeau, 1981). Therefore, hostage management techniques are important. The same techniques that decrease the hostage taker's anxiety can be used to reassure, calm, and instruct hostages. Bolz and Hershey (1979) suggest that if the following information is given to hostages, it will maximize their chances of emerging safely, without bodily harm.

1. Don't be a hero; accept your situation and be prepared to wait.
2. The first fifteen to forty-five minutes are the most dangerous for all concerned. Follow the instructions of your captor. The longer you are together, the less likely the captor will be to hurt you.
3. Don't speak unless spoken to and only if necessary. Try to be friendly if possible, but not phony.
4. Try to get rest. Sit if you can. If the situation goes on for a long time, try to sleep if you can.
5. Don't make suggestions to the hostage taker. If your suggestion goes wrong, he or she may think you planned it that way.

6. Don't try to escape unless you are absolutely sure you can make it. Even then, rethink it before you try.

7. If anyone needs special medication, inform your captor.

8. Be aware of everything you see and hear. Try to remember the number of captors, their descriptions and conversations, their weapons, and the number and identities of other hostages. If you are released, your information will help the police.

9. If you are permitted to speak on the phone, be prepared to answer yes or no to questions asked by the police.

10. Don't be argumentative toward captors or other hostages. Express a cooperative attitude.

11. Don't turn your back on your captors unless directed to do so, but don't stare at them either. Eye contact can be good. People are less likely to harm someone they are looking at.

12. Be patient. Even though the police may appear to be doing nothing, they are engaged in a complete program that is designed to rescue you unharmed as soon as possible.

13. If you believe a rescue is taking place or you hear noise or shooting, hit the floor and stay down. Keep your hands on your head. Do not make any fast moves.

T. Strentz (1987) points out that today more Americans are being held hostage or have been held by international terrorists gangs than all other nationalities combined. He feels that the time has come to prepare Americans to face the too-real possibility of becoming hostages; "only complete familiarization with and preparation for terrorism can equip anyone to survive a confrontation with dignity." To this, we add our own advice to seek professional help when the incident is over, even though you have come through apparently unscathed. Professional help reduces the severity of any psychological damage

incurred during the incident and prevents development of additional pathology. Professional help is recommended as a routine follow-up to any hostage experience (Russell, 1989).

After It Is All Over

Whether captors surrender or are overpowered, how the negotiator deals with them afterward is as important as how he or she dealt with them when negotiation took place. The negotiator should talk with hostage takers quietly, just as he or she did when the pressure was on, and even praise them for being cooperative in letting the hostages go. Tell them they made the right choice in surrendering. Roughness, violence, or verbal putdowns are inadvisable since there is a chance the police may deal with the hostage takers again, especially if the situation involves a mental case or a family fight (Danto, 1978).

The Selection of Hostage Negotiators

How does one select an effective hostage negotiator? The most important characteristic is to really care about people. Negotiators must be able to make people comfortable, communicate effectively with them, and create in them a feeling of trust – the feeling that they really matter and will not be deceived. The stressful nature of the job requires that negotiators be psychologically stable and able to perform well under pressure. They must have a sense of humor – they'll need it. They must convey, physically and psychologically, what the military refers to as "command presence." In civilian terms, this translates to an appearance of maturity and effectiveness, someone who commands respect. Negotiation is a human act. Others will respond to negotiators based partially on their self-confidence and the image they present (Nielson & Shea, 1982). As manipulators, they must be flexible and adaptable under stress. But they cannot be "bullshit artists" because the hostage taker will quickly see through such insincerity.

Cooper (1977) has stated that "experienced negotiators are agreed that success in their endeavors is dependent to a large extent upon the creation of a bond of trust with the hostage taker. Such a bond is not easy to forge and there is much evidence to suggest that it tends to be personal to the individual negotiator rather than attaching to the institution or interest he represents."

Schlossberg, the originator of the hostage negotiator concept, says that hostage negotiation today is still more an art than a science. In a recent seminar (1989) he described the "state of the art" as follows. "Today you start with a male negotiator. After approximately three hours we replace him with a female negotiator. The minute the female gets on the phone, the whole personality of the criminal changes." Schlossberg theorizes that this switch in negotiators possibly sets up a Daddy-Mommy fantasy, with the female negotiator entering as the understanding Mommy after Dad has said his piece.

Moral Dilemmas for Police

Hostage situations often present moral dilemmas to police administrators and commanders. For example, is a visit or phone call from the president, governor, or other important official in response to a hostage taker's demands a precedent to be avoided, or is it negotiable? After apprehension, should promises be honored that were made under duress in return for surrender? Should hostage takers be permitted to leave the original site of the hostage incident, especially if they go outside the original jurisdiction? If a clear shot is available at a hostage taker who is about to leave the jurisdiction in accordance with negotiation promises, should that shot be taken? Would steps taken to terminate a hostage incident be different if the hostage was an illustrious public official or personality rather than an ordinary citizen who just happened to be in the wrong place at the wrong time? Do all lives in a jail or prison hostage situation have equal weight (for example, the

lives of murderers, pimps, rapists, robbers, and those on death row)? These questions have no clear-cut answers, since they involve moral issues and personal value judgments. It should only be noted that when police commanders are faced with these issues, they must consider the precedent that will be set by whatever action they choose.

Effects of the Hostage Experience

Effects on Victims

At 10:15 A.M. on Thursday, August 23, 1973, the quiet routine of the Sveriges Kredit Bank in Stockholm, Sweden, was destroyed by the chatter of a submachine gun. As clouds of plaster and glass settled around the sixty stunned occupants, a lone, heavily armed gunman called out in English, "The party has just begun." The "party" was to continue for 131 hours, permanently affecting the lives of four young hostages and giving birth to a psychological phenomenon subsequently called the *Stockholm syndrome* (Strentz, 1987; Schlossberg, 1989). The Stockholm syndrome describes the automatic, unconscious, emotional response to the trauma of becoming a hostage victim. It consists of the following three stages of behavior: (1) the hostages begin to identify with their captors and to have positive feelings toward them; (2) the hostages begin to have negative feelings toward the authorities; and (3) under the right conditions, the hostage takers begin to develop positive feelings toward their hostages.

Strentz (1987) has studied hostage situations and interviewed many victims and finds that hostages typically go through four stages: denial, delusions of reprieve, busywork, and taking stock. The first and immediate defense mechanism is *denial.* They react as if the traumatic incident is not happening to them. They gradually begin to accept their situation but find relief for their anxiety by viewing the situation as temporary, believing that the police will soon come to their rescue (*delusions of reprieve*). If freedom does not occur soon, many hostages become engaged in *busywork*, such as methodically counting and recounting windows or knitting. Sooner or later all hostages begin to reflect upon their past life (*taking stock*), vowing to change for the better.

While the vast majority of hostages experience this sequence of emotional events, the Stockholm syndrome occurs only in a few because time is the critical factor in its development. Strentz (1987) and Schlossberg (1989) describe the syndrome as regression to a very early level of development. Hostages become like infants who cannot feed themselves, cannot speak, and have no locomotion, putting them in a state of extreme dependency and fright. The infant has a parent who sees to its needs, and the infant begins to love the parent for fulfilling these needs. Similarly, hostages' every need – in fact, their very lives – are gifts from the captor. Hostages become as dependent as they were when they were infants, once again living with a controlling, all-powerful adult and threatened by the outside world. The behavior that worked as a dependent infant surfaces again as a coping device. They identify with the captor as a means of self-protection, sometimes even going so far as adopting the captor's values and philosophy.

Most hostage takers, including terrorists, cannot inflict pain or death on another human being unless the victim is dehumanized. When a captor and hostages are locked together in a relatively small space, a process of humanization usually begins. Hostages can gain the empathy of their captors, which lessens the captors' aggression. However, if hostages are held in isolation (locked in another room; hooded, tied or gagged; or forced to face the wall, away from captors in the same room) then they have been dehumanized, making it easier for captors to harm them. As long as hostages are isolated from captors in any of these ways, the Stockholm syndrome will not develop, regardless of the time involved. The Stockholm syndrome has both a positive and negative impact on hostage negotiations. The stronger the syndrome, the less likely the

hostage taker will kill hostages, especially if the syndrome has advanced to the third stage. On the other hand, information coming from hostages may be consciously or unconsciously falsified. Hostages also may act counter to police commands during an assault. It is possible for the syndrome to be so strong that a hostage offers him- or herself as a human shield for the captor. There are also documented incidents of released hostages making their way back through the barricades to reenter the hostage situation. Finally, the syndrome may affect the negotiator's performance, especially if a hostage fails to seize an opportunity to escape or attempts to interfere with the negotiator's efforts. However, in spite of these negative aspects, negotiators should attempt to foster the Stockholm syndrome to effect safe release of the hostages. Since reaching the third stage may save lives (the hostage taker develops positive feelings toward the hostages), negotiators should attempt to humanize the hostages to the hostage taker in every possible way. For example, they may ask the hostage taker to get information on the names of hostages, the names of their relatives or children, or their medical condition. They can ask the hostage taker to allow hostages to talk on the phone. They can discuss some of the hostages' family responsibilities. Any action negotiators can take to emphasize that hostages are human beings may help captors to develop feelings of empathy for them.

Just as a crime victim's problems do not end with the offender's capture, a hostage's tribulations do not end as well. Experience suggests that these victims go through stages similar to those of rape victims: the immediate stage, the pseudo-adjustment stage, and the resolution and integration stage (Chapter 10). Victims also demonstrate some of the same feelings seen in other crime victims, such as self-blame, guilt, fear, and anger. This is why we routinely recommend professional counseling for everyone who has undergone a hostage experience. There are actually three victims in every hostage situation: the hostage; the indirect hostage, such as a family or airline; and the co-victim, such as the state, represented by the police. After termination of a hostage situation, Middendorff urges that attention be given to all three victims. Finally, it is critical that hostage victims be debriefed by a law enforcement aide and a psychologist or psychiatrist (if available). Victims should understand that these interviews are part of the routine, and afterward they should be given a phone number to call twenty-four hours a day if the need arises.

Effects on Negotiators

Research has shown that negotiators experience a variety of emotions, including anger toward suspects and hostages, empathy and sorrow, boredom, fatigue, and discomfort (Mirabella & Trudeau, 1974). All police negotiators pay a personal price when they attempt to induce the Stockholm syndrome. "Hostages will curse him as they did in Stockholm in August in 1973. They will call the police cowards and actively side with the subject in trying to achieve a solution to their plight, a solution not necessarily in their best interest or in the best interest of the community . . . a hostile hostage is a price that law enforcement must pay for a living hostage" (Strentz, 1987).

Special Factors Involved when the Perpetrator Is an Officer

According to police officers that have experience dealing with hostage/barricaded incidents involving a police officer-perpetrator, there are marked differences in dealing with such situations versus the usual situation, where John Q. Citizen is involved. As one veteran negotiator states: "It is a brand new ball game!" Unfortunately, there is little, if any, written information detailing these perceived differences (Russell & Zuniga, 1984).

The Hostage Negotiator

In the very rare but problematic situation when the hostage taker is a police officer, the hostage negotiator must accept responsibility for the conduct of the negotiations. He or she must be alert and observant at all times. The negotiator must literally "walk on eggs" with every statement made to the hostage taker, knowing that the wrong word, even the wrong inflection, may turn the situation into one of violence. The negotiator must be in command at all times and, simultaneously, be concerned with the welfare of the hostages. In some instances the negotiator may have to deal directly with the hostages, particularly if the captor is using one of the hostages to do the talking. While carrying on a conversation with the hostage or hostage taker, the negotiator must receive and process information and intelligence from outside sources, then integrate this material into his or her negotiating approach. New information may dictate a radical change in negotiating tactics – perhaps just as the negotiator is getting comfortable in the situation. Few other situations place so much stress on one person, and for so long a period (the average hostage situation lasts about twelve hours).

SWAT Members

Members of SWAT may spend hours looking through a rifle sight, trying to get or maintain a visual picture of the perpetrator. When the target is a fellow officer, emotions and tension can run even higher than usual. In one incident, a SWAT member was given a green light to shoot the subject – a police officer that had earlier killed his partner. The subject had emerged from a car with a weapon, but the SWAT member did not fire. As he later explained, the suspect had placed the rifle down and no longer constituted a threat. When a lieutenant who was present at the scene but did not have command responsibility recounted this incident to us, we were told that the SWAT officer refused to fire because it was a fellow cop. Later conversation with another lieutenant who had operational command and who gave SWAT the green light confirmed that the SWAT member did not fire because, as he was squeezing the trigger, he observed the officer-perpetrator laying down his weapon so that he no longer constituted an immediate threat. The interesting thing is that the lieutenant and the other officers who told us the story apparently found no difficulty in accepting the first reason – the member of SWAT didn't shoot because he couldn't kill a cop. This may indicate the possibility that in such instances, a SWAT officer may be unable to carry out their assigned duties. This is even more likely if the SWAT member personally knew the officer. In some small rural areas, every officer present may know the perpetrator and his or her whole family.

Other Officers

The situation of a police officer-perpetrator constitutes a special stress for all officers involved, not just the negotiator and SWAT. Officers on the outer perimeter, traffic control, and even those hearing the incident over the police radio are markedly affected. Some officers may know the officer involved. Some may have worked with him or her, perhaps as a partner. Some may even know the officer as a friend.

Police Dependents

Situations of police officer-hostage takers are very stressful to the dependents of all law enforcement personnel – the so-called police family. Media coverage may aggravate the problem. Immediate family members of officers involved may be placed under severe and prolonged stress as a result of the incident.

The Mechanics of Hostage Negotiations with Officer-Perpetrators

In this chapter we have listed three common mistakes that negotiating officers in hostage negotiations must avoid: losing patience, prematurely initiating tactical action,

and making value judgments about the hostage taker. When the perpetrator of the hostage/barricaded incident is a police officer, it becomes even easier to make one or more of these mistakes.

The task force commander or negotiator may feel the need to resolve the situation quickly. As one experienced negotiator remarked, "There is a tendency to get it over with as quickly as possible because it involves a cop." This same negotiator, looking back upon the incident that he helped negotiate, realized that he had compromised his own safety because of his desire to "get the thing over with." He also remarked, "I really couldn't believe that another cop would ace me." The danger on the other side of the coin is that necessary action, such as making the decision to give SWAT the green light, may be delayed because of the compelling desire to give the involved officer "one more chance before. . . ."

The negotiator who couldn't believe another cop would kill him illustrates the error of making value judgments about the hostage taker because he or she is a police officer. Negotiators may refuse to admit to themselves that the officer-hostage taker presents a real danger. This is especially true if they have known the officer as a partner or a friend.

If the perpetrator is trained in hostage negotiation techniques, negotiators face another major problem. This perpetrator knows what negotiators are trying to do. He or she knows what SWAT is doing and what the task force commander is probably planning. In one incident the negotiator said: "The guy kept telling me, 'Don't give me that bullshit . . . that's the bullshit I used out on the street.' He kept trying to play games with my mind."

In hostage situations involving John Q. Citizen, we are taught that time is in our favor. But is this true when negotiations involve an officer-perpetrator? In certain cases this is false: time actually works against us. As an example, consider the following.

The situation started with an officer making a phone call to his ex-wife, telling her of his depression and that he was really looking forward to spending Christmas Eve with her and the children. When his ex-wife informed him that this would not be possible since she would be with her new boyfriend, he made some remark to the effect that he might as well end it all and hung up. This remark made her think that he might be contemplating suicide. She then asked a deputy friend from another agency to go by and check on the officer's welfare. When the deputy came by, the officer did not wish to admit him into his home. The officer told us later, "I didn't want to see him. . . . I didn't want him to see me like this" (he had been crying). The deputy, having been refused admission and being concerned about his friend's depressed and agitated state, notified the officer's commander. The commander tried to establish contact with his subordinate but was unsuccessful. Now the situation seemed to merit a maximum response. The commander called in the agency's negotiation team. The team responded from another city two hundred miles away. This necessitated diverting an airborne department aircraft from its original destination to pick up the agency's chief hostage negotiator. A request was made for a police psychologist to go to the airport, to be transported by helicopter to the scene. You begin to get the picture? Now everybody is in the act.

Further information about the incident was being carried over the police radios of several agencies. The barricaded officer, who had a radio at his home, was monitoring the radio. He became embarrassed. He saw his job being threatened (the only thing he had left) as more and more law enforcement personnel kept getting involved. The incident was now a major event. In this case, time works against a successful resolution of the case. As more personnel became involved, the threat to the officer's job increased (at least in his eyes) and he became more and more embarrassed to admit the true facts. Circumstances had painted the officer into a corner. It wouldn't have taken much more for him to decide

that suicide was the only honorable alternative left. In fact, he admitted these feelings to the psychologist after the incident was resolved.

Psychological Effects

Officers involved in a hostage/barricaded situation in which an officer is the perpetrator experience a number of emotions relative to their involvement. Some are angry that by his or her actions, the officer is placing their lives and the lives of their fellow officers in jeopardy. "It pissed me off that this officer would make me chase him Code 3 against heavy traffic, endangering my life in addition to his own. You get angry at the officer very much like when cops go to family fights that involve other cops. They don't like to be involved and they feel some anger towards the officer for creating the situation they now have to handle" (Russell & Zuniga, 1984).

Such situations make officers aware of their own vulnerability, very much as a police funeral makes every officer aware of the danger he or she faces daily. The officer who has gone "10–8" is not, in the eyes of fellow officers, much different from themselves. They too have had their share of family problems, work problems, and so on. "Well, it sort of upset me because I got family problems too. I have problems on the job. What if I would desert some day? If he broke under the pressure, maybe it will happen to me. I'm sure he didn't want to and I don't want to either, but it might happen." And then there is the question of future trust: "If he comes back on duty, I don't know that I could ever trust him again. Supposing he goes off the deep end when I need him?"

The psychological effects on SWAT members in an ordinary hostage/barricaded situation are considerable. In spite of the best preparation and plans, very often there are demanding and uncomfortable situations: It is too cold, too hot, there is no water, no cover, no room, dangerous conditions, and so on. When the perpetrator is an officer, there are additional strains. One SWAT member said: "When you are looking down the sights for a half hour or so, it's hard enough when the person in your sight is just John Q. Citizen, but if he's a police officer, there is lots of added stress there. It's an added stress that you don't need. Like you said about other officers getting angry. I get mad too, that there is a fellow officer making me go through this bullshit!"

We must also consider the psychological effects on commanders, including the chief. They may have to decide whether this officer can return to duty once he or she has received treatment. Like the subject's fellow officers, they may wonder if the officer can be trusted in the future. This becomes not only a personnel problem for the chief or the administrator, but also one involving a question of negligent retention. If something happens in the future involving this officer, the question may arise as to whether he or she should have been retained on the force with such a past history of violence and emotional instability. These decisions are not easily made.

We must also consider the psychological effects on the officer-perpetrator. An officer who creates a hostage/barricaded situation has gone farther in "crossing the line" than John Q. Citizen under similar circumstances. Rightly or wrongly, police officers are expected to exhibit much more maturity and self-control than the average citizen. If officer-perpetrators were worried about their job in the past, they certainly have more cause to be worried now. Many officers are convinced that having gone this far, there is no way they can retain their job with their agency, nor is there any chance of getting a job with another law enforcement agency. Thus their future looks very bleak. The job may have been the only thing they had left, and now they have blown that. It is at this time that the potential for suicide – always an impulsive act – is high.

Finally, we must consider the psychological effects on the officer perpetrator's family. They will have to endure the frequently distorted media presentation of the event. They will have to face other officers and their families, friends, and neighbors. They will feel isolated and alone. The stress may create further problems in an already problem-ridden marriage. It may create problems with the children as they face the taunts of classmates and friends. There may be problems dealing with the general public, including threatening/obscene phone calls, letters, and other harassment.

Lessons Learned

An officer-perpetrator incident should be contained as much as possible, especially in regard to getting others involved. The police radio should be used sparingly when an officer is involved. Rely on the telephone wherever possible. Other police personnel should be mobilized as little as possible. There should be an immediate debriefing after the situation is over, not only for those officers directly involved (such as negotiators and SWAT personnel), but also for those officers on the inner and outer perimeter. A short briefing for the troops at each roll call might go far to minimize the adverse impact of the situation and prevent rumors and misinformation. Officers involved may need help similar to officers involved in post-shooting trauma. Don't forget the commanders! They have been under considerable stress too, especially those at the scene. If officer-perpetrators are to get help and return to duty, fellow officers may need guidance on how to relate to them and what to expect of them. The question of whether they can be trusted may have to be approached openly for some officers, particularly those who will be working closely with them.

The most important question seems to be whether there is any way to prevent such occurrences. In all cases we are familiar with, officers have given clear signs of depression, emotional instability, and family problems. This means that supervisors – particularly first-line supervisors – must be alert to such clues so officers can receive help at the earliest possible time. Although our sample is small $(N = 6)$, a profile begins to emerge of the troubled officer type:

- An older officer (late twenties to mid-thirties).
- Over five years in the department or in police work.
- Family problems (including problems with girlfriend or boyfriend).
- Often is known to police, who have had to respond to family fights at his or her residence.
- On the verge of divorce. Recently divorced or separated (one to two years or less) (may have a similar situation with a live-in girl- or boyfriend).

- Generally known as a "good officer" but supervisory problems have begun to emerge because of the effect of personal problems on his or her work.
- Loves police work and is very threatened by the potential of losing his or her job.
- Drinking has increased. Violent behavior (verbal and/or physical) emerges when drunk.
- In family fights there is an increasing tendency toward physical violence.

All of us must be aware of the prodromal clues to violent behavior that might result in a troubled officer initiating a hostage or barricaded situation.

SUMMARY

The primary objective in any hostage situation is to negotiate the safe release of the hostages and ensure that no one gets injured or killed, including the hostages, police officers (and other emergency personnel present), innocent bystanders, and hostage takers. The author has described the types of hostage situations, the personalities likely to be involved in each type, hostage negotiation techniques, and the characteristics of successful negotiators. We have discussed the effects of hostage taking on victims and negotiators. We have noted the special factors involved when a police officer is the perpetrator.

Since creation of the hostage negotiator concept, many such teams throughout the United States have handled thousands of situations without losing a hostage, police officer, or perpetrator. This testifies to the effectiveness of the approach described in this chapter and to the importance of negotiation as the most humane, compassionate, and effective way to handle hostage-taking barricaded subjects. Negotiation saves lives, prevents needless bloodshed, and represents professional police work at its finest.

BIBLIOGRAPHY

Alexander, Y., & Gleason, J. (1981). A terrorist organization profile: A psychological role model. In *Behavioral and quantitative perspectives on terrorism*, Special Operations and Research. Unit, FBI Academy. New York: Pergamon Press.

Arcaya, J. M. (1988). The Police and the emotionally disturbed: A psychoanalytic theory of intervention. *Journal of Police and Criminal Psychology, 4*(1), 31–39.

Caram, P. (1987). *Negotiating with the Middle-Eastern mindset*. New York Authority Police Department, Hostage Seminars, ALETA.

Fowler, R., Devivo, P., & Fowler, D. 1985. Analyzing police hostage negotiations: The verbal interactional analysis technique. *Journal of Emotional First Aid, 2*(2), 1628.

Froman, L., & Glorioso, J. May, 1984. Applying communications theory to hostage negotiations. *Police Chief,* 59–60.

Gilmartin, K., & Gibson, R. June, 1985. Hostage negotiation: The bio-behavioral dimension. *Police Chief,* 46–48.

Hoffer, E. (1963). *The true believer; Thoughts on the nature of mass movements*. New York: Time.

Jenkins, B. June, 1985. The threat of terrorism in the United States. *Police Chief,* 48.

Nielson, R., & Shea, G. August, 1982. Training officers to negotiate creatively. *Police Chief,* 65–67.

Olin, W. R., & Born, D. G. January, 1983. A behavioral approach to hostage situations. *FBI Law Enforcement Bulletin,* 19–24.

Reed, B. T. (1988). Neuropsychological considerations in hostage negotiations: Introductory concepts. In *Police psychology: Operational assistance,* ed. Reese & Horn, pp. 225–231. Washington, D.C.: FBI.

Reiser, M. (1982). *Police psychology.* Los Angeles: LEHI Publishing Co.

Russell, H. E. (1989). *How to improve your chances of survival if taken hostage.* Unpublished manuscript.

Schlossberg, H. June, 1989. *Hostage negotiator seminar* presented in Tucson, Arizona.

Soskis, D., & Van C. Zandt (1986). Hostage negotiation: Law enforcement's most effective nonlethal weapon. *Behavioral Science and the Law, 4*(4), 423–435.

Strentz, T. November, 1987. A hostage psychological survival guide. *FBI Law Enforcement Bulletin,* 1–7.

U.S. Department of State. (1984). *Patterns of global terrorism: 1983.* Washington, D.C.: Office for Combatting Terrorism, U.S. Department of State.

Chapter 19

BEHAVIORAL ASPECTS OF CONFLICT SITUATIONS

Police officers frequently respond to calls involving people in conflict. Whether these situations involve family differences, barroom brawls, or neighborhood arguments, all the conflict management skills of the officers are required to achieve a satisfactory resolution without escalating the situation. The adverse results of such escalations range from citizen complaints to assaults on officers (Shea & Harpool, 1988).

FAMILY DISPUTES

For most police officers, involvement in a family dispute is an all-too common experience. Research conducted in the 1970s by a major California police department showed that in a six-month period, officers responded to more than 16,000 family disturbance calls, requiring more than 8,000 man hours. Twenty-five percent of all assignments were calls to family disputes (Schnabel, 1982). More important, these calls often result in jeopardy to the officer's life. Twenty-two percent of all police officers killed nationally and about 40 percent of those injured were handling a family dispute at the time. Approximately one-third of all homicides and other reported assaults take place within the family. Family disturbances also are frequently associated with suicide and child abuse.

The chief of the department studied noted "due to the high incidence of family dispute calls, especially assignments which involve the same persons on a repeated basis, a casual attitude may develop even in seasoned officers. This can prove to be just as dangerous as the inexperienced officer's lack of requisite

knowledge in dealing with the unique problems posed in family crisis settings" (Schnabel, 1982, p. 39).

Prior to 1966, no law enforcement agency in the United States had a training program to teach officers to intervene effectively in family disputes. Dr. Morton Bard implemented the original family crisis intervention study in 1967, with his training of "family cops" in the New York City Police Department. In the 1970s and 1980s, many departments saw the need for this training, and other programs were initiated.

Although training methods differed among programs, the goals were similar: (1) to improve police capability in restoring family order during a crisis, while at the same time minimizing the chance of police or citizen injuries; (2) to help families resolve tensions that can lead to disputes by referring them to appropriate community social health and mental health agencies; (3) to reduce the number of repeat calls from chronically fighting families by providing solutions before serious physical injuries result (there is a much higher risk of injury arising from incidents characterized by a history of repeat calls); (4) to enhance police-community relations by providing excellent services to families in crisis; and (5) to establish a liaison between the police and other community agencies that provide specialized services to families in crisis so that the need for future police intervention can be reduced.

Police training programs for handling domestic disputes should last a minimum of forty hours, preferably eighty hours. The following subjects should be covered: (1) necessary tactics and practices to ensure the safety of the officer and the family; (2) interviewing techniques emphasizing how to observe both verbal and nonverbal communication patterns and to assess content; (3) characteristics of a stable family relationship and factors that cause a stable situation to deteriorate; (4) aspects of human behavior that can have a special impact on the family, such as alcoholism and job loss; (5) social, legal, medical, and mental health agencies available within the community to accept referrals, the procedures for referral, the type of cases each agency handles, the agency's requirements for eligibility for its services, and the hours the agency is open; and (6) role playing of typical family dispute situations, using volunteers as well as officer trainees.

Handling Family Disputes

In order to deal effectively with family disputes, officers must prevent injury, restore order, and assist disputants in finding lasting solutions to eliminate the need for repeat police callbacks. The officers' approach to family fights is one of problem solving and crisis management – not arrest and prosecution. In diffusing a family conflict, officers should follow these basic procedures:

1. Be alert to the high danger potential of a family conflict and approach it with full safety precautions.
2. If at all possible, do not go alone. Wait for backup.
3. Survey the scene before leaving your patrol vehicle. If possible, do a drive-by to check out the immediate area.
4. Park away from the house. If the disputants are outside the house or in the street, try to move them inside.
5. Approach the residence with full caution. Look in the window if possible, listen to see what's going on; never stand in front of the door when you announce your presence.
6. Prevent injury. Once inside, officers should position themselves between the two (or more) parties in conflict. Be alert for objects that might be used as weapons (real weapons such as guns or knives, or potential weapons such as pots and pans).
7. Separate the disputants from each other. If possible, each person in the argument should be kept out of hearing and visual range of the other. If this cannot be done, the officers should insist that one person speak at a time.
8. Introduce yourselves, using full name and title, and address both parties of the dispute as Mr. and Mrs. This is important because it helps create a tone of politeness that may calm the highly emotionally charged atmosphere of the conflict.
9. Avoid overt threats, and convey the clear impression that you are there to help solve the problem, not necessarily to arrest somebody or even to decide who is right or wrong. The traditional approach, before family crisis training was available, was to warn the family "If I have to come back again, somebody's ass is going to jail." Officers arrive at a family fight with authority invested in their role. There is usually little need to stress this authority, since it speaks for itself.
10. Try to create an atmosphere favorable for discussion by removing your hat, sitting down, asking the disputants to sit down, turning down your radio,

and looking directly at them. These actions will demonstrate to disputants that you expect to discuss the general situation rather than the fighting between them.

11. Take steps to exclude outsiders unless someone present can be useful in resolving the fight or calming participants.

12. Demonstrate firmness but indicate that you are open to discussion and have a fair attitude toward all participants. Often one side or the other will try to use or exploit the officers, especially if he or she is the one who called the officer to the residence.

13. Ask diversionary reality questions to tone down the hostility and anger, helping disputants make contact with reality. For example, the officer might ask how many people live here, where the children are, etc.

14. Find out the facts. Officers should identify the facts of the family disturbance (whether a crime has been committed, whether there are court orders involved, who was the caller, and so on).

15. Reinforce calm behavior, and make every effort to allow the parties to back down gracefully and save face.

16. Make every effort to resolve the conflict that led to the dispute. In addition to these specific actions, the following techniques can be used to resolve family disputes (Goldstein et al., 1977).

Mediation

In mediation, the goal of officers is to help disputants solve their own crisis rather than trying to solve it for them. Mediation involves the following steps:

1. Officers inform disputants that they must solve their problems themselves, but they are there to help.

2. Officers avoid suggesting solutions. Instead, they solicit suggestions from disputants as to how they think their problems can be solved.

3. Officers check proposals with the other disputants until there is acceptance or compromise.

4. Officers avoid criticizing the disputants and encourage them to follow through on the agreed-upon solution.

Negotiation

In negotiation, officers suggest solutions, compromises, or other means of dealing effectively with the crisis. They help disputants bargain but remain neutral. For example, if two officers are present in a husband-and-wife dispute, one officer might suggest a solution while talking with the husband, while the other officer does the same while talking with the wife. The two officers can then bring the disputants together and help them negotiate a solution or compromise.

Counseling

Counseling a husband and wife in a family dispute takes time, training, and experience. Problems that lead to family fights do not develop overnight. They are often long-standing and will not be easily resolved, especially in the stress of the crisis. Officers may have to be satisfied with helping the disputants acknowledge that they have a problem and encouraging them to get help.

Referral

If disputants need help, referral to a community agency may be appropriate. The greatest problem associated with referrals is non availability of community agencies at the time of critical need. Family disputes often occur late at night, early in the morning, or on weekends and holidays, when most agencies are closed. As a result, police officers must be familiar with the resources available in the particular community, hours of availability, services offered, and eligibility requirements of those agencies most frequently used.

When referring someone, officers should remember that they are involving a third party whom the disputants do not know and may not wish to contact. Therefore, they may have to overcome some resistance to following the referral suggestion. This will be easier if officers let the disputants know that they understand their problem and their feelings about it and tell them that the chances are good the agency can help. Officers should give disputants all appropriate referral information in writing and make sure that they understand it. They may offer to call the agency to facilitate the referral. If this is not appropriate, officers should obtain a commitment that they will contact the agency at the earliest possible opportunity. A follow-up call to the disputants may also be advisable and may assist in a successful referral.

Arbitration

If officers have tried mediation, negotiation, counseling, and have suggested referral but none of these has been acceptable to the disputants, they may then have to impose a solution directly. Since this will be the officers' solution, they must realize that it is the least desirable method for resolving family disputes and that it results in the highest number of return calls. Therefore, arbitration should be used only as a last resort.

In arbitration, officers should first think of all possible solutions to the problem and review in their heads the strengths and weaknesses of each. They must be aware of any personal biases that may affect their consideration of possible solutions. Having reviewed all the solutions they can think of, they choose the one they feel is best and, if possible, discuss it with a partner. The officer (or the officer and a partner) make the final decision, then tell the disputants to follow it and spell out the consequences if they do not.

Legal Aspects

Currently legal and civic groups demanding stronger police action in domestic confrontations besiege police departments. The courts also are beginning to examine the problem. In one case, action was brought against the New York City Police Department, as well as probation and family court personnel, alleging that police officers intervening in domestic disputes did not make arrests even if physical evidence of an assault was present (*Bruno v. Codd* 1977). In another case, the Oakland, California, Police Department was accused of an inadequate response to women in general, and black women in particular, who were victims of domestic violence (*Scott v. Hart* 1977). In this case plaintiffs alleged that they were deprived of equal protection when police failed to respond to calls from women who were assaulted by their spouses, former spouses, or boyfriends, while responding to calls from those assaulted in non domestic situations.

Traditionally, police have maintained a policy of non arrest in domestic violence cases whenever possible. Although this policy was never intended or perceived to be discriminatory by police departments, these recent court actions suggest that police will have to take a careful look at their policies and be ready to defend them or amend them.

Landlord-Tenant Disputes

Police are usually called in landlord-tenant disputes because nobody else is available, but they have little or no training in the complexities of landlord-tenant law. As a result, officers often see this as a waste of time, and the citizen is disappointed because officers do not have a legal solution. However, police cannot ignore these calls, since they often lead to violence and other serious criminal offenses. Most disputants seeking police assistance lack the motivation, sophistication, or money to seek a lawful settlement.

The most common abuses perpetrated by landlords are lockout of a tenant, usually accompanied by the lock-in of the tenant's possessions; seizures of a tenant's property; removal of doors or windows; trespassing (the landlord enters the tenant's premises without permission); and termination of services (the tenant's gas, electricity, or water is cut off).

Abuses most commonly perpetrated by tenants are destruction of the landlord's property, refusal to pay rent, and accumulation of garbage.

Handling Landlord-Tenant Disputes

Effective handling of landlord-tenant disputes requires that officers know and understand the relevant penal code provisions. This will enable officers to intervene, not by making an arrest, but rather by explaining to the parties what conduct is unlawful and suggesting alternate lawful solutions. For example, if the landlord has locked out the tenant, officers can explain that a lockout is unlawful and suggest that the landlord consult an attorney or go to small claims court. If the landlord is unwilling to desist, officers can make it clear that the tenant can initiate criminal proceedings.

The Oakland, California, Police Department has established a landlord-tenant intervention unit to achieve a settlement of such disputes by referring the parties to other agencies, such as small claims court. Early settlement is the goal, since it deters future violence. Establishment of this unit followed a sixteen-month experimental landlord-tenant dispute settlement program in which the department found that effective police involvement in such disputes prevented both minor and serious offenses, some violent, that might have occurred had parties been left to themselves. Officers can be trained to identify the causes of landlord-tenant disputes, refer these disputants to the proper agencies for resolution, and, in some cases, achieve settlement without the necessity of referral.

The Community Mediation Service

Another innovative approach to handling a variety of disputes that usually required police intervention, or those that can lead to serious crime, is the community mediation services of the Pima County (Arizona) Victim Witness Program. The objectives of this service are to present viable alternatives to resolve, without violence, disputes involving families, neighbors, and landlords; and to settle a problem quickly in order to reduce repeated law enforcement involvement.

Most people do not want to take friends or relatives to court, lose time from work, pay a fine, or go to jail. This program is an organized effort to assist police by providing another place where both parties in a dispute can sit down in a nonthreatening environment with a mediator and talk about ways of reaching an agreement. It takes police officers out of the mediation role while providing a specialized referral resource.

SUMMARY

In this chapter, the author discussed conflict situations and their management. It is important for police officers who are called upon to handle these situations to recognize that they are not called as proxy psychologists but to preserve the peace, prevent injury, and assist people in crisis to find solutions. However, because so much of their work involves dealing with people in crisis situations, police officers have a significant opportunity to contribute to the mental health and safety of the community by learning how to perform effective conflict management through mediation, negotiation, counseling, referral, and arbitration.

BIBLIOGRAPHY

Bard, M. (1970). *Training police as specialists in family crisis intervention.* Washington, D.C.: National Institute of Law Enforcement and Criminal Justice.

Bard, M., & Zacker, J. (1973). Effects of conflict management training on police performance. *Journal of Applied Psychology, 2,* 202–208.

Bruno v. Codd. (1977). 90 Misc. 2-Adv. Sh. 1047, 396 NYS ad 974.

Goldstein, A. P., et al. (1977). *Police crisis intervention.* Kalamazoo, MI: Behaviordelia.

Nierenberg, G. I. (1968). *The art of negotiating.* New York: Cornerstone Library.

Schnabel, P. H. June, 1982. Response to family disturbances. *Law and Order,* 39–42.

Scott v. Hart. 1977. No. C76-2395, N.D. Cal.

Shea, L., & Harpool, A. (1988). Tactical communication training for conflict diffusion. In *Police psychology,* ed. J. Reese & J. Horn, pp. 379–390. Washington, D.C.: U.S. Department of Justice, FBI.

Steinmetz, S. K., & Straus, M. A. (1974). *Violence in the family.* New York: Dodd, Mead.

Chapter 20

BEHAVIORAL ASPECTS OF CRISIS INTERVENTION WITH VICTIMS

In his presidential address to the ninety-first annual meeting of the American Psychological Association, M. Siegel (1983) focused on the growth of crime and violence in the United States, with particular attention to its victims. Citing E. Chelimsky work (1981), he said that "rates of crime and victimization seem to rise continually, in good years or bad, in prosperity or recession, in Republican or Democratic administrations. . . . The rate of violent crime (usually based on murder, robbery, rape, and assault as a composite index) more than doubled in the 1960s, tripled by the late 1970s, and continues to increase rapidly. So, of course, does the number of victims."

Why should police officers be interested in victims? First, due to the high number of unreported and unsuccessfully prosecuted crimes, officers will find many victims unwilling to report or cooperate as effectively as they might. Victims may be fearful, hostile, confused, or ignorant of what to do. Officers who are first to arrive on the scene and interact with the victims set the tone for the follow-up activities of other investigative officers. Their knowing how to handle victims and witnesses will not only lead to a more positive attitude by victims toward the police, but also can facilitate their cooperating more fully with the prosecution and testifying in court if necessary.

Second, studies of stressful situations involving prisoners of war, Vietnam veterans, and survivors of natural and man-made disasters have shown that the individuals involved suffer deleterious effects on their mental and physical health. C. J. Frederick (1986) states that except for rape, victims of violent crime have received little attention. However, with the introduction of a new diagnostic entity, post-traumatic stress disorder, crime victims are receiving more recognition. While every victim of a crime does not develop major psychological problems secondary to the event, all victims can profit from the immediate compassion and understanding intervention on the part of those caretakers who are usually the first persons the victim encounters during the crisis (police officers and medical personnel). Although police officers are not mental health professionals, the victim's extreme vulnerability can enable officers to be of great help, not only in handling the immediate effects of the crisis but also in the final resolution and integration of the experience.

The Psychology of Victimization

People are victimized in various ways. When people become victims as a result of chance events or circumstances over which they believe they have no control – such as crime – they usually feel helpless. Society also plays a role in how victims feel. For example, when a child comes home from school and tells his parents that the teacher was mean and made him sit in the corner, a common parental response is to inquire "What did you do to deserve it?" From experiences such as this, many people grow up thinking that if something bad happens, they deserved it. Bad things do not happen to good people. Therefore, if something bad happens, the victim must have precipitated it.

Society sometimes regards victimization as contagious. Many believe that being a victim happens to somebody else. Often people don't wish to associate with those to whom bad things happen because it may rub off.

Dr. Morton Bard (1982), a specialist in victimology, testified before the President's Task Force on Victims of Crime that "society's disregard of crime victims, until recently, directly flowed from their stigmatized status." He described society's view of victims as "losers in a competitive society, with an inner conviction that the victim is somehow to blame for what has happened." All these beliefs may contribute to the feelings of self-blame that most victims experience. The burglary victim, for example, tells himself, "If only I had had those locks replaced." The rape victim asks, "Why did I ever go to that bar in the first place?" Some of this self-blame may be displaced onto police officers. "Where were you when I needed you?" or "This is what you're paid to prevent" are examples of victims' attempts to avoid self-blame.

As a result of the feelings of helplessness and loss of control over one's own life, anger at the offender would be a natural reaction. However, the victim may be too fearful to either directly express the anger or acknowledge it to him- or herself. This is understandable when one considers that the victim has been placed in great danger by the offender and may be hesitant to express anger because of a fear of retaliation. Victims may handle this anger in several ways. It may be directed against the self, in which case depression may result. As victims search to make sense out of nonsensical acts, they may use rationalization. They may ask over and over again, "Why would anybody do such a thing as this?"

Finally, victims often use denial. Like heart attack victims who may deny that they are having an attack by thinking it is heartburn or muscle strain, crime victims often behave as if the crime has not occurred. A car theft victim may walk blocks trying to find his car before he is willing to admit that it probably has been stolen. The rape victim may deny its impact by appearing very cool and collected, as if the experience has made no impression.

Crisis Intervention with Victims

M. Bard and K. Ellison (1974) , J. L. Greenstone and S. C. Leviton (1982), and Harold Russell (1986) have pointed out that all crimes against persons are not only violations of the law but also violations of the victim's self-image, his or her sense of identity and worth. Individuals may view their possessions as an extension of their personality — the outermost layer. A crime such as burglary generally hurts victims only at this outermost layer: their property. A crime such as armed robbery involving personal contact with the robber and threat to the physical self of victims invades the second personality layer.

Aggravated assault and robbery invade the third layer of the personality. Victims are physically as well as emotionally injured. Rape goes to the very core of the self. It penetrates beyond bodily harm, into victims' basic beliefs, values, and emotions. This may account for M. Siegel (1983) belief that "crime victims are often shocked by the depth and severity of their reactions. . . . To the crime victim, a reasonably safe and secure world has become a violent and deadly place" (p. 1271).

The emotional reactions experienced by victims become crises when existing defenses and problem-solving techniques are not adequate; victims feel helpless and unable to cope. Effective crisis intervention by officers can be of immeasurable assistance in the criminal investigation, while at the same time helping prevent serious emotional consequences to the victim.

The ABC Model*

Whenever officers intervene in a crisis situation, whether with victims or with individuals involved in such crises as domestic disputes, suicidal behavior, and/or auto accidents, they should have a plan of action that will provide them with a structured approach. We will offer a model – the ABC model – in a moment. But first, how do officers determine that an individual is in crisis? What are the symptoms? **Emotional symptoms**, there may be a display of extreme emotions (screaming, crying, hysterics, severe depression). There may be incongruent emotions. For example, people may verbally deny feeling upset but display uncontrolled body trembling. They may claim no anger but clench their fists and lock their jaws. **Physical symptoms**, there may be a display of extremes (that is, frozen into immobility or a state of frenzied activity). There may be physical symptoms with incongruent emotions (for example, rigid body but flitting eyes). **Situational symptoms**, if an individual is a victim of a crime, even a relatively minor one where no one was injured and nothing was taken (breaking and entering), the experience can still be emotionally upsetting. When the individual is a rape or assault victim, trauma can be devastating. It is impossible to cover every form of victimization, but the following ABC model* for victim intervention is a generic approach suitable for all of these situations. The letters stand for:

A. Achieve contact
B. Boil down the problem
C. Coping through inventory

Here's How It Works

Officers' first step is to achieve contact with the subject. They do this by introducing themselves, the agency they are with, and stating the purpose of the contact. For example, "I am Officer Smith with the city police

and I'm here to help you." They then collect as much information as they can regarding the subject and nature of the event. They begin by asking the person his or her name and what he or she would like to be called. They then try to boil down what happened (for example, How do you see it?), focusing on the here and now (for example, What is most important to you *right now?*). Officers then try to have the victim cope with the situation (What can you think of as a solution? What else can you think of? In what way do you think this will help? What do you want to happen right now? Is there anything you would like to ask me?). Having a structured approach, even a loosely structured one as in the ABC model, gives officers some plan of action, some sense of direction that may prove useful in dealing with victims.

Victim Intervention Techniques

M. Silbert (1976) has described a ten-point checklist of techniques for officers to use in field management of victim situations. Frederick (1986) lists twelve intervention responses that are of use to police officers. We have combined and edited these two lists as follows:

1. **Officers should introduce themselves by full name and title.** This is important in any police encounter with a victim, since it offers him or her a choice of calling officers by name or rank. This gives the victim a certain amount of control, and a first small step toward regaining a sense of mastery over the situation. The personal and behavioral demeanor of officers can mean a great deal, since the victim tends to model his or her behavior on that of officers as authority figures.
2. **Briefly verify the crime.** This should be done quickly without detailed discussion. Obtain only the necessary information,

such as the type of crime being dealt with, whether it involved a weapon, how many people were involved, and whether the criminal had transportation. Officers may explain to the victim that later another officer will be interested in the details, but right now only this basic information is needed. Officers might remark, "Do you think you can help me?" giving the victim another choice.

3. **Recognize the victim's ordeal and reassure him or her of immediate safety.** Since victims are often confused and unable to appreciate the presence of the police and what it means for their safety, even though there are several squad cars with emergency lights flashing, it may be necessary for officers to constantly reassure the victim that "it is safe now," "the police are here," "we have officers in the area," "you are safe." Repeating the word *safe* is important, since it brings the victim back to the reality of the moment instead of allowing him or her to ruminate about what has happened. The reassurance of safety is also important because the victim, with feelings of guilt and self-blame, may view police officers with mixed emotions — glad to see officers as protectors, but also afraid of them as punishers or blamers. Officers who show empathy immediately will help counter any negative feelings of the victim toward the police. Officers should remember that, to the victim, the ordeal is important, no matter how routine they may consider the case. Even if it is the officers' third purse-snatching of the day, they must realize that to each of the victims the crime is unique. To convey empathy they might say, "You've been through a terrible ordeal; I know it's been a shock to you. You're safe now."

4. **Verify the victim's physical well-being.** All injuries may not be visible,

particularly assaults. Elderly victims may have vague or nonspecific complaints. Police officers should verify the victim's well-being immediately or as soon as the victim is calmed down sufficiently to assist. If hospitalization is required, an ambulance should be called and officers should administer whatever emergency first aid is required. If the victim is injured and asks about his or her condition, officers might reply, "We're going to get you checked out then arrange for anything you may need." This is not to give the victim false information but to try to build trust and hope. Burdening the victim with additional worries is not conducive to his or her welfare.

5. **Solicit the victim's help in identifying the suspect.** Questioning that seems to lack sensitivity and support can compound the trauma and add insult to injury. Demanding that the victim identify or describe the suspect immediately may cause further trauma rather than eliciting useful information. Crime victims, particularly in an assault, have experienced a loss of control over their environment. Officers can help a victim overcome an emotional block resulting from this loss of control by offering choices. Instead of demanding or simply asking what the suspect looked like, officers might say something like: "I'd like to ask you a few questions about what happened, then I'll explain what we're going to do. I need your help with one thing right now: finding the suspect. There are other officers waiting to look for him right now. The more information you can give me now, the better chance we have of finding him. Do you think you can calm down enough just to help with this? Good." These words have several effects. First, the frequent use of the word *now* helps reinforce the present reality for the victim. The crime is over. He or

she is safe. Officers need the information now to help others in the field. Soliciting the victim's help in this manner offers a choice because officers ask for help rather than demand it. When officers ask if the victim is calm enough to help, they again offer a choice. When they respond to the victim's affirmative nod with "Good!" they are reinforcing positive behavior.

6. **Diffuse crisis emotions.** Disclosure of negative or upsetting information can cause great anxiety, even panic. Officers should set up a calm atmosphere, modulate their voices, be active listeners, and introduce reality slowly.

7. **Establish the elements of the crime.** After the initial moments of crisis have passed, it is time for officers to begin establishing the exact elements of the crime so that they may fill out the report. They should be flexible in filling out the report so that they do not give the victim the impression that they are making demands that the victim must meet. The victim should be allowed to proceed at his or her own pace in describing what has happened. Officers should provide encouragement and reassurance and continue to offer the victim choices. They should ask "Can I make notes while I'm asking the questions?" or "I have to fill out this report. Would it be all right if I make notes and write down your answers on this report form?"

8. **Keep the choices simple.** The availability of choices is such an important tool in psychological first aid that it is important that choices not be complicated. The proper response for a simple choice is yes or no. Choices that require more complicated answers are less effective.

9. **Explain the procedures that will follow.** Police officers tend to forget that although they are familiar with the procedures that follow, the victim is not. In crisis situations, it is especially important that a victim understand what will happen and why, because his or her feeling of helplessness is so pervasive. Even if the victim does not ask what will happen next, it is important for officers to say that a follow-up detective will call as the case progresses. Officers should answer all of the victim's questions. Even though justification may not be necessary, an explanation is always helpful.

10. **Every victim should be encouraged to seek professional help.** Officers should convey the impression that seeking psychological assistance is normal. They might say, for example, "These things take their toll on everyone." "It's best to get some professional help now to make sure you're doing okay." "A little help now will prevent serious problems later."

11. **Preserve the crime scene and collect physical evidence.** This procedure is standard and will not be discussed.

Nonverbal Intervention Techniques

Sometimes what is said is less important than the way it is said. Nonverbal communications often determine how words are interpreted. Some of the most important features of nonverbal communication follow.

Body Posture. The way we position our bodies tells a lot about how sincerely interested we are in what the speaker is saying. If we incline our heads and sometimes the whole upper part of our body toward the speaker, this indicates that we are really listening. On the other hand, if we lean back we may communicate disinterest. The victim may entirely judge officers' attitudes from this nonverbal message.

In handling victims, officers should sit down, if at all possible, and encourage the victim to do so. Sitting down helps reduce tension and relaxes the victim.

Distancing. Officers should maintain an optimal distance when talking to the victim. If officers stand too close or too far away, the conversation is likely to be uncomfortable. Officers should stand close enough to express feelings of empathy and interest, yet far enough back to avoid threatening the victim. The farther away one stands, the greater the feeling of formality and disinterest. Police officers must judge the victim's responses to determine if the distance is too great or too small.

Eye Contact. Because of guilt and self-blame, a victim often will avoid eye contact. If officers keep looking directly at the victim's eyes, there will usually be an improvement in his or her response. Eye contact communicates encouragement and support. If officers are looking around the room or at a notebook, this may indicate disinterest and perhaps even impatience. If they have to write something, they should look up frequently and make eye contact, especially when asking questions.

Touching. Touching can be crucial in diffusing a crisis or instigating a further upset. Officers should be careful about touching victims, particularly those who have experienced a sexual assault. They may place a hand close to the victim – for example, on a table. This allows the victim a choice. Officers should not draw back if the victim touches them for emotional support.

Verbal Intervention Techniques

The importance of nonverbal behavior does not decrease the importance of verbal techniques.

Vocalization. Victims often speak hesitantly and softly or not at all. As a result, it is important for officers not to overwhelm the victim with their voices. Officers should speak softly and slowly, avoiding any voice tone or pace that may communicate impatience or lack of interest.

Active Listening. Officers should show that they are really interested, particularly when the victim has an obvious need to ventilate emotions. Allowing silence, offering reflective comments, and providing timely clarifications and summaries are three major tools in active listening.

Silence is extremely important to victims in crisis, since it gives them time to collect thoughts and to phrase them comfortably before responding to questions. Victims often are confused and need a moment or two to orient themselves to the question before coming up with an answer. A rape victim may have special difficulty in answering questions that are embarrassing and perhaps degrading. Officers themselves are often uncomfortable asking these questions. Sometimes the victim's reported uncooperativeness occurs because officers are uncomfortable and do not know how to ask these questions sensitively. Officers who are uncomfortable in asking a rape victim details of the crime should consider acknowledging this discomfort, thus increasing the likelihood that the victim will respond in a helpful manner.

Reflective comments also demonstrate that officers are actively listening. They encourage the victim to express emotion. Both the content and feeling of what the victim has said can be reflected back through active listening. For example:

> *Victim:* He jumped right through the window. . . .
> *Officer:* You mean he just burst right in? (Reflecting *content.*)
> *Officer:* I bet that was frightening. (Reflecting *feeling tone.*)

Timely clarifications and summaries are another means of demonstrating to the victim that officers are actively listening. Moreover, timely clarifications and summaries help to tie up random emotions for the victim. Rather than interrupting repeatedly to clarify, these summaries should be done after the victim has finished a segment of a story. For example, officers may summarize what was said, then ask, "Do I have it right?"

Diversionary Reality Questions. These questions force victims to deal with reality, thus reducing their distress. They should be simple, realistic, and non threatening (for example, "How many people live here?" or "How many children are there?").

Personalizing Statements. Using words such as I think or I feel will personalize statements and create an environment of empathy toward the victim. If officers are accepting of the victim through personalized statements, this is reassuring. Since the police are often viewed as representatives of society, an understanding approach will reduce the victim's concern about society's reaction. Officers also should capitalize on their prestige as protectors by reassuring victims that they are safe from further occurrences and from retaliation by the perpetrator. This is especially important with rape or assault victims, whom offenders often warn that they will return to kill if the crime is reported. In such cases, a clear and repeated statement such as "In my experience as a police officer, rapists do not generally return to harm anybody" is critical.

State the Obvious. As we have mentioned several times, victims need constant reassurance that officers are concerned for their safety and that they understand and empathize with them. Stating "I'm here to help you. You are safe now" or "I know this has been a dreadful experience for you" may seem obvious to officers, but it is important for the victim to hear these words of reassurance.

Accident Victims

Police officers frequently will have to deal with victims of situations besides crime, such as severe auto accidents and medical emergencies. Although the major responsibility in these situations often falls on paramedics (or

other medical personnel), police officers should be aware of the following.

Relaxation

It is important to relax the victim if at all possible. A simple technique that works well is to tell the victim to take a deep breath and let it out slowly. Officers who appear calm and relaxed will be more able to get the victim to relax.

Reassurance

Like victims of crime, accident victims need continual reassurance that everything possible is being done for them and everything will turn out all right. Officers should not lie but should take the opportunity to assure the victim that they are there to help, that an ambulance is on its way, and that others who are involved are being taken care of, if necessary. Officers and paramedics have a tendency, while concerning themselves with those showing physical signs of injury at accidents, to ignore other survivors who do not show symptoms. Yet these people may be suffering very traumatic emotional damage.

Positive Statements

Officers should make only positive statements relative to the condition and future of the victim. The fact that a victim may be unconscious does not relieve officers of this responsibility. Hypnosis research indicates that what is said under these circumstances, even if the victim is unconscious, can have a significant effect on the victim's chance of survival. Avoid statements such as "He'll never make it" or "I've never seen such a bad injury."

The Citizen-Observer Victim

We should remember that the ordinary citizen who may observe a crime or crisis situation is also a type of victim. The observer, too, can become highly emotional. Officers may first have to calm down an emotional citizen-observer before they will be able to carry out other necessary police duties. Goldstein and associates (1977) offer several techniques to calm citizen emotions in crisis situations.

1. **Show understanding.** By tone of voice, facial expression, and gestures, officers show that they understand the feelings the citizen-observer is experiencing and how strongly he or she is experiencing them. For example, they may say, "It can be awfully frightening when something like this happens. You're really feeling very angry and upset."

2. **Be a model.** If officers respond calmly to the crisis, their appearance of control serves as a model for the involved citizen.

3. **Reassure.** Using reassurance, officers should give the citizen reasons why he or she should feel calmer (for example, "I've handled many like this," or "We've got the situation under control"). Reassurance works especially well in calming a situation if officers have first established themselves as nonhostile authority figures.

4. **Encourage talking.** It is difficult for anybody to yell, scream, cry, fight, or behave emotionally if, at the same time, he or she is trying to answer questions. Encouraging the person to talk is an effective means of calming him or her down. Sometimes police officers may encourage the person to talk about the crisis itself. This can be a form of ventilation. However, if talking about the crisis gets the citizen more agitated, officers may calm him or her by asking numerous questions and taking notes at a deliberately slow pace.

5. **Use distraction.** Distraction is useful although its effect may be temporary. Distraction may be accomplished by asking a favor (for example, "May I have a glass of water?"), asking a question totally irrelevant to the situation (for example, "Can you tell me where

you got that particular item?"), or asking a question relevant to the crisis situation but opposite to what the citizen is likely to expect (for example, "Do you really want me to take him to jail?").

6. **Use humor. Humor can help keep the crisis in perspective and cool tempers in a very tense situation.** However, humor must be used cautiously. Because of the emotional nature of the situation, it may not be appreciated. At no time should officers attempt to use ethnic humor.

7. **Repeat or outshout.** Sometimes calmness does not work. When someone is very upset and is only aware of his or her own feelings, the person is often unresponsive to the feelings and presence of others. Officers may have to repeat themselves several times or even outshout the citizen in order to be heard. They may slam a clipboard loudly to get attention.

8. **Use physical restraint.** When calm conversation, repetition, and outshouting have not worked, and when there is a threat of physical danger, officers may physically have to restrain and subdue the highly aggressive citizen. The minimum force required should be used.

9. **Use trust in others.** In a crisis, it may be appropriate for officers to ask someone else to help them by speaking to the citizen and attempting to calm him or her. This may be a trusted friend, relative, or neighbor. However, officers have to be careful in using a trusted acquaintance, first making sure that this person will not aggravate the crisis.

10. **Temporarily ignore, if there is a more pressing need.** Sometimes officers can calm the emotional citizen by temporarily ignoring him or her while handling someone in more acute distress, such as a bleeding accident victim. This reminder of reality may help calm the emotional citizen.

Death Notification

Police officers frequently have the difficult task of notifying families that a loved one has died. There is no easy way to do this, and it never gets any easier regardless of how often officers have done it. In general, the most effective approach seems to involve frankness and empathy. Officers should state clearly that the individual has died so that there is no doubt of what is being said. Officers should anticipate a variety of reactions to this news, ranging from calm, almost stunned acceptance, to hysterics (J. E. Hendricks, 1984). Officers should not draw back if the family member wishes to embrace them. They should be prepared to spend some time with the people to whom they have delivered the news. Many jurisdictions have crisis or outreach workers that officers can call to the scene. They will be able to handle the situation, freeing police officers to return to duty.

Notifying a police family of the death of a police officer is perhaps the most difficult thing an officer ever has to do. F. Stillman (1986) refers to police survivors as "invisible victims" and urges police psychological units to become involved in meeting their needs. He also states that injured officers, disabled officers, and officers who have had to kill fall into this "invisible victims" classification and require psychological assistance.

Intervening Crisis Workers as Victims

J. L. Greenstone and S. C. Leviton (1986) caution that it is not sufficient to learn crisis management procedures without also attending to the specific sources of stress and tension that may impinge on interveners, and thereby affect their ability to do the intervention efficiently and effectively. They warn that crisis workers (police officers) and the victim alike are subject to the same or similar stressors and thereby may both fall prey to them. Burnout was first noticed in professionals whose jobs required them to deal constantly with people in crisis. We shall devote more discussion to this stress and other stressors in later chapters.

SUMMARY

In this last chapter in the section on crisis situations, the author focused on one of the central figures in any crisis – the victim. As a result of a crime, accident, medical emergency, or other crisis, any citizen can have an emotional response that must be handled by officers. The generic ABC model gives officers a structured approach to crisis intervention in a variety of situations. The skill officers' show will reduce emotional trauma to the victim, enhance his or her cooperation with police, and lessen the severity of the crisis. Effective crisis intervention by police officers can "make the difference between averting a serious psychological disorder or experiencing one which may be so disabling that it can undermine the individual's effectiveness and happiness for years. At worst, it can lead to overt acts of suicide. Thus, psychological first aid provided by sensitive agents can be truly life saving" (C. J. Frederick, 1986, p. 346). Learning the necessary skills requires an understanding of the psychology of the victim and the adoption of approaches and techniques described in this chapter.

BIBLIOGRAPHY

Bard, M. 14 September, 1982. *Testimony presented at a public hearing of the President's Task Force on Victims of Crime*, Washington, D.C.

Band, M., & Ellison, K. May, 1974. Crisis intervention and investigation of forcible rape. *Police Chief, 41*(5), 68–74.

Brammer, L. M. (1973). *The helping relationship: Process and skills.* Englewood Cliffs, NJ: Prentice-Hall.

Chelimsky, E. (1981). Serving victims: Agency incentives and individuals' needs. In *Evaluating victim services*, ed. S. E. Salasin. Beverly Hills, CA: Sage.

Duncan, T. S. (1985). *Domestic crisis intervention for law enforcement officers.* Lawrenceville, VA: Brunswick Publications.

Ehly, S. (1986). *Crisis intervention handbook.* Washington, D.C.: National Association of Psychologists.

Fields, R. (1981). Research on victims. In *Evaluating victim services*, ed. S. E. Salasin. Beverly Hills, CA: Sage.

Flint, R. T. (1975). *The psychology of victims.* Schiller Park, IL: Motorola Teleprograms.

Fowler, R. (1984). Crisis case analysis. *Emotional First Aid: A Journal of Crisis Intervention, 1*(3), 66–70.

France, K. (1982). *Crisis intervention: A handbook of immediate person-to-person help.* Springfield, IL: Charles C Thomas.

Frederick, C. J. (1986). Post-traumatic stress responses to victims of violent crime: Information for law enforcement officials. In *Psychological services for law enforcement*, ed. J. T. Reese & H. A. Goldstein, pp. 341–350. Washington, D.C.: U.S. Government Printing Office.

Goldman, S. R., & Killam, E. W. November, 1982. Another aspect of rape prevention. *Law and Order*, 42–45.

Greenstone, J. L., & Leviton, S. C. (1986). Referrals: A key to successful crisis intervention. *Emotional First Aid: A Journal of Crisis Intervention, 3*(2).

Hendricks, J. E. (1984). Death notification: The theory and practice of informing survivors. *Journal of Police Science and Administration, 12*(1), 109–116.

———. (1985). *Crisis intervention: Contemporary issues for on-site interveners.* Springfield, IL: Charles C Thomas.

Kinder, G. (1982). *Victim: The other side of murder.* New York: Delacorte Press.

Klyver, N., & Reiser, M. (1983). Crisis intervention in law enforcement. *Counseling Psychologist, 11*(2), 49–54.

Pearce, J. B., & Snortum, J. R. (1983). Police effectiveness in handling disturbance calls: An evaluation of crisis intervention training. *Criminal Justice and Behavior, 10*(1), 71–92.

Plummer, D. L., Jenkins, J. O., & Hampton, L. A. (1984). Rape and intervention strategies. *Crisis Intervention, 13*(3), 104–113.

President's task Force on Victims of Crime. (1982). *President's task force on victims of crimes: Final report.* Washington, D.C.: U.S. Government Printing Office.

Russell, H. E. May, 1986. *Victimology.* Presented at the Arizona Law Enforcement Academy.

Salasin, S., ed. (1981). *Evaluating victim services.* Beverly Hills, CA: Sage.

Sanders, C. M. (1989). *Grief: The mourning after: Dealing with adult bereavement.* Somerset, NJ: John Wiley.

Siegel, M. December, 1983, Crime and violence in america: The victims. *American Psychologist, 38*(12). 1267–1273.

Silbert, M. (1976). *Crisis identification in management: A training manual.* Oakland, CA: California Planners.

Slaikeu, K. A. (1984). *Crisis intervention: A handbook for practice and research.* Boston: Allyn & Bacon.

Sparks, R. F. (1982). *Research on victims of crime: Accomplishments, issues and new directions.* Rockville, MD: NIMH, Center for Studies in Crime and Delinquency.

Spates, C. R. (1981). *The mental health needs of victims: A review of the literature and recommendations for research* (Contract No. 379508166). Washington, D.C.: National Institute of Mental Health, Mental Health Services Branch.

Stillman, F. (1986). The invisible victims: Myths and realities. In *Psychological services for law enforcement*, ed. J. T. Reese & H. A. Goldstein, pp. 143–146. Washington, D.C.: U.S. GPO.

Symonds, M. (1980). The second injury to victims of violent crime. *Evaluation and Change* (special issue), *20*, 36–38.

Walker, L. E. A. (1989). Psychology and violence against women. *American Psychologist, 44*(4), 695–702.

PART VI

THE STRESSES OF POLICE WORK

Chapter 21

JOB-RELATED STRESS

In his opening remarks to one of the first seminars ever held on police work and stress, Karl Goodin, chief of the Cincinnati Police Department, observed that "policing . . . is one of the most stressful jobs in the occupational picture today." Chief Goodin continued:

> I have been a policeman for almost twenty years. During that time, I have seen many of my fellow police officers incapacitated by health problems, heart attacks, ulcers, chronic headaches, mental depression, and even suicide. They have been stricken in numbers that seem unduly large when compared to friends in the business world and in government service agencies other than police.
>
> The situation is a paradoxical one because police officers begin their careers as healthy men and women. They enter the profession as the healthiest and most physically fit people in any single occupation, yet year after year they are struck down at comparatively young ages when early health history would seemingly point to above-average longevity.
>
> Figures show that career police officers, both active and retired, die younger than those in most other occupational groups and suffer a particular high incidence of health problems. Why? The work is relatively clean; there are no poisonous industrial fumes to breathe or noxious chemicals to handle; it is certainly not monotonous compared to assembly-line work. Even though police officers run the risk of being killed in the line of duty, that is a relatively minimal risk. Their job is actually safer than a good number of others, such as iron workers or farmers.
>
> Why do they suffer health problems? Stress is the reason named again and again by occupational researchers as the major factor causing health problems in police officers.
>
> Stress. What causes it? Why is it such a prevalent condition in law enforcement officers' life? (1975, p. 275)

This chapter seeks to present answers to some of these questions. It will not present a comprehensive review of the topic. Readers are directed to the bibliography at the end of the chapter for references to specific and/or additional areas of interest they may elect to study further. The author will limit the discussion to the following: a brief review of the early history of stress research; a set of definitions; stressors in the police environment and in the personal life of police officers; the psychological and physical symptoms of stress; and ways that police departments and individual officers can reduce the adverse effects of stress.

Historical Background

It was not until the Civil War that environmental stress was recognized as an important etiological factor in certain physical and emotional conditions. Surgeons of both armies became aware of soldiers who presented certain behavioral patterns. They were listed in the sick book excessively, got into fights, went absent without leave frequently, and refused to obey rules and regulations. These psychological, physical, and behavioral symptoms were the products of stress and resulted from pathological interaction between the soldier and his environment. The military study of stress continued in World War I, World War II, Korea, and Vietnam. Much of what we know today about the impact of stress on police work was first noticed in combat situations.

In civilian medicine, the study of stress was based on the work of nineteenth-century French biologist Claude Bernard, who pointed out that the internal environment of our bodies – our blood pressure, heart rate, oxygen level, the amount of red cells in the blood – must maintain consistency and that all these must shift periodically to meet the demands of life. If adaptation to a change in condition does not occur, disease or even death may ensue. Dr. Bernard's work was extended by Harvard physiologist Walter D. Cannon, who discovered "the wisdom of the body," describing the internal mechanisms of adjustment in body functions as responses to environmental changes. Cannon was especially interested in the emergency reactions of the body – how the body deals with sudden life-and-death situations. In one classic experiment, he studied the reaction of a cat suddenly confronted by its proverbial enemy, the dog. The cat immediately went into an emergency response. Adrenaline was released into the bloodstream, as was an almost identical hormone called noradrenalin, leading to a variety of physiological reactions. Blood-clotting mechanisms were accelerated, more sugar appeared in the blood, rates of circulation and breathing increased, more red blood cells were released from the spleen, senses became keener, the digestive system went into temporary inactivity, and sphincters contracted. Cannon noted that all these responses were very useful and adaptive because they prepared the body for maximum effort – to either fight or flee to ensure survival. Cannon observed that a variety of emergency situations could trigger this pattern of adaptive responses (for example, pain, physical injuries, and intense emotion).

The word *stress* was virtually coined by an Austrian-born physician, Hans Selye, who founded the International Institute of Stress in 1978. As a young medical student, Selye was impressed with what he called the "sameness of sickness," what many different patients had in common as they appeared depleted of energy, listless, haggard, and drawn. He later demonstrated that these final manifestations of stress were the product of a three-stage process: the alarm stage, the resistance stage, and the exhaustion stage. Together they constituted the *general adaptation syndrome* (GAS). Selye pointed out that no living organism can exist in a continuous state of alarm; and that should stress continue, the animal will either develop a disease or die.

Definitions

Stress has been defined as "the nonspecific response of the body to any demand placed upon it" (Reese & Bright, 1987, p. 277). When we refer to stress, we are talking about the effect that certain environmental features have upon a person. Police officers do not exist in a vacuum but in a social world, surrounded by others significant to them, such as family, friends, fellow police officers as well as the citizens and criminals with whom they interact during their tour of duty. The physical aspects of their environment also surround them, indoors and outdoors, which can either be stressful or nonstressful. When we speak of stress as the product of the interaction of people with their environment, we are really concerned with *stressors* in the environment – anything that produces an autonomic nervous system response in the individual. What is the autonomic nervous system and how does it work? The autonomic nervous system controls all hormonal glandular activity, which influences such functions as breathing, blood pressure, and pulse rate.

A person has two nervous systems: the central nervous system, consisting of the brain and the spinal cord; and the autonomic nervous system. Most conscious, voluntary behavior is associated with the central nervous system (for example, reading, writing, and firing a weapon). But while you are reading this page, thinking about the material and perhaps making notes, your body is also engaging in autonomic nervous system activity (breathing, maintaining blood pressure at a certain level, and secreting hormones).

The autonomic nervous system consists of the sympathetic and the parasympathetic divisions, which work in tandem. The sympathetic division alerts people and gets them ready to make a maximum effort. When the stimulus for an autonomic nervous system response is no longer present, the parasympathetic division is activated to restore the individual to his or her former homeostasis. The autonomic nervous system functions as an *emergency response system* (Chusid, 1982, p. 278).

Humans have survived and dominated this planet because of two features: a superior brain and the autonomic nervous system response mechanism. When primitive man rounded a bend in the trail and came face to face with a large animal, the autonomic nervous system responded immediately: more adrenaline was secreted, breathing changed rapidly, digestion dramatically stopped, the spleen produced more red blood cells so more oxygen could be carried through the body, the sphincter muscles contracted − placing primitive man in an alert position for a maximal effort in running or fighting.

Today, not many police officers worry about meeting lions or tigers during a normal tour of duty, but the autonomic nervous system response is still there, operating as an emergency response mechanism. Functioning as needed, it causes changes in officers' biology. Instead of fending off giant animals, today's police officers may get involved in a dangerous family fight or a bloody, fatal automobile accident. They may face the stress of working under incompetent or hostile supervisors. Each stressor in officers' environments can evoke an autonomic nervous system response.

Case Example. The police officers start their day at a certain level of tension. They receive a call to an accident with injuries. They switch on the emergency equipment, code 3. Immediately, simultaneously, their bodies also go code 3 because the autonomic nervous system response has been evoked. They arrive at the accident scene and take whatever measures are necessary. When they are finished they go code 4, turn off the emergency equipment, make their report, and resume patrol.

The officers' bodies do not turn off as easily. The parasympathetic division of the autonomic nervous system takes longer to come down from its level of tension. Their tension levels have not returned down to the precall level when they get another call. This time it's a bad family fight. After nearly being knifed by an irate husband, the officers end up arresting him and putting him in handcuffs. Once again they have gone code 3, both in their police equipment and their bodies. Once again when the emergency is over their procedures return to code 4, but their bodies do not go code 4 as easily as the equipment. Hence, their present level of tension, while not as high as a few moments ago, is still considerably higher than when they started this tour of duty.

It is very important for officers, family, and the counselors who work with police officers to understand code 3 biology. Police officers' tension level may be very high at the end of a tour. They don't want to go home if that means listening to more problems. They may want to stay at the station and exchange war stories with other squad members or join other police officers in a "choirboy rehearsal." Biologically, they need to release their tension gradually before they are able to go home and assume their role of spouse and parent.

We believe that police officers themselves have a code 3 personality. If you ask a hotel clerk, "What kind of night did you have last night?" she may reply, "Wonderful." You ask, "What happened?" She replies, "Nothing happened. No one checked in, no one checked out, no one rang the phone. I read my book, dozed a little, and had a marvelous night." Ask a police officer what kind of a night he had and he says, "Wonderful." You ask, "What happened?" He replies, "We had three rapes, two homicides, three shootouts, and five narcotic busts." The police officer likes that kind of action. He has a code 3 personality.

STRESSORS IN POLICE WORK

Author Joseph Wambaugh has said, "The physical dangers of being a cop already are vastly overrated by TV and movies, while no one pays attention to the more serious emotional dangers on the job that drive cops to divorce, suicide, alcoholism and drug addiction in greater numbers than any other vocational group" (Terry Eisenberg, 1975). Hans Selye (1978a) reinforces this view when he remarks, "It may be said without hesitation that, for policemen, the most important stressors are emotional, especially those causing distress." Reese and Bright (1986) state: "There is no doubt, however, that it [police work] is among the most emotionally dangerous jobs in the world" (p. 50).

Terry Eisenberg (1975), a psychologist and former police officer in the San José Police Department, appears to have created the most comprehensive list of job stressors. It is based on his own experiences while working as a patrol officer in a metropolitan area for over two years. He identifies over thirty alleged or implied sources of psychological stress and organizes them into six categories: (1) intra-organizational practices and characteristics; (2) inter-organizational practices and characteristics; (3) criminal justice system practices and characteristics; (4) public practices and characteristics; (5) police work itself; and (6) police officer himself or herself.

Intraorganizational Practices and Characteristics

Eisenberg (1975) describes those features within a police organization that may provoke and encourage the development of psychological stress among police personnel, particularly patrol officers. The following conditions represent sources of psychological stress.

Poor Supervision

Because of the paramilitary nature of police organizations, supervision plays an especially important role in the work of police officers. This is especially true of first-line (sergeant) supervision. Supervisors who are incompetent, always go by the book, are overly demanding, manipulate others for their own advantage, or fail to back up subordinates in delicate and critical situations can substantially contribute to subordinates' psychological stress. In too many police agencies, officers appointed to supervisory status receive no training for the new role. Even if training is offered, it is administered some time after officers have already assumed the role, made decisions, and directed subordinates. Except perhaps in very large departments, police officers are quite restricted in their ability to get out from under such supervisors. As Eisenberg (1975) states, "The importance of the supervisor [sergeant] in the life of a patrol officer cannot be underestimated" (p. 281).

Absence or Lack of Career Development Opportunities

Most police officers start and end their careers as patrol officers; however, when they start, most do not anticipate ending their careers in this way. Most aspire to go higher in the organizational chain and would admit to at least occasional fleeting fantasies of someday becoming chief. However, promotional opportunities are limited. In addition, the promotional process often lacks objectivity, which generates more frustration. Specialized assignments within the patrol officers' rank are also limited and are sometimes awarded on a buddy system.

Excessive Paperwork

The volume of paperwork that ordinary officers have to contend with is incredible. One call lasting twenty minutes may generate two hours (or more) of paperwork. Much of it, to officers at least, seems absolutely unnecessary.

UNACCEPTABLE POLICY

Many times police officers find certain department policies offensive, threatening, and/or unreasonable. Many of these policies center around two important issues: the use of force and minority recruitment. Officers may worry about getting involved in a shooting (or some lesser use of force). Even though they took action they thought was appropriate at the time, they find that their action is now being censored by command, possibly even being reviewed by the county attorney to determine if criminal charges should be filed. In such cases, officers see themselves as having fewer rights than the hoods they arrest. This is because, as police officers, they must answer any and all questions about the incident, even to the extent of having to take a lie detector test. Although this may violate their constitutional rights as persons, failure to consent to these procedures may subject officers to punishment or even termination for disobeying departmental rules and regulations.

Department policies concerning minority recruitment may threaten or offend other officers who see the policy as reverse discrimination. Various interest groups may demand concessions and threaten to sue in court if their demands are not met. This elicits hostility toward the special interest group from other officers, who may see these demands as unreasonable and selfish and not in the best interest of the department.

Inter-Organizational Practices and Characteristics

Eisenberg (1975) second category refers to those features between or among police agencies that may lead to stress, such as *jurisdictional isolationism*. Law enforcement agencies tend to operate within a particular jurisdiction, and boundary lines between jurisdictions are often jealously guarded. Although mutual aid agreements may exist, each agency is an island unto itself and often does not share with other agencies information concerning emergency crisis conditions, equipment, and criminal activity.

Although police officers in different agencies may get along well together as individuals, particularly at the patrol level, command personnel often do not reflect this cooperation. Further, when an issue depends on loyalty to the organization, even cooperation between individual officers may disappear. All local police (city, county, state) are suspicious of federal law enforcement agencies.

Criminal Justice System Practices and Characteristics

Within this category are stress-related conditions that arise from the actions of agencies within the criminal justice system (for example, adult probation, juvenile probation, juvenile court, parole, corrections facilities, municipal and superior courts). Those within the criminal justice system often acknowledge it to be anything but a system, even though the agencies share a common mission. Stressors include the following.

Ineffectiveness of the Corrections System

Most police officers see the corrections system as having failed in its mission to rehabilitate, punish, or restrain lawbreakers. Police officers continually find themselves arresting the same people for the same offenses. Consequently, a sense of meaninglessness develops along with the feeling that "They don't care. Why the hell should I?"

Unfavorable Court Decisions

Over the past few years law enforcement personnel have considered certain court decisions to be too restrictive and antagonistic to their mission. Not only do these court decisions seem to overprotect the rights of the criminal at the expense of both the police and the victim, but delays and continuances in the judicial process further frustrate police officers. Most officers view plea bargaining, a necessity in today's crowded court schedules, as a negative procedure in which those guilty of serious crimes are allowed to plead guilty to lesser crimes, thus mitigating or even putting aside their sentence.

Another source of frustration within the courtroom setting involves scheduling officers' appearances in court. With rare exceptions, scheduling fails to take officers' on- and off-duty time into consideration. Although there is compensation for overtime, appearing in court usually interferes with officers' personal lives. This is particularly stressful when officers work shifts other than days. Having to appear in court during the day can severely disrupt sleep and other personal activities. Once they are in the courtroom, defense attorneys often attack officers. This can make them feel that they are being treated more as criminals than as police officers.

PUBLIC PRACTICES AND CHARACTERISTICS

Eisenberg (1975) refers to the sources of stress outside of law enforcement and the criminal justice system that can affect police officers.

Distorted and Unfavorable Press Accounts of Police Incidents

Police officers know the importance of reporting the news to the public, but they become very sensitive after they have been burned a few times by irresponsible or malicious reporters. Accounts of a police incident in the local newspaper may be distorted by incompleteness, error, and/or antipolice bias, resulting in the department and its members looking bad in the eyes of the public.

Unfavorable Minority and Majority Attitudes

Minorities sometimes see the police as oppressors. Allegations of brutality and racism are common. Majority members of the community may complain about slow response time, discriminatory police practices/services, insufficient manpower, and so on.

Derogatory Remarks by Neighbors and Others

Derogatory remarks are particularly hard to deal with, since they directly affect an officer's spouse and children. An officer's children may be referred to as "pigs" or "piglets." Children themselves sometimes make derogatory remarks about the parent's profession, particularly teenagers who are rebelling against authority. If the husband is an officer, his wife may be cornered at neighborhood gatherings and told of the terrible experiences endured by a neighbor or friend by some brutal or insensitive police officer. Donovan (1978) states that many children of police officers commit suicide every year, "pressured by the taunts they receive by being cops' kids" (p. 384).

The Ineffectiveness of Referral Agencies

Police officers encounter daily many situations where community services other than police intervention are required. In some jurisdictions, there is a lack of referral agencies; in others, the referral agencies that exist are perceived as ineffective. Many helping agencies (other than the police) work only from 8 A.M. to 5 P.M. (and seldom on weekends or holidays). Resources in the private sector are usually unavailable to police officers' "clients" because they cannot afford them.

DEMANDS OF POLICE WORK

Role Conflict

Police work presents officers with many conflicting roles. Serving the public sometimes conflicts with their mission to enforce the law. Maximizing efficiency in enforcing the law sometimes conflicts with guaranteeing the individual citizen's constitutional rights. The police officers' role may conflict with the role of parent or friend. The public wants officers to be highly visible when crime or danger threatens; otherwise they would prefer not to see them. These role conflicts in law enforcement work have significant consequences for development of stress.

Shift Work

Shift work is a major stressor, not only in terms of the adverse effects it has on officers' family lives but also in terms of their personal health. People function best when they have a regular work schedule. Changing shifts every month, every three months, or whatever time period the department mandates is very disruptive to biological rhythms. Anyone who has worked "swing" and "graveyard" shifts can testify to the major adjustment in body functioning required. The biological stress of shift work is often expressed in symptoms such as constipation, sleep difficulty, depression, fatigue, and digestive disorders. The change from day shift to swing or midnight also requires numerous personal and occupational adjustments. Related issues, such as court time and holdover assignments, create additional disruptive influences in officers' lives. Shift work also tends to force police families to associate only with each other, since other families are not available for recreation and company during such odd hours.

Police administrators, having come up through the ranks, accept shift work as a normal part of the job. Shift plans are developed with major emphasis on what the military calls "the needs of the service" and show little, if any, consideration for the social, psychological, and/or physiological impact on the officers. Although no published controlled experiments have been conducted in any police agency, it has been reported that many officers resign because of their inability to adapt to rotating shifts (O'Neil, 1986). All research on fatigue indicates that a large number of officers appear to be suffering from chronic fatigue attributable to shift changes and the social, psychological, and physiological disruption associated with night work. There is also a significant relationship between the number of nights worked and citizens' complaints of brutality (O'Neil, 1986).

Fear and Danger

Whether police officers acknowledge it or not, police work involves dangerous acts that can provoke fear and lead to serious injury, disability, or even death. Although the actual frequency of these incidents is quite low in relation to number of police contacts throughout the country on any given day, the tension is still there because officers are aware from the beginning of training that there is no such thing as a routine stop. An officer going down a dark alley in response to a prowler may never see the prowler and may never even have to draw his gun; but fear, apprehension, and tension are there. The autonomic nervous system is in action. This is a stressor.

Crisis Situations

People in the helping professions are subject to *burnout*. This subject is covered in Chapter 22.

Sense of Uselessness

Officers who seriously desire to help people often find themselves frustrated through no fault of their own. They often are unable to resolve the problems of the people with whom they come in contact.

Fragmentation of Police Work

Police work is like working on a production line, with each person making one contribution to the total product. There are few opportunities for follow-up on a case and little, if any, feedback from other police personnel, such as detectives, on cases that patrol officers were originally involved in.

People's Pain

The street is full of people who suffer both physically and mentally. Brutality, pain, and death are normal and usual and, to police officers, eventually routine. However, no matter how long officers have been on the force or how much pain they have seen, they still react emotionally when dealing with battered children, sexually abused victims, or badly beaten older people.

Rapid Changes

Police officers' working environment can change from complete boredom to a life-and-death struggle in a matter of seconds. Television and movies rarely show the long periods of boredom that exist in police work, the endless patrolling and filling out of the proper forms. Yet at almost any time, an immediate response to a dangerous situation may be required. When officers have to move fast and shift gears that rapidly, they're under stress!

Responsibility

Police officers must take responsibility for the consequences of their actions. A mistake, even if accidental or unintended, can call for disciplinary action, civil litigation, or even criminal prosecution. Officers constantly must be aware of their actions, their appropriateness, and their possible adverse consequences.

SPECIAL TYPES OF POLICE OFFICERS

Eisenberg (1975) discusses five types of police officers whose uniqueness adds to the stressors already described.

Incompetents

Police officers who manage to get through the required training but are unable really to work on the street are subjected to severe stress far beyond that experienced by average officers. Some of these incompetents leave police work voluntarily. A few are eventually discovered and dismissed, but most stay in police work and attempt in various ways, most of them maladaptive, to cope with their own incompetence.

Fear-Ridden

Although all police officers experience fear in certain situations, there are officers for whom fear is a constant burden. They are afraid for their own physical well-being. Such police officers (the wimps) usually do something early in their careers that shows their lack of courage. From then on they become the object of ridicule and derision by their peers. Nobody wants them for a partner and nobody wants them as backup. The stress on these officers is even greater than usual because their actions deprive them of the support and positive recognition given other police officers.

Nonconformists

Police departments, like other paramilitary structures, demand conformity from their members and allow little deviation from established norms. Like the military, law enforcement is more than a job. It is a way of life that is lived with others in the police family. If officers do not conform or are in some significant way different from their peers, the stress will be severe. The result is exclusion from the company and support of fellow officers.

Minority Officers

Minority police officers have special pressures. They are exposed not only to the ordinary stressors common to all officers but also to the stress associated with the rejection and skepticism from citizens of their own ethnic background. Minority officers often have to fight a long, hard battle before they are fully accepted by fellow officers as equal members of the police family.

Female Officers

From their very first days at the academy, female officers are also subject to unique stressors. Most female officers feel that they must excel, particularly in the physical and self-defense portion of the training, to prove to male colleagues that they can back them up in a time of need. In addition to this pressure to succeed and be accepted, female officers have the problem of how to deal with a professional environment in which most cohorts are men. Female officers may be exposed to ridicule, sexual innuendo, and even sexual harassment. Some female officers handle this pressure with no trouble. Others sometimes respond by trying to "outmasculine" the men. When they do, they not only surrender their femininity but also try their best to hide it. By not completely being themselves, they create a tremendous stressor on their emotional well-being.

Prior to the mid-seventies, female recruits entering the academy had few role models to emulate, if any. But the 1980s saw a significant change. Women are now patrolling the streets in nearly all cities, and many female officers have attained high supervisory positions, up to and including chief. Gail Cobb became the first American female officer to die in the line of duty. Her death was "dramatic evidence of women's increased involvement in law enforcement" (Stratton, 1984, p. 193). On a happier note, Captain Kathleen Brennan of the Pima County Sheriff's Department was recently appointed head of that department's SWAT Team. She is the first female officer in Arizona to receive such an assignment and is perhaps the first in the nation. Sheriff Dupnik said she was selected for the job because "she was the best choice" (Durazo, 1989).

It is obvious that we have not exhausted the list of stressors in police work. Even today, we still do not know all the psychological dangers and stressors in police work, or their consequences. What we do know, however, is that a lack of awareness of the impact of stress can be very dangerous. When people are unaware of threats to their well-being, they are less able to cope with the stress that confronts them. To cope successfully with stress on an individual or departmental level, police officers must be made aware of the nature of job stress and of its consequences. Awareness alone will do much to mediate the adverse effect of stressors in police work.

PSYCHOLOGICAL AND PHYSICAL SYMPTOMS OF STRESS

Selye (1978b) emphasized that "in our life's events, the stressor effects depend not so much upon what we do or what happens to us, but on the way we take it." Reese (1987) echoes Selye in noting that "much of the [stress] problem lies in perception . . . overload and/or over commitment comes from outside not within." Each of us may react differently to certain stresses with our own unique pattern of physical and psychological symptoms that tell us we are under stress. Almost any psychological or physical symptom may develop as a result of stress. We are all familiar with the feeling of being uptight: gritted teeth, tense forehead and neck muscles, fluttering eyelids, shallow breathing, cold hands, and butterflies in the stomach. Beyond these common symptoms, the list of physical sequel of stress is endless. So too is the list of psychological symptoms. We may become irritable, anxious, fearful, tense, and depressed.

All police officers should learn to recognize the specific way that their body tells them they are under stress. As Reese (1987) states, "It is necessary to get the officer to recognize symptoms and to adequately cope, not self-medicate, drink, tranquilize, or withdraw" (p. 37). By careful self-observation, officers can gradually develop an instinctive feeling that tells them when they are running above or below the stress level that corresponds to their own nature. No refined chemical tests or monitors can do more.

Individual Stress Reduction Techniques

Here are some things officers can do, as individuals, to reduce the adverse effects of job stress.

Anticipation, Avoidance, Rehearsal

Reese (1987) states that the degree of effectiveness with which one reacts to situations is what separates professionals from amateurs. The professional has learned to be an "intentional reactor." An intentional reaction involves "assessing a situation in advance so that, even though the individual's reactions appear natural, they are purposeful and appropriate." This involves learning various proactive skills for greater self-control. Taking steps to be an intentional reactor in situations

involves deciding in advance what one has to do in that particular situation. Going through this mental preparation prepares one to act more effectively and also reduces one's stress level.

Officers should try to anticipate stressors in their environment and, if possible, avoid them. If this is not possible, police officers should rehearse their responses to the anticipated stress. All of us have had the experience of waiting for an important interview to take place. During the wait, we try to anticipate questions that will be asked and rehearse our answers to them. Officers may lessen the stress of responding to calls by rehearsing what they will do when they arrive on the scene, recalling similar situations, and remembering what they did in the past that was either effective or ineffective.

Attention to Diet

The diet of the average police officer is a nutritionist's nightmare. It consists of fast foods – doughnuts, coffee, hamburgers, french fries, and milk shakes – eaten under the most adverse conditions and usually with the background noise of the ever-present police radio. Officers may have to terminate their meal quickly to answer a 10–52 (accident with injuries), in which they will be exposed to sights, smells, and tensions hardly conducive to digestion. The role of diet as a stress reducer cannot be discussed in detail here. However, as an example of the importance of this subject, let us consider just one food, refined sugar, which makes up a large part of what police officers eat.

Insufficient sugar consumption or an overactive pancreas can cause *hypoglycemia*, or low blood sugar. When a person eats sugar, the pancreas releases insulin, which regulates the body's glucose levels. Hypoglycemics may display a bewildering array of symptoms, including depression, impotence, alcoholism, violence, dizziness, and headaches. For hypoglycemics, life may be a series of rollercoaster highs and lows. Highs correspond with the midmorning coffee break, when a sweet roll and coffee with sugar brings a blast of energy. A feeling of lethargy and fatigue follows this when the blood sugar level drops. Two common ways to relieve symptoms are to eat more sugar, which provides temporary relief, or to release adrenaline into the system. Since violent outbursts stimulate the flow of adrenaline in the body, a hypoglycemic may actually satisfy a critical body need through anger.

If we apply this knowledge to stress and police work, we may conclude that it may be more valuable to refer officers who have an abnormally high number of citizens' complaints to a physician for a fasting blood sugar test rather than to refer them to the officer of internal affairs for investigation. The officers' irritability and tendency to use too much force, which may be the basis of most citizens' complaints, may be associated with what they are eating rather than with personality factors. In our seminars on job-related stress, a nutritionist is always on the program by popular demand. Her presentation is always received with interest and is followed by demands for further information on the importance of diet in modulating stress reactions.

Exercise Program

It is ironic that police officers in even the smallest department must pass a demanding physical before acceptance, yet too few departments pay attention to maintaining physical fitness after training is complete. Numerous studies have shown that police officers are often overweight and out of shape. This can lead to serious consequences. For example, in the Pima county sheriff's department, a young deputy was transferred from patrol to detectives. After staying in detectives for about two years, he was transferred back to patrol. The first day on patrol, he was called to a neighborhood disturbance and engaged in a fight with a citizen. The citizen knocked the officer to the ground and managed to break away and dash back into his

house, where he obtained a .357 Magnum and came out shooting. He wounded the officer before the officer killed him. It developed that this citizen was not a criminal, but rather a very depressed person who had been drinking heavily and expressing suicidal thoughts after his wife had left him. The citizen may have chosen this way to die.

At first the deputy seemed to be adjusting well to the stress of the shooting. The department psychologist saw him in the hospital as he was recovering from his wound and reported that he seemed to be experiencing no problem. However, a short time later, the deputy left Tucson and flew to Chicago. Upon arriving there, he called the FBI and informed them that he was wanted for murder in Tucson. He persisted with this self-accusation, turning himself into the Chicago police. Finding that he was a deputy, the Chicago police took up a collection and paid for his fare back to Tucson. However, he got off the plane at one of the stops and did not return to Tucson until later. When he did appear, he resumed calling the FBI and other law enforcement agencies, saying that he was a murderer and should be placed in prison and punished. Eventually it was necessary to confine him to a hospital psychiatric ward. The psychiatrist in charge stated that the officer was experiencing considerable guilt related to what he perceived as his lack of physical fitness. He told the psychiatrist that if he had maintained his physical fitness while he was in detectives, the citizen could not have pressed him to the ground, broken away, and gotten his gun. He therefore blamed himself for the citizen's death.

In Chapter 23 we will discuss in more detail this postshooting syndrome, but the point here is that police officers need to stay in shape in order to carry out the physical activities demanded of them. All officers should assume responsibility for their own physical condition and engage in a continuous planned program of physical fitness. Police officers might involve their spouse and perhaps the whole family in a physical fitness program. Brisk walking is the world's least expensive sport. It offers an opportunity for the family to do something together, it doesn't take much money, and everybody feels better and becomes healthier.

Private Time

Everyone needs some time to be alone. Married couples need private time to be alone by themselves. Some of this private time can be spent on an exercise program. Time for reflection and conversation is a must for any officer.

Relaxation

If Americans knew how to exercise properly, how to eat properly, and how to relax, a large part of our health problems would disappear overnight. Most people have never experienced true relaxation. They perceive relaxation as not being uptight. Relaxation is much more than this. Many books are available to teach you how to relax. One of the best is *The Relaxation Response*, by Harvey Benson (1975). Benson discusses the principles of relaxation and gives many exercises, from deep muscle relaxation that can be done at home, to quick, simple relaxation exercises to be performed at the office and in the car.

Other relaxation techniques can be helpful — for example, listening to soothing music, meditating, or reading an interesting book. Once you learn to relax by one or more of these methods, practice relaxation several times a day. It doesn't have to take a long time; under certain stressful situations, even a few seconds can suffice. We teach recruits to relax when faced by stress simply by putting the index finger and thumb of each hand together, taking a deep breath, and saying to themselves "Relax, relax, relax." Troopers tell us that this single technique has been very helpful in stressful situations.

Adequate Sleep

Adults do best when they have had not less than seven hours of sleep and not more than

eight hours. In forming habits for better health, it is important to pay attention to getting adequate sleep — a factor often overlooked by action-oriented people, particularly in their youth. In regard to forming habits for better health, Dr. Lester Breslow (1980) reported an interesting study of seven thousand residents in Alameda County, California, over the past thirty years. The study's purpose was to establish statistical evidence of a link between peoples' daily life-style and health habits and their general health and life expectancy. Breslow and his colleagues questioned the participants on seven habits they thought might have a relation to health: (1) cigarette smoking; (2) moderate or no use of alcohol versus heavy use; (3) moderate or strenuous exercise versus little or none; (4) seven or eight hours of sleep versus less or more; (5) eating moderately, so as to be neither obese nor too thin; (6) eating breakfast; and (7) eating regularly at certain mealtimes rather than snacking during the day.

The results were striking. Breslow found that "for every age, those who followed seven of the habits had better physical health than those who followed six . . . and so on, down to those who followed three habits who were found to have better health than those who followed from zero to two" (p. 294). Perhaps even more interesting was the finding that a man of sixty who followed all seven health habits had about the same physical health as a thirty-year-old man who followed from zero to two of the habits. Life expectancy findings were equally startling. "We found that a man at age 45 who was following zero to three of the habits can expect to live to 67 years old, while a man of 45 who follows six to seven of the habits has a life expectancy of 78" (p. 294). The fact that life-style changes can result in an increase of eleven years in life expectancy gives some indication of the health strategy that everyone ought to follow.

Positive Thinking

One of the common elements of most mental illnesses is a negative self-image. Fortunately, most of us are not mentally ill. However, all of us, to a certain extent, engage in negative thinking, programming ourselves for failure or responding negatively to stressors. All of us do a lot of self-talking. We do this every day, but unfortunately, many times we don't tell ourselves favorable things. We tend to cut ourselves down, to find fault with ourselves. What we have to do is to change this negative self-talk to positive.

It is clear that it is not the stress but how one interprets it that makes the significant difference. Stress can be both positive and negative in its influence. Selye (1978b) has coined the term *eustress* for the good kind of stress that makes you come alive, that challenges you to do your utmost. By positive thinking, you can convert negative stress into positive experience.

> I think there's another better way to handle stress that involves taking a different attitude towards the various events in our lives. Attitude determines whether we perceive experiences as pleasant or unpleasant. In adopting the right attitude, one can convert a negative stress into a positive one – something I call a eustress, employing the same prefix for good that occurs in such words as euphoria and euphonia. (Selye, 1978b, p. 295)

Selye developed the concept of eustress in association with the following experience. At the age of sixty-five he developed a type of cancer whose cure rate is practically zero. Here's how Selye reacted to this news:

> I was sure I was going to die, so I said to myself, "All right now, this is about the worst thing that could happen to you, but there are two ways you can handle this; either you can go around feeling like a miserable candidate on death row and whimper away a year, or else you can try to squeeze as much life as you can." Selye chose the latter and then a "strange thing happened. Years went by, then two, then three and look what happened. It turned out I was that fortunate exception." (Siegel, 1986)

Recent scientific research offers evidence that positive thinking can be a potent force in preventing disease and in recovering from disease (Locke & Colligan, 1988). Another attitude that, in conjunction with positive thinking, helps to relieve stress, may be summed up as follows: "Don't sweat the small stuff." This phrase comes from the experience of a business executive who told of an earlier time when, as a salesman, he had picked up a young hitchhiker along a mountain road. Shortly after picking him up, the salesman found himself behind a big truck. Since it was only a two-lane country road, there was no opportunity to pass. Without realizing it, the salesman found himself getting upset because of his inability to pass the slow-moving truck. As his annoyance was reaching a peak and he was considering passing the truck, even though it might be dangerous, he looked over at the young hitchhiker, who was apparently very relaxed. The young man, noticing his glance, looked back at him and said, "Don't sweat the small stuff." Now a business executive, the salesman states that this was one of the most valuable bits of advice he had ever gotten, and from that time on he tried to see things in perspective. Remember, none of us, not even police officers, is irreplaceable. When something seems to get you really uptight, back off, relax, and "Don't sweat the small stuff."

Stress Reduction at the Department Level

As we indicated in our discussion of intradepartmental stressors, there is much that a police organization can do to look within itself, identify unnecessary stressors, and eliminate or moderate them. For example, when officers are being investigated by the office of internal affairs, they are understandably under great stress, particularly if there is a possibility of termination or criminal prosecution for their actions. In our American tradition, officers, like other accused persons, must be presumed innocent, yet many departments make no allowance or provision for keeping officers informed of the investigation's progress.

Certainly, there may be some facts about the investigation that cannot be made available at a particular time. We are not talking about that. We are talking about unnecessarily allowing officers to "twist slowly, slowly in the wind" while their fate is being decided, as a Nixon aide once phrased it.

The department could initiate certain administrative changes involving the use of "tickler files" to ensure that the investigation and paperwork proceed without unnecessary delay. Using these files, the department could inform officers at any time of the status of the investigation, thus relieving them of unnecessary stress. Every department would profit from a review of all standard operating procedures in order to eliminate or change unnecessary or stress-provoking ones. Another way for police departments to reduce stress is to work constantly to improve selection procedures so that only those with high stress tolerance are hired. After candidates are hired and placed in the academy, they should undergo a field training and evaluation program so that candidates who are not suitable can be terminated before they become permanent employees. There should be an active in-service training program to acquaint officers with the subject of job-related stress. The department can assist the spouses' auxiliary in holding annual stress management seminars for officers' spouses.

Supervisors, particularly first-line ones (sergeants), should be trained to detect signs of adverse stress reactions in their personnel so they may be assisted or referred for assistance. Many departments now have an in-house mental health professional or have contracted with the private sector to provide counseling services (Chapter 24). Officers and their families should be encouraged to take advantage of these services; confidentiality should be assured. It is helpful if the professional has an office away from the station so that those who come will not have to make their visits known to other officers. There is nothing bad about seeking assistance. However, it is realistic to recognize that police officers may be suspicious that seeking help may result in a negative entry in their personnel jacket.

Edward C. Donovan (1989) makes an appeal for peer counselors to aid the department psychologist.

> Peer counseling works in the law enforcement vocation. It works when others don't and for a simple reason. Peer trusts peer but not outsiders. The police vocation is a closed society that will not let outsiders (nonpolice) in . . . the unwritten rule of suffering in silence about all that passes before your eyes and never speaking to others outside the vocation is seldom broken. So who else can a cop who is in trouble with himself talk to but another cop, someone who knows where he's at and how he's feeling about being there. (Donovan, 1978, p. 25)

Similarly, Horn and Solomon (1989) consider peer support to be a key element for helping officers cope with critical incident trauma.

Given the importance of exercise in stress reduction, departments need to sponsor on-duty exercise programs. Information and counseling regarding physical fitness needs should be available to officers and their families. We have emphasized the importance of diet in stress reduction. Department cafeterias and nutrition staff should be encouraged to comply with up-to-date concepts in nutrition through the food that they provide. Just as candy, pop, and other junk foods have been taken out of many school cafeterias and food-dispensing machines, the same could be done in police cafeterias and snack bars.

SUMMARY

This chapter has presented information on stressors in police work. The author discussed how stress may have a positive or negative value. How it affects individual officers is, to a large extent, up to the officers themselves. It is not the event but how officers perceive it that determines how much stress they experience and whether they experience it positively or negatively. Stress experienced in a positive way can make one tougher and more able to deal with stresses found on the job or in the family.

It is first necessary to identify stressors and to note which ones you react to, how they affect you, and what actions you can take to prevent adverse effects, while retaining the positive results from dealing effectively with the stressor. These stress-reducing actions include: (1) anticipation, avoidance, rehearsal; (2) attention to diet; (3) exercise program; (4) private time; (5) relaxation; (6) adequate sleep; and (7) positive thinking. Finally, the author discussed certain actions that the police department can take to reduce or eliminate unnecessary stressors in the police environment.

BIBLIOGRAPHY

Bayley, D. H. (1986). The tactical choices of police patrol officers. *Journal of Criminal Justice, 14*, 329–348.

Benson, H. (1975). *The relaxation response.* New York: William Morrow.

Breslow, L. 3 November, 1980. Forming habits. *Arizona Daily Star.*

Chollar, S. April, 1988. Food for thought. *Psychology Today*, 30–34.

Chusid, J. G. (1982). *Correlative neuroanatomy and functional neurology*, 18th ed. Los Altos, CA: Large Medical Publications.

Davidson, M. J. (1980). The coronary-prone type A behavior pattern and the policeman: A cross cultural comparison. *Journal of Police Stress, 1*, 39–41.

Debro, J. March, 1983. Stress and its control: A minority perspective. *Police Chief*, 106–115.

Dietrich, J. F. (1989). Caring for the dying: A police officer's privileged vocation. *Police Stress, 9*(1).

Dietrich, J. F., & Smith, J. (1986). The nonmedical use of drugs including alcohol among police personnel: A critical literature review. *Journal of Police Science and Administration, 14*(4), 300–306.

Donovan, E. C. (1978). Need some help, Doc?" *Journal of Police Stress, 1*, 25.

_____. August, 1989. *Research communications.*

Dunlavey, M. A. July, 1982. Stress and the police. *Law and Order*, 63–66.

Durazo, A. 6 June, 1989. Lt. Kathleen Brennan named 1st Female Commander of Co. Sheriff's SWAT Team. *Arizona Daily Star*, 1B.

Eisenberg, T. November, 1975. Labor management relations and psychological stress. *Police Chief*, 1954–1964.

Geiger, F. J. May, 1982. Stress reduction techniques . . . for the Chief of a small department. *Law and Order*, 56–66.

Gentz, D. (1986). Stress – A psycho-semantic perspective. In *Psychological services for law enforcement*, ed. J. H. Reese & H. A. Goldstein, pp. 439–442. Washington, D.C.: U.S. Government Printing Office.

Goodin, K. 8 May, 1975. Police stress. Presented at a conference on Police Stress. National Institute of Occupational Safety and Health, Cincinnati, Ohio.

Greller, M. M. November, 1982. Police stress: taking a department-wide approach to managing stressors. *Police Chief*, 44–48.

Horn, J. M., & Soloman, R. M. (1989). Peer support: A key element for coping with trauma. *Police Stress, 9*(1), 25–26.

Hunt, M. 11 June, 1989. When little things go wrong. *Parade*, 8–9.

Kankewitt, B. (1986). *The shattered badge.* New York: Methuen.

Kirschman, E. F. (1986). An ecological approach to emotional disability in police. In *Psychological services for law enforcement*, E. J. T. Reese & H. A. Goldstein, pp. 451–458. Washington, D.C.: U.S. Government Printing Office.

Locke and Colligan (1988). *The healer within: The new medicine of mind and body.* New York: E. P. Dutton.

Luxenburg, J., & Johnson, D. L. January, 1983. Personality type and job stress. *Police Chief*, 52–56.

Miller, A., et al. 25 April, 1988. Stress on the job. *Newsweek*, 40–45.

Mitchell, J. (1988). Stress recovery: An interview with Jeffrey Mitchell. *Public Management, 70*(11), 6–8.

O'Neil, P. S. (1986). Shift work. In *Psychological services for law enforcement*, ed. J. T. Reese & H. A. Goldstein, pp. 469–476. Washington, D.C.: U.S. Government Printing Office.

Parker, D. A. (1986). A procedure for simple insight-oriented stress reduction. In *Psychological services for law enforcement*, ed. J. T. Reese & H. A. Goldstein, pp. 479–482. Washington, D.C.: U.S. Goverment Printing Office.

Reiser, M. (1982). *Police psychology.* Los Angeles: LEHI Publishing Co.

Revkin, A. May, 1983. Taking the stress out of shift work. *Police Magazine*, 2–4. 12 November, 1977.

Russell, H. E. (1986). *Job related stress in police work – An update.* Manuscript.

Schaefer, R. B. May, 1983. The stress of police promotion. *Management – FBI Law Enforcement Bulletin*, 2–4.

Selye, H. (1978a). The stress of police work. Journal of *Police Stress, 1*, 7–9.

_____. (1978b). On the real benefits of eustress. *Psychology Today*, 60–70.

Siegel, B. S. (1986). *Love, medicine and miracles.* New York: Harper & Row.

Stratton, J. G. (1984). *Police passages.* Manhattan Beach, CA: Glennon Publishing Co. p. 332.

Sugar plays role in tension, violence. *Tucson Citizen*, p. B-1.

Tucson Medical Center. Summer, 1982. *For your good health*, pp. 1–2.

Wagner, W., & Larson, J. September, 1982. Stress: Causes, symptoms, illness. *Law and Order*, 66–76.

January, 1982. Workshop: Deadly force. *Police Chief*, 78–90.

Chapter 22

SPECIAL STRESS SITUATIONS

Certain situations and conditions found in police work constitute special stressors and merit attention. The author has selected six of these areas for discussion: use of deadly force, critical incidents, burnout, special assignments, marriage, and retirement.

THE USE OF DEADLY FORCE

Police officials are very aware of the problems inherent in the use of deadly force. In 1980 Chief Joseph S. Dominelli, president of the International Association of Chiefs of Police, said: "The use of deadly force is the most awesome and frightening duty ever imposed upon a police officer in a democratic society. No other occupation group, outside of military forces in wartime, is authorized by law to make a life and death decision under the split-second pressure of circumstances facing the police officer at the time he reaches for his service weapon." Statistics indicate that in the United States six hundred criminals are killed each year by police (Baruth, 1986). Some of these killings are done in self-defense, some are accidental, and some are to prevent a serious crime. A few represent serious abuses of police power (Cohen, 1980). On the other side of the ledger, approximately one hundred officers are killed in the line of duty each year. In 1988, the last year for which statistics are presently available, 159 officers lost their lives (Donovan, 1989). Many lose their lives in that split second required by the processes of perception, evaluation, decision, and action that every officer exercises

prior to using deadly force (Dominelli, 1980). Not only do officers have to face the stress from the shooting itself, but they also have to worry whether it will be judged a "good shooting" by investigators and administrators who will review and judge their every action (or lack of action) in the cold, unemotional reality of the next day. In most jurisdictions, the use of deadly force by police is subject to no less than five legal sanctions: (1) civil action in a local or state court; (2) criminal action in a local or state court; (3) federal civil rights action under Section 1983 of Title 42 of the U.S. Code; (4) federal criminal action under Section 242 of Title 18; and (5) departmental disciplinary action. Recently, in Tucson a police officer was found innocent of manslaughter in a criminal court but was judged liable in a civil court (along with the city he worked for). He subsequently lost everything he owned. The relationship of deadly force incidents to lawlessness is shown by the following analyses of the situations in which they occur:

1. Disturbance calls: 32%
2. Robbery in progress: 21%

3. Burglary in progress: 20%
4. Traffic offense: 8%
5. Personal dispute and accident: 4%
6. Stake-out and drugs: 4% (Blau 1986).

These statistics are based on 1982 incidents. Undoubtedly today's statistics would show a much higher prevalence of incidents in the "stake-out and drugs" category.

Critical (Traumatic) Incidents

A critical incident may be defined as any incident that induces, or has the potential to induce, an emotional shock capable of creating "substantial and lasting damage to the psychological well being of an individual" (Blak, 1986, p. 311). A police shooting; a police officer shot; a high-speed pursuit through city streets; discovering the body of a raped and/or physically abused child – all are examples of events that would emotionally shock any police officer, even though the officer may deny such feelings. Officers are human beings and are not immune to human reactions. Many police officers can now recognize and admit to such feelings as fear, anger, anxiety, doubt, but this was not always the case. In fact, as J. G. Stratton (1984) observes, police academies stress the violent and dangerous, and tell recruits that this is what the job is-what you get paid for. A nonemotional response is a necessity.

Post-Shooting Syndrome

The identification of post-traumatic stress disorder in the context of the police use of deadly force is one example of how mental health professionals have made a major contribution to law enforcement (Zeling, 1986). Dr. Michael Roberts, a consultant to the San José, California, Police Department, was one of the first to call attention to the *post-shooting syndrome*. He pointed out that for many new (and even some experienced) officers, the confrontation between the officer and an armed felon that results in the felon's death is

the ultimate myth of police work: This hero myth comes from movies, television, and from our cultural fiction involving the bad guy, the marshall, and "high noon." Perhaps even more important is the support that this hero myth receives from locker room values and the war stories told in police bars.

A San José police officer says that most police officers think that sometime they may have to shoot somebody. "Driving around, you think what if this would happen? . . . finally it happens to you and a lot of things you thought would happen don't. You imagine a blazing gun battle after which you go over and roll him over with your foot and blow the smoke from your gun" (Cohen, 1980). What really happened is that when this officer had to shoot a man, it took four rounds from his .357 Magnum before the suspect dropped. The officer then grabbed some gauze from the first aid kit and tried for fifteen minutes to resuscitate the victim.

The etiology of the post-shooting reaction lies in the emotional discontinuity between officers' expectations about the shooting and the reality of it. Officers' expectations revolve around the fantasy of a heroic, man-to-man confrontation. In reality, most police shootings do not involve a heroic situation. More often, it is a lopsided contest. Further, if the person is not a felon but a disturbed, mentally ill citizen, or if the shooting is accidental, the psychic trauma for officers may be even more severe.

Some officers involved in shootouts state that they hated all the adulation they received from their fellow officers afterward. One officer says, "You can't really talk to someone who hasn't been there. They want to hear the gory details, not about your problems handling it, because it's heavy and it reminds them that it could happen to them" (Cohen, 1980). Most officers are terribly afraid that they might have to shoot someone, so they are anxious to talk to an officer who has, hoping that whatever gave him the guts to pull the trigger will rub off on them. The following are some of the adverse reactions that officers involved in shootings may demonstrate:

1. **Sensory distortion.** Time slows down; everything happens in slow motion.
2. **Flashbacks.** Many things subsequently occur that instantly remind you of the shooting – another shooting, the sight of a body in the street. You live it over and over.
3. **Fear of insanity.** Officers may have this fear because of symptoms in (1) and (2) above.
4. **Sorrow over depriving a person of life.** It is very difficult to break the cultural and religious prohibition against killing. Even police officers who have previously killed in military combat state that a police shooting is entirely different. Detective Dan Sullivan of the Santa Barbara, California, Police Department states that "in a war, that's what you're there for . . . to wipe them out. Police work isn't like that. You are certainly not on a search and destroy mission" (Cohen, 1980).
5. **Crying.** This usually happens outside the police environment because the macho image does not permit tears.
6. **Grasping for life.** Officers become very concerned about their families, their home life, being loved and accepted by others – a sort of guilt reaction to the shooting.
7. **Nightmares.** One officer reported frequent nightmares in which the suspect kept coming at him, looming ever larger and ever nearer while the officer frantically pumps bullets into the apparition.
8. **Heightened sense of danger.** A shooting brings officers face to face with their own mortality. No longer can they entertain the idea that "It won't happen to me." For some officers, this has resulted in their leaving law enforcement. Although exact statistics are not available, it has been reported that between 50 to 80 percent of officers involved in shootings have left police work (Baruth, 1986, p. 307).

9. **Anger and hate toward the victim/ suspect.** Solomon and Horn (1986) state that this is the second most frequent and severe post-shooting reaction. Officers curse the victim/suspect for "making them do it," but this anger may mask the feelings of fear and vulnerability that the incident aroused in officers so that the curse more properly may be expressed as "goddamn you for making me feel so vulnerable."
10. **Isolation/withdrawal.** Officers may think that no one will understand what they are going through. They don't want to risk being ridiculed or put down. Peer support from another officer who has gone through a shooting experience can be most helpful at this time.
11. **Fear and anxiety about the next time it happens.** One officer who shot a suspect who he thought was armed (but wasn't) expressed fears that the "next time maybe I'll hesitate to shoot and this time the asshole will have a gun and he'll blow my f---- head off."
12. **Fear that they will be fired, criminally charged, or sued in civil court.** These are frequent reactions. Police policies and procedures may add unnecessary stresses to officers involved in a shooting. Delays in completing the investigation, a negative attitude, or lack of support from supervisors and/or administration can compound the psychological damage. One undercover narcotics officer had to endure a post-shooting investigation that began in May and dragged on until he was finally cleared of any wrongdoing in August. In this time the stress on the officer and his family was so severe as to result in a divorce.

Increasingly, officers involved in shootings find themselves before grand juries or in civil or criminal court. These legal proceedings make psychological intervention more difficult because officers become preoccupied with the legal ramifications of what they say to the psychologist rather than trying to express feelings about the shooting. Officers involved in shootings frequently seek immediate legal representation, either through their own lawyer or perhaps a lawyer from the Fraternal Order of Police. In the Tucson, Arizona, Police Department (TPD), confidentiality of the interview has to be assured, not only to officers but also to their attorneys. Even if this is the case, an attorney may decide that it is not in the best legal interests of his or her client to participate in such sessions.

In one incident, the senior author (HER) was called to the site of a shooting that involved a senior sergeant. This was the fourth time in his career that this sergeant had been involved in a shooting. The first time he said that the department had the "get back on your horse" philosophy, in which he was given a pat on the back, reassured that he was a good cop, and told to report for duty the next night. For the second shooting he got some time off because he was severely wounded and ended up in the hospital for several months. The third shooting did not actually involve any gunfire, but weapons were drawn. This last shooting, to which the author responded, involved a family fight. The young wife was firing a rifle at the officers and other people in the immediate vicinity. The sergeant was one of three officers who fired in return. The victim did not die but was severely injured and taken to the hospital. Asked about his reaction to this shooting, where a member of the behavioral science unit (BSU) was present but actually did next to nothing (in contrast to the other situations where no help was available), the officer stated that "just knowing that you were there made the difference . . . it helped." Officers involved in a shooting may not be open to therapeutic help until some time has passed. First they are interviewed by homicide detectives and other personnel (internal

affairs) about all aspects of the shooting. They are usually fatigued at the end of this process.

While they may express appreciation at the help being offered, they prefer to go home to their spouses and family, get some rest, then come in to talk. At this time, while the officers are undergoing investigation, attention should be paid to the spouse and other family members. Undoubtedly this is also a period of great stress for them; they may profit from help. In addition, assistance given to them at this time may enable them to be of more help to their loved one. In 1981 Dr. S. A. Somodevilla, a psychologist for the Dallas, Texas, Police Department, invited officers who had been involved in shootings at any time during their career to meet in Emotional Trauma Groups to reduce post-shooting trauma. Fifty-two officers responded, and from their initial meetings, information was developed that led to a department standard operating procedure (SOP) covering police shootings.The behavioral sciences unit of the Tucson Police Department has initiated a post-shooting support team comprised of officers who have been involved in shootings. These officers volunteer their own time for training and assistance to fellow officers who have been involved in shootings. Recommendations of Somodevilla's Emotional Trauma Groups (Somodevilla, 1986) and those of TPD's BSU are combined as follows:

1. **One officer from the post-shooting support team (PSST) will be on call to lend support and reassurance to officers involved.** (If more than one officer is involved, one or more additional officers from the PSST will be available.)
2. **Officers' families will be informed immediately of their condition.** It is best, if possible, for the officer involved to make the call.
3. **Officers will be removed from the scene immediately or as soon as possible.** They may be recalled to the scene for interviews when the necessary personnel have arrived to interview them.

4. **Some reassurance from someone in authority that the officers acted correctly should be provided.** However, everyone must fully realize that this support from a supervisor is only an opinion and may be negated by higher authority at some later time.

5. **Officers should have access to an attorney.** If the department psychologist has a Ph.D. or M.D., this usually does not present any significant difficulty. However, attorneys may not allow any interaction between their clients and master's-level psychologists, PSST members, and/or peer counselors. This is due to the legal question of whether client/doctor confidentiality would extend to the nondoctoral therapist.

6. **When police shootings occur, officers' weapons are seized for ballistics.** Officers feel embarrassed, angry, even fearful, when they lose their weapon. When Tucson's post-shooting support program first began, the responding PSST or behavioral science unit member took replacement guns to the scene to give officers whose weapons were taken. The program has had such strong support that now the first-line supervisor routinely carries a replacement weapon to the scene.

7. **The supervisor in charge should prepare material that can be presented to all shifts at briefings.** This material should identify the incident, officer(s) involved, what happened, and what action was taken to put the officer on sick leave, suspension, and so on. These measures should counteract the rumors that spring up and receive wide circulation following any police shooting incident. In this briefing, other officers should be advised that an officer has gone through an experience that can be traumatic and that they should be sensitive to the feelings the officer may have. Joking and prying would be ill advised.

8. **Establishment of clear, timely feedback to the officers is highly desirable.** Officers should not have to hear that the subject has died on local TV news.

9. **Officers should be officially informed that they do not have to answer any questions from the media.** In many cases, they will be forbidden to make a statement.

10. **Mandatory time off after a shooting is imperative.** One day should be routine; more days can be authorized if requested by officers, the commander, or the police psychologist. Officers generally feel that more than one day is not helpful because they need to "get back on the horse."

11. **At TPD, we began the program by requiring officers involved in a shooting to report to the BSU within twenty-four hours.** However, it was soon concluded that this added an unnecessary burden on already stressed officers. The policy was then changed to require the BSU to contact officers within twenty-four hours. This has worked out quite well.

12. **Proactive treatment is important.** Like the Dallas PD, TPD decided to disseminate information about post-shooting trauma and the PSST team to all personnel. This was accomplished by mandatory in-service training. In addition, cadet classes at ALETA (Arizona Law Enforcement Training Academy) have added a two-hour course entitled "Mental and Emotional Preparation for Shooting" to the regular firearms training. One hour of this class is devoted to post-shooting trauma and the resources available to officers who become involved in shootings (larger agencies assist smaller agencies throughout the state). Written material also is distributed. However, at ALETA police chaplains do not offer material on "Thou Shall Not Kill," as is done in

the Dallas program. This seems an idea worth copying.

One final note before leaving this subject. Our experience in the Tucson Police Department indicates that occasionally it can be very helpful to have a "volunteer wife," whose husband has been through a shooting experience, available to talk one-on-one with the wife of an officer involved in a shooting. The BSU routinely offers to provide this service to the shooter's wife. It seems obvious that similar support for police officers from the psychological services unit, peer counselor, or other volunteer helpers should be used to counteract the adverse psychological effects inherent in other types of critical incidents.

Burnout

Burnout refers to a syndrome of emotional exhaustion and cynicism that frequently occurs among individuals who do "people work" and who spend considerable time in close encounters with others who are experiencing chronic tension and stress (Maslach & Jackson, 1979). J. T. Mitchell (1989) defines burnout as "a descriptive word that implies the loss of an energy source and the useless remains of a once functional system." There are two types of burnout: gradual and rapid onset. Mitchell's gradual burnout appears to be what we have labeled career burnout.

Career burnout is not unusual, since almost everybody gets burned out to some degree. However, when people are constantly working in stressful situations and are responsible for those with whom they are working, they become especially susceptible to burnout. Over time, people working in a constantly stressful situation may begin to dislike and distrust those with whom they have contact. They may wish that they never existed. This can even happen to professionals who are normally sympathetic and concerned about the welfare of their clients. In addition to feeling negative about clients, workers may begin to feel negative about themselves and

may question whether their work has any meaning or value. This happens to nurses, doctors, psychologists, and others in the helping professions. But what about police officers who are constantly exposed to powerful and often-violent emotional stimuli associated with death, assault, rape, and murder?

J. G. Stratton (1984) observes that in the first few years after the academy, young officers may see all their expectations about the job go up in smoke. If disillusionment is too great, officers may become bitter toward the job and the department. This bitterness and resentment may be carried over to the streets and affect the way they interact with the public.

Dr. Donn Hupler, a former Albuquerque, New Mexico, police officer, notes that most techniques used by police officers to distance themselves from people and their problems have a depersonalizing or dehumanizing quality. For example, the police vernacular is replete with words that dehumanize (maggot, scumbag, basket case, and so on). Intellectualization is another defense mechanism that helps police officers handle emotionally charged situations. For example, the police officer may say about the woman who died in the flaming car, "She's better off dead. With those injuries, she'd have been a vegetable"; or about the suicide, "If I had his problems, I would have blown my head off too."

Police officers also utilize physical distancing to remove themselves from the emotional punishment associated with their work. Officers do not like to be touched. Devices such as sunglasses, an impersonal tone of voice, aloofness, and such statements as "It's not my problem, lady" serve the purpose of keeping others at a distance. In addition, officers may distance themselves further by aggressive gestures, such as resting a hand or elbow on the butt of their gun. In many ways the message comes through that officers are not really interested and do not want to get involved. Officers who go by the book are also defending themselves against stress. They cop out from taking responsibility for their decision or action by retreating to "the book" and stating with all the rigidity associated with military regulations, "I've got a job to do, lady," and "That's the way the law is."

J. T. Reese (1987, p. 34) describes burnout as "a disease of commitment, ironically causing a lack of commitment." There are three stages of burnout: (1) the stress stage (an imbalance between resources and demands); (2) the immediate, short-term emotional response to this imbalance (strain); and (3) changes in attitude and/or behavior which represent defensive coping. Of course, individual officers have different responses to the same stressors. Some officers seem capable of handling enormous amounts of stress, while others have a low stress-tolerance threshold. Burned-out officers can be recognized by their pessimistic outlook and negative feelings about everything. "Everything sucks," "the department sucks," "the job sucks," "the family sucks," and so on. "Paradoxically," remarks Reese (1987), "the more negative the attitudes and approach of the officer become, the more his burnout symptoms intensify. Thus, he reinforces his own counterproductive behavior" (p. 34).

What can be done to prevent officers from developing burnout? The best defense against burnout is gaining an understanding of its symptoms and causes. Dr. Gilmartin's chapter presents valuable information relative to the causes and effects of job-related stress and how to handle it. Reese (1987) presents several things individual officers can do when they find themselves experiencing the early warning symptoms of stress. The most important is for officers to change from the position of helpless victim to that of active participant in their recovery. Some of Reese's suggestions to the officer are:

> Share your worries and frustrations with a trusted friend; avoid "ain't it awful" sessions over coffee, etc; avoid self-medication (alcohol, drugs, etc.); eat properly and get an adequate amount of rest; take things one at a time; do something of value for someone else; learn to accept those things you cannot change; find something to look forward to each day; and balance your activities. Divide

your day into time for business, family, and time for you. (1987)

E. S. Rosenbluth (1986) notes that each of us has an individual body chemistry, a heredity that creates differing abilities to utilize the forty-odd nutrients required daily for our bodily cells to operate at peak efficiency. When one of these nutrients is absent or in short supply, the ability to handle stress is reduced. By knowing about and paying attention to our body's chemistry, we can manage our consumption of food and drinks in the way most conducive to good health and increased stress tolerance in resisting stress-related illness.

J. G. Stratton (1986) cites some things that departments can do to assist the officer in preventing and/or handling burnout. Among these suggestions are: (1) departments should encourage officers to continue their learning. Personal growth is a major defense against burnout; (2) administrators need to provide avenues of communication from the bottom to the top. Officers often feel that there is no way for their ideas to be heard by top management. Captains and above should spend some time with the troops to get an idea of what's going on in the streets and with the officers; and (3) departments should choose their field training officers (FTOs) with care because it is from these FTOs that recruits will build their own image of what police work is and what they should be as officers. FTOs should appreciate the skills and knowledge these new officers bring to the department. We also suggest that officers be allowed a stress day – a day not deducted from ordinary leave time or sick leave, but just an extra day now and then for officers to use when they feel they just can't buckle on that leather and go out and face the world one more time.

Rapid Burnout

According to J. T. Mitchell (1989), rapid burnout occurs "when people are exposed to overwhelming stress for even relatively short periods of time. It occurs when the emergency service worker has used up most or all of his energy and still is not able to cope adequately with the situation." Individuals, in effect, are totally exhausted and unable to continue to operate effectively at the scene (although they may continue to deny this emphatically). Their continued presence may actually present a source of danger to themselves, fellow workers, and people they are trying to help.

Supervisors should be aware of the symptoms of rapid-onset burnout and be ready to remove personnel if these symptoms occur: (1) psychological: high anxiety, increased irritability, depression, lack of emotional control, hyperexcitability, apathy, feelings of isolation; (2) physical: severe fatigue, tremors, headaches, gastrointestinal upset, excessive sweating, chills, symptoms of shock; or (3) thought: poor concentration, indecisiveness, confusion, slow thinking, loss of objectivity, forgetfulness, inability to express thoughts clearly. If these symptoms appear, the supervisor should ask workers to take a break (or order one if necessary), point out to them that fatigue is lessening their ability to function effectively, promise they can return to the scene if they take a rest and improve, provide physical comforts (food, drinks, lavatory facilities), provide a place to rest away from the carnage, provide blankets, dry clothes, and so on. In addition, the supervisor could allow workers to ventilate emotions, allow them some quiet time alone, and remove them completely from the scene if their symptoms seem excessive. Workers should also be told that if they push themselves too far, they also could become casualties, thus adding more victims to the already overburdened evacuation chain.

Special Assignments

It is a common belief among police officers that certain assignments, such as narcotics, homicide, internal affairs, and airborne, present their own special stresses. The following is a brief discussion of some of the special stresses that officers in those assignments encounter. Increased knowledge of these special stresses can be preventive.

Narcotics

Undercover narcotics work is one of the most dangerous and stressful jobs in police work. "Narcs" must create and play a role that is not only dangerous but also puts them in daily intimate contact with the dregs of humanity. As one narc remarked, "We associate with the scumbags — humanity at its worse." Because of the nature of their work, narcs may become paranoid and have feelings of guilt because of the deception they must practice. They learn to manipulate their way in and out of different situations — a trait useful in a narcotics assignment, but one that can present problems if carried over into other assignments. They may feel alienated from other police officers, not only because their true identities are unknown to other officers, but also because other police officers do not understand how big the problems are that narcs face every day.

Narcs believe that, except for themselves and a few colleagues, no one else realizes that the pushers and criminal elements associated with drugs could take over society. As a result, they become vulnerable to the "savior complex," in which they see themselves standing alone against the forces of evil. They begin to resent directives from police administrators and the supervision of their own bosses, feeling that they prevent narcs from achieving their goals. Because of the critical importance of the problems they are dealing with, they may become convinced that the ends justify the means. They may become sarcastic, cynical, chronically angry and hostile, and even scared. They may be intensely frustrated when they see weeks or even months of dangerous undercover work finally culminate in an arrest that comes to naught when the arrestees plea bargain their way out of prison. The hours may create a special stress on their marriage or on their relationship with a boy- or girlfriend. Neighbors, not knowing the nature of narcs' assignments, may wonder about the spouses who receive these scummy-looking characters at all hours of the day and night. Finally, narcs may have much less freedom and opportunity to talk about their work than other colleagues, further increasing their stress.

Michel Girodo, professor of psychology at the University of Ottawa and consulting psychologist to a number of law enforcement agencies, conducted extensive research relating to undercover police operations. Girodo (1985) reminds us that the primary focus of many law enforcement activities is not interrupting the transaction between the dealer and the user but is mainly directed at "foreign cultivation, importation, manufacture, theft, and high level wholesalers" as the targeted links in the drug trade. This emphasis necessitated the development of new, "sophisticated investigative techniques for gathering evidence against money launderers, drug-profit diversion schemes, as well as for following the flow of moneys and assets that form the trafficker's resource base" (p. 299).

Undercover operations can last a day or two, most frequently weeks or months; some may go on for years. The most challenging covert operations (and therefore, perhaps, the most stressful), according to Girodo, are those that (1) extend over a long term, (2) require agents to move to a new geographical area, (3) require that agents immerse themselves in an organized criminal subculture (street or high level), and (4) necessitate a wholesale transformation in role and personal identity.

Psychological Risks

The most immediate and potentially fatal danger is, of course, that agents' covers are blown and their true identities discovered. But there is also the psychological injury to their egos because of the shame, embarrassment, and feelings of failure that follow such an unmasking. When threats are made against agents, relocation and additional security compound the stress of reentry into their old role. Girodo (1984b) points out that mental disturbances arising from the stress of undercover work create problems not only for agents and their department, but also have important legal implications. First, what is the department's responsibility in connection with the question of "adequate training"? This becomes important should psychological and/or physical injuries arise out of an assignment and the agent claims disability compensation and/or retirement because of job-related stress. Second, there are important legal implications about the possible connection between an agent's mental disturbance and his or her ability to gather credible and valid evidence using undercover investigative techniques.

Girodo (1984c) carried out an extensive investigation designed to assess the extent and type of psychological disturbances attributable to undercover work. Most of the research was carried out on federal narcotic officers. They found no incidence of psychotic disorders in the subject agents. They also determined that there were no cases of multiple personality (a popular misconception associated with the role-playing nature of the work). The vast majority of psychological disturbances fell into the categories of personality disorders and neurotic/situational adjustment reactions.

Personality Disturbances

Behavioral and personality changes arising from undercover work can be classified into five areas (Girodo, 1984c):

1. **Role generalization.** This refers to the tendency to use the language and social style of the infiltrated subgroup. It can extend into minor changes in attitude and deportment, somewhat like behavioral differences seen in a young man before he goes to boot camp and when he returns home immediately thereafter.
2. **Medalist syndrome.** This is more typical of agents in high-level operations.

The agent develops "an inflated ego, an exaggerated feeling of importance, and an idyllic but spurious sense of entitlement which is communicated throughout the department" (Girodo, 1984c, pp. 60–61).

3. **Primate syndrome.** This is a more serious type of character distortion usually associated with infiltration of motorcycle gangs, street subcultures, and other lower-level fringe groups. Agents may become direct participants in violence and sordid conduct. When they return to regular police duties, they may display long hair, crude language, and poor impulse control. Agents who were more controlled and reserved before the undercover assignment may not show these outward signs of disturbance but may take it out on their families, with increased aggression and temper outbursts.

4. **Rhetorical drama.** This describes more of a process than a psychological state. The undercover role persists or suddenly reemerges. It always occurs in public and has a theatrical quality. This seems to be designed to attract attention and garner recognition from peers and supervisors of their undercover work. "Social dramas that are enacted are rhetorical statements designed to validate the special status skilled undercover agents expect" (Girodo, 1984b, p. 61).

5. **Acute paranoid disorder.** Because of hostile and alien social contexts, lack of information, peer group isolation, uncertainty, threats, and mutual suspicion, a supervigilant attitude and generalized anxiety can develop. Two kinds of operational evidence-gathering consequences have been seen. Agents are so overcome by real or imagined fears that they back away from the target and fail to make contact with anyone in the target group except for one or two nobodies on the periphery. Their ventures are deliberately low risk and reactive rather than proactive. Also, paranoid fear can lead to agents becoming overly assertive, initiating, or aggressive in their approach. They charge into the target group in such an aggressive way that they either get them angry or get "burned" on the spot, or they like the agents' style and want them to assume a leadership position and initiate criminal activity. Agents whose fear and anxiety make them overly aggressive are inviting falsification and possible perjury after the undercover assignment is completed (Girodo, 1984b, p. 61).

Neurotic Adjustment Reactions

Normal depression, with its characteristic lack of drive, motivation, and interest in regular police duties, is a common reaction in agents coming off an undercover assignment. This is an emotional rebound from the intense dedication and emotional investment agents have made in their former assignment. Sometimes one sees a clinical depression that is more serious and merits treatment. There are two possible causes of this clinical depression: the agents have an underlying predisposition that makes them more susceptible to stress experienced in the undercover job, or conflicts with other team agents and supervisory personnel.

In certain operations loneliness combines with fear of failure or physical harm to arouse strong dependency needs. When agents perceive an unsupportive supervisor or unappreciative fellow agent, anger and hostile feelings can lead to depression, especially if there is no healthy way for this hidden anger and hostility to be expressed. When combined with aggressive impulses, these hidden feelings can lead to anxiety and depression (Girodo, 1985).

The use of undercover agents requires a careful balancing of law enforcement objectives and the agents' emotional health. Not every officer is suited to this work. Those who are selected should receive training not only in undercover techniques, but also in recognizing conventional and unique signs of psychological stress.

> In the past five years sufficient psychometric, behavioral, and clinical data have been collected to allow for the development of a three-tiered comprehensive approach to the question of selection/screening, training, and the primary, secondary, and tertiary prevention of psychological distress in undercover agents (Girodo, 1983, 1984c). This model recognizes that as long as the undercover technique remains in use, one can apply psychological knowledge to: (1) reduce the incidence of health disturbances; (2) identify early warning signs of stress and intervene before they develop into more severe symptomatology; and (3) where the first two are unsuccessful, provide special assistance to those who have not gone through their undercover experience emotionally unscathed. (Girodo, 1985, p. 308)

G. M. Farkas (1986) reports the results of a recently declassified study by the FBI of seventy-six agents with extensive undercover experience. Results suggest that the major sources of stress in deep undercover work were supervisor/subordinate relationships, role requirements of undercover officers, and strain on marital and social relations. Major symptoms were paranoia, change in attitudes toward certain laws, sympathy for the criminal target, and "corrosion" of the agent's value system (p. 433). Farkas also reports the results of two experiments undertaken by the Honolulu Police Department to ascertain the nature and degree of distress relative to deep undercover work. Study results show clearly that a variety of psychological symptomatology is associated with such assignments. Symptoms most commonly reported were anxiety, loneliness/isolation, oversuspiciousness, and relationship and marital problems. Thirty-two percent of the sample (82 officers) said their psychological problems were of sufficient magnitude that contact with a department psychologist would have been desirable (G. M. Farkas, 1986).

J. C. Cheek and T. Lesce (1988) caution that undercover officers must assume responsibility for monitoring their own degree of stress so as not to exceed their tolerance threshold, thus posing a danger to themselves and their fellow agents.

Homicide Detail

Dr. Parke Fitzhugh, a psychiatrist for the Dade County, Florida, Police Department, states that "homicide detectives on the average are one of the last groups to seek professional help . . . they're under a great deal of stress, but generally, they've only gotten to me when they've been referred and they're at a crisis." Another homicide detective has said about his work, "I'll get a case today that looks really hot, but the next day, I'll have another one I'll have to chase, the next day, there's another. The detective gets frustrated and demoralized – he has leads on his own cases that he's not able to follow" (*Tucson Citizen* May, 1981).

Compounding the strain is the public's demand that violent crimes be solved, particularly if the homicide involves a child or a sexual attack. Homicide detectives see all the blood and gore that other police officers do not have to deal with at close range or over a long period of time. Often homicide detectives have to notify the victim's loved ones of the death. A further unique strain upon homicide detectives is that they must investigate shootings in which other police officers have been involved.

Sexual Assault Detail

Reese and Goldstein (1986) claims that "rape investigators can, and often do, become vicarious victims – stressed, altered, and in some cases destroyed by the crimes they investigate. . . . Rape investigators routinely see the worse manifestations of human behavior. They deal with molested children, sexual assault of the elderly and defenseless, senseless beatings and murder, rape, and mutilated bodies." These experiences can lead to marked feelings of depression, despair, and discouragement, especially when they see the same crimes, the same brutality over and over again. It is here that the defense mechanism of isolation of affect occurs as a protection against the horror and revulsion of such scenes. A hardening process occurs that enables officers to deal with all the misery and brutality. This isolation of affect can carry over to family life, creating more problems and stress.

Another stress comes from officers' constant interaction with victims of rape and assault. Reese notes that investigators must deal with the shocked relatives and friends and, if the victim is still alive, with a woman probably at the most traumatic time in her life. Eventually officers must deal with their own emotions and be cognizant of how they can negatively carry over to their own family. Burnout in sex crimes assignments is frequent, especially in units specializing in sexual assaults against children.

Internal Affairs

Many picture internal affairs officers as headhunters who get pleasure out of proving that a fellow officer has committed a criminal act or violated departmental regulations. While this may actually be true of some, the authors' experiences indicate that the average internal affairs investigator is more desirous of proving an accused officer's innocence. In small departments where all officers know those assigned to internal affairs, the personal element can be an added stress because there is less social distance. In larger departments, most officers do not know the internal affairs personnel as individuals. Nevertheless, the stress level for internal affairs investigators is still high, and many ask to be relieved after a year or two on the job.

Airborne Law Enforcement

In the past few years, an increasing number of police departments have added helicopter units.

With the advent of this relatively new addition to the armamentarium of law enforcement agencies has come a variety of issues with which police administrators must deal. These include the selection of appropriate personnel as helicopter pilots and observers, training of personnel for performing area law enforcement functions, and identification of sources of psychological stress encountered by police personnel stemming from the airborne law enforcement function. (Sultan et al., 1980, p. 311)

An opinion survey designed to identify problem areas and sources of psychological stress in airborne law enforcement indicated that these activities present stresses unique from those encountered by field officers on tional activity of flying in an air support division was a significant stressor because of the danger involved. Another unique stressor was the relative inaccessibility to supervision while in the air. On the ground, officers in a critical situation can request and receive speedy assistance from a supervisor. Airborne officers, who have only radio contact with supervisors on the ground, must rely on their own judgment. Finally, the potential for serious injury – even death – resulting from a helicopter crash adds another stress for airborne personnel.

Patrol

Although patrol is not usually considered a special assignment, stress researchers have identified fatigue as one of the major magnifiers of stress in police work. Since patrol officers in the field are susceptible to fatigue, especially during the late-evening and early-morning watches, patrol work can create stress. Fatigue is a state of weariness resulting from prolonged or intense physical, emotional, or mental effort. It tends to increase directly with the amount of time a person functions at a given task and can vary in severity from simple drowsiness to a numbing lack of awareness brought on by a particularly long or stressful tour of duty. Villa (1981) states that administratively controlled variables such as overtime, shift rotation, and off-duty court or educational commitments can cause significant, dangerous levels of fatigue, even in young field officers.

> For many field officers, especially those who are professionally motivated, a typical work week might include the following work-related activities after normal working hours: six hours of school and two hours of study, ten hours of court appearances and eight hours of overtime due to unusual occurrences and personnel shortages. This typical 66-hour work week might easily be extended to 90 or more hours in the case of highly motivated officers working in high crime areas. (p. 312)

Fatigue tends to increase anxiety and fearfulness, thus lowering the person's ability to deal appropriately with the many complex situations common to field experience. Fatigue also tends to lower the quality of the officer's decision making and increases the probability of a less adaptable decision than usual. Fatigue may be a critical factor tipping the balance in a "shoot/don't shoot" situation by decreasing the officer's ability to analyze the situation appropriately. Further, the same late-night and early-morning hours when officers are more likely to be fatigued are also the times when they are more likely to use force or be the victims of violence. Police administrators must control variables contributing to officer fatigue so this self-generating cycle, where "overtime contributes to fatigue; fatigue increases the likelihood of injuries and illnesses; injuries and illnesses create a need for overtime assignments" may be interrupted (Villa, 1981, p. 313).

Police Marriages

J. G. Stratton (1984) notes that being a police officer is not easy, but being married to one is not easy either. Stressors impinging upon police marriages are many – physical danger, shift work, dealing with people in trauma – and can exert an adverse effect on the most stable of police marriages.

Do cops actually have a higher rate of divorce than other professions and the general population? The popular view within law enforcement circles is that they do. But M. B. Saper (1980) states, "It would be a mistake to conclude that police officers have more frequent or more severe marriage problems than persons in other professions" (pp. 28–29). M. Reiser (1982) remarks that rumors and misinformation about police divorce rates have been passed on from one generation of cops to another. His surveys in the Los Angeles Police Department in 1971 and 1977 revealed that the divorce rates for sworn personnel were "comparatively low" (p. 160). The cops' divorce rate of 27.57 percent was considerably lower than the divorce rate for California (51.9%) and slightly lower than the national average (31%).

In the past decade, much has been written about police marriages and the police family (Madamba, 1986; Reese, 1987; Reiser, 1982; Stillman, 1986; Stratton, 1984). There has been growing awareness that, as in the military, the family, not the individual officer, must be the focus of concern. If officers' spouses are happy with their mate's choice of police work as a career, this will go a long way toward ensuring twenty to thirty years of service. If spouses are not happy with their mate's choice, eventually officers may have to choose between a police career and marriage. One will have to go. As Stratton (1984) remarks:

> Police wives are remarkable women. What appears as terrible stumbling blocks to a relationship, they seem to handle as a matter of course. People mention the "woman behind the badge" and the "supportive" role of the wife. This presents a distorted picture. Police wives stand at least equally with their husbands in keeping their relationships growing, their households happy, and their children healthy. Frequently the importance and difficulty of this role goes unrecognized by law enforcement administrators. (p. 314)

However, this does not imply that police wives are not frequently upset by their officer husbands. Here is what some police wives the authors have talked to have to say:

> "My husband spends all his time at the job. He seems to have no time for the children and me."

> "The only friends we have are his friends and these are other policemen. I have lost all my friends because with his hours, we don't have any opportunity to do things with anybody except other cops. Not only that, but he doesn't seem to be very happy going out with anybody except a cop."

> "My husband treats his kids like they were some punks on the street. They feel that they can't talk to him because he will not listen. He just tells them to do something because that's the way it is."

> "Isn't it true that a cop's most important person is his partner? Well, what if his partner is a female cop? Isn't there a danger that I'll never be able to compete with her? How can they help but form a strong emotional attachment to each other?"

Speaking at a seminar to the wives of other officers, one wife said:

> A subject we all can relate to, is that sometime feeling that the job is first, and all else second. To some guys, this job is a mistress, or a terrific hobby which they can do and enjoy almost everyday. How can you help but NOT become resentful? Here we are up to our necks in housework, babies, diapers, and everyday crisis while they drive away to meeting people from all walks of life. They get to talk with (are you ready for this) REAL ADULTS! What we wouldn't give some days to talk with someone over ten years old. They get to eat dinner out, while you're home dodging mashed potato fights and spilled milk. "They only get to grab a hamburger here and there," you say. Well, I'd settle for a bun with shoe leather, as long as it comes with a large order of PEACE and QUIET. (Colson, 1979)

What is it about police work that seems to spawn these types of complaints from police wives? Reiser (1982) states that men in police work are part of a fraternity that has strong, cohesive, in-group values and pressures to con form. Because of the stresses involved in police work and the mutual interdependencies required to survive, there is a premium placed on manliness and physical adequacy. Additionally, this largely male fraternity places a high value on one's ability to hold liquor, to seduce women, and to be unbeatable in a fight. Extramarital sexual affairs are not only condoned but expected because of this macho image. Barbara Bennett, in an insightful article entitled "The Police Mystique" (1978), compiled a lengthy list of all the unwritten "shoulds" that police feel they must live up to. This list contains five general attributes that work together to form the police mystique and perpetuate its unwritten code.

1. **It's us versus them.** Cops are different — at home, on the street, after work. Cops aren't especially liked, and they are misunderstood by their wives and by the public. Cops feel most at home with other cops.
2. **Silence is security.** Keep your mouth shut: Accept things as they are; don't get too involved, and don't take risks. According to Bennett, this results in an unwritten commitment to noncommitment.
3. **Keep your cool.** The facade of "don't let it show" is important, demanding behavior that is superhuman and unrealistic. We know that all people have emotions and need them, even cops. Like others, an officer's fight-or-flight response is triggered in stressful situations. Unlike others, officers usually cannot run or flee, and as a result are not able to release tensions. When seen in a counseling office for marital problems, police officers often present the image of the tough guy whom nothing can affect. Beneath that rugged exterior is often a very caring person who feels

deeply but does not know or cannot remember how to let his wife know that. In this stage of the relationship, the wife often stops seeing the concerned, caring man hidden inside. She no longer knows how to penetrate the shell. Eventually she may no longer care to. In this kind of marriage the police officer is likely to go home and find that his wife has packed up and left without any warning.

4. **Stay on top.** This cluster of attitudes and stereotyped behavior defines policing as a macho profession. The profile of a cop turns out to be a "Marlboro man" – rough and rugged, traveling free with a cigarette in one hand and a rifle in the other.

5. **Sex is survival.** This idea is closely related to the macho expectations that pressure most officers. It also includes archaic sexual ideas – the belief in two kinds of women (those that do and those that don't) and two kinds of sexual codes (one for husbands, one for wives). These sexual dichotomies only perpetuate game playing and one-sided sex. When human sensitivity is stifled, both sexes lose.

These elements are part of the unwritten code of behavior of police officers. They subtly pervade the police environment and exert influence on the marriages of these officers, often playing a role in the marital problems besetting police couples. Other pressures on police marriages derive from some of the stresses mentioned in the previous chapter. For example, a police officer's unusual hours may make it impossible for him or her to attend a daughter's graduation, a son's special Little League game, or a spouse's birthday party. Or a factor like the easy availability of credit can cause financial strain if the couple does not know how to handle money correctly.

Because of the rigid structure of the police organization, officers may carry feelings of

frustration and anger home from the job and displace them onto their spouse and children. Other problems may arise because they are unable to cope with family problems after seeing nothing but problems at work all day. All they desire is peace, quiet, and a little tender loving care. At the same time, this is a family, and officers have a responsibility to become involved in the daily problems of family life. If communication is not open between officers and spouses, each may feel resentment toward the other. The officer sees the spouse as nagging, and the spouse sees the officer as uncaring.

Drinking may become a problem. Not only is alcohol a stress reduction device, but it also elicits peer approval because it suits the macho image. But do police officers drink harder and more often than civilians? Edward Donovan, the officer who began the Boston Police Department's stress reduction program, gives an emphatic "yes" to that question. He was a cop at twenty-six and a drunk at twenty-nine; he left his wife and seven kids; he contemplated suicide. He straightened out and twelve years ago began the Boston Police Stress Program to help other cops with similar problems (Kankewitt, 1986). Every cop – as well as anyone who aspires to be a police officer – should read Donovan story, *The Shattered Badge.*

A study by V. E. Pendergrass and N. M. Ostrove (1986) provides firmer evidence that police officers may indeed consume more alcohol than the general population. Male officers consumed more than female officers, but the latter seem to be moving toward heavier drinking. One interesting finding was that consumption did not decrease with age or rank, so whatever conditions support heavy drinking continues throughout the police career.

Due in large measure to Donovan's pioneering work, some police departments are now beginning to recognize this problem (Stratton & Wroe, 1980). Programs exist in some larger agencies for alcoholic police officers. These have usually been started by recovering alcoholic officers who managed to convince an administrator of the program's value. In all cases we are aware of, treatment is based on the principles of Alcoholics Anonymous (AA). Recovering alcoholic police form a special chapter of AA that is designed to appeal to police officers in the community, active and retired.

As with other alcoholics, alcoholism is only part of the officers' problems. However, unless officers first complete an alcohol recovery program, trying to help them with marital, family, financial, and other problems is doomed to failure. Since there is almost no chance that alcoholics will quit drinking or enter such a program until virtually cornered into it, on several occasions we have advised commanders to order the officers to a hospital detoxification center for treatment. While everyone, including alcoholic officers, knows this order can be refused, it cannot be done without some jeopardy to their jobs. So far we have had no refusals or even questioning of an order, probably because alcoholic police officers at that point are, as one said, "sick and tired of being sick and tired."

In 1974, Dr. Bruce Danto, psychiatrist for the Detroit Police Department, focused attention on a little recognized and understood problem of police marriages: the police widow. What happens to the widow and children of police officers who are killed in the line of duty or who die in accidents or from stress-related illnesses? According to Danto, police wives are familiar with death expectations, since they know about the danger inherent in police work. They have seen their husbands with various work-related injuries and, with wives of other officers, have shared the experiences of loneliness, doubt, and fear. Nevertheless, even though she recognizes the possibility of death, the widow of a slain police officer is still the victim of an event whose probability she has denied. While rationalizing that this is the lot of a policeman's wife and family, she still displays all the clinical features of bereavement that are shared by any widow in any situation.

Widows' feelings of abandonment should be of significant concern to a police department. Many departments offer little meaningful contact with survivors. The widows in Danto's study complained that there were few warm feelings from police officials, who they felt should check regularly with them on an ongoing basis to show that the police department cared. Widows felt that they had belonged to a police family, only to learn that they were without a family once their officer husband died. There were also bitter feelings expressed toward the community, which they felt was unappreciative of the policeman's real job, expecting him to lay his life on the line for little reward and even less recognition. Danto's study suggests that police departments should pay more attention not only to the widows of slain officers, but also possibly to the widows of officers who die after retirement. Since departments are making efforts to encourage the feeling of the "police family" and "we take care of our own," measures to carry out this policy should extend to widows. The Fraternal Order of Police (FOP) and other similar organizations should look to this area to create needed and innovative programs.

Not much, if any, progress has been made in this area. F. Stillman (1986) writes:

> When killed in the line of duty, our "silent" victim leaves behind a family that has been inordinately assimilated into the police profession. Yet rather than being embraced by the police community, these police survivors become grim reminders of the ultimate police obligation. Police funerals and presentations of awards and metals often heal the organizational wounds but not the personal grief of survivors. Police survivors often report feeling like outcasts from this "work family." (p. 144)

In the spring of 1984, the first national seminar was held for law enforcement survivors. Approximately 40 families attended, some from as far away as Guam and Hawaii. Survivors expressed anger, bitterness, despair, and, especially, frustration. They felt wronged not only by police departments, but also by the whole criminal justice system and society in general. War stories included such incidents as the widow being informed by the media about her husband's death; a community's sympathies being with the murderer of her husband (an officer who was killed by a saber-wielding maniac); or an officer who died at his desk of a heart attack but whose death was ruled as accidental and treated unceremoniously.

Stillman observes that other victims (rape, murder, survivors, abducted children, drug addicts, even animals) have support groups that work to secure their rights and provide support in traumatic times. Too many times the police family is left to endure tragedies all by itself, with no one helping to heal the wounds. Stillman suggests that police psychological units get involved with such families, not only to give direct support to the family, but also to make police administrators and other mental health professionals aware of their needs.

Domestic Violence

For years, law enforcement agencies denied the presence of any appreciable alcohol/drinking problems among law enforcement personnel, yet experts in this field know that 10 percent of any given population (including police officers) will show signs of moderate to severe alcoholism. Accumulating evidence of alcoholism among police personnel forced law enforcement administrators to acknowledge the problem. Programs were undertaken to address this issue and give officers the help they needed to overcome dependence before it developed into a situation that threatened the career of the officer, the welfare of his family, and the community he served.

Approximately eight years ago, the United States Marine Corps (USMC) discovered, through surveys ordered by a concerned command, that there was a problem of domestic violence within the corps. Domestic violence was interfering with the mission of the corps and was responsible for the loss of

many excellent top-functioning noncommissioned officers. The corps approached Dr. Peter Neidig and asked him, in effect, to tell command how widespread the problem was, who it involved, and how the violence could be stopped. Neidig discovered that domestic violence is a much more common problem among marine families than ever supposed; military personnel involved in domestic violence were usually top-performing personnel, not the "dirtbags" as many had suspected; and domestic violence was preventable – it could be stopped. Like everything else, the earlier it was detected, the easier and more successful the task. Neidig came up with a short, practical program: two hours per week for twelve weeks. The goal of the program was simply to stop the violence. If additional treatment/counseling programs were desired, referrals could be made to appropriate resources. However, the aim of his program was to simply stop the violence. The program has been in operation in the USMC and in the other service branches for several years and has proven successful in reducing violence in domestic conflicts.

We are convinced, through extensive experience with law enforcement personnel, that domestic violence is also a problem in a considerable number of police families. This conclusion is strengthened by the reaction of police officers who have been involved with Neidig's program. These officers have voiced enthusiasm for the possibility of making this domestic violence containment program available to police families. A domestic violence survey conducted with 438 officers and 118 spouses (not necessarily those of the 438 officers) was undertaken to assess the need for such a program for law enforcement families. A preliminary analysis of the data from officers reveals that 10 percent admitted to overt acts of physical violence in their marriage (such as throwing, smashing, hitting, or kicking something; pushing, grabbing, or shoving the marriage partner; and so on). Twenty-two percent admitted to more "serious" physical violence (such as beatings, using a knife or gun on the marriage partner; suffering injuries that necessitated medical attention; or injuries that resulted in having to take time off from work). In the case of the spouse, 23 percent admitted to overt physical violence and 20 percent identified "serious" physical violence in the marriage. Thus 43 percent (nearly half) of the spouses have experienced some form of physical violence in the marriage. We

expect that the results of this survey (Russell et al., 1988) will enable us to approach police administrators and trainers and impress upon them the fact that there is a serious and widespread problem of domestic violence within police families. Unless addressed and stopped, there will continue to be headlines like the following one from a recent issue of the *Arizona Daily Star:*

OFF-DUTY OFFICER IN FAMILY DISPUTE IS KILLED BY POLICE

Duncanville, Texas (AP) – An off-duty Dallas police sergeant was shot to death by police in this suburb yesterday as he brandished a gun and tried to enter his home after an argument with his wife, authorities said.

Retirement

One of the most stressful stages in police officers' careers is retirement. When they joined the force, the promise of voluntary retirement with a pension immediately payable was seen as a major benefit. If young recruits (and later young police officers) thought about retirement at all, it was to assign it to sometime in the hazy future. If asked what they were going to do when that magic day arrived, they most likely would say, "I'm just going to kick back and enjoy myself." Reality is quite different. When that magic day approaches and they can "pull the pin," many are ambivalent – even those who have been successful. Stratton (1984) states that for many, "it means a lowered standard of living. The Bureau of Labor has estimated that a retiree needs between 70-80 percent of his working income to maintain the same standard of living after retirement. For some, it is the end of their central purpose in life, a loss of power and prestige. For those who have been failures, it destroys any lingering hope or fantasy of a late blooming success" (p. 332).

We also would add that retirement may bring a loss of personal identity. In many

ways, our job determines not only what we do but who we are; what our values are; our likes and dislikes; our circle of friends. Police work defines officers' roles. Suddenly, with retirement, the police officer role is gone. Since the children have probably left by now, officers' role as parent is gone as well. Whatever the badge and gun meant to them as tokens of power and status is also gone. If they are forced into retirement, either by age or their own feeling that they should get out while they are still young enough to do something else, they go from an active, clearly identified existence in a very familiar world to a state of identity diffusion in a very unfamiliar world. In no other occupation except the military is there such an abrupt cutoff in the sense of belonging and usefulness. There is an old expression in law enforcement: "The door hits you in the ass when you leave." Some police retirees become so despondent that they consider or actually commit suicide.

The answer to this retirement problem is, of course, advance planning. Stratton (1984) recommends that officers start thinking about retirement five years before their eligibility date. We believe that officers should start thinking about retirement the day they leave the police academy's recruit class. Planning for retirement at such an early date is probably impossible, but thinking about what one wants to do when one retires is never begun too early. Too many times police officers, who state that the main reason they are retiring is that they've had it up to here with their job, end up taking a similar job with the medical examiner's office, the county attorney's investigative division, and so on. In most cases they do this because no other jobs are available to them that offer comparable pay.

Some departments, especially those with in-house psychologists, already are addressing this problem and setting up programs to assist officers in making the transition between active duty and civilian life. In those areas where there are local colleges and universities, a department's efforts can be assisted by vocational guidance personnel and facilities normally found in the university setting. But it is the individual police officer and spouse who must take primary responsibility for changing the stress of retirement into the opportunities of retirement.

Disability Retirement

Workers' compensation laws were passed to ensure that employees (and dependents) would have a means of support if they are laid off work because of job-related injuries. Such benefits are designed as a temporary, fill-in measure with the expectation that employees will return to work. If employees are police officers and feel that they can no longer perform their duties, they may apply to the police pension board for a disability retirement. The board may recommend a disability retirement to the city (county/state) Civil Service Commission, which has the final say.

Physical injuries and conditions are usually quite easy to rule on because of the medical evidence introduced. However, emotional trauma is often quite difficult to measure. Officers may be seen as malingerers who are trying to con the system into granting undeserved benefits. Since a single officer's retirement benefits can cost the pension system between one and two million dollars, it is easy to understand the need to award disability pensions only to those who truly deserve them.

Stratton (1986) observes that

> In recent years, stress has replaced the "bad back" as the piranha of the compensation industry, voraciously chewing up large chunks of benefit funds. Because of the great emphasis placed on police officer stress in the last decade, and because police work is so obviously emotionally stressful, disability claims based on stress-related conditions have sky-rocketed in the 1980s. The problem is compounded by the lack of familiarity with police work that characterizes psychologists and psychiatrists who are not in the police field. (p. 527)

A police officer who is claiming job stress as a basis for disability retirement walks into a doctor's office for an evaluation. The doctor asks, "What do you do for a living?" The claimant replies, "I'm a police officer" and the doctor says, "Gee, you must be under a hell of a lot of stress, aren't you?" The claimant emerges with the doctor's findings that he is no longer able to perform the duties of a police officer (which the doctor really knows nothing about – except what the claimant told him) and recommends the granting of a disability pension. Stratton (1986) notes that in California, the provisions of the Labor Code governing the awarding of disability pensions so liberally favor the claimant that practically all cases are granted pensions. Approximately 50 percent of California law enforcement officers retire on disability.

SUMMARY

In this chapter, the author discussed situations and conditions of police work that are associated with special stress, including the use of deadly force, post-shooting trauma and other critical incidents, burnout, special assignments, police marriages, and retirement. Experienced officers can certainly think of other special stresses the author may not have covered. While there is ample evidence to indicate how and why police officers encounter significant stress on and off the job, the author also believes that police officers do a disservice to themselves and their profession by being more negative about these stresses than is called for.

For example, regardless of whether police divorce rates are high, if officers and their spouses believe that this is true, when marital problems occur, couples may simply bow to the inevitable and seek the divorce they expected to experience in the first place instead of putting effort into solving these problems or seeking professional help. As anyone who has been married for longer than a few weeks knows, marriage is something that you need to work at. A successful marriage is the result of mature people compromising, understanding, and communicating with each other. This is true of police marriages as well as other marriages. They can work – they do work – they do last. They do not have to end in divorce.

Let us be realistic but also optimistic. We need to emphasize that police officers are, by selection and training, physically and psychologically healthier than civilians. Most police officers appear to be more satisfied with their jobs than civilians. With positive thinking, the morale of police officers will improve, thus reducing stresses associated with negative thinking.

BIBLIOGRAPHY

Appelbaum, D. May, 1983. Looking down the wrong side of the gun: The problems of the police use of lethal force." *Police Chief,* 55–59.

Baruth, C. L. (1986). Pre-critical incident involvement by psychologists. In *Psychological services for law enforcement,* ed. J. T. Reese & H. A. Goldstein, pp. 305–309. Washington, D.C.: U.S. Government Printing Office.

Bayley, D. H. (1986). The tactical choices of police patrol officers. *Journal of Criminal Justice, 14,* 329–348.

Bibbins, V. E. (1986). The quality of family and married life of police personnel. In *Psychological services for law enforcement,* ed. J. T. Reese & H. A. Goldstein, pp. 421–426. Washington, D.C.: U.S. Government Printing Office.

Blak, R. A. (1986). A department psychologist responds to traumatic incidents. In *Psychological services for law enforcement,* ed. J. T. Reese & H. A. Goldstein, pp. 311–314. Washington, D.C.: U.S. Government Printing Office.

Blau, T. H. (1986). Deadly force: Psychosocial factors and objective evaluation – A preliminary effort. In *Psychological services for law enforcement,* ed. J. T. Reese & H. A. Goldstein, pp. 315–318. Washington, D.C.: U.S. Government Printing Office.

Boelte, E. R. (1989). Marriage survival: A proactive approach to improving the law enforcement marriage. *Police Stress, 9*(1), 13–15.

Brown, M. F. May, 1983. Shooting policies: What patrolmen think. *Police Chief,* 35–37.

Callahan, M. (1983). Entrapment, inducement, and the use of unwitting middlemen. *FBI Law Enforcement Bulletin, 52*(12), 17–24.

Caron, N. A., & Kelly, R. T. January, 1983. The Kansas City Police Department PreRetirement Planning Lecture Series. *Police Chief,* 47–49.

Cavanaugh, J. L., & Rogers, R. (1984). Malingering and deception. *Behavioral Sciences and the Law, 2*(1), 3–118.

Cheek, J. C., & Lesce, T. (1988). *Plainclothes and off-duty officer survival.* Springfield, IL: Charles C Thomas.

Cipriano, R. F. July, 1982. Firearms and law enforcement officers killed: An alternative. *Police Chief,* 46–48.

Cohen, A. (1980). I've killed that man 10,000 times. *Police, 3,* 4.

Daley, R. (1981). *Prince of the city.* New York: Berkeley.

Daviss, B. May, 1982. Burn out. *Police Magazine,* 9–18.

Deadly force to apprehend escaping felons. May, 1983. *Police Chief,* 29–34.

Derogatis, L., Lipman, R., & Covi, L. (1973). An outpatient psychiatric rating scale. *Psychopharmacology Bulletin, 9,* 12–28.

Dolezal, S. 21 November, 1982. Being a good cop: Is it good enough?" *Detroit Free Press.*

Dominelli, J. S. (1980). Quoted in Newsletter of *International Association of Chiefs of Police 6,* 1.

Donovan, E. Summer, 1989. List of names of police officers killed in 1988. *Police Stress.*

Duchesne, L. W., & Vasil, V. L. May, 1983. Responding to use of deadly force: The rollout team. *Police Chief, 50*(5), 34–41.

Ericson, R. B. (1982). *Reproducing order: A study of police patrol work.* Toronto: University of Toronto Press.

Farkas, G. M. (1986). Stress in undercover policing. In *Psychological services for law enforcement,* ed. J. T. Reese & H. A. Goldstein, pp. 433–440. Washington, D.C.: U.S. Government Printing Office.

Freudenberger, H. J. May, 1982. Coping with job burnout. *Law and Order,* 64–66.

Girodo, M. (1983). Undercover operators and law enforcement stress: Getting the pendulum to return. *R.C.M.P Gazette, 45,* 26–28.

Girodo, M. (1984a). Entry and re-entry strain in undercover agents. In *Role transitions,* ed. V. L. Allen & E. van de Vliert, pp. 169–179. New York: Plenum.

_____. (1984b). *Undercover identity: A social self in search of an audience.* Paper presented at the International Interdisciplinary Conference on Self and Identity, University of Cardiff, Wales. July.

_____. (1984c). *Psychological factors in undercover narcotics agents.* Paper presented at the Drug Conference of the International Narcotic Enforcement Officers Association, Albany, New York, October 6–12.

_____. (1985). Health and legal issues in undercover narcotics investigations: Misrepresented evidence. *Behavioral Sciences and the Law, 3*(3), 299–308.

Kankewitt, B. (1986). *The battered badge.* New York: Methuen.

Law OKs murders in California?" May, 1983. *Police Chief,* 42.

Madamba, H. J. (1986). The relationship between stress and marital relationships in police officers. In *Psychological services for law enforcement,* ed. J. T. Reese & H. A. Goldstein , pp. 463–470. Washington, D.C.: U.S. Government Printing Office.

Maslach, C., & Jackson, S. E. May, 1979. Burned-out cops and their families. *Psychology Today,* 59–62.

Mitchell, J. T. (1989). *Surviving critical incident stress.* Seminar held in Tempe, Arizona, August 23–24.

Moorman, C. B., & Wemmer, R. C. May, 1983. Law enforcement officers murdered in California: 1980–81. *Police Chief,* 42–54.

Neidy, P. H., & Friedman, D. H. (1984). *Spouse abuse: A treatment program for couples.* Champaign, IL: Research Press.

Neilsen, E., Eskridge, D. L., & Willoughby, E. L. July, 1982. Police shooting incidents: Implications for training. *Police Chief,* 44.

Pendergrass, V. E., & Ostrove, N. M. (1986). Correlates of alcohol use by police personnel. In *Psychological services for law enforcement,* ed. J. T. Reese & H. A. Goldstein, pp. 489–496. Washington, D.C.: U.S. Government Printing Office.

Petrone, S., & Reiser, M. February, 1985. A home visit program for stressed police officers. *Police Chief,* 36–37.

Reese, J. T., & Goldstein, H. A., eds. (1986). *Psychological services for law enforcement.* Washington, D.C.: U.S. Government Printing Office.

Reiser, M. (1982). *Police psychology: Collected papers.* Los Angeles: LEHI Publishers.

Rosenbluth, E. S. (1986). Police bBurnout – Increasing durability to stress illness through the body's own chemistry. In *Psychological services for law enforcement,* ed. J. T. Reese & H. A. Goldstein, pp. 501–513. Washington, D.C.: U.S. Government Printing Office.

Saper, M. B. February, 1980. Police wives – The hidden resource. *Police Chief,* 28–29.

Sarbin, T. R. (1984). Role transition as social drama. In *Role transitions,* ed. V. L. Allen & E. van de Vliert, pp. 21–37. New York: Plenum.

Somodevilla, S. A. (1986). Post-shooting trauma: Reactive and proactive treatment. In *Psychological services for law enforcement,* ed. J. T. Reese & H. A. Goldstein, pp. 395–398. Washington, D.C.: U.S. Government Printing Office.

Stillman, F. (1986). The invisible victims: Myths and realities. In *Psychological services for law enforcement,* ed. J. T. Reese & H. A. Goldstein, pp. 143–146. Washington, D.C.: U.S. Government Printing Office.

Stratton, J. G. (1984). *Police passages.* Manhattan Beach, CA: Glennon Publishing Co.

_____. (1986). Worker's compensation, disability retirement: The police. In *Psychological services for law enforcement,* ed. J. T. Reese & H. A. Goldstein, pp. 527–531. Washington, D.C.: U.S. Government Printing Office.

Stratton, J. G., & Stratton, B. T. May, 1982. Law enforcement marital relationships: A positive approach. *FBI Law Enforcement Bulletin,* 6–11.

Stratton, J. G., & Wroe, B. October, 1980. Alcoholism programs for police. *Journal of Law and Order*, 18–24.

Van J. Maanen. November, 1980. Beyond account: The personal impact of police shootings. *Annals of the American Academy of Political and Social Science, 452*(12), 245.

Villa, B. J. Spring, 1981. Management control of fatigue among field police officers. *Journal of Police Stress*, 38–41.

Williams, C. (1987). Peacetime combat: Treating and preventing delayed stress reactions in police officers. In *Post-traumatic stress disorders: A handbook for clinicians*, pp. 267–283. Washington, D.C.: Disabled American Veterans.

Zeling, M. (1986). Research needs in the study of post-shooting trauma." In *Psychological services for law enforcement*, ed. J. T. Reese & H. A. Goldstein, pp. 409–410. Washington, D.C.: U.S. Government Printing Office.

Chapter 23

THE BROTHERHOOD OF BIOCHEMISTRY: ITS IMPLICATIONS FOR A POLICE CAREER

As the field of behavioral sciences has grown over the past decades, significant attention has been given to the study of the stressful effects of life as law enforcement officers. The main theme of these studies concerning police stress revolves around two major approaches. The first approach points out the stress reaction and its potential long-term effects. This involves educating police officers about the stress reaction and revolves around Hans Seyle's concept of the general adaptation syndrome (GAS; the physiological processes through which the body attempts to adapt to everchanging challenges). The second major approach in teaching law enforcement officers about stress is to present a list of potential stressors or events that precipitate the stress reaction. This list usually becomes somewhat a litany of the daily negative events that officers are exposed to, such as the inhumanity of man toward his fellow man, the inefficiencies of the criminal justice system, sedentary life-style, poor nutritional habits, and so on. While this information is indeed valuable, it appears to miss the major concept of the stress reaction for law enforcement officers. It points out stress as a negative event to be avoided. But in reality, most officers find that in the beginning years of their career, experiencing this stress reaction in mild dosages makes the career exciting and very attractive. If you asked a large number of law enforcement officers why they chose or

stayed with their career, you would probably hear such answers as "Cop work gets in your blood," "It's exciting and a different thing to do each day," "I couldn't stand just working behind a desk," and so on. However, what attracts law enforcement applicants and young cops to the job in the first half of a police career may be their undoing when the novelty has worn off. When police officers state that "cop work gets in your blood," they may unknowingly be describing a very potent physiological change that all police officers experience when first approaching their job. This physiological change appears to be so entrenched in the police role that it might be impossible to separate this physiological change from the role itself. It has been said that police work creates a brotherhood. Today this brotherhood is not exclusively a male domain, but it is a closed social unit that extends membership only to other cops. Cops may not understand the procedures, equipment, or geographical terrain in which other officers perform their duties, but they certainly understand the physiological sensations involved in the job. For example, a cop from Maine and a cop from California accidentally meet in O'Hare Airport and start sharing experiences and telling "war stories." Each officer might have difficulty visualizing the external events taking place in the narrative told by the other (the setting, temperature, type of community the call took place in, and

277

so on), but he or she would have no difficulty in understanding the "internal environment" of the call: how it felt to work that particular call – the physiology of the call. The brotherhood of police is actually a "brotherhood of biochemistry." Cops understand how other cops feel in similar situations because "they've been there." They've experienced similar physiological sensations, and they've made critical decisions in these physiological states. The physiological sensations cops experience on the street are characteristic of the stress reaction. Without these sensations, police work would not be as attractive to young cops. In fact, they might find it boring and mundane.

Hypervigilance

Consider how the police role is developed in young cops. It begins with the manner in which law enforcement officers are required to view the world. If you take cops in Anytown, U.S.A., and put them behind the wheel of a patrol unit, they are required to view the streets and the community from a different perspective than citizen drivers. Cops realize that "I better pay attention out here! I could get my butt kicked or get somebody else or myself killed if I'm not paying attention!" This reality forces young officers to take a different view of the world from civilians. When viewing the world while in this new work role, officers experience a new physiological sensation – an increase in alertness, an increased sensation of energy and aliveness. This new perceptual style goes beyond just "paying attention." It includes looking, and watching sections of the community that other people would ignore or consider neutral. In the interest of their own safety, officers have to view all encounters as potentially lethal. This newfound perceptual style, with its emphasis on officer safety, carries with it a parallel physiological and psychological state. As mentioned previously, young officers feel increased sensations of energy, aliveness, and alertness. They find themselves becoming quick-witted in the presence of fellow street cops. Friendships

develop quickly, and camaraderie is intensified among people with whom they share potential jeopardy. During the developmental years, young officers experience firsthand the physiological stress reaction, but it is not seen as a negative reaction. On duty, the associated sensation of physiological intensity is viewed as pleasant and enjoyable. They find their job so attractive that it is difficult to leave at the end of a shift. What is unwittingly taking place is that young officers are developing an on-duty style of *hypervigilance.* This style, though necessary for the survival of law enforcement officers, often leads to the long-term destruction of an effective personal life. Officers go on duty, experience increased energy, alertness, quick-wittedness, and camaraderie, and enjoy their tour. However, for every action there is an equal and opposite reaction. Officers who experience an on-duty physiological "high" find that when they get off duty and return home, this hypervigilant reaction stops, as they literally plunge into the opposite reactions of detachment, exhaustion, apathy, and isolation. Thus officers experience the police stress reaction – an emotional ride on a biological roller coaster.

The "biological" roller coaster describes the extreme psychophysiological swings that police officers experience on a daily basis. One can assume that average citizens live on a more even keel, but police officers are denied this stability. Because of the degree of emotional intensity of law enforcement – the increased sensations of alertness required while on duty, followed by reactions of an equal magnitude in the opposite directions while off duty – the police officer's life is characterized by the extremes of highs and lows. This pendulum-like swing occurs daily. Going to work initiates an increased sensation of involvement, energy, and alertness – coming home, a sensation of apathy, detachment and boredom. The biological reason this roller coaster takes place lies in the autonomic nervous system that controls all the body's automatic processes: heart rate, blood pressure, body temperature, and so on. The autonomic nervous system has two branches that act in tandem. The sympathetic branch (Chapter 21) alerts the body to potentially intense situations, causing increased alertness, awareness, and the "fight or flight reaction" (like taking a bunch of "uppers"). The parasympathetic branch controls the body's quiescent or peaceful counterreactions (like taking a bunch of "downers"). This biological roller coaster cycles daily for young officers in the first years of their careers as they polish police skills. It produces high-activity, highly involved police officers, but leaves them with underinvolved, apathetic personal lives. It can be said in no uncertain terms that the first victims of this biological roller coaster are not the officers themselves but their families. The officers alternate between being "heat seekers" at work, where the more intense the call, the more they're drawn to it, and being "couch potatoes" at home. Once the police role is unplugged, there remains only a listless detachment from anything related to a personal life.

The "couch potato" phase of the biological roller coaster can be documented easily by interviewing police spouses during the first decade of the officer's career. Although the faces and names change, the stories remain almost identical.

> "She's different now that she's a cop. We used to do so many things together, but now she gets off duty and I can't even speak to her."

> "He comes home from work, collapses on the couch, turns on the television set – I can talk to him for five minutes and he doesn't even hear me."

> "You know, we drove 150 miles last weekend to go visit my mom and dad. I don't think she said two words to me on the whole trip."

> "We walk through the mall on his days off and he barely grunts to me, but then he

sees two or three of his buddies working off-duty and you can't shut him up: 'Hey, what happened last night? Did you guys arrest that asshole? I heard you come up on the air.'"

As officers begin experiencing the biological roller-coaster ride, they begin heavily investing in the police role. Their family and personal relationships become thin, frazzled, and very fragile. The police wife laments, "I don't know how much longer I can keep this family together. He comes home angry every night: 'Everybody on earth is an asshole.'"

> "I swear she'd rather be at work than at home. She starts getting ready for work two hours before she has to be there. Sometimes I think she's married to the job and not to me."

The police family begins reverberating with this biological roller coaster. Police officers' life-styles change drastically. These elevated sensations while on duty are necessary. Officers do not have the luxury of viewing the world as primarily peaceful and benign.

Officers' very existence depends on their being able to perceive situations from the perceptual set of hypervigilance. They must interpret aspects of their environment as potentially lethal that other members of society see as unimportant. Without hypervigilance, police officers would be seen as "not good cops." However, the tragedy is that while law enforcement officers are trained to react during the upper phase of the biological roller coaster, there has been very little training done or education provided on how to adapt to or avoid the pitfalls of the bottom half of the ride. In the first decade of a police career, the valleys of the roller-coaster ride destroy the emotional support systems and the family support systems – systems that will become increasingly important if officers are to survive the second-half of a police career.

Social Isolation

Unknowingly, law enforcement officers begin cycling around this roller coaster. Work becomes increasingly attractive, relationships and friendships occurring on duty become highly intense, while old relationships that existed prior to becoming a cop are dropped or are maintained only minimally.

For decades, law enforcement officers have deluded themselves concerning this letting loose of old friendships by rationalizations, such as "Only other cops can understand me" and "Everybody else just wants to tell me about that cop who gave him a ticket." However, in reality, young cops often get together and talk about the job and to share "war stories." These gatherings vicariously return officers to the elevated highs of the biological roller coaster. Speaking to the schoolteacher next door or the welder who used to be your friend is "not exciting." Young heat-seeking cops love to tell war stories and hear them from others. Through such dialogues, roller-coaster valleys are avoided, and "cop talk" returns officers to the elevated reaches of energy and alertness, and draws them back into the "brotherhood of biochemistry." The sharing of war stories amounts to little more than "adrenal masturbation."

Young officers become very comfortable only with other police officers, their social isolation from other aspects and relationships in their lives increases, and they become comfortable only within the sphere of this hypervigilant, narrow police role they all share. Here's how social isolation develops. At the start of their careers, young cops believe that the world is divided into "good people" and "bad people." The socialization pattern of the police academy soon has the officers redesigning this dichotomy to "good people" (cops) and "other people." The "other people" soon become "assholes." Young officers begin seeing the world as just cops and "assholes," but soon have a rude awakening when they find that veteran cops sometimes refer to officers from other agencies as "assholes." The

social isolation pattern deepens. Now the world is divided into "cops in their department" and "assholes." Social isolation continues to narrow until it's "uniform cops in my district or precinct on swing shift"; everybody else is an "asshole." After a few years, the average cop concludes, "it's me and my partner" and the "rest of you are assholes." Eventually he says, "I'm not so sure about my partner. Sometimes he can be a real asshole."

The longer people are cops, the more unconsciously reactive they become to situations in which they do not feel completely comfortable. The physiological sensation of being in potential jeopardy is experienced in the abdominal area, triggered by a branch of the tenth cranial nerve: the vagus nerve. When cops experience this physiological sensation while dealing with another person, it's easy to project negative values onto the other person immediately and label him or her an "asshole." If asked, cops would probably say "I just had a gut feeling this guy's an asshole." Thus, a defensive physiological reaction designed to permit officers to survive becomes a socially isolating event that threatens officers' personal emotional survival.

The Lives of Cops

After approximately two years on the job, officers are riding this biological roller coaster daily and consider most of the outside world "assholes." While these two reactions are going on, however, officers are typically doing their job, have high on-site activity, are enjoying police work, and in many ways, although still quite naive to the realities of the long-terms effects of a police career, could be experiencing the "golden years" of their own individual law enforcement career. They enjoy going to work, they are highly energized and enthusiastic, enjoy coworkers, and will state "I love my job." This fragile lifestyle and paranoid way of perceiving the world will typically come crashing down on officers in the not too distant future. Officers find themselves staying away from home for longer and longer periods of time. If the shift ends at midnight, cops realize that once they walk through the doors of their house, the exhaustion, apathy, and bottom half of the roller coaster will hit them hard; unwittingly they spend more time away from home. Younger officers in smaller police departments find themselves going down to the department on their days off just to see what's happening. The economic realities of police management can be quite exploitive of young cops' overinvested, biological enthusiasm. Sometimes the hardest thing about managing young cops is not in getting them to come to work but in getting them to go home. Many small police departments actually could not exist without this overinvestment by young officers and also by nonreimbursed reserve officers whose only payment is a ride on the biological roller coaster. These officers have overlearned the social perceptual style that comes with assuming a police role. The longer they are cops, the more they interact only with other cops, all learning to see the world in only one manner.

Young officers continue to overinvest in their police role. For the first few years, this overinvestment leads to an exciting, enjoyable, dynamic job. Very often, early in their police careers, officers not only isolate themselves from nonpolice friends, but also overindulge in their professional role by listening to scanners while off duty or on days off. One of the potential hazards of this overidentifying and overinvesting in the police role is financial. From the beginning, cops learn the financial realities of a police career: "You're never gonna get rich being a cop." Off-duty work can be an extremely seductive lure for many police families. Officers can provide the necessities and a few extra luxuries of life by working an extra two or three shifts per week, either as security at the local shopping mall or doing point control for construction projects. Although the extra cash certainly helps, the additional time away from home spent in the police role continues the officers' overinvestment and leaves little time for them to develop competencies in other

social roles and to build a personal life for themselves and their family.

This overinvestment in the police role goes beyond justifiable pride in the profession. Officers begin linking their sense of self-worth to the police role in what at first glance appears to be a basically benign sense of pride. However, this creates an intense form of emotional vulnerability for average police officers. When you ask a group of cops who controls their police role, young cops often say, "I do." The older, wiser cops respond, "I wish I did." This link of self-worth to the police role creates a social dynamic that turns many enthusiastic, energized police officers into cynical, recalcitrant employees who resist administrative direction. As external administrative authorities alter their police role and the inevitable decline occurs, their sense of self-worth also takes a tumble. Police officers do not control their police role and must admit, upon reflection, that it is controlled by administrative authorities. Not until after the first several years of police work do the realities of this type of administrative control hit home. Then there is a "rude awakening." This vulnerability is particularly salient to specialized police officers – the narcotics agent, canine officer, or detective in some special assignment.

This psychological phenomena of having your sense of self-worth controlled by other individuals leads to very normal feelings of defensiveness and resistance. This linkage explains why police officers, after the first few years, may grow to resent administrative authority, mainly because they are so vulnerable to the changes that can take place in their police role. This resentment and resistance to administrative control leads to an occupational pseudoparanoia, in which officers begin making such statements as "I can handle the assholes on the street but I can't handle the assholes in the administration." Although the streets contain physical danger, the major psychological and emotional threat comes from those who control their police role, with its emotionally overinvested sense of self-worth.

Emotional Vulnerability

Hypervigilance and the biological roller coaster, combined with the emotional overinvestment in the police role, create emotionally vulnerable individuals. For the first four or five years, officers are overly enthusiastic about the job, eating, sleeping, and breathing police work. But with eight or nine years on the job, they find themselves increasingly resentful, resistant, and hostile toward a police career. However, they have invested so much financially and emotionally in the sense of security a police retirement provides that they can't let go. Former young heat seekers become cynical dinosaurs whose constant lament is: "Just wait until I get my twenty in — then I can get the hell out of here."

Regardless of which theorist is discussing the concept of stress, the crucial elements in defining stress appear to be any given situation where subjects have high demands placed on them and low control over those demands. Police officers, particularly those who do the best job and care the most about their police role, are extremely vulnerable to police stress. The best officers are those most susceptible to the stress of the biological roller coaster. Those officers who practice good officer safety skills and are hypervigilant and observant are the ones most likely to have an elevated sense of involvement on duty. They are also the ones most likely to have the biological roller coaster come crashing down during their off-duty time. They go from "heat seeker" to "couch potato." It's during this off-duty, down time that any significant intervention must take place. However, during this down time, when officers are experiencing apathy and detached exhaustion, they are least likely to implement any change. Life is in neutral. If officers do anything, it will probably be to complain about the job. In breaking the stress cycle, officers must take control over those aspects of their lives that they can control. Average cops do not control their police role. However, they can control, at least to a larger extent, their own personal life.

It is the surrender of their personal life to the biological roller coaster and off-duty depressionlike states that causes the strong vulnerability of the police stress response. Officers find themselves feeling less and less comfortable off duty, even while becoming more and more cynical about the job. The only time they feel alive and involved is at work. So the overinvestment in the police role continues, and they become more and more vulnerable to having this overinvested role taken away from them without a well-developed personal life to cushion the blow. This highly vulnerable emotional state typifies the personal lives of a significant percentage of law enforcement officers. Officers need to recognize the vicious cycle and make appropriate changes in their life-styles.

Controlling One's Life

It is very difficult for average law enforcement officers to make a realistic appraisal of how much of their personal life they really do control. Their immediate rationalization is to say "I'm a cop twenty-four hours a day." But, in reality, with some planning and proactive effort, they are capable of controlling a significant percentage of their time each day. They can develop separate, noncop personal lives. This is usually not done easily because when officers are off duty, the biological roller coaster robs them of spontaneity or enthusiasm. What do average cops want to do when they get off duty? "Nothing. Absolutely nothing!"

Several ineffective methods of breaking this cycle have surfaced, and in all likelihood the average cop has experimented from time to time with all of them. They focus on getting officers out of the off-duty valleys of the biological roller coaster and back to the more elevated states associated with on-duty status. Some officers heavily invest in special response team assignments, where staying on duty for longer periods of time permits them to experience even more than average levels of hypervigilance. The narcotics officer or SWAT officer is an excellent example of the extreme heat seeker. But such actions are an inappropriate way of attempting to regain control. For married police officers, promiscuity and/or other relationships that are initiated while in the police role permit officers to extend inappropriately the sense of aliveness and energy and to avoid the pitfalls of apathy and detachment at the opposite end of the roller coaster. Gambling, substance abuse, "choir practices" – all are escape mechanisms that go far beyond just permitting officers to "unwind." They allow overinvested police officers to avoid facing the realization that home, in contrast to the emotional on-duty high of the biological roller coaster, is a place and time of detachment, isolation, and depression, and is to be avoided at all cost.

Family Impact

As the police socialization process evolves over the years and hypervigilance becomes the normal perceptual set for police officers, the police family does not go unscathed. The family also learns to overidentify with the police role. Pride in being a police family may become of pathological importance in maintaining the police perceptual style as a primary family identifier. The result is that any variable that emanates from the workplace is of increasing importance to the family's well-being and happiness. As the officer and family begin putting more and more of their eggs in the basket marked "police role," a drastic effect looms on the horizon. Because more law enforcement officers are on the receiving end of orders than are on the giving end, police families become vulnerable to the actions of individuals outside the family who have an important role in controlling the family identity.

The overimportance of the police role leaves the police family feeling hypervulnerable to any changes that impact the officer's police role. If there has been overinvestment in the police role and a concomitant narrowing of support systems to only the police culture, changes such as removal from an assignment

can send the vulnerable police family into crisis. Police families also fall victim to the couch potato syndrome. They become deficient in planning skills. "We like to be spontaneous" becomes a catch phrase for a lot of police families, even though "spontaneity" might be something the family has not experienced socially in years. Hobbies are forgotten, vacations are not planned, trips away from the police role are not experienced. The cycle of overinvestment in police work, the biological roller coaster, and apathy toward and disregard for a personal life may even cost police officers their families during the first decade of their career. This leaves them without vital support systems and compounds their isolation as the second decade of a police career unfolds.

Case Example. Officer John Miller was a sixteen-year veteran of a two thousand-man police force. During his career, he had served in several capacities, from patrol officer to detective. For the past nine years he had been a canine officer. During this time John earned the respect not only of the street cops but also of his superiors. It was a rare individual indeed who did not speak of John as an officer to be admired and looked up to. John had high job satisfaction, was well respected by other canine officers, and appeared to be heading toward his twenty-year retirement as a police success story. John also had a well-functioning police family. He had been married for seventeen years. This marriage had produced two children, a son and daughter, fourteen and twelve years old. The family was heavily invested in John's role as a police officer, particularly in his specialty of canine officer. The children had grown up with police service dogs as members of the family. On two occasions over the past decade, the family had traveled, once to California, and another time to the southeastern United States, to bring back prospective canines for the dog unit. These trips occurred as part of the family vacation. The family also had imported a dog from Germany at their own expense. Beyond a doubt this was a police family — a canine-oriented police family. On more than one occasion, the children had been proud to have their father bring the highly trained dogs to their elementary and junior high schools to perform canine demonstrations.

Suddenly, John found himself under the supervision of a new captain. The new command officer had certain ideas of his own involving the cross-training of bomb dogs and narcotics dogs. John adamantly opposed this idea. John tried to approach his new captain with tact but was met with an authoritarian narrow-mindedness. The captain ordered John to take his experienced drug dogs and cross-train them as bomb dogs. Again, John tactfully attempted to explain to the captain that once a dog is certified to alert to one narrow range of olfactory sensation, cross-training would confuse the animal and reduce its total efficiency, producing a dog of only limited serviceability. When this approach was rebuffed, John tried to make it clearer by pointing out to the captain that if a cross-trained dog sat down (meaning that he's found something), they wouldn't know whether to evacuate the building or get a search warrant. The captain failed to appreciate the humor in his approach, and John found himself unceremoniously ordered out of the canine unit and returned to uniform patrol, assigned to a part of the city where he had begun work sixteen years prior. This unexpected transfer hit John quite hard and also his wife and children. The transfer meant that not only was John no longer a member of the specialized canine unit, but that all city-funded equipment, including the dogs, would be turned back to the city for assignment to another officer. John took the transfer hard.

When he started his new assignment as a patrol officer, he did so with cynicism and hostility. This was the first time in sixteen years that John did not enjoy going to work, and he rapidly grew to hate it. His sick leave increased as did the number of citizen complaints. On more than one occasion John found himself receiving verbal discipline from

his watch commander (an officer with whom he attended the police academy sixteen years prior). John's new lieutenant attempted to perform intervention and supervisory counseling by stating "John, I know that the manner in which you were handled at Special Operations [canine] was maybe not the best way. This is field operations and it's a new deal over here. I need you as a leader. We have a lot of young cops out here and I'm gonna need your seniority and your leadership." To this John responded, "Lieutenant, you can count on me being here. I have four years to go till I retire, but don't count on me for anything else." John's behavior continued to deteriorate, evidenced not only by a lack of adequate investigation for field calls, but also by a general decline in his performance as a police officer.

While deterioration was taking place at work, John's family also was beginning to suffer. His wife and children bounced back from the transfer much sooner than John did. His wife advised John, "You have four years to go here and then we can do what we want to do. Let's just finish it out." To which John responded, "I'm not gonna make four years with these assholes."

Several months after John's transfer from canine, he encountered an old police friend who had retired and become chief of police in a small rural department in the same state. When John and his old friend began commiserating over old times, his friend advised him, "If you come to work for me in my department you can start working your dog the day you arrive." John was rather enthusiastic about this job proposition even though it meant a 40 percent reduction in pay and relocating almost 250 miles away in a small rural community. John's wife took the news of a potential move with a marked lack of enthusiasm. "John, we've lived in this city almost our whole life. Our children were born here. Our parents are here, and our home is almost paid off. Let's just do four more years with the department then decide what we want to do. I don't think we can take a 40 percent cut in pay and still make ends meet." Thus, John and his wife began several months of confrontation over his accepting the chance to work with a dog again in the new town. Now not only was the workplace exceedingly unhappy for John, but for the first time in seventeen years of marriage, home had become a place of confrontation and tension. After several months of constant debate at home over whether or not to relocate to the new city, and simultaneously operating under closer and closer administrative scrutiny due to his deteriorating police performance, his wife finally gave in, saying "If the only way I can keep this family together is to move to that town, then I guess we just have to go."

John and his wife sold their home, where they had lived for sixteen years, transferred the kids to a school district of questionable quality, and attempted to re-create a new life in an isolated part of the state away from friends and family. The state in which the family lived had statewide certification for peace officers and a statewide public safety retirement system, so his retirement rights were intact. John continued to work toward his last four years of a police career.

Shortly after arriving in his new department, John found the grass was not always greener on the other side. His old friend the chief required all officers to undergo a field training program. John was assigned a field training officer who had approximately two years of police experience. Although John was typically an easygoing and open-minded individual, he found the young officer's habit of personal editorializing about officer safety more than he could bear on a daily basis. John soon began getting into confrontations with this young officer. This was reflected in his daily evaluations and eventually brought John to the attention of his old friend, the chief. The chief attempted to counsel John by saying "John, look. Just go through the field training program. Learn how we do business here, and as soon as you're through the program, we'll start working on your getting a canine unit up on the streets." To this, John

responded, "I thought I was gonna work a dog as soon as I got here." The chief advised him at this point that his canine unit would not be funded until the next fiscal year – approximately seven months away. Feeling angry and betrayed, John confronted the chief. "You brought me way the hell up to this Godforsaken spot by telling me I could work the dog. Now you're saying I can't have one for seven months. That's b.s."

Soon John was given the choice of conducting business the way the chief wanted or finding employment elsewhere. John went home and advised his wife that they were leaving the town after only two months. His wife responded positively, believing that they were returning to their old city where John had rehire rights inasmuch as he had given notice to his former employer. John responded, "I'm never going back there to work for those assholes even if I only had four days, not just four years." John quit his job and found employment in a twenty-man police force, again at the opposite end of the state. This time he traveled to his new employment without his family; his wife elected to return to the city where his police career had begun. John found himself divorced, two hundred miles away from his children. At first he saw them every other weekend, but as the months passed he visited less and less frequently. John became involved in a live-in relationship with a dispatcher who worked in his new department.

After a year and a half working as a canine officer in the new department, a new mayor and city council were elected. The day they were sworn into office, they terminated the chief of police and the entire police force, including John. Now, at forty-one years of age, with eighteen years toward a twenty-year retirement within the state, John found himself with high blood pressure and impaired vision, and unable to pass a required preemployment physical for state law enforcement officers. Two years away from retirement eligibility, John went to work as a security guard in a power plant 300 miles away from the city where he practiced law enforcement for sixteen years.

He began to drink excessively and became a hostile, cynical, and emotionally broken man.

John's case can be considered a tragic consequence of the police stress cycle and a prime example of how vulnerable a police officer becomes if he welds his sense of self-worth to his police role – a role he himself does not control. Obviously John lost perspective along the way by overinvesting in his role as a canine officer. More important, he also lost a wife, a day-to-day relationship with his children, a satisfying police career, and ultimately his retirement. How in a little less than two years did a satisfied, enthusiastic, happily married police officer become an angry, cynical, depressed, alcohol abusing individual who, in all likelihood, will never realize a police retirement and who, without professional counseling, will not be able to put the pieces of his life back together?

By studying John's case, average cops can learn the tragic consequences of law enforcement overinvolvement, the consequences of the "brotherhood of biochemistry." It's important to step back from John's case and point out where he made mistakes that average cops unfortunately often replicate with little, if any, awareness of their own vulnerability.

If you were a friend of John's, what would you have advised him to do along his downward spiral and career-ending decisions? Would you have told him to just go along with the captain and cross-train the bomb and dope dogs, knowing that it would yield a dog that was unserviceable? Would you have told him to just bear it the next four years? Do it by "standing on your head" if you had to, just complete your four years? It won't do any practical good for John, or any other police officer, to point out that the captain who ordered the training was "an asshole" or that the chief of the small town who promised John an immediate position as canine officer and then reneged, was also "an asshole." It won't help to blame the mayor, city council, and all the registered voters who ousted the chief and all his officers, for John's misfortune.

Somewhere during this tragic cycle, John should have taken control of his life and assumed personal responsibility. John is like a large number of other law enforcement officers heavily invested in the police role – highly vulnerable because he had placed all his eggs in the basket marked "canine officer" – in a basket held by someone else. In John's case the basket was held by a captain who, in all likelihood, was not highly competent. Nonetheless, when the basket fell, John and his family sustained the damage – not the captain.

What would you have told John? Would it have helped to tell John to start putting some eggs in a basket marked "John and family?" Maybe John, his wife, and the children could have started an independent canine training service. Perhaps John could have channeled his enthusiasm into other aspects of life that the police department did not control. John was a victim of police stress because he, like other victims, had no control over his fate. Police officers who overinvest in their police role, no matter how benevolent their intentions, run the risk of becoming another "John." How often have competent, enthusiastic officers had a positive productive career changed by a transfer, a demotion, a loss of status or prestige in the department? Whom do those officers turn to? Because of the job's biological roller coaster, they have failed to develop a personal life. Where do the officers escape to? Where do they feel in control? It's obvious that the police department controls the police role. If officers have abdicated a personal role, where do they find emotional serenity, peace, and tranquility? They don't. Instead, with other burned-out cops, they find camaraderie and shared cynicism and hostility toward the police department. Although John's case is a tragedy, it's by no means an isolated example.

Overcoming the Brotherhood

The first step in helping officers to achieve emotional survival is to teach a "proactive life-style." "Render onto Caesar the things that are Caesar's," but take the reins of your life fully in hand and develop a personal life. For most police officers, this requires a written, preplanned personal master calendar that the family keeps posted someplace visible and central to the family. Often it is put on the refrigerator with magnets. This preplanned master calendar permits the family to put *in writing* several things each week that they can look forward to. These activities do not require significant expenditures. Bowling, walks, physical exercise, or even quiet time to read can give officers control over at least one aspect of their lives. Usually it's this block of time, the off-duty time, that young officers throw away so haphazardly. Many officers will view the suggestion of attempting to develop a proactive personal life with uncertainty and rationalize away any possibility of doing so by statements such as "Yeah, every time you plan something, some jerk down at the department's gonna call you back," or "I took a vacation once and when I came back I was transferred." Many times these rationalizations are true, but does this require a police family to surrender control of its own time? If they make the fatal mistake of giving up control, they're surrendering to the role of victim. Police officers who plan together with their families have a proactive, self-controlled lifestyle that gives them something to look forward to each day, no matter how small the event. While a certain percentage of these plans are going to be canceled by call-outs, court dates, and overtime, the majority will take place if officers plan them.

Without proactive planning for a personal and family life to break the stress cycle and roller-coaster ride, many police families find themselves not looking forward to "doing things" but rather to "buying things." These police families find themselves purchasing new cars, guns, and other "large-ticket items." It sure feels good to buy a new car! Every sense, every process is stimulated. The feel of the seats, the steering wheel, the smell of the car is all very stimulating – somewhat like the upper highs of the biological roller coaster.

However, these buying highs are short-lived. After the novelty wears off, the payment lingers on. Police families who do not plan things to do typically tend to buy impulsively. Thus, the biological roller coaster has some very definite drawbacks in the world of impulse economics. The second major element to emotional survival for a police family is to recognize and satisfy the intense need for physical exercise. Selling physical fitness programs to cops certainly is not one of the easiest undertakings. Many an older street cop responds to the suggestion of jogging with cynical statements, such as "If they want me to run, why did they give me a patrol car?" However, physical fitness is an officer's number-one means of breaking the deleterious impact of the biological roller coaster. The downward side of the ride and the resultant off-duty depression is the body's way of attempting to metabolize adrenaline-related stimulants that are produced during the on-duty "high." Fuels that are not metabolized through exercise will typically lead to explosive outbursts of anger and hostility at home. "The flying toaster and small appliance syndrome" is the label given to these outbursts of anger that occur in police families due to the combination of both sedentariness and unresolved anger and hostility. The old military expression "The more you sweat in peace, the less you bleed in war" suggests that regularly scheduled exercise is one way of beating the cycle of stress-related depression. It also gives police officers the capacity to practice biological "officer safety" effectively on a daily basis, thus maintaining a balanced sense of alertness on duty.

The extreme physical and emotional swings initiated by the biological roller coaster result in shortened life expectancy. Repeatedly, studies demonstrate that police are more susceptible to injury and death from stress-related breakdown than from any other factor. In the civilian population, 55 percent of all deaths are attributable to heart disease. Among police officers, the three leading causes of nonaccidental disability retirements are heart and circulatory disease, back disorders, and peptic ulcers. Police work cannot only be survived but can offer a rewarding career of service to others. However, individual officers must assume responsibility, through self-motivation, to seek the necessary attitudinal change. It is essential for police officers to have a systematic program of physical exercise, not only to break the stress-related cycle, but to provide what cardiologists label "cardioprotective resistance."

Cops need to have a self-initiated regular period, approximately thirty to forty-five minutes per day, of aerobic exercise – rhythmic and repetitive exercise that places emphasis on the exchange of oxygen and carbon dioxide and not on the development of musculature (like weight lifting). Cops who exercise feel a greater sense of self-satisfaction and control over their own destinies. There are days when officers come home from work and don't feel fit to rejoin the human race. Anger, hostility, and the desire to just "sit in front of the tube and pop a cold one" dominate all other thoughts. Taking a half-hour to work out physically increases their sense of self-worth, self-esteem, and physical well-being. Average cops may agree with the benefits of physical exercise, but their problem is "How do I find time to do it? I'm already stretched thin." This is where they should go back to step one in our tips for officer emotional survival and schedule a time *in writing* on the calendar. Biking, jogging, walking, and swimming not only permit officers to have some energy left for a personal life but also lead to lower physiological thresholds under stress that produce better decisions in those life-and-death situations police officers have to face.

The third element of emotional survival that police officers and their families need to build revolves around the development of other alternative, nonpolice roles. Police officers who, for the first several years of their career could not get enough of police work, unfortunately become those who do not have a personal life, nor do they know how to

develop one. The novelty of cop work has worn off, yet there's no well-developed, balanced personal life to fall back on to recharge the batteries. The contrast between the following two case histories emphasizes the value of developing a personal, balanced life-style.

Case Example. James Martin was a nineteen-year veteran on the day he was killed in the line of duty. When officers were dispatched to his residence to notify his wife and two teenage daughters, they were met with the predictable reactions of emotional devastation that comes with the news of hearing that your loved one will not be returning. The officers on this particular call, after providing whatever support they could to the family, found it necessary to use the telephone. When they approached the telephone, they found taped on an index card under the kitchen telephone the message, "This is a career, not a crusade." Months later when the officers followed up to see how the family was doing, the index card was still taped below the telephone. They asked the officer's widow what the card meant. She responded: "He loved being a cop and he was very good at it, but he had seen so many of his friends become obsessed with police work and how it cost them their families. We vowed never to let that happen. He loved putting bad guys in jail and he loved being a cop, but he also loved being a husband and a father. We always found time to have our time together. We might have had our Christmases on December 26 or Thanksgiving dinners on Saturday, but we always had them. We never surrendered being a family. I miss him very much. But I can look back and say we had a good life together." It's obvious that this family planned for time together and that the officer had developed other interests. Although this officer tragically lost his life in the line of duty, he left behind an emotional legacy of two children and a wife who not only share the pride of having been a police family but the love of having been a functioning, caring family unit. Police work does not always need to take control of family time.

Case Example. Not all stories have the same ending, however. The author (KG) while visiting another city to conduct police training, was approached by the police chief of a nearby small law enforcement agency and asked to become involved in a situation concerning one of their officers who was terminally ill. Initially the author thought the request was to provide some psychological assistance to the officer. However, the chief advised that the difficulties were not with the officer himself, but with his son. The problems revolved around the fact that the son, who was twenty-three-years of age, had not spoken with his father since he was eighteen, when he left the house under significant family strain. The chief further advised that he himself had approached the young man and found him totally unwilling to even consider speaking with his father, who wished to make peace with his son. The chief angrily expressed his feeling that the son was being unreasonable ("This kid's some kind of an asshole").

The author was requested to approach the son to negotiate some sort of peace between him and his terminally ill father. The following day, the author met with the young man, telling him that he (the author) was there in his capacity of police psychologist to talk with him about his father. The boy interrupted: "You're here to tell me my dad's dead, aren't you?" The author's response was "No, I'm not. But you really ought to go see him." This impulsive, highly directive statement resulted in an angry response. Immediately the young man shouted, "You have no right to come here and tell me what the hell I ought to do. You don't know anything about the situation. Why don't you just leave!" When the author requested him to explain why he was so unwilling to see his father and attempt to reach some form of final understanding, the young man stated: "Do you know how many times my father ever came to watch me play football in high school or wrestle? I'll tell you. Not once! Do you know how many times he attended a Cub Scout meeting or a Boy Scout meeting or a Little League game? Not once! The only thing I can remember about my father when I was growing up was that he was never home, and he was always angry. If I stepped out of line, I was told that I was going to grow up to be just another one of the little assholes that he sees everyday."

The young man ventilated his hostility, adding that he saw no reason to go into town to visit his father. He said he felt sorry for his mother and would come back to town to help her after his father passed away. The author attempted numerous strategies to get this young man to rethink his position. For two hours the son continued to express his feelings that the time for creation of some relationship between him and his father had long passed. It became obvious that this young man remained adamantly entrenched in his position and was not going to contact his father. When the chief of police was advised that the officer's son would not go to see his father, the chief expressed anger and hostility toward the young man. The chief described the officer who was dying, saying "I've known him for over twenty years. He's one of the best cops I know, just a fine human being. I'll give you an example of what kind of man he is. There's not a family in our town here who, at Thanksgiving, goes without a food basket, and that's because he almost single-handedly coordinates this program. At Christmas he receives the names of needy families from the schools and welfare offices, and he sees that each family has a food basket and each child has a toy under the Christmas tree. He's active in our bicycle safety program and in the school resource program." As the chief was speaking, it became obvious to the author that he was describing an entirely different man from the one the son had. The chief was describing a life that he had shared with this officer at the upper reaches of the biological roller coaster where the officer was involved — participating in activities and enthusiastically sharing his life with those around him. The officer's son, however, was describing a life spent at the lower reaches of the biological roller coaster – an apathetic, disinterested, emotionally detached, angry father. It was apparent that the chief of police and the officer's son were speaking about two entirely different people psychologically. The tragedy of this second case history is that the son never did travel to the hospital. The officer died, and the son probably looks back on his deceased father with a very different emotional legacy from those of the children of our officer whose professional and personal credo was "This is a career, not a crusade."

SUMMARY

If law enforcement officers are to survive the "brotherhood of biochemistry," they must look at both their on-duty and off-duty life-styles and take charge of the events in their lives that they can control. Proactive goal-setting, an active aerobic exercise program, and nurturing and developing other roles in life besides the hypervigilant police role should enable officers to manage their life-style more effectively. To survive police stress, officers need to know what they can control and to surrender what they cannot control. Their emotional and physical well-being requires them to take a realistic review of their day-to-day life-style and to make whatever alterations are necessary to ensure a well-balanced, healthy personal life.

PART VII

CONCLUSION

Chapter 24

THE ROLE OF THE MENTAL HEALTH PROFESSIONAL IN POLICE WORK

In the last decade there has been an increasing demand for mental health professionals to work with or for police agencies. This is not surprising, since police officers are so often in the role of front-line caretakers for the community's mentally ill. An article discussing the work of the San Francisco Police Department's Mental Health Unit concluded "police may provide the most consistent mental health care in the community" (Taft, 1980). This is one of the few police units in the country to deal exclusively with people who are mentally ill. The Los Angeles Police Department has a Mental Evaluation Detail (MED), a round-the-clock unit that receives all reports involving mentally disturbed people, advises officers, and acts as a liaison with the various mental health and medical facilities in the city.

The extent of the problem that the mentally ill present to police is indicated by the fact that in one year, the San Francisco Police Department processed approximately 3,200 emergency detention cases in which a person was taken to a mental health center and a report was filed. In addition, there were innumerable crisis "800" calls (radio code for insane persons), family disturbances involving mental cases, and probably thousands of suspects arrested on criminal charges that stem from mental illness. In total, it is estimated that the department handles over 10,000 insane person incidents each year (Taft, 1980). Further,

any cutback in funding for mental health services increases the burden on the police.

All mental health professionals should take an active interest in how the police handle mental cases. If the police are effective – not as pseudopsychologists or psychiatrists but as police officers – then the quality of mental health care in the community will be significantly higher. Opportunities for involvement of mental health professionals in police work are multiple and extend beyond the employment of a police psychologist. In areas where police departments do not have their own mental health resources, mental health professionals may become involved in the selection and training of police officers to ensure that only emotionally stable applicants are admitted into the police academy and that, while there, they learn how to deal humanely and effectively with mental cases. Community psychologists also may come to the aid of their local police department and other emergency service workers in times of great stress. An example of such an incident is the crash of an Air Florida flight into the 14th Street Bridge in Washington, D.C.

Mental health professionals may also work with police when employed to perform a certain function. For example, a psychologist may be hired to administer and interpret psychological tests and give clinical evaluations for screening purposes. In the Tucson Police Department, each applicant is given psychological tests and is interviewed by a local psychologist in private practice who has considerable experience in evaluating police officers. The clinical interview lasts approximately fifty minutes. If the psychologist finds that additional testing and interviews are needed, they are given, with the professional sometimes spending up to six hours with each applicant. There is a set fee for each applicant for this service, regardless of the amount of time spent.

A police department may employ a mental health professional to offer counseling to police officers and their families. The Arizona Department of Public Safety has contracted with a group of private practitioners, who offer a certain number of counseling hours at a fixed price per hour to members of the department. Nevertheless, these services provide only limited resources to police agencies. Further, consultants often are inadequate because of their lack of police knowledge and their short-term involvement. In our judgment, the best solution is for a police agency, if possible, to hire a full-time, in-house police psychologist or otherwise qualified mental health professional. There are several advantages to this arrangement. First, the psychologist and department will get to know each other, becoming familiar with each other's needs, expectations, and methods, and building the sense of trust necessary for a successful relationship. This will be true not only in terms of the department and the psychologist, but also between the people of the department and the psychologist.

Another advantage to a full-time, in-house psychologist is availability twenty-four-hours a day, seven days a week. This availability, plus a continued presence and visibility in the station and in the field, develops a feeling of familiarity and trust among the officers.

Police Psychologist

Discussion of the role of police psychologists may be introduced most appropriately by quoting from DePue:

If I only knew then what I know now – This phrase is especially appropriate to characterize the present day application of behavioral sciences to law enforcement. . . .

The behavioral science discipline of political science has contributed to our understanding of topics ranging from the threat of terrorism to corruption in government. Sociology has provided tools to assist us in assessing the strengths and weaknesses of groups within our communities, as well as the communities themselves. Criminology has provided the framework to determine the scope of the crime problem and the nature of the offender. But, perhaps the greatest contribution to the state of the art has been made in the field of psychology.

From a rather modest start in such areas as interview and interrogation, the practical applications of psychology have mushroomed, touching nearly every aspect of police work. Improved police recruitment, selection, and screening techniques have been developed. Officer self-control such as dealing with anger and fear are examples of internal problems being addressed. Programs for stress management in law enforcement have been molded into police practices and administrative procedures. Techniques for more effectively dealing with hostage situations have been developed, modified, and refined. Improved methods of understanding victims and witnesses have been developed, especially in dealing with children. New insights into the criminal personality have enhanced law enforcement understanding and interpretation of behavior exhibited during crimes. Criminal personality profiling and investigative analysis have contributed to early identification, apprehension, and incarceration of serial violent offenders. Crisis intervention, conflict management, and hypnosis are still other examples of psychology in action in law enforcement. The list goes on and on.

Armed with the information available today, I could have done a far better job as a police officer and administrator in the 1960s. I know now that I could have detected crimes that must have certainly gone undetected. My interviews and interrogations could have yielded greater results. Offenders in many of my cases could have been identified, located, and apprehended earlier in their criminal careers. Victims, witnesses, and perpetrators could have been handled with more professionalism and safety for all concerned. As an administrator, I could have dealt with personnel matters more effectively and provided for training and support services that addressed unique policing problems as well as debilitating personal problems. (Depue, 1988)

Before proceeding to cite services performed by today's police psychologists, it is necessary to present our basic philosophy of how department psychologists should approach their duties and responsibilities. In the chapters on stress, the author referred several times to the belief that the police system is in many ways like the military. Like any military organization, the police department has an assigned mission. The police chief, like the military commander, is given certain resources (personnel and equipment) to accomplish this mission. The role of any technical support personnel (legal, medical, psychological) is to support the organization in accomplishing its mission, just as the role of the military psychologist is to support the command and the troops in the field. This is the identical mission of the police psychologist within the police department. Thus, the primary responsibility of the police psychologist is to the department, not to the individuals comprising that department. This does not preclude performing clinical services for employees, confidentiality, or having the welfare of the "patient" constantly in mind. In our opinion, these are not mutually exclusive goals. However, the police department is not a therapeutic or rehabilitative agency. It is a law enforcement agency with a definite, restrictive function. Police departments cannot afford to throw away personnel, but neither can they afford to keep officers on the street who are ineffective and emotionally unstable. Not all police psychologists and administrators hold this view. Many believe it is difficult, if not

impossible, to utilize psychological services effectively for both management and clinical functions. They argue that psychologists' involvement with management undermines their capacity to develop the rapport with police employees that must exist if employees are to use clinical services. They also believe that a strong relationship with employees may bias the psychologists' input to management (Morris, 1980). However, the author does not perceive this as an unavoidable conflict. Those two functions are not mutually exclusive. As Morris (1980) finally concludes, after delineating these potentially conflicting functions:

An effective Combination of management consultation and direct services, on the part of PSU [Psychological Services Unit], does appear feasible. The same principles [autonomy, identification, avoidance of decision-making, input at the policy level] which support effective consultation also support the rapport with officers. A well-planned and regulated involvement in both direct services and management provides the psychologist with a greater comprehension of the whole range of system phenomena; both his counseling and his management input should be enhanced.

Scope of Activities

According to the observations of several experienced police psychologists (DePue, 1979; Morris, 1980; Reiser, 1982; Russell, 1983; Stratton, 1984), services provided to police departments by mental health professionals may include the following.

Psychological Screening

Mental health professionals may evaluate job applicants' emotional stability, intellectual and interpersonal skills, and suitability for police work. This evaluation may be done by a department-employed psychologist or by professionals outside the department whose services are contracted specifically for this purpose. The latter seems preferable because a psychologist's approval or disapproval of a candidate is generally only one part of the selection process. Should the department still hire the candidate who is disapproved by the psychologist, friction between the candidate and the department psychologist may result if the candidate learns of this disapproval. As J. G. Stratton (1984) has pointed out, the major problem with psychological screening is that few of the tests have been adequately validated for this specific population. Many, including the most frequently used, the Minnesota Multiphasic Personality Inventory (MMPI), were originally devised for use with mental patients. To assume that they have validity as a selection device for police candidates may be inappropriate. Caution should be exercised in using any of the results and, in particular, in relying on them to the exclusion of other available data. It is interesting to note, however, that the Supreme Court of the State of New York ruled that the city of New York did not have to rehire a probationary police officer who was fired in 1983 because of his poor score on the MMPI (Flanagan, 1986).

It is the author's belief that the department psychologist should *not* become involved in the psychological screening of department applicants. This should be delegated to another psychologist. The department psychologist can then claim to have absolutely no influence on the acceptance or rejection of a particular candidate (such as the child of a sergeant or lieutenant).

Training

The department psychologist is involved in recruit training, in-service training for veteran officers, and education for specialized activities, such as handling sex crimes. Bull and Horncastle (1988) note "in policing it is typically the case that little evaluation is undertaken of the effectiveness of training." Jaywardene (1982) commented: "A large number of studies have limited themselves to a detailed description of programming designed to provide improvement in the area of concern. From

these descriptions the improvement in police function had to be inferred."

The department psychologist may assist in evaluating the validity of courses taught in the police academy (for example, in determining whether a particular course is necessary or whether it is accomplishing its stated goals). The psychologist also may help students overcome academic problems by improving their study skills and/or teaching them to use self-hypnosis techniques in learning situations.

Criminal Investigation – Hypnosis and Profiling

The department psychologist's skills are becoming more useful in certain aspects of criminal investigation. One relatively new and controversial area is investigative hypnosis. This technique dates back to the early 1960s, when the Israeli police used hypnosis to catch terrorists after finding that witnesses to acts of terrorism could recall far more under hypnosis. For example, at first people could not remember someone putting down an ordinary-looking bag; under hypnosis, the same witnesses gave a more accurate description of who was carrying what and who sat where. Some also demonstrated a photographic memory. They were able to recall who came on a bus with them, at what stop, and what was being carried. Some even remembered the registration numbers of cars that were in the area prior to an explosion. Most important, they were able to construct composites (identity pictures) of people they "saw" while under hypnosis (Reiser, 1982).

After the success of the Israeli police, Dr. Martin Reiser of the Los Angeles Police Department began to use hypnosis as an aid to investigation. Reiser formed an institute to teach hypnosis to other police psychologists and select police investigators. Investigative hypnosis became controversial, particularly in reference to the admissibility in court of evidence obtained through its use. Court concerns have led many law enforcement agencies to restrict its use to clinical and police psychologists and psychiatrists rather than to allow hypnosis by police officers trained as hypno-investigators.

Hibler (1987) states that the current policy of federal investigative agencies now requires that only mental health professionals who have been trained in hypnotism (usually psychologists or psychiatrists) manage all trance aspects of the hypnosis sessions.

> The use of professionals is important for several reasons. First is concern for the well-being of interviewees who may have been subjected to great trauma. Federal agencies want to be certain that witness' or victims' re-identification with the crime does not adversely arouse emotions. Further, there is the desire to assure that subsequent trial testimony regarding hypnosis is provided by an expert. Likewise, investigative experts should handle details of the case. Accordingly, specially trained investigators participate in what has come to be known as "a team approach." . . . The roles of each are specified in a standardized script, which sequences the course of the interview in consideration of both hypnotic and forensic factors. Additionally, all interviews are videotape recorded so that there is a clear record of all that occurs.

An unexpected use of hypnosis by the Tucson Department psychologist occurred when a female cadet was referred, in desperation, from the Arizona Law Enforcement Training Academy. It seems that this woman had successfully completed all aspects of the recruit course (in fact, she was number one academically) except for qualifying on the firearms course. The best she could achieve was a score of 106 out of 300. She needed 250 to qualify. The psychologist enlisted the aid of Detective Seng, a peer counselor, from the behavioral science unit, who had been a firearms instructor. It was determined that anxiety was overriding her training and concentration. Hypnosis was employed, and the next day she shot a 296. She has consistently shot at or near that level since that one hypnosis session. Other officers (including a captain who is a competitive shooter) have found hypnosis to be of help in improving their shooting. Recently Seng (1989) initiated a study to determine the value of employing group hypnosis training with recruit cadets as part of the regular firearms course. Preliminary results indicate a significant, positive influence on range performance of those cadets undergoing the group hypnosis sessions. Another new development in criminal investigation that benefits from the expertise of the police psychologist is profiling of criminal suspects. "Criminal personality profiling is the study of unsolved crimes in an attempt to provide the behavioral and personality characteristics of unidentified offenders" (Horn, 1988). One of the most famous suspect profiles was by James Brussel, a psychiatrist who described the "mad bomber" who was plaguing New York City because of his hatred for Con Edison (the utility from which he had been discharged). The extent of Dr. Brussel's accuracy was such that in describing the then-unknown suspect, he told detectives that when this person was arrested, he would be "wearing a double breasted suit with all buttons carefully buttoned" (Ault & Reese, 1980).

The rationale behind profiling is that behavior reflects personality, and that by examining behavior, the investigator may be able to determine what kind of person would commit this kind of crime. Knowledge of the likely personality characteristics of offenders will enable investigators to identify possible suspects and develop an effective approach to them (Douglas et al. 1987). A pilot project initiated by the behavioral science unit (BSU) of the FBI Academy at Quantico, Virginia, involved psychological criminal analysis. The initial project was aimed at formulating criminal offender profiles by interviewing incarcerated felons who had exhausted all appeals (Kessler & Douglas, 1980). This led to an ongoing systematic study, the criminal personality interview program, designed to identify the salient characteristics, motivations, attitudes, and behavior of offenders involved in specific types of crime.

The FBI Academy's BSU has profiled the nuisance (obsessive-compulsive) offender

(Reese, 1979), the fire setter (Rider, 1980), and the lust murderer (Hazelwood & Douglas, 1980). Currently the federal investigative profilers are part of the National Center for the Analysis of Violent Crimes at the FBI Academy. The team approach requires thorough, professional, accurate work from investigators, forensic pathologists, laboratory technicians, and profilers (Horn, 1988). The pathologist team member contributes to the profiling effort not only by conducting the routine autopsy of homicide victims, but also by analyzing the perpetrator's postmortem manipulation of the victim (Zeling, 1988).

Counseling

Given the high-stress nature of police work, one of the immediate and everpresent needs of the department is for someone to do professional counseling with police officers and their families. The police psychologist is seen as the most likely individual to offer such services. But if psychologists see their role primarily as therapists, little time will be left for other duties, and their impact on the total department will be minimal.

The author believes that the most productive service for psychologists to offer is crisis intervention, not long-term treatment. In most communities adequate mental health resources are available to all citizens, and mental health practitioners in the private sector are available under many health insurance plans. These resources should be used. The department psychologist can maximize these resources by doing liaison work between the community's mental health resources, including private practitioners, so that police officers and their families can be referred to professionals who have some understanding of police work and the police culture, and who have a desire to work with law enforcement personnel.

One answer to providing counseling services to police personnel is to use peer counselors. Eddie Donovan, the Boston cop who started the stress program of the Boston Police Department and who founded the International

Law Enforcement Association, was one of the first to point out the need for peer counseling. "Peer counseling works in the law enforcement vocation. . . . Peer trusts peer but not outsiders. The police vocation is a closed society that will not let outsiders (nonpolice) in – the unwritten rule of suffering in silence – is seldom broken. So who else can a cop who is in trouble with himself talk to but another cop . . . someone who knows where he's at and how he's feeling about being there" (Donovan, 1978).

Linden and Klein (1988) believe "Police peer counseling is an idea whose time has arrived and an approach whose implementation is being well accepted by police officers." They believe the role of peer counselors should be expanded to involve peer counseling in support groups for new recruits and their spouses, teaching in the police academy, in-service training for police officers handling posttraumatic incidents, and providing retirement counseling. They have developed a peer training program in California that has been approved by the California Commission on Police Officers Standards and Training (POST). To date, this program has trained well over three hundred officers throughout California and has been widely acclaimed by those officers.

Liaison with Mental Health Facilities

The department mental health professional can serve as a liaison to the mental health facilities in the community. An ability to move freely between the law enforcement and mental health systems not only can facilitate the referral of officers and their families to community agencies but also can assist field officers handle and dispose of difficult mental cases encountered in the streets. With the cooperation of various hospitals and clinics, standard operating procedures can be developed for the police department relative to the handling of mental patients and involuntary commitment. This cooperation benefits both systems and the people they serve.

Field Emergencies

Psychologists and other mental health professionals employed by the department should be available on a twenty-four-hour basis to help officers in the field handle subjects barricaded in defiance of authority, violent mental cases, suicides, officers involved in critical incidents, and emergency services personnel who have been subject to extraordinarily severe stress (such as plane crash, floods, or other disaster situations).

Command Consultation

Police psychologists should offer consultation to all levels of command relative to the department's mental health and morale. They should be available to advise management on factors affecting police performance, such as working environment, communication, leadership, and supervisory techniques. This consultation can be offered in formal meetings and presentations or in single, informal sessions with lieutenants, captains, or sergeants. Morris (1980) notes that the effective use of psychologists in management depends mainly on them having administrative support and adequate autonomy, on their avoidance of a direct role in decision making, and on their involvement at the policy or procedural level.

Applied Research

There is a need in all police departments for applied research designed to answer pressing contemporary problems. Some major research projects currently under way in various police departments involve development and validation of physical fitness tests; study of accident proneness in police officers; personality variables associated with marksmanship; personality characteristics of officers assigned to vice, motor, SWAT; and use of biofeedback and treatment in musculoskeletal disorders. Other questions we consider important include how to select a narcotics officer, what makes a good juvenile officer, and how to

evaluate an officer's performance in the prevention of violence and crime (rather than the usual evaluation of efficiency based on the number of arrests made and citations issued).

Job Evaluation

When police mental health professionals are asked to evaluate an officer's job performance, the question is most often "Is he fit for duty?" Stratton (1984) notes that sergeants usually conduct the evaluation of personnel in their field assignments. Supervision is always a difficult task, and this is even more true in police work. Cops operate independently and are rarely seen by, or spend much time with, sergeants or higher-level supervisors. Sergeants might be reluctant to criticize or put pressure on officers they supervise when they may have been partners with these same officers, working with and depending on them before they became sergeants. A sergeant who hesitates to hold an officer accountable for below-average performance may allow field performance to deteriorate to a point that termination is the only solution. Stratton states that "although it is very necessary at times for a particular officer to be psychologically evaluated for fitness, often such requests result from the supervisor's failure to hold the officer accountable for his work. Rather than discharge him, an attempt is made to 'pass the buck' to a psychologist" (Stratton, 1984–present).

The author has had similar experiences. Frequently, line commanders will attempt to solve administrative or disciplinary problems by using mental health professionals to "wash the dirty linen." When an officer has such problems, the mental health professional should refer him or her back to command, noting that this officer is cleared psychologically for any disciplinary and/or administrative action that is deemed appropriate by command. Stratton (1984) concludes that "although it seems that supervision may be complicated, often the psychologist should not be involved in evaluating how effectively the employee should do his job; rather it should be the task of the first-line supervisor, difficult though it may be."

Selection for Special Assignments

Police agencies may request the advice of psychologists in evaluating officers for special assignments, such as SWAT, hostage negotiation teams, or sex crimes. Some police agencies have asked psychologists to sit in on promotion boards. In our judgment, psychologists and other mental health professionals have little to offer in these cases. The best predictor of a person's behavior is past behavior. Police officers, particularly senior patrol officers, sergeants, and lieutenants, can do a much better job than most mental health professionals in selecting personnel for these assignments or for promotion. Here again, our advice to in-house police psychologists is to stay clear of any kind of selection process.

Review of Mental Cases

One of the important duties of mental health professionals may be to go through the officers' daily reports involving mental cases to determine which individuals are likely to be dangerous to officers or others. These people's names can then be placed in the computer with an appropriate notation so the dispatcher can warn street officers of any factors threatening their own safety or the safety of others if they are called to deal with these subjects at a later date.

Program Models

In the past few years, four types of program models involving mental health professionals have emerged. They include the Dallas Program, the Tucson Program (1974–1984), the Multi-Department Program, and the Tucson Metro Behavioral Sciences Unit (1984–present).

The Dallas Program

The Dallas Police Department operates its own psychological service unit, staffed by a civilian employee of the department and master's-level psychologists recruited from the ranks of sworn personnel. The unit's budget is included in the overall police budget. Therefore all personnel are under the command of the chief of police.

The Tucson Program (1974–1984)

A civilian psychologist who was not an employee of the police department or the city of Tucson headed the behavioral science unit of the Tucson Police Department. He was a full-time member of the staff of the Southern Arizona Mental Health Center, a bureau of the State Department of Health Services. The city contracted for his services from the state. A sworn member of the police department, a master's-level sergeant with eighteen years of department service assisted him in the unit.

In the author's judgment, the Tucson model offers certain advantages. First, since the psychologist was an independent contractor and did not report to the chief of police, he was autonomous as far as operation of the BSU was concerned. Although he had to satisfy the chief of police, other command personnel, and the troops themselves, no one in the police department made up his efficiency report or in any way had a direct bearing on whether or not he kept his job. If the contract was not renewed, he was still a full-time employee of the state and would be assigned other duties. Again, since his chain of command was outside the police chief's chain of command, he was free to advise the chief on matters within his expertise without concern for backlash.

Another advantage to a police department considering this model is that a local mental health agency may be contacted to ascertain if any staff member would be interested in working with the police in the role of police mental health professional. If a staff member expresses interest, a contract can be made for six months or a year. Thus the police department can try out the new person without too much problem letting him or her go should the person not work out. It also should be noted that the contract might call for a certain number of hours, thus making it possible for the police department to have a fully qualified professional without having to provide a full-time salary in a limited police budget. Further, a local mental health agency might be able to provide this service at cost, which is considerably less than the cost of employing a private psychologist as a consultant.

The Multidepartment Program

Another model that may be especially suitable for small departments is for several of them to pool their resources and hire one mental health professional to provide services to all (Chandler, 1980). The psychologist can be centrally located and can provide services on an as-needed basis to the several departments that have contracted for these services. The Law Enforcement Clarification Center in Rockford, Michigan is located in a small town and serves all law enforcement personnel in twelve counties. The center is located in a big white house converted for office use and is not connected to any local police department. People from any department may come and go and not be noticed. It is important for small police departments to consider this model, since services involved in selection, training, and counseling may be needed more in small than in large departments. If one person is ineffective in a ten-person department, it will be more devastating than if one person is ineffective in a two thousand-person department.

The Tucson Metro Behavioral Science Unit (1984–present)

When Dr. Russell left the Tucson Police Department, its behavioral science unit became a "metro" unit, serving both the Tucson Police Department (TPD) and the Pima County Sheriff's Department (PCSD). The unit currently consists of one full-time psychologist and one peer counselor in both the TPD and the PCSD.

Referrals for Counseling Services

How do officers (and their families) avail themselves of the services of these psychological units? In the TPD and the PCSD, any officer, civilian employee, or member of the family may contact the Metro Behavioral Science Unit (MBSU) at any time. The confidentiality of the doctor-patient relationship applies not only to the clinical psychologist, but also to the sergeant members of the MBSU with only two exceptions. First, if the counselor is told that a felony has been committed, this cannot be kept confidential, since the counselor could be charged with being an accessory to a felony. The other restriction on confidentiality concerns dangerousness. Because police officers carry badges and guns, the client is told that if at any time the counselor becomes concerned about the safety of the office or of any citizens, steps will be taken to address this issue. This may simply involve informing the officer's commander that the officer has come for counseling without revealing the details. Clients are told that should any such step become necessary, they will be told exactly what the counselor proposes to say to the supervisor and that they will have the opportunity to modify the counselor's proposal if they disagree.

A person may also come in contact with the MBSU through referral from a supervisor. In this situation, the officer is told that interviews are confidential but that the supervisor will require some feedback. This may consist of nothing more than telling the supervisor that the officer is coming for counseling. The officer is told that any information given to the supervisor will be with the officer's permission. In our experience, this has presented no problem in the five years the unit has been in operation. Finally, if officers are the subject of an internal affairs investigation, they are not seen in the MBSU but are referred to a psychologist outside the two agencies for evaluation.

Selecting the Police Mental Health Professional

If you are a member of a police agency interested in employing a mental health professional, perhaps with the objective of starting a behavioral science unit in the department, how do you select the professional you will use? We will use a psychologist as an example. While employment interviews offer some assistance, there are other important considerations.

First, review the educational and vocational background of the applicant. If this person has graduated from an accredited program in clinical psychology, you probably do not have to worry about professional qualifications. It is hoped that in the not-too-distant future, some universities will have graduate programs centered around police psychology as a specialty. Ascertain whether the applicant has had experience with law enforcement agencies as an officer, employer, or consultant. Work in a military setting would also be favorable. Of course, you should complete a thorough background check by contacting references and past places of employment to ascertain skills and character. Do not accept claimed academic background or degrees without verification from the colleges or universities named. The arrest record always should be checked.

The best advice the author can offer is to ask the candidate to spend a couple of days in the department, riding with some senior patrol officers who are good officers and good judges of people. Expose the applicant to sergeants whose opinion you trust and allow interaction with several first-line supervisors and field commanders. After the candidate has spent time riding and interacting with these officers, ask them questions such as "Do you like the applicant?" "Would you trust this person's judgment?" and "Would you go to see this person if you had a problem?" This approach probably will yield the most valid selection of a psychologist who can relate well to department personnel and who really likes to work with police. Such a psychologist will be an asset to the department.

If you are beginning a program, it is vital that the first psychologist you select be able to perform well and relate effectively. If the first psychologist fouls up, it will be a long, long time before that negative experience will be forgotten, thus setting back by at least several years the implementation of any behavioral science program in the department.

Program Benefits

Schilling (1978) contends that experience demonstrates that a BSU returns far more than its original cost. "These units have established impressive track records for reducing the cost of internal investigations, limiting the cost of sick time benefits and decreasing the supportable grounds for liability litigation. They also produce savings in the cost of replacing employees who would be lost to the agency without rehabilitation."

In evaluating the worth of these programs, the author must also note the humanistic benefits to police and their families from available counseling services and stress management programs. These services help police officers do their job more effectively and safely, with fewer adverse effects on themselves and their families. Benefits also accrue to the public, since services offered by the police mental health professional and associates reduce the likelihood of abrasive police-citizen contacts and increase the possibility of more efficient and satisfying services to the public. Although a cost analysis of these BSUs has not been done, there seems to be little doubt that the value of these services far exceeds their cost, especially when they are provided by in-house personnel.

Statistics from a recent article on civilian job stress indicate that many large corporations spend more than $200 million a year on medical benefits for employees. A large percentage of such medical expenses is caused by stress-related conditions. Legal costs are also involved. Americans filed a record number of stress-related worker's compensation claims in 1987 (Miller, 1988, pp. 40–45). Police officers are increasingly seeking disability discharges based on various medical and emotional claims, ranging from heart attacks allegedly caused by job stress, to a claim by one deputy in California that her personality wasn't suited for police work, causing her to be a chronic mental disability case. Surely the availability of a psychological service unit within a police department should prove to be cost-effective if it addresses only some of these situations.

SUMMARY

In this chapter the author discussed the role of the mental health professional in police work. In the last decade there has been an increased tendency for police departments to employ mental health professionals, especially psychologists. The in-house psychologist with multiple responsibilities is preferred over the part-time consultant who is hired on a contractual basis to provide limited counseling or other specific services. In addition to counseling services, the police mental health professional may participate effectively in a wide range of functions, such as screening, training, research, liaison with mental health agencies, consultation, and field emergencies. The author described four models for these programs that have emerged within the last few years (Dallas, Tucson BSU, Multi-Departmental, and Tucson Metro BSU). Recent experiences in departments with behavioral service units indicate that these programs are cost-effective.

In selecting a police mental health professional, the most important factor is whether the applicant will be accepted by department personnel as someone they can work with, trust, and discuss problems.

Before closing this chapter, the reader's attention is directed to an article by Park Dietz and J. T. Reese (1986) on suggested strategies for police psychologists to follow to minimize role conflicts when providing mental health services and consultation to law enforcement agencies. The article discusses common dilemmas faced by mental health professionals who work on behalf of law enforcement agencies. It focuses on issues relating to informed consent; conflicts in values, norms, or their relative importance; and to the erosion of professional identity. Ten strategies police psychologists may use to reduce their risk of confronting ethical dilemmas or of experiencing role conflicts while working on behalf of law enforcement agencies are provided.

The police psychologist should also be aware of certain new legal considerations in screening police applicants and in evaluating an officer's fitness for duty that pertain to the concept of vicarious liability. C. L. Flanagan (1986) observes:

> Within recent years there has been an impressive increase in the number of high risk occupations (e.g., law enforcement agencies, Nuclear Regulatory Commission, fire departments). Such screening is somewhat different from that performed by most psychologists, mainly because the purpose of the evaluation and the dangerous type of errors that can be made (e.g., hiring an armed police officer who is a danger on the streets). In addition to the finely honed clinical skills needed for such screening, the psychologist must keep abreast of legal decisions. Thus, further complicating the matter, the psychologist who is not trained as a lawyer must be able to link psychology and the law.

Finally, this subspecialty has been accepted in the field of psychology itself. The American Psychological Association now has a Police and Public Safety Section within Division 18 (Psychologists in Public Service). Soon, it is hoped, there will be graduate training programs in police psychology at universities and professional schools of psychology. There is also a need to develop supervised intern training programs and postdoctoral fellowships in this specialty.

The strongest support for the new police psychology has come from the FBI's Behavioral Sciences Unit at the FBI Academy, Quantico, Virginia. The Veteran's Administration did much to hatch and protect the then-embryonic clinical psychology profession. The FBI's BSU has been the patron of this new police psychology specialty. Police psychologists look forward to its continuing support.

BIBLIOGRAPHY

Ault, R. L., & Reese, J. T. March, 1980. A psychological assessment of crime: Profiling. *FBI Law Enforcement Bulletin,* 22–25.

Chandler, J. T. February, 1980. The multi-department: Police psychologists. *Police Chief,* 34–36.

Dietz, P. E., & Reese, J. T. (1986). The perils of police psychology: Ten strategies for minimizing role conflicts when providing mental health services and consultation to law enforcement agencies. *Behavioral Sciences and the Law, 4*(4), 385–400.

Douglas, J. E., et al. (1987). Criminal profiling from crime scene analysis. *Behavioral Sciences and the Law, 4*(4), 401–421.

Flanagan, C. L. (1986). Legal considerations in psychological screening for high risk occupations. *Public Service Psychology, 11*(6), 13.

France, K. (1982). Crisis intervention: A handbook of immediate person-to-person help. Springfield, IL: Charles C Thomas.

Hazelwood, R. R., & Douglas, J. E. April, 1980. The lust murderer. *FBI Law Enforcement Bulletin,* 18–22.

Hibler, N. S. March, 1987. In McNeil, J. E., et al. Hypnosis and identi-kit: A study to determine the effect of using hypnosis in conjunction with the making of identi-kit composites. *Journal of Police Science and Administration, 15*(1), 63–67.

Horn, J. M. (1988). Criminal personality profiling. In *Police psychology: Operational assistance,* ed. J. T. Reese & J. M. Horn, pp. 211–223. Quantico, VA: U.S. Department of Justice, FBI.

Leff-Simon, S. I., Slaiken, K. A., & Hansen, K. (1984). Crisis intervention in hospital emergency rooms. In *Crisis intervention: A handbook for practice and research,* ed. K. A. Slaiken. Boston: Allyn & Bacon.

Miller, A., et al. 25 April, 1988. Stress on the job. *Newsweek,* 40–45.

Porter, B. April, 1983. Mind hunters. *Psychology Today,* 44–52.

Reiser, M. (1982). *Police psychology.* Los Angeles: LEHI Publishing Co.

Ressiler, R. K., et al. September, 1980. Offender profiles: A multidisciplinary approach. *FBI Law Enforcement Bulletin,* 1–5.

Russell, H. E. June, 1983. *The Tucson Police Department's Behavioral Sciences Unit.* Presented to advanced management class, Arizona Law Enforcement Training Academy, Tucson.

Scott v. Hart. 1977. No. C76-2395, N.D. Cal.

Stratton, J. (1984). *Police passages.* Manhattan Beach, CA: Glennon Publishing Co.

Trotter, R. J. (1987). Psychologist with a badge. *Psychology Today, 21*(1), 26–30.

Zelig, M. (1988). Analysis of post-mortem manipulation of homicide victims to enhance psychological profiles. In *Police psychology: Operational assistance,* ed. J. T. Reese & J. M. Horn, pp. 437–447. Quantico, VA: U.S. Department of Justice, FBI.

INDEX

A

ABC model, 228
Aberrant sexual behavior, 94. *See also* Rape
Aberration, 95
Abnormal behavior, 34. *See also* Mental illness
Abraham, Karl, 73
Accident victims, crisis intervention with, 232
Acrophobia, 58
Active listening, 231
Acute paranoid disorder, 264
Acute paranoid psychosis, 122
Addiction, 118–119. *See also* Drug-dependent behavior
Affective disorders, 73–74
Aggressive mob, 188
Agoraphobia, 59
AIDS, 126, 135
Airborne law enforcement, 266
Alcohol, 119–120
    cocaine and, 126
    teenage crowds and, 197
Alcoholic hallucinosis, 121
Alcoholics Anonymous, 126
Alexander, Y., 237
Allen, Scott W., 177
American Academy of Pediatrics, 137
American Psychiatric Association, 47, 179
American Psychological Association, 265
Amisir, 229
Amphetamines, 122
Anatomy of Melancoly (Burton), 165
Andison, F.S., 139
Anger management, 150
Anger rape, 101
Anolik, S.A., 88
Anonymity, in mob, 204
Antisocial personality disorders.
    See Psychopaths
Anxiety, 26–27. *See also* Neurotic disorders;

Stress situations
Anxiety neurosis, 54–55
Arab terrorists, 218
Arcaya, J.M., 208
Arif, A., 142
Arizona Law Enforcement Training Academy, 192
Assault, 162
Ault, R.L., 301
Autonomy, personality and, 18
Avoidance, as stress reduction technique, 248

B

Barbiturates, 122
Bard, Morton, 227–228
Bardo, Robert John, 164
Barricaded subject, 201
Barth, J., 136
Baruth, C.L., 318
Baxter, A., 106–107
Behavioral science unit, 290
Beigel, A., 138
Bell, T.J., 136
Belson, W., 139
Bennett, Barbara, 268
Bent, Dan, 154
Bernard, Claude, 288
Bernheim, Hippolyte-Marie, 60
Bertholf, M., 142, 146
Bianchi, Kenneth, 98
Bias crimes. *See* Hate crimes
Binder, A., 190
Binging, cocaine and, 158
Biopsychosocial model, 10
Bipolar psychoses, 74
Blak, R.A., 298
Bleuler, Eugen, 69–70
Blind flight, in mobs, 196
Body posture, as crisis intervention technique,

230–231
Bolz, 203
Bondage, masochism and, 98
Borderline personality disorder, 43
Born, D.G., 271
Boston Police Stress Program, 294
Boston Strangler. *See* DeSalvo, Albert
Brady, James, 176
Brennan, Kathleen, 274
Breslow, Lester, 297
Brick, J.R., 196
Bright, 286
Brotherhood of biochemistry, 277–290
Brothers, J.T., 195–196
Bruno v. Codd, 220
Brussel, James, 301
Bull, 300
Bundy, Ted, 88
Burgess, Ann W., 101
Burnout, 260–261
Burton, Robert, 185
Bush, George, 96

C

Cameron, N., 130
Campus-event crowd, 198
Cannon, Walter D., 20–21, 240
Caplan, G.M., 151
Caplan, Gerald, 183
Caram, P., 205
Career burnout, 260–261
Career development, lack of as stressor, 241
Casual crowd, 120
Catatonic type of schizophrenia, 80
Celebrity murder, 163
Chandler, C.L., 202
Chandler, J.T., 301
Changes in Role Concepts of Police Officers (Sterling), 8
Charcot, Jean-Marie, 60
Cheek, J.C., 281
Chelimsky, E., 226
Child molestation. *See* Pedophilia
Choirboys (Wambaugh), 149
Chusid, J.G., 136–241
Citizen-observer victim, crisis intervention with, 232-233

Civil War, stress and, 239
Clark, Ramsey, 137
Claustrophobia, 59
Cleckley, Hervey, 84, 86
Cobb, Gail, 299
Code of conduct, 198
Code 3 personality, 200
Cohen, A., 256–257
Cold turkey, 125
Colgate University, 222
Colligan, 298
Colson, 267
Columbia University, 201
Combat psychiatry, 288
Community-oriented policing. *See* Proactive policing
Community support, riots and, 195
Compensation, 29
Compulsive Personality Disorder, 50–51
Conflict, 25–26
Conflict situations, 220–225
Confrontation, in riot process, 189
Conscious, 21
Constitutional factors, in normal personality development, 19
Constitutional psychopathic inferiority, 70, *See also* Psychopaths
Contagion, in mob, 194
Controlling group, riots and, 196
Conversion neurosis, 60–61
Cooper, 284
"Copycat" suicide, 180
"Copy cat violence," 140
Cornell University, 222
Corrections system, stress from, 250
"Couch potato" phase, of biological roller coaster, 300
Court decisions, stress from, 253
Covey, R., 231
Cowan, Fred, 141–142
Crack, 125
Criminal justice system, stress from, 253
Criminal Personality, The (Yochelson and Samenow), 78
Crisis intervention with victims, 226–235
Critical incident stress debriefing (CISD), 183–184
Cronin, Lawrence, 164

Cross-dressing, 96
Crowd control, 194. *See also* Riot behavior
Cuadrado, M., 118

D

Dalby, J.T., 130
Dallas Program, 300
Dances, crowd control at, 196
Danger: stress from, 241
Danto, Bruce, 211
Date rape, 101
Deadly force, as stressor, 255–256
Death notification, 225
Death of police officer, 288
Defense mechanisms, 27
Defusing, in critical incident stress debriefing, 183–184
Delayed response, to disaster, 180
Delinquent behavior, 111–115
Delirium tremens, 121
Delusional disorder, 137
Delusions, 35
Demobilizations, in critical incident stress debriefing, 184
Denial: as defense mechanism, 30
Depressed group, as disaster reaction 180
Depression: in abnormal behavior, 55
Depressive drugs, 157–158
Depressive neurosis, 55–56
Depue, 291
DeSalvo, Albert, 86
Developmental factors, 19–20
Deviant behavior, 14.
    See also Abnormal behavior
Deviations, as aberrations, 123
Devivo, P., 284
Dietz, Park, 300
Disability retirement, 273
Disaster Research Center, 183
Disasters, behavior and, 177–185
Disorganized asocial personality disorder, *See* Paranoid schizophrenia
Disorganized type of schizophrenia, 71
Dispersed mob, 196
Displacement, 28
Dissociative neurosis, 61–62

Distancing, as crisis intervention technique, 274
Diversionary reality questions, 198
Divorce, in police marriages, 294
Dominelli, Joseph S., 290
Donovan, Edward C., 7, 244, 252
Douglas, John E., 103
Drive-by shootings, 148
Drives, 24
"Drone" officers, 164
Drug dependence, 118
Drug-dependent behavior, 117–127,
    See also Alcohol; Crack
Duarte, C., 140
Dubin, William, 152
Duke, Tony, 9
Duncan, B.J., 160
Dupnik, Sheriff, 299
Durazo, A., 299
Durkheim, Emile, 156
Dysthymic disorder. *See* Depressive neurosis

E

Ego, 20–21
Ego ideal, 21
Eisenberg, Terry, 242
Elderly, suicide among, 172
Emergency response system, 284
Emotional anesthesia, 67
Emotional disturbances, 70.
    See also Mental illness
Emotional Trauma Groups, 300
EMS personnel, 205
Enrique, V., 196
Environmental factors, in normal personality development, 21–22
Epicureans, 186
Erikson, Erik, 21–22
Escape mob, 190
Escape routes, riots and, 191
Etherington, C.A., 109
Eustress, 299
Event-oriented crowd, 184
Exhibitionism, 98–9
Eye contact, as crisis intervention technique, 231

F

Falaret, Jean Pierre, 81
Family disputes, 221
Family of police officer: brotherhood of
    biochemistry and, 277-290
Fantasy, 31
Farago, L., 13
Farberow, N.L., 157
Farkas, G.M., 280
Fatigue, from patrol, 283
FBI, 100
Fear:, stress from, 245
Female officers, stress and, 247
Ferracuti, F., 138
Fetishism, 96
Fichtner, M., 180
Field training officers, 275
Fight or flight reaction, 27
Filson, C.R., 131
Final decision phase, in violent police citizen
    encounters, 162
Finn, P., 146
Fisher, D., 88
Fitzhugh, Parke, 281
Fitzpatrick, 208
Fixated pedophile, 120
Flanagan, C.L., 302
Flanders, 202
Flashbacks, from hallucinogens, 63
Football games, crowds at, 18
Forth, A.E., 98
Fowler, D., 202

L

Laughlin, Henry P., 35
Law Enforcement Clarification Center, 300
Law Enforcement Training and Information
    Network, 114
Learned drives, 28
Lee, M., 142
Leff, 41
Lesbians, hate crimes against, 145
Lesce, T., 281
Levinson, J., 203
Leviton, S.C., 21
Levy, R., 5

Levy, Terry, 182
Lewis, J.M., 221
Lewis, L.M., 221
Libido, 20
Librium, 151
Linden, 29
Litman, R.E., 183
Locke, 261
London Metropolitan Police, 7–8
Los Angeles Suicide Prevention Center, 187
Lunde, 201
Lust murderer, 101
Lysergic acid diethylamide (LSD), 123

M

Madamba, H.J., 284
Mainlining drugs, 125
Major depressive disorder, 74–75
Majority attitudes, stress from, 251
Mantell, Michael, 177
Marijuana, 124
Mark, G.T., 196
Martorana, J.A., 118
Marx, Marilyn, 126
Mask of Sanity, The (Cleckley), 84
Maslach, C., 273
Masochism, sexual, 97–98
Mass murder, 141
McGinnis, J., 182
McMains, 200
McNeil, T., 146
McPherson, L.M., 195
Matthews, R.A., 38
Medalist syndrome, 279
Megaree, E.I., 135, 142
MEN (Men Evolving Nonviolently), 180
Men Against Rape, 180
Mental activity, levels of, 22–23
Mental Evaluation Detail (MED), 293
Mental health professional, 293–304
Mental illness, 40
    hostage situations and, 204–205.
    See also Abnormal behavior; Neurotic
    disorders
        Personality disorders
    Psychopaths; Psychotic disorders
Meredith, N., 137

Mescaline, 123
Methadone, 126
Methedrine, 125
Mezer, R.R., 24
Michelson, R., 201
Middendorff, 211
Milavsky, W.R., 139
Mild tranquilizers, 123
Military experience, stress and, 178
Miller, A., 234
Mills, C. Wright, 34
Minnesota Multiphasic Personality Inventory
    (MMPI), 98
Minority attitudes, stress from, 245
Minority officers, stress and, 247
Mirabella, 210
Mirasol Task Force,
Mitchell, Jeffrey T.,162, 177
Mixed violence, 137–140
Mobs, 187–199, *See* also Riot behavior
Monahan, J., 178
Monroe, R.R., 136
Morenz, Barry, 173
Morris, 303
Mott, Colonel, 178
Multi-Department Program, 302

N

Narcissistic personality disorder, 42
Narcotics, 123
Narcotics work, 262–263
National Center for Health Statistics, 199
National Institute of Drug and Alcohol
    Abuse, 120
National Institute of Mental Health, 188
National Survey on Drug Abuse, 122
Need gratification, 20
Negotiators, in hostage situations, 201
Neidig, Peter H., 136
Neighborhood Watch, 6
Neighbors, stress from, 251
Nelson, F.L., 176
Neurotic adjustment reactions, to undercover
    narcotics work, 263
Neurotic disorders, 53–65
New Briarfield Apartments, 6
Nielsen, E., 175

Nielson, R., 207
Nonconformists, police as, 254
Nonpolice roles, for stress reduction, 301
Nonshy murderers. See Undercontrolled
    personality
Nonverbal techniques, for crisis intervention,
    231
Nostalgia, in Civil War, 196
Novelty, in mob, 195
Nylen, C., 180

O

Oakland Men's Project, 177
Obsessive-compulsive neurosis, 56–58
Office for Combatting Terrorism, 209
Olin, W.R., 202
O'Neal, P., 87
O'Neil, P.S., 245
On-scene support services, 205
Open conflict, in riots, 189
Opiates. See Narcotics
Organic personality disorder, explosive type,
    75–76
Organized nonsocial personality.
    See Psychopaths
Ostrove, N.M., 287
Overactive reaction, to disaster, 199
Overcontrolled personality, 160
Overinvestment, in police role, 30

P

Panic: in mobs, 195
Panic attacks, 64–65
Paperwork, as stressor, 248
Paranoid behavior, 129–134
Paranoid personality disorder, 49–50
Paranoid schizophrenic, 61
Paraphilias, 77
Passive-aggressive personality disorder, 48–49
Pathological anxiety, 28
Pathological intoxication, 117
Patrol, as stressful, 266–267
Patton, George, 13
Pedophilia, 105–106
"Peeping Toms." *See* Voyeurism
Peer counselors, 26

Pendergrass, V.E., 269
Pennsylvania Psychiatric Center, 181
Pep pills, 121
Persecution, feelings of as abnormal behavior, 47
Person, Ellen Spector, 84–85
Personal involvement, professional attitude and, 10
Personality development, normal, 20
    See also Defense mechanisms;
        Developmental factors
Personality disorders, 47–51, 77
Personalizing statements, as crisis intervention technique, 235
Phobic neurosis, 58–60
Pierson, 202
Pima County (Arizona) Victim Witness Program, 224
Pittsburgh Steelers, 214
Police psychologist, 294–295
Police widow, 288
Policy, as stressor, 148
Political terrorism, hostage situations and, 218
Polydrug abuse, 119
Polygraph, psychopaths and, 8
Positive thinking, stress reduction and, 250–251
Postincident functions, of critical incident stress debriefing, 183
Postshooting syndrome, 256–257
Post-traumatic stress disorder (PTSD), 62-64
Pott, Jack, 167
Power rape, 98
Precipitating incident, to riot, 195
Preconscious, 22
Preincident functions, of critical incident stress debriefing, 184
President's Commission on Law Enforcement and the Administration of Justice, 5, 8
President's Task Force on Victims of Crime, 228
Press, stress from, 149
Price, S., 8
Prichard, James, 83
Primary drives, 28
Primate syndrome, 279
Prisoners: hostage situations and, 204
Private time, stress and, 259

Proactive life-style, brotherhood of biochemistry overcome by, 281
Proactive policing, 2
"Problem of the broken window," 8
Problem-oriented policing. *See* Proactive policing
Prodomal clues, 186
Professional attitude, 14
Profiling, 296
Projection, 29
PROMIS, 150
Propaganda, mob agitated by, 190–191
Psychic numbing, post-traumatic stress disorder and, 67
Psychological crowd, 188
Psychological first aid, to disaster victims, 181–182
Psychological screening, 295
Psychopathic personality disorder, 8
Psychopaths, 81
Psychotic disorders, 77 *See also* Affective disorders; Schizophrenic disorders
Pyromania, 67

Q

Quaaludes, 120
Quainton, 200

R

Rape, 100-103
Rapid burnout, 261–262
Rationalization, 28–29
Reaction formation, 29
Reactive policing, 8
Reagan, Ronald, 164
Reed, B.T., 136
Reese, J.T., 89
Regressed pedophile, 106
Regression, 31
Rehearsal, as stress reduction technique, 256
Reid, W.H., 88
Reiser, M., 170
Relaxation, stress and, 260
Relaxation Response, The (Benson), 260
Repression, 30
Residual type of schizophrenia, 69

Resnick, H.L.P., 195
Retirement of police, 272–273
Rhetorical drama, from undercover narcotics
    work, 263
Rider, 303
Riordan, J., 211
Riot behavior, 187–199;
    riot control, 187–199.
    See also Crowd control
Rioter, 189–19
Roberts, Michael, 268
Robinson, R., 206
Rock concerts, crowd control at, 198
Rogers, R., 86
Role conflict: mental health professional and, 24
Role generalization, from undercover
    narcotics work, 263
Role of police officer, 1–2
Roman Holiday phase, 189
Ronstadt, Peter, 9
Rosenbluh, E.S., 275
Rowland, L.W., 38
Rubenstein, E.A., 139
Rule, Ann, 92
Rumors, mob agitated by, 197
Russell, Harold E., 97, 211

S

Sadism: psychopath and, 97
Sadistic rape, 101
Samenow, S., 95
Sanchez, José E., 88
San Ysidro mass execution, 75
Saper, M.B., 267
Sardino, Thomas J., 194–195
Schaeffer, Rebecca, 173
Scharf, P., 17
Schilling, 30
Schizoid personality disorder, 42
Schizophrenic disorders, 69–73
Schlossberg, Harvey, 200
Schmidt, W., 75
Schnabel, P.H., 220
Schneidman, Edwin S., 157–158, 160
Schuckit, M.A., 117
Scott, B., 5
Scott v. Hart, 224

Secondary drives, 28
Secondary gain, neurotic disorders and, 65
Self-hypnosis technique, 300
Selye, Hans, 247–248
Seng, 304
Serial rape, 101–102
Sex crimes, 100–110, *See also* Aberrant sexual
    behavior
Sexual assault detail, 265–266
Sexual homicide, 103
Sexuality, 100
Shades of Gray, 35
Shah, Idries, 188
Shah, S.A., 135
Shattered Badge, The (Donovan), 286
Shea, G., 200–207
Shea, L., 8
Shell shock, World War I and, 240
Shiftwork, stress from, 245
Shore, D., 131
Show-of-force principle, in handling mentally
    ill, 41
Siegel, M., 227
Signal anxiety, 62
Silberman, C., 178
Silbert, M., 228
Silver, J., 76–78
Simon, 41
Singer, R.D., 139
Siporin, M., 195
Situational factors, in normal personality
    development, 21–2
Situational trauma, neurotic disorders and, 64
Skin popping, of narcotics, 122
Sleep: loss of and suicide, 160
Smith, W., 174
Snorting, of narcotics, 122
Social isolation, of police officers, 280
Social violence, 135
Socrates, 18
Solomon, J., 111
Solomon, R.M., 264
Somodevilla, S.A., 258
Soskis, D., 202
Special assignments, 262
Speck, Richard, 136
Speedball, cocaine and, 130
Spellacy, F., 136

Sports crowds, 196
State University of New York at Albany, 222
Steadman, H.J., 186
Stephens, Darrel, 9
Stephens, K.S., 109
Sterling, J.W., 8
Stevens, W.R., 102
Stewart, E., 5
Stillman, F., 270
Stockholm syndrome, 203
Stoller, R.J., 94–95
Stratton, John G., 13, 137, 261
Strentz, T., 206–211
Stress: job-related, 239–254, *See also* Brother
    hood of biochemistry; techniques
        reducing, 277–290
Stressors, 240
Student demonstrations, 196
Subculture of violence, 140
Sublimation, 32
Substitution, 31
Sudden murder, 162
Suggestibility, in mob, 195
Suicide, 156–173; autoerotic fatalities and,
    110
Suicide, Le (Durkheim), 156
Suicide plan, 179
"Suicide potential," 179
Suicide prevention centers, 180–183
Suicidology, 157
Sullivan, Dan, 269
Sullivan, Harry Stack, 54
Sultan, 282
Superego, 21
Supervision, as stressor, 246
SWAT when police as hostage taker, 214
Syndromatic communication, suicide clues
        from, 180–181

T

Taft, 304
Taking stock, hostages and, 209
Talk-down cure, 136
Task force approach, 6
Techniques for Dealing with Child Sexual Abuse

(Baxter), 106
Teenagers, suicide and, 162,
        See also Delinquent behavior
Television, violence and, 139
Texas Adoption Project, 88
Texas Research Institute of Mental Sciences,
    136
Thompson-Pope, S.K., 126
Thou Shalt Not Kill, 181
Toch, H., 172
Tolchin, M., 182
Tolerance, drugs and, 119
Tracks, drugs and, 121
Training, by mental health professional, 295
Transsexual, 96–97
Transvestitism, 96
"Triad of depression," 180
Trudeau, 202
Trust, personality and, 23
Turkat, I.D., 156
Turner, J.T., 146

U

Unattached children, 179
Unconscious, 25
Undercontrolled personality, 143
Undercover narcotics, 262–263
Undifferentiated type of schizophrenia, 69
Uniform Crime Reports, 138
Universities: crowds at, 195
University of Kansas, 195
University of Oklahoma, 197
Uselessness, stress from sense of, 253

V

Valium, 123
Van Zandt, C., 202
Verbal techniques for crisis intervention, 231–
    232
Vietnam War, stress, 62
Villa, B.J., 266
Violence, 135–153
Vocalization, as crisis intervention technique,
    234

Voyeurism, 99–100

W

Wambaugh, Joseph, 242
Warning period, before disaster, 205
Warren, J.I., 103
Washton, A.M., 118
Weissberg, M., 112–136
Wensyl, J.W., 206
West, Donald J., 106
Westermeyer, J., 133
Westphal, Kurt, 58
White, Robert W., 22
Whitehouse, J.E., 6
Whitman, Charles, 135
Wilcox, Brian, 140
"Wildings," 143
Wilkinson, C.B., 187

Williams, T., 63
Wilson, James Q., 9–10
Wilson, R. Reid, 65
Wimps, police officers as, 254
Wish, E.D., 118
Wolfgang, M.E., 138–139
Wroe, B., 286

Y

Yochelson, S., 108
Yudofsky, B., 76–78
Yudofsky, S.C., 76–78

Z

Zeling, M., 263
Zimbardo, P.E., 163
Zuniga, 216

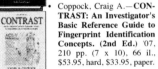
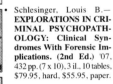

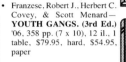
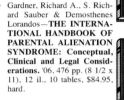
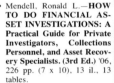
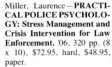

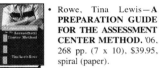
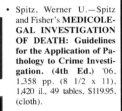

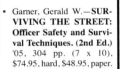
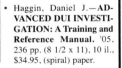

Sept. 18/07